Mastering Hurst Cycle Analysis

A modern treatment of Hurst's original system of financial market analysis

By Christopher Grafton, CMT

Hh

HARRIMAN HOUSE LTD

3A Penns Road
Petersfield
Hampshire
GU32 2EW
GREAT BRITAIN

Tel: +44 (0)1730 233870
Fax: +44 (0)1730 233880
Email: enquiries@harriman-house.com
Website: www.harriman-house.com

First published in Great Britain in 2011

Copyright © Harriman House Ltd

The right of Christopher Grafton to be identified as the author has been asserted in accordance with the Copyright, Design and Patents Act 1988.

ISBN: 978-0857-190-62-8

British Library Cataloguing in Publication Data
A CIP catalogue record for this book can be obtained from the British Library.

All rights reserved; no part of this publication may be reproduced, stored in a retrieval system, or transmitted in any form or by any means, electronic, mechanical, photocopying, recording, or otherwise without the prior written permission of the Publisher. This book may not be lent, resold, hired out or otherwise disposed of by way of trade in any form of binding or cover other than that in which it is published without the prior written consent of the Publisher.

No responsibility for loss occasioned to any person or corporate body acting or refraining to act as a result of reading material in this book can be accepted by the Publisher, by the Author, or by the employer of the Author.

Designated trademarks and brands are the property of their respective owners.

Printed and bound in Great Britain by CPI Antony Rowe, Chippenham

Set in Sabon and RotisSansSerif

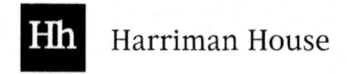

Hh Harriman House

七転び八起き

Nana korobi, ya oki

"Fall down seven times – get up eight."

Contents

Praise for *Mastering Hurst Cycle Analysis*	xi
About the author	xiii
Acknowledgments and thanks	xv
Introduction	**xvii**
1. The Properties Of Cycles	**1**
Introduction	3
Basic Quantities	5
Visualising Period and Amplitude	8
How Cycles Combine	10
Properties of Market Cycles	17
Conclusion	39
2. Basic Tools I: Valid Trendlines	**41**
Trend and Trendlines	43
The Concept of Trendlines	45
Trend Direction	48
Trend Strength	54
The Real Nature of Trend	56
The Valid Trendline (VTL)	61
The Key Role Played by VTLs	65
Conclusion	74
3. Basic Tools II: Displaced Cycles – The FLD	**77**
Introduction	79
Properties of the FLD	80
Plotting the FLD	83
Applying FLDs	86
FLD Combinations	96
Conclusion	101
4. Isolating Market Cycles I	**103**
Introduction	105
Cycle Envelopes	107
Phasing Analysis Set Up	115
Conducting a Phasing Analysis	121
Conclusion	138

5. Isolating Market Cycles II — 141
Introduction — 143
Spectral Analysis — 145
Phasing Analysis – Daily Chart — 152
Conclusion — 163

6. Selection, Set Up And Entry — 165
Introduction — 167
Creating a Shortlist — 169
Scanning Charts — 178
Entering the Trade — 190
Short Selling — 199
Conclusion — 207

7. Managing Open Positions — 211
Introduction — 213
Case Study – JPMorgan Chase 2002/2003 — 214
Conclusion — 234

8. RSI And Elliott Wave — 235
Introduction — 237
RSI and Elliott Wave – the Basics — 238
Case Study I: Gold, November 2008 — 249
Case Study II: Euro/USD, January 2010 — 260
Conclusion — 269

Conclusion — 273

Appendices — 283
Appendix 1: Elliott Wave Patterns — 285
Appendix 2: FLD Code — 295
Appendix 3: Inverse Moving Average Code — 301
Appendix 4: Cycle Envelope Code — 303
Appendix 5: Diamonds Grid and Numbers — 307
Appendix 6: Final Diamond Placement Code — 321
Appendix 7: Discrete Fourier Transform Code — 331
Appendix 8: Volatility Index code — 345
Recommended further reading — 347
The Sentient Trader — 348

Index — 349

List of figures and tables

Figure 1.1 – Sine waves showing period, amplitude and phase difference — 5
Figure 1.2 – Mass spring oscillator — 9
Figure 1.3 – Damped oscillation — 10
Figure 1.4 – Head and Shoulders Top and Double Bottom Composite (78 week plus 18 week) — 11
Figure 1.5 – Complex composite consisting of four component cycles (156, 78, 18, 9) — 13
Figure 1.6 – Individual components of the complex composite wave in Figure 1.5 — 14
Figure 1.7 – 80-day cycle in the FTSE 100 — 15
Figure 1.8 – Composite with 5° trend added — 16
Figure 1.9 – Composite with 15° trend added — 17
Figure 1.10 – Set of harmonic and synchronised proportional waves 54, 18 and 9 unit periods — 19
Figure 1.11 – Non-harmonic and non-synchronised waves (lacking proportionality for emphasis) — 19
Figure 1.12 – Vibrating string showing even harmonic levels — 21
Figure 1.13 – Harmonic waves in phase showing synchronisation of troughs and dispersion of peaks — 22
Figure 1.14 – FTSE 100 showing tendency for sharp bottoms and rounded tops — 22
Figure 1.15 – FTSE 100 bar chart 1 July–21 October 2010, with gaps for non-trading days — 27
Figure 1.16 – Dow Jones Industrial Average 1900-2010 — 29
Figure 1.17 – DJIA 1900-1921 — 30
Figure 1.18 – DJIA 1921-1942 — 31
Figure 1.19 – DJIA 1942-1962 — 32
Figure 1.20 – DJIA 1961-1982 — 33
Figure 1.21 – DJIA 1982-2002 — 34
Figure 1.22 – DJIA 2002-2010 — 35
Figure 1.23 – Tokyo Stock Exchange TOPIX Index 1949-2010 — 37
Figure 2.1 – Different ways to position trendlines — 46
Figure 2.2 – S&P 500 Daily bar chart December 2009 to October 2010 — 49
Figure 2.3 – S&P 500 Daily bar chart February 2010 to October 2010 — 50
Figure 2.4 – S&P 500 Daily bar chart February 2009 to October 2010 — 51
Figure 2.5 – S&P 500 Weekly bar chart January 2005 to October 2010 — 52
Figure 2.6 – S&P 500 Monthly bar chart 1970 to October 2010 — 53
Figure 2.7 – S&P 500 Trend Mix October 2010 — 54
Figure 2.8 – S&P 500 Index March 2009 to October 2010. Trend strength — 55
Figure 2.9 – Sine wave showing horizontal trend channel — 58
Figure 2.10 – Sine wave showing uptrend channel — 58
Figure 2.11 – Sine wave showing downtrend channel — 58
Figure 2.12 – Composite cycle (156, 78, 18, 9) showing the trend underlying the 156-day cycle — 59
Figure 2.13 – Trend underlying the 78-day cycle of the composite — 60
Figure 2.14 – Trend underlying the 18-day cycle — 60
Figure 2.15 – Trend underlying the nine-day cycle — 60
Figure 2.16 – VTL-downtrend (red), VTL-uptrend (blue) — 63
Figure 2.17 – Correct and incorrect VTLs — 64

Figure 2.18 – British Airways showing Valid Uptrend Lines	67
Figure 2.19 – British Airways showing Valid Downtrend Lines	71
Figure 2.20 – British Airways with non VTLs	73
Figure 3.1 – Sine wave with an offset replica	81
Figure 3.2 – Example of an 18-day FLD	84
Figure 3.3 – Example of a 31-day FLD	85
Figure 3.4 – 70.5-day FLD in Vedanta Resources (VED.L) February to September 2010	87
Figure 3.5 – 70.5-day FLD downward cross in Vedanta Resources (VED.L) on 28 April 2010	90
Figure 3.6 – 70.5 day FLD upward cross in Vedanta Resources on 9 July 2010	92
Figure 3.7 – Offset sine waves with no underlying trend	94
Figure 3.8 – Offset sine waves with underlying uptrend and downtrend	95
Figure 3.9 – FLD rising cascade DJ Eurostoxx 50, 11 December 2007	97
Figure 3.10 – Through the rising cascade DJ Eurostoxx 50, 18 January 2008	98
Figure 3.11 – FLD falling cascade DJ Eurostoxx 50, 14 June 2006	99
Figure 3.12 – Through falling cascade DJ Eurostoxx 50, 12 July 2006	100
Figure 4.1 – Comparison of conventional and centred moving average, Boeing (BA) daily	108
Figure 4.2 – Detrending a 14-day moving average to isolate shorter components	111
Figure 4.3 – Boeing 1998-2003, showing three 80-week cycles with MAs	112
Figure 4.4 – 40-week moving average bands, Boeing 1998-2003	113
Figure 4.5 – 40 and 80-week cycle envelopes, Boeing1998-2003	115
Figure 4.6 – Setting up the chart for phasing analysis	116
Figure 4.7 – Phasing analysis of the 54-month cycle, Boeing 1998-2003	121
Figure 4.8 – Phasing analysis of the 18-month cycle, Boeing 1998-2003	122
Figure 4.9 – Phasing analysis of the nine-month (40-week) cycle, Boeing 1998-2003	125
Figure 4.10 – Detail of grids 190 to 240	127
Figure 4.11 – Detail of grids 151 to 194	127
Figure 4.12 – Phasing analysis of the 20-week cycle in Boeing 1998-2003	129
Figure 4.13 – Phasing analysis abstract for the 10W cycle	132
Figure 4.14 – Abstract from weekly phasing model, Boeing (BA) 3 July 2003	136
Figure 4.15 – Phasing analysis final version, Boeing weekly bar chart, 1998-2003	138
Figure 5.1 – Composite of sine waves showing components and phasing analysis	146
Figure 5.2 – Periodogram of composite cycle	147
Figure 5.3 – Full phasing analysis of Boeing daily chart, 3 July 2003	149
Figure 5.4 – Periodogram on Boeing price data July 2002 to July 2003	150
Figure 5.5 – Boeing daily July 2002–July 2003 with Ehlers' DFT	151
Figure 5.6 – Abstract from Boeing weekly phasing analysis	153
Figure 5.7 – Phasing analysis of 20W cycle Boeing, July 2002–July 2003	154
Figure 5.8 – Phasing analysis of the 80D cycle	156
Figure 5.9 – Phasing analysis of 40D cycle	157
Figure 5.10 – Phasing analysis of 20D cycle	159
Figure 5.11 – Right translation in the S&P 500, 2003-2007	161
Figure 5.12 – Left translation in the S&P 500, 2000-2003, decline	162

Figure 6.1 – Rolls-Royce candlestick chart showing VI and ATR	174
Figure 6.2 – Caterpillar initial scan weekly chart – periods and amplitudes	179
Figure 6.3 – Caterpillar initial scan weekly chart - underlying trend	184
Figure 6.4 – Caterpillar final scan weekly chart	186
Figure 6.5 – Detail of Caterpillar weekly chart, 28 October 2005	187
Figure 6.6 – Caterpillar final scan daily chart	188
Figure 6.7 – Caterpillar – trading the 20W cycle post VTL Break	195
Figure 6.8 – Telefonica declining into the 2002 nest of lows	197
Figure 6.9 – Telefonica rounding the 2002 nest of lows	199
Figure 6.10 – Verizon 20-week cycle, 25 May 2006	201
Figure 6.11 – iShares Spain ETF	205
Figure 6.12 – Market Vectors Egypt ETF, 4 February 2011	207
Figure 7.1 – JPMorgan Chase weekly phasing analysis, 23 August 2002	215
Figure 7.2 – JPMorgan Chase second cycle low and recovery: late 2002-early 2003	218
Figure 7.3 – JPMorgan Chase daily, September-December 2002: trading the recovery	220
Figure 7.4 – JPMorgan Chase the next 20W cycle set up	224
Figure 7.5 – JPM trade: first leg – 2 April 2003	227
Figure 7.6 – JPM trade: second leg – 27 May 2003	229
Figure 7.7 – JPM trade: final leg – 26 June 2003	232
Figure 7.8 – JPM trade overview	233
Figure 8.1 – The first and second derivatives of price	240
Figure 8.2 – The five subdivisions of an impulse motive wave	244
Figure 8.3 – A common corrective wave: the zigzag	246
Figure 8.4 – Full cycle with higher low showing common 62% retracement	248
Figure 8.5 – Gold spot weekly phasing analysis	250
Figure 8.6 – Gold spot with weekly RSI	252
Figure 8.7 – Gold spot weekly Elliott Wave analysis	256
Figure 8.8 – Gold post-analysis, December 2010	259
Figure 8.9 – Euro-USD weekly phasing analysis, January 2010	261
Figure 8.10 – Euro-USD weekly Elliott Wave analysis, January 2010	263
Figure 8.11 – Euro-USD daily Elliott Wave analysis, January 2010	266
Figure 8.12 – Euro-USD weekly RSI analysis	267
Figure 8.13 – Euro-USD daily chart post entry	269
Table 1.1 – Data extract for composite cycle	13
Table 1.2 – Data for composite cycle in Figure 1.5 - first four time units	15
Table 1.3 – Simplified Nominal Model showing calendar days and trading days	26
Table 1.4 – Dow Jones Industrial Average Periodicity 1903-2010	36
Table 1.5 – TOPIX periodicity 1949 to 2010	38
Table 2.1 – Average cycle periods, British Airways - as of 20 July 2009	70
Table 3.1 – FLD Projections summary	94
Table 4.1 – Boeing price data for the ten days to 29 November 2010	109

Table 5.1 – Periodogram key data	147
Table 5.2 – Detail from the daily phasing model	160
Table 6.1 – RV and ATR values among DJIA members, 28 October 2005	175
Table 7.1 – Phasing model JPMorgan Chase, 17 March 2003	226

Praise for *Mastering Hurst Cycle Analysis*

"This book is highly-recommended for any market analyst or trader who wishes to add cycles to their analytical toolbox. This is a clear and concise introduction."

– Bill Sarubbi, Fund Manager, Cycles Research Investments LLC, Vienna

"Cycles are one of the most underutilised, and yet most rewarding, sources of information available to an analyst or investor. If it is possible to anticipate a reversal, and track it in real time, then eager investors should want to know about it. Until relatively recently, cycles have not been properly understood, so there has been a dearth of practical knowledge. This gap is now being filled by dedicated researchers such as Chris Grafton. His book brings together the ideas of one of the pioneers of cycle analysis – the engineer, J.M. Hurst – and presents them in an easily understandable and very useable form. Once mastered, the techniques explored in the book should be a source of significantly enhanced market understanding and very profitable investment."

– Tony Plummer, Author, *Forecasting Financial Markets*, Director, Helmsman Economics Ltd

"I really like this book. It takes the excellent original idea of Hurst and brings it right up-to-date in the modern computer era. It explains cycles and harmonics and shows how to construct Valid Trend Lines and Lines of Future Demarcation. It does not pretend that this subject is easy, but does explain it with very clear charts and writing. The work shows the relationship to Elliott waves and RSI oscillations. There are some clear worked examples and ideas of how to put on and manage a trade. Most investors will find it a useful addition to their knowledge. Well done Chris Grafton."

– Robin Griffiths, Technical Strategist, Cazenove Capital Management

"Through clear, straightforward explanations of the tools and up-to-date market illustrations, Grafton makes Hurst cycle analysis accessible to today's trader. Readers gain not only a thorough understanding of cycles but also the skills to begin implementing cyclic analysis immediately."

– Julie Dahlquist, Ph.D., CMT, Editor of the *Journal of Technical Analysis* and co-author of *Technical Analysis: The Complete Resource for Financial Market Technicians*

"J.M. Hurst's Cyclic Principles are perhaps the most powerful yet misunderstood concepts about the workings of financial markets in the history of financial trading. Published in the 1970s, Hurst's work has survived into the 21st century because it is so powerful and effective, but the application of his principles and the practice of his trading methodology have been shrouded in a cloak of arcane mystery. Christopher Grafton has done a great service to the 21st century trader by thoroughly presenting Hurst's work in a format that replaces the pencil, eraser and chart pad with a computer. Armed with the tools that Grafton includes in the book (and an understanding of how to apply them) the reader will be well placed to start honing their analytical skills and putting this powerful theory to profitable use."

– David Hickson, creator of Sentient Trader – Hurst Trading System (www.sentienttrader.com)

About the author

Christopher Grafton is currently Director, Principal Analyst and Systems Developer at Vectisma Ltd., an independent market analysis firm focusing on Japanese equities with a global macro overlay, based in England. Previously, he has held positions on the sell side at several investment banks in London and Tokyo and also worked as an analyst and trader for a London based hedge fund specialising in Japanese equities. Christopher speaks fluent Japanese, is a member of the Market Technicians Association, is a successful systems designer, programmer and trader, and holds the Chartered Market Technician designation.

Acknowledgments and thanks

My editors at Harriman House, Stephen Eckett and Craig Pearce; Physics postgrads at Imperial College and University College London: Paolo Barletta, Shaun Thomas, Chris Willis, Alastair Dunn, Alexey Lyapin, James Burnett, Marten Tolk as well as Jessica Chan at the Royal College of Music for their academic insights; Tim Grafton, for website and various technical input; Jeremy Du Plessis, Head of Technical Analysis, Updata Plc., for technical support and for allowing the use of Updata charts throughout; Corey Sheres, TradeStation, for technical support; John Ehlers, MESA Software for guidance on spectral analysis techniques; Mark Cotton at 7G Trading Tools (**www.7GTradingTools.com**) for translation into TradeStation Easy Language; Andrew Cardwell, President, Cardwell RSI Edge LLC, for advice on RSI; Jeffrey Kennedy, Chief Commodities Analyst, Elliott Wave International, for advice on Elliott Wave theory; Robert Prechter, President, Elliott Wave International, for allowing the reproduction of Elliott wave figures; Tony Plummer, Helmsman Economics Ltd., for sharing his insights and for reviewing the work; Bill Sarubbi for advice on the causes of cycles and for reviewing the work; Julie Dahlquist, Ph.D., CMT, senior lecturer, Department of Finance, at the University of Texas at San Antonio College of Business, for reviewing the work; Robin Griffiths, Technical Strategist, Cazenove Capital Management, for reviewing the work; David Hickson, creator of Sentient Trader, for reviewing the work; Giles Sarson, North Square Blue Oak, for feedback; James Ferguson, Chief Strategist, Arbuthnot Securities, for his fundamental take on the markets; Rob Roy, President Cain Brothers Asset Management, for general support and encouragement; Brent Smith, Redburn Partners, for technical input; Malcolm Pryor, for pointing me towards Harriman House; Christina, for artistic input; and finally Dako, Ollie, Charlie, Lottie and Pete for their support and forbearance.

Introduction

Overview

My experience in financial markets has been gained on the sell side broking Japanese equities for investment banks in both London and Tokyo; and on the buy side as an analyst and trader for an equity long-short fund.

My interest in market analysis drew me towards the Market Technicians Association in New York and I hold their CMT designation. I am also currently preparing a thesis for the International Federation of Technical Analysts' Master of Financial Technical Analysis (MFTA).

My knowledge of Hurst cycle analysis comes principally from studying Hurst's original material. J.M. Hurst was an American aerospace engineer in the 1960s who applied his understanding of mathematics, computing and engineering to market cycles. The workshop-style course he produced in the early 1970s described in detail the practical application of his cyclic principles to real trading. Apparently only 250 copies of the course were ever produced and after a few years of private seminars, Hurst seems to have simply vanished.

Twenty-five years later Traders Press[1] republished Hurst's original work. However, because Hurst's course was written before personal computers were widely available the content is rather difficult for the modern market technician to implement. It is also hard work; but having said that, the course is pretty much essential reading for any serious student of market cycles.

The code for all of the indicators used in this book is provided in two programming languages in the appendices. More may be added in the future if there is demand.

The purpose of this book is to get you to the stage where you can perform cyclic analysis on any freely traded financial instrument quickly and effectively on your own system. Do not expect to find it easy to begin with, because it is not. In a short time however you will find that the pieces start falling together, you get the knack and the skills become second nature. Eventually you will not remember why it seemed so hard to start with.

Hurst Cycle Analysis is part art, part detective work and part science, and once you have mastered it you will benefit from the outstanding results it is capable of producing. And, what is more, you will begin to see the markets in a completely new light.

How this book is structured

Chapter 1 – The Properties of Cycles

This chapter explains the basic physics of cycles and examines Hurst's principles. We look at the way cycles combine in the market, how they relate to one another harmonically, why they tend to synchronise at certain times and how there tends to be a more or less uniform set of cycles operating throughout the price history of all freely traded financial instruments.

Chapter 2 – Basic Tools I: Valid Trendlines

In this chapter we examine the concept of trend and look at traditional ways of drawing trendlines. We then consider a more robust definition of trend and look at the concept of the *Valid Trendline*. We will go on to learn how Valid Trendlines are constructed, why they are a more objective measure of trend and how they are used to uncover cycles in the market.

Chapter 3 – Basic Tools II: Displaced Cycles – The FLD

Here we follow on from the last chapter with a brand new tool: the *Future Line of Demarcation* or *FLD*. We will look at how this indicator is put together and then learn to use it to identify past and future reversals, project prices and reveal underlying trend.

Chapter 4 – Isolating Market Cycles I

In this chapter we get to the core element of Hurst's system: phasing analysis. We will look at how cycles are isolated in weekly market data and introduce the concepts of *cycle envelopes* and the *phasing model*.

Chapter 5 – Isolating Market Cycles II

Here we will continue the lesson on phasing analysis, but on the daily chart. We will consider the role of *spectral analysis*, a mathematical tool used to help uncover the dominant cycle. We will also look at the concept of *peak translation* and examine how it can be used to help uncover trend.

Chapter 6 – Selection, Set Up And Entry

In this chapter we will start applying what we have learnt so far to actual trading. The concept of *relative volatility* will be introduced and we will look at ways to screen long lists of securities to make them a more manageable length. We will look at ways to scan charts quickly and then move on to the setting up and entering of trading positions. The concept of risk within the context of Hurst's techniques will also be covered and you will be shown how to set stops and target prices.

Chapter 7 – Managing Open Positions

In this chapter we will look at how to manage trades using cyclic principles. You will learn why a good entry can make the trade easier to manage as well as how to control risk. We will also consider how to exit positions.

Chapter 8 – RSI And Elliott Wave

Here we will consider how to combine RSI and Elliott Wave to improve results in Hurst cycle analysis. We will explore the subject of momentum, and some advanced RSI techniques will be introduced and applied to cycles. We will also see how the Elliott Wave principle applies to cycle work and note some of the similarities.

Conclusion

A summary of all of the material covered in the book.

Appendices

Diagrams of Elliott Wave Patterns and code for the Hurst indicators in the Updata and TradeStation programming languages.

Endnote

[1] www.traderspress.com

1 THE PROPERTIES OF CYCLES

Introduction

There are recurring cycles in financial markets[2] which share common characteristics. Although cycles in the real world are rarely uniform, they can always be defined in terms of fundamental quantities. Understanding these physical properties helps us to be able to identify and interpret market cycles. Because Hurst was an engineer by training, he drew heavily on the principles of physics to develop his system of cycles-based market analysis.

The three basic quantities of cycles are *amplitude*, *period* and *phase*. These describe the size and the timing of a cycle. There tends to be a proportional relationship between the length of a cycle and its amplitude. Simply put, the longer the time between adjacent lows of a cycle, the further it tends to rise and fall. Also, when the phase of a cycle is known, we can say how far along its path it is at any given time. We can use this value to say when a cycle will reverse, or we can use it compare the progress of one cycle to that of another.

In this chapter we will cover the basic physics of cycles. This might seem somewhat removed from the markets, but a sound understanding of the nature of cycles is essential if you are to become a skilful cycles analyst.

*

Hurst observed that market action is a composite of multiple cycles. Once you have understood the elements of individual cycles, you need then to grasp how they combine with one another. Casual observers of market cycles sometimes complain that as soon as a cycle has been identified it vanishes, inverts or seems to morph into something else. These apparent inconsistencies can be accounted for by the interaction of a multiplicity of different cycles of varying magnitudes. You will be shown not only how cycles build upon one another, but also how the underlying trend, which itself is just a straightened out section of much longer cycles, can distort the picture.

Although at any given time there are many different cycles operating in the market, they belong to a finite set. In other words instead of there being infinite variety there appears to be a family of a relatively small number of related cycles. Interestingly we see this set of cycles not only in financial markets, but also in many other diverse natural phenomena. This makes the task of isolating cycles considerably easier because, at any one time, we know roughly what we should be looking for. You will be shown the cycles that make up this nominal model as well as the results of a long range study of two major market indices that helps illustrate the concept.

To simplify matters further, rather than being randomly distributed, cycles are related to one another. Most readers will be familiar with the idea of harmonics in music, but this also applies to market cycles. Hurst observed that longer cycles tend to be multiples of shorter cycles, usually by two. There are a few exceptions and at times this relationship is more difficult to see than at others, but the application of this principle makes identification of cycles much more straightforward.

Additionally, cycles tend to coincide at lows making periodicity easier to determine. These principles of *nominality*, *harmonicity* and *synchronicity* are the bedrock of Hurst cycle analysis and provide a basic framework of predictability. Of course, markets are big, complicated mechanisms and they do not always conform neatly to theoretical expectations. We will also therefore need to look at how and why the model occasionally deviates from the norm.

By the end of this chapter you should understand the basic properties of individual cycles; know how multiple cycles interact with one another; and be familiar with Hurst's principles of cyclicality. Once this foundation is in place you will be ready to start studying the powerful set of tools employed in Hurst cycle analysis.

Basic Quantities

Cycles Defined

A cycle is defined in terms of amplitude, period and phase. Figure 1.1 shows two perfect sine waves with these three basic quantities labelled.

Figure 1.1: Sine waves showing period, amplitude and phase difference

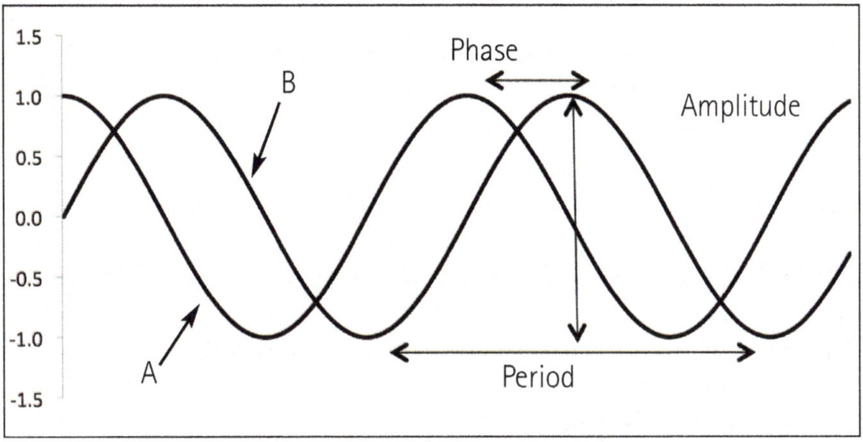

Amplitude

The first property we are going to look at is amplitude, or the height of a cycle. In physics, a cycle is defined as a repeating fluctuation of an observed variable, described by a sine wave around a central value. This sounds a bit convoluted, but is very straightforward. In financial markets, the observed variable is price and the central value is the long-term average price. In other words, price tends to fluctuate rhythmically around a mean.

A full cycle describes a path through time from a trough to a peak and then back again to the level of the previous trough. In physics, amplitude is defined as the absolute difference between the central value and the peak or trough. In market analysis, however, it is the distance between these two extremes. In Figure 1.1 the amplitude is two as the values change from -1 to +1.[3]

Velocity and acceleration

The amplitude of a cycle is a measure of its size or power. In the market it is represented by price change. All cycles, whether big and powerful or small and weak, display exactly the same characteristics: the speed of a cycle is zero at its trough and again at its peak, and it is at its maximum halfway up or halfway down.

The acceleration of the cycle, on the other hand, is greatest as it comes out of the turns and least when it is midway between peak and trough in either direction. Thus, *regardless* of amplitude, a cycle's speed is lowest at either extreme when its acceleration is highest; and conversely, a cycle's speed is highest mid-way along its path when its acceleration is lowest.

Period

The time after which the pattern of a cycle starts repeating itself is the length or period of the cycle. In Figure 1.1 this is the distance between the two adjacent troughs shown. If a cycle has a period of 20 days, for example, one full revolution from low to high and back to low takes 20 days to complete. A nine-month cycle takes nine months to complete, an 18-year cycle takes 18 years to complete, and so on.

Frequency

The frequency of a cycle is the reciprocal of the period and shows how many times it fluctuates in a given time. In physics the convention is to describe cycles in terms of frequency and the standard measurement is hertz, or one cycle per second.

In market analysis, however, we talk in terms of period. If the cycle period is short, then the frequency is high. If the cycle period is long, then the frequency is low. For a cycle with a period of 20 days, we would say that the frequency is 1/20th of a cycle per day. Thus in ten days the cycle would have completed half a full revolution. This brings us on to the final basic property of cycles: phase.

Phase

If you imagine two cycles with the same period, but peaking at different times, then the time shift between these two cycles is the phase. Two cycles are in phase if their lows correspond. Otherwise they are out of phase.

In physics, if two cycles have a constant phase difference, then they have the same frequency and are said to be coherent. Coherence is a measure of cyclic correlation and is central to another concept that will be examined when we look at the interaction of different cycles: that of constructive and destructive interference.

If both cycles in Figure 1.1 are given a period of 20 days and Line B is offset from Line A by a quarter of a period, then the phase difference between the cycles is five days (one quarter of 20).

If we think of Line A as being in the lead, then having topped first it is already halfway down as Line B reaches its peak. Similarly, when Line A bottoms, it is already halfway up as Line B reaches its trough.

This sort of relationship is often described in inter-market analysis when referring to the phase of the commodity market cycle in terms of the bond market cycle or when looking at sector rotation in the stock market and so on. However, the concept of phase is also the basis for one of the most powerful tools in Hurst analysis: the *FLD* or *displaced cycle*, which will be examined in detail in chapter three.

Phase in the market

It is possible to talk about the phase of a single cycle, providing a reference point in time is chosen. The usual way to express phase in the market, however, is in terms of time elapsed since the occurrence of a cycle trough.

For example: *prices are currently five days along a 20-day cycle* is a description of phase. This is useful information, because if we are five days along in a 20-day cycle, then – other things being equal – we know not only that the cycle is going up strongly, but also that it is another five days from a top. Alternatively, if the cycle phase is 15 days, then we know that it is five days past the top, going down strongly and another five days from the next low.

This concept is central to another key tool in Hurst's system: the *phasing model*, which will be introduced in chapter four.

Proportionality

Hurst observed that with the exception of very long cycles, amplitude and period tend to be proportional.[4] What this means, for example, is that an 80-day cycle can be expected to have roughly twice the amplitude of a 40-day cycle; a 20-day cycle can be expected to have twice the amplitude of a 10-day cycle, and so on.

This makes sense, after all you would expect an 18-month long cycle to be able to push prices up or down further than would a 20-day cycle. Thus, if you believe that a very long cycle has just bottomed, it is reasonable to assume that, other things being equal, there will be a proportionally large move out.

Of course there are times when this relationship appears to break down, for example in a long consolidation pattern, but this can be explained in terms of the action of other even longer cycles, as will be covered when we discuss the concept of *summation*.

Visualising Period and Amplitude

Physical models

Although physics analogies should be seen as learning tools rather than be taken too literally, using physical models can give us a better feel for market cycles. The following examples will help you picture what we have covered so far.

One intuitive way to visualise period, amplitude and proportionality is think about dropping a bouncy ball so that it falls to the ground. The ball is released, accelerates downwards to its maximum speed and bounces off the ground. Before it reverses direction its speed is briefly zero and when it reaches the top of its bounce its speed is once again briefly zero.

The greater the height of the drop – amplitude – the longer the time between initial bounces – period – before friction absorbs the ball's kinetic energy and brings it to rest. Drop the ball from lower down, however, and the bounces are shorter and quicker, i.e. the frequency is higher. If you were to plot the ball's path as a time series on a graph it would look very much like cyclic motion.

Mass spring oscillator

Although the bouncing ball example helps to illustrate the proportional relationship between amplitude and period, the behaviour of a true cycle is subtly different. In the ball's case, the force of acceleration and deceleration acts either straight up or straight down, i.e. the bounce and gravity.

The acceleration of a true cycle, on the other hand, is always towards the centre of its oscillation, in other words it reverts to the mean. This can be demonstrated with a mass spring oscillator as shown in Figure 1.2.

Figure 1.2: Mass spring oscillator[5]

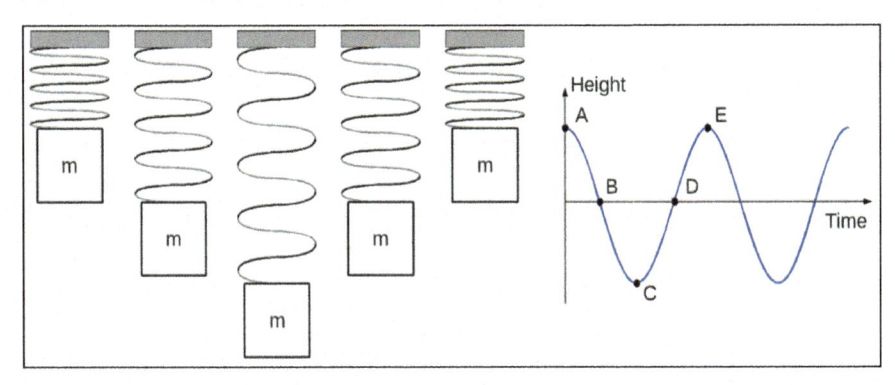

When the load (m) attached to the spring is released it initially falls due to gravity, stretching the spring (A to B on the graph). At point B the forces acting on the load become balanced and the speed is at the maximum. The load then continues down at a slower speed as the spring's restoring force exerts itself, stops briefly (at point C), after which the evolution of its motion is reversed. At point E the load returns to the initial height finishing one cycle and starting a new one.

Assuming the rigidity of the spring is constant the mass of the load will determine the length of the period (and conversely the frequency of the swings) as well as the vertical displacement (amplitude) which will be in direct proportion.

Note that at the low (point C) and high (points A and E) the speed is zero. Unlike the ball the maximum speed, as we noted earlier, is in the *middle* (points B and D) and this is the crucial point to remember when we start looking at market behaviour.

Shock absorbers

We can take this idea a step further. Think of the suspension in a car travelling down a road and hitting a bump. The size of the bump determines the initial amplitude and the car spring will continue to oscillate as the car travels along.

Unlike a laboratory mass spring oscillator, these oscillations will be damped by the shock absorbers and will decay as shown in Figure 1.3, like a pendulum in syrup. On the other hand, if the energy lost to friction is replaced, for example more bumps of the right size and in the right spots on the road, then plotting the motion of the end point on the spring as the car drives along will replicate the same sine wave we saw in Figure 1.1.

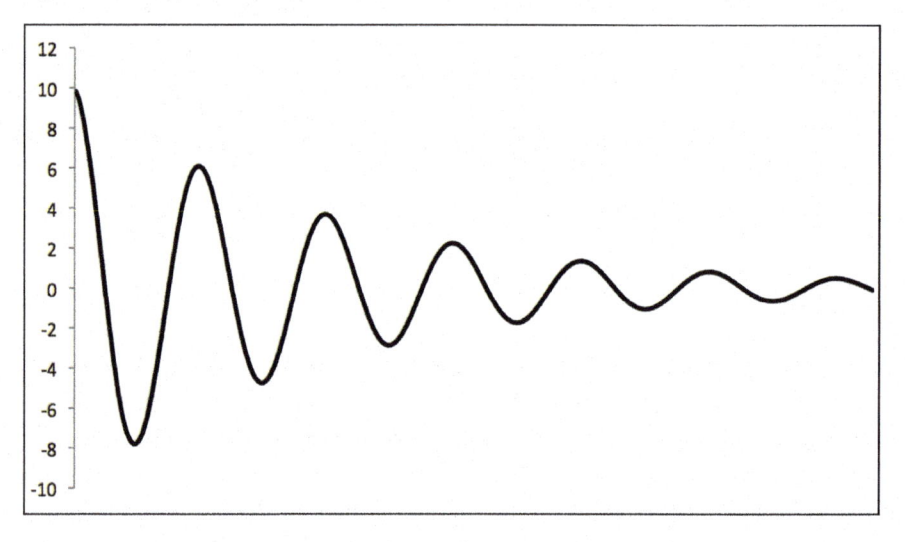

Figure 1.3: Damped oscillation[6]

How Cycles Combine

Now that you have a better feel for the characteristics of individual cycles it is time to look at the behaviour of multiple cycles. Hurst's insight was that the market is a composite of numerous cycles of varying magnitude interacting with each other. Each cycle is separate and yet they combine in a specific way to create price patterns and the overall shape of market action.

The way cycles combine is by simple addition: the value of a short cycle at any given time is summed with that of a long cycle, which in turn is summed with an even longer cycle and so on to the upper limit. What we perceive as price movement is simply all of these cycles added together. In physics this is known as superposition. Hurst referred to it as the *Principle of Summation*.

Summation

Let us say that the two sine waves in the middle and lower charts of Figure 1.4 are an 18-month (78 week) and an 18-week cycle respectively. The value of each of these cycles at each point in time is summed to create the composite curve at the top.

Two price patterns in the composite should immediately be obvious: a Double Bottom and a Head and Shoulders top.

Figure 1.4: Head and Shoulders Top and Double Bottom Composite (78 week plus 18 week)

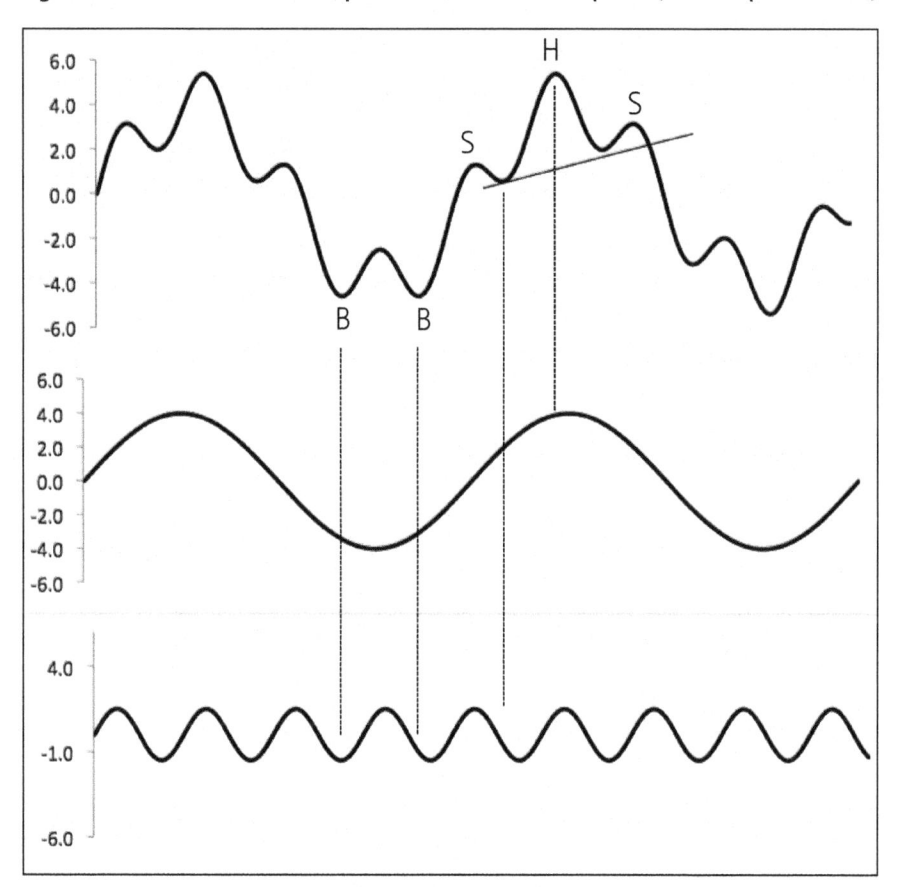

Creating a composite cycle

The patterns that show up in the composite are just the result of the two cycles interacting in the following manner:

- Starting in the middle of the chart, the 18-week cycle runs up along the advancing leg of the 18-month cycle. The second trough of the 18-week cycle occurs halfway along the 18-month cycle's up-leg and temporarily pulls it down to create the left shoulder. This is an example of so called destructive interference.

- The peaks of both cycles then superimpose to create the head, which is an example of constructive interference. The 18-week cycle then runs down the decline of the 18-month cycle with the third peak of the shorter cycle pulling the longer cycle down to form the right shoulder.

- Notice also how the composite cycle seems to lengthen in the decline and how the middle section is the steepest and longest. Note also during this stage that the second crest of the 18-week cycle does not overlap the first trough of the 18-week cycle. These are features of a five-wave decline that should instantly be recognisable as an impulse wave to students of Elliott Wave.

As for the double bottom, the sharp lows are the 18-week cycle superimposing onto the 18-month trough – another example of constructive interference – and the intervening peak that defines the double bottom is the 18-week cycle showing through the composite cycle – which again is destructive interference.

Table 1.1 gives the values of each cycle at each point in time and illustrates how the composite is derived. For example, the first bottom (B) in the composite has a value of -5, which is the sum of -1 (18 week) and -4 (18M). The left shoulder (S), has a value of +1, the sum of +1 and 0; the Head (H) has a value of +5, the sum of +4 and +1. Notice that the trend component in this example is zero, i.e. it has no impact on the shape of the composite.

Table 1.1: Data extract for composite cycle

X-axis	78W	18W	Trend	Sum
	A	B	C	(A+B+C)
0.00	0.00	0.00	0.00	0.00
0.50	0.16	0.26	0.00	0.42
1.00	0.32	0.51	0.00	0.83
1.50	0.48	0.75	0.00	1.23
2.00	0.64	0.96	0.00	1.61
2.50	0.80	1.15	0.00	1.95
3.00	0.96	1.30	0.00	2.26
3.50	1.11	1.41	0.00	2.52
4.00	1.27	1.48	0.00	2.74
4.50	1.42	1.50	0.00	2.92
5.00	1.57	1.48	0.00	3.05

Complex composites

Obviously the market is more complicated than this: first, there are many more possible components; and secondly market cycles are not perfect sine waves. Nevertheless, the process is the same.

Figure 1.5 shows a composite curve not dissimilar to what you might see in actual market data. This has been created by adding together four perfect sine waves. Let us say that these component sine waves have periods of 156, 78, 18 and nine days and that their respective amplitudes are in proportion, as shown in Figure 1.6.

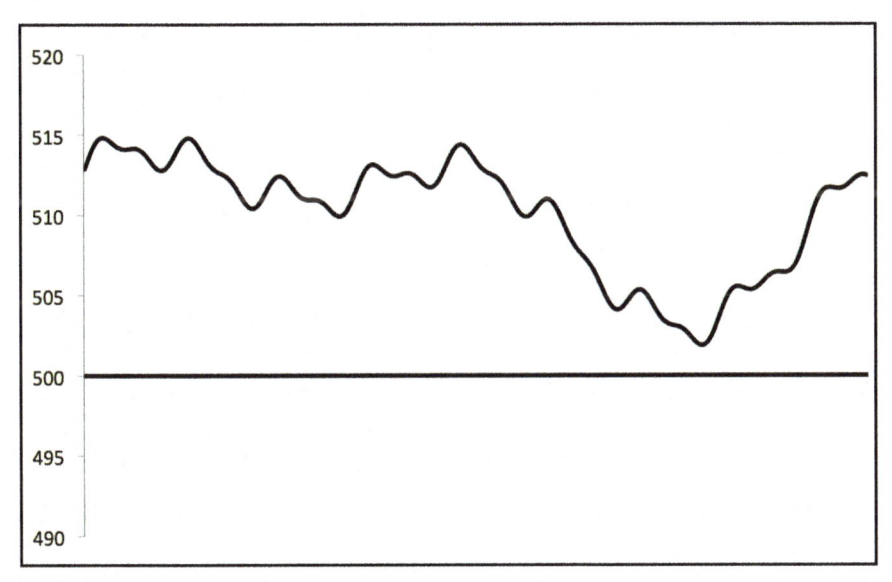

Figure 1.5: Complex composite consisting of four component cycles (156, 78, 18, 9)

Figure 1.6: Individual components of the complex composite wave in Figure 1.5

156-day cycle

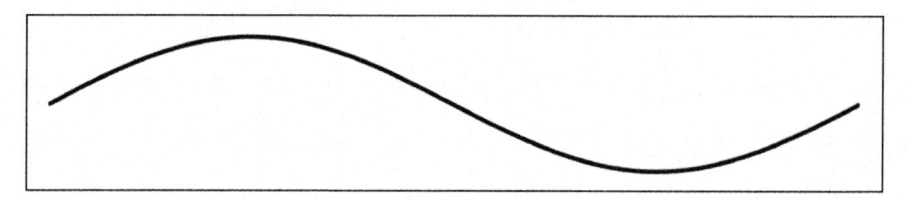

78-day cycle

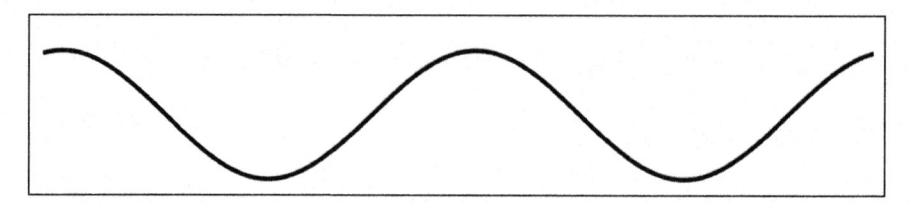

18-day cycle

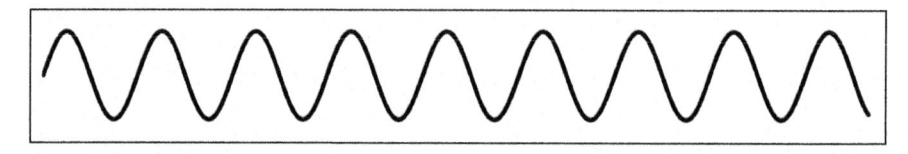

Nine-day cycle

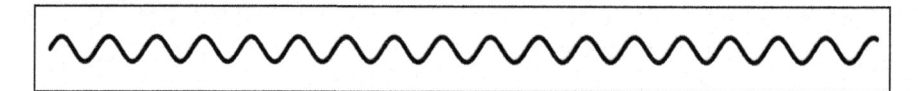

Underlying trend (composite of all cycles longer than 156 days)

Again you can see how the value of each cycle at each point in time is simply added together to create the composite. Table 1.2 shows the detail of the first four time units. The final column is the sum of each cycle value and this has been added to a constant (K) of 510 to enhance visibility.

Table 1.2: Data for composite cycle in Figure 1.5 - first four time units

X-axis	156D	78D	18D	9D	Trend	Sum+K
0.00	0.00	2.88	0.00	0.00	0	512.9
0.50	0.08	2.91	0.17	0.17	0	513.3
1.00	0.16	2.94	0.34	0.32	0	513.8
1.50	0.24	2.96	0.50	0.43	0	514.1
2.00	0.32	2.98	0.64	0.49	0	514.4

The effect of underlying trend

Figure 1.7 shows the FTSE 100 Index daily bar chart from March 2009 to September 2010. The sine wave with a period of 80 days shown in the lower window looks to be a pretty close approximation to the cycles in the price data.

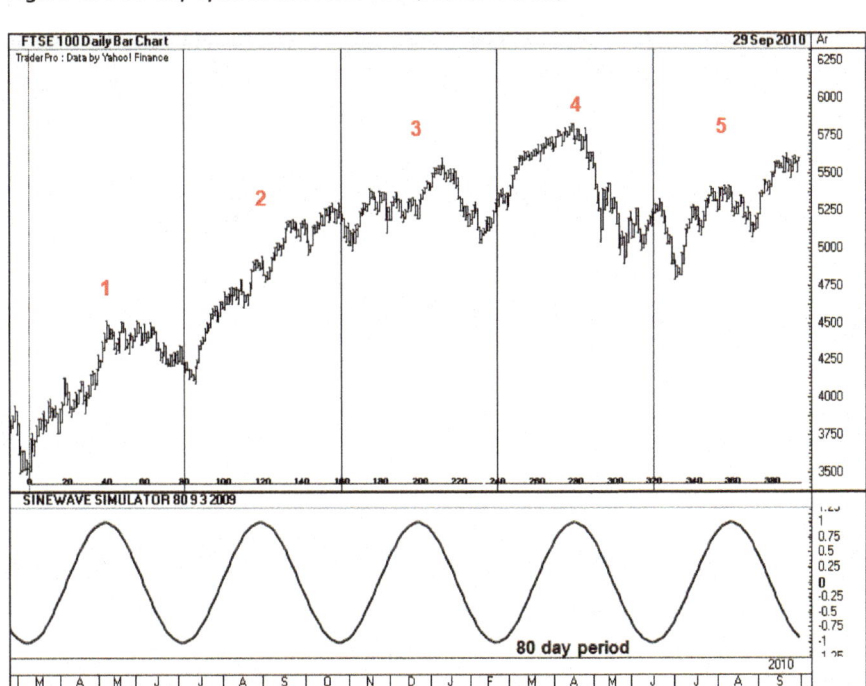

Figure 1.7: 80-day cycle in the FTSE 100 (Source: Yahoo)

Despite the uniformity of the dominant cycle running through the FTSE 100 here, each numbered cycle looks slightly different. The second low of the first cycle is much higher than the first. The second cycle hardly looks like a cycle at all. The fourth shows a longer period and a lower second trough, and so on.

The reason for this distortion is the presence of underlying trend or, more correctly, the action of the sum of all longer cycles.

In stage one the underlying trend has just turned up, causing the second higher low; in stage two the trend is now firmly up obscuring the fluctuation of the cycle; and finally in stage four the trend has turned down, causing the cycle to extend and form a second lower low.

Swamped cycles

Figure 1.8 shows the same composite we were just studying (Figure 1.5) but this time a 5° trend has been added. All that has been done here is to add a set of values that plots a diagonal line across the chart. The value of each cycle is then added to the value of this new line at each point in time. The fluctuations seem to be muted.

Figure 1.8: Composite with 5° trend added

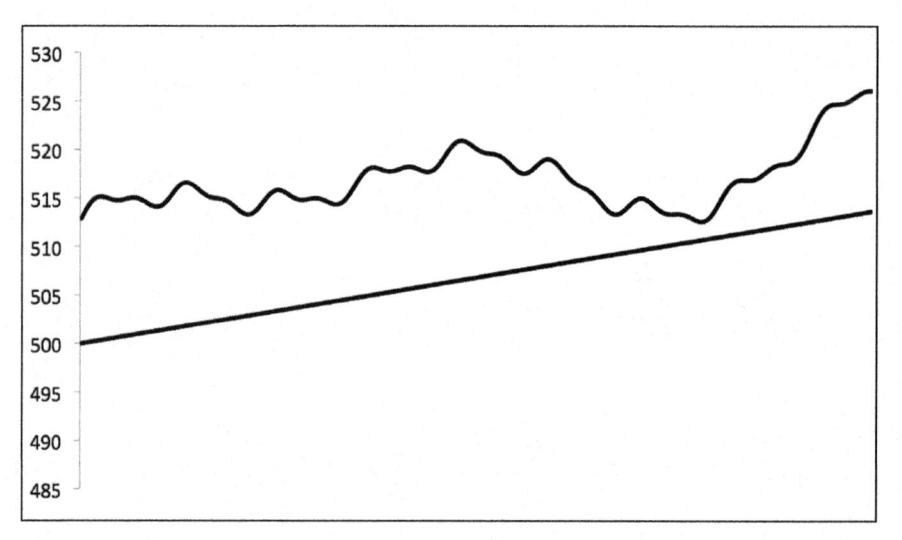

Figure 1.9 shows the same composite, but this time a 15° trend has been added. This time the cycles' fluctuations are much less apparent. The cycles are still there, it is just that they have been swamped by the underlying trend.

The stronger the trend component the more pronounced is this effect. This is one of the reasons some market observers are suspicious of cycles and bemoan the fact that they seem to come and go.

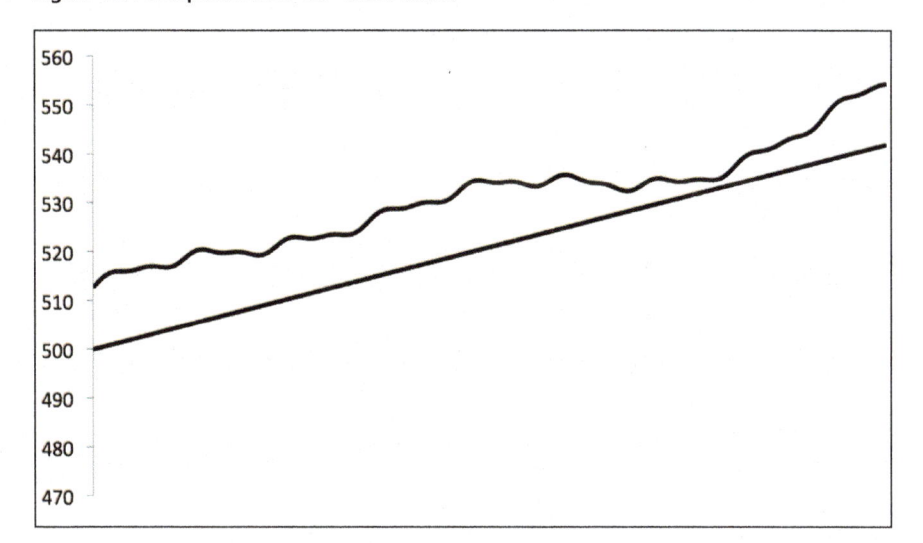

Figure 1.9: Composite with 15° trend added

Properties of Market Cycles

Hurst's principles

Hurst observed that market cycles, and indeed cycles in many other naturally occurring phenomena, are governed by a set of core principles which all fall under the broader heading of the *Principle of Cyclicality*. These principles are as follows:

1. *Harmonicity*: cycles typically tend to be related to one another by multiples of two, although in certain cases by a multiple of three.

2. *Synchronicity*: cycle lows tend to converge: in other words the trough of a long cycle will coincide with the trough of all shorter component cycles. Although, apart from commodities, this is not the case for cycle peaks, which tend to be more dispersed.

3. *Nominality*: there is one more or less uniform set of cycles from very long to very short.

4. *Variation*: deviation from the norm is to be expected: cycle periods and amplitudes vary over time.

5. *Commonality*: these principles are applicable to cycles in all markets across the entire price history.

It is worth remembering here that although Hurst used the word *principle* he did not mean *physical law*, like the law of gravity or the law of thermodynamics, but rather *strong tendency*. Occasionally the influence of strong fundamental factors or price shocks will temporarily distort the picture. This is to be expected: forecasting the market is not an exact science.

1. Harmonicity

We have seen that price action is a composite curve of a multiplicity of different cycles. Adding sine waves together on a spreadsheet and generating a composite curve is easily done. Pulling that composite apart again and identifying the components is less easy. Extracting cyclic information from market data is harder still.

The main purpose of Hurst cycle analysis and the subject of this book is how to extract cycles from market data and form conclusions about what path they will follow beyond the end of the data.

Isolating component cycles would be made very much more difficult were it not for the strong tendency of cycles to form harmonic relationships.

Harmonics example

A useful way to conceptualise waves (cycles) in market action is to imagine you are sitting on a beach near a busy fishing port. You watch three types of vessel going past at regular intervals – a cargo ship, a ferry and a trawler – with the wash from each of these breaking onto your beach as waves.

- Every 54 minutes a cargo ship passes and produces a big wave.
- Every 18 minutes a ferry passes and produces a lesser wave.
- Every nine minutes the trawler passes and produces a much smaller wave.
- The cargo ship is three times the size of the ferry and the ferry is twice the size of the trawler.
- The wash created is proportional to the size of the boat, there is a 3:2:1 harmonic relationship and the waves are synchronised.

You could represent these three waves graphically as in Figure 1.10. Notice that there are two full revolutions of the short cycle (red) to one revolution of the mid cycle (blue) and there are three full revolutions of the mid cycle to one of the long cycle (black). The cycles are harmonically related and the pattern produced is pleasing to the eye.

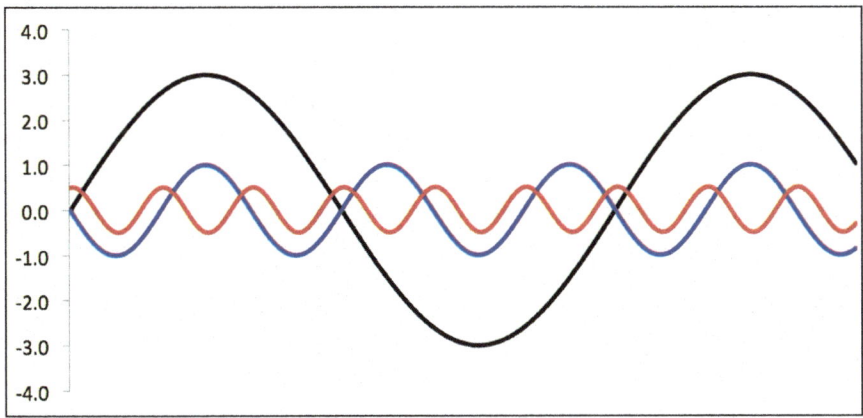

Figure 1.10: Set of harmonic and synchronised proportional waves 54, 18 and 9 unit periods

Figure 1.11 on the other hand shows three cycles lacking harmonicity. This is a much more confused and seemingly random picture and were market cycles arranged in this way we would have a hard job extracting useful information. Fortunately, however, they are not.

Figure 1.11: Non-harmonic and non-synchronised waves (lacking proportionality for emphasis)

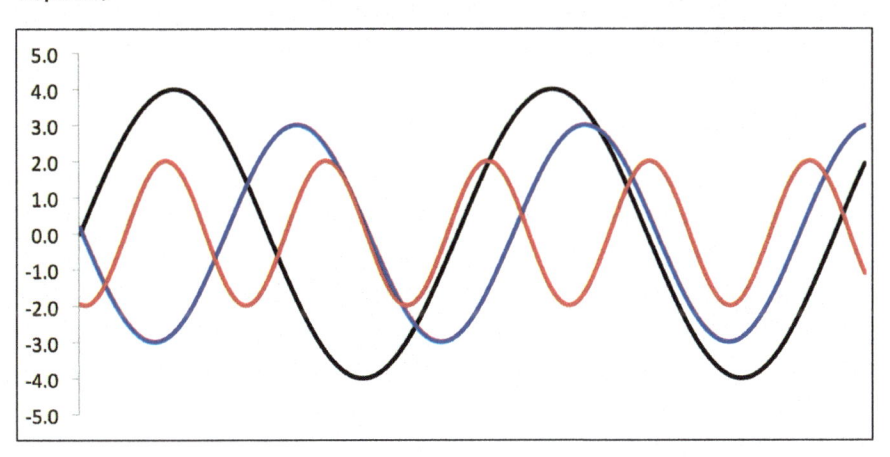

Market harmonics

Multiples of two

The periods of market cycles, and indeed many other naturally occurring cycles, are typically related to one another by a factor of two. Any given cycle tends to be half as long as its closest longer neighbour and twice as long as its closest shorter neighbour. Thus, if you have identified an 80-day cycle, you can expect it to break down into two 40-day cycles. If you are looking at a 40-day cycle, you should be looking for two 20-day cycles, and so on.

Going the other way, if you have found a 20-week cycle in the data, you should be looking for another 20-week cycle to make up a 40-week cycle. If you are looking at a 40-week cycle expect it to be the first half of an 80-week cycle, and so on. Naturally, this makes the job of searching for cycles much more straightforward. If you have found one, you should be able to find the others.

Multiples of three

Hurst identified two exceptions to this: the 54-month cycle breaks down into three 18-month cycles and the 54-year cycle (sometimes called the Kondratieff wave) breaks down into three 18-year cycles. Why this should be so is uncertain.

It should be noted that certain respected analysts have identified three as the base harmonic rather than two[7], and this may well be a suitable area for further research. In our experience however, using the relationship of two as the base gets the required results more often than not.

Sometimes market cycles are difficult to read and a cycle other than the 54 month will seem to break down into three harmonics rather than the usual two. It is not unheard of, but it is the exception. If you do come across this, you will often find a way to make a harmonic two work without too much contortion. This sounds a bit shoot from the hip, but it will become clear when we look at isolating market cycles in chapters four and five.

Harmonics in music

A rough analogy for market harmonicity can be made with music. Figure 1.12 is a graphical representation of the frequency of a vibrating string showing the second, fourth and eighth harmonics.

When an instrument produces a note, the fundamental pitch is accompanied by a series made up of harmonics (or overtones). The relative intensity of these harmonics determines the timbre of each note, that is to say the characteristic piano or violin sound.

Harmonic series exist because when a string (or column of air) vibrates, it does so by vibrating at several frequencies simultaneously – each resulting in a harmonic. Like the markets, these frequencies only occur at integer multiples of the fundamental frequency and that is why all harmonic series follow the same pattern, irrespective of the fundamental pitch[8]. The difference between these harmonics and those of cycles, of course, is that it is the nodes that coincide here rather than the troughs.

Figure 1.12: Vibrating string showing even harmonic levels

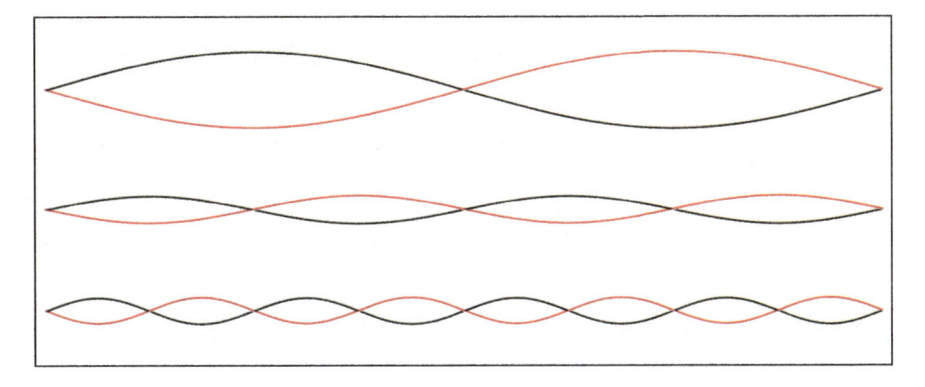

Synchronicity

Cycle troughs tend to converge giving them a sharp appearance. If cycles have a harmonic relationship then their troughs will have to coincide periodically, which goes some way to explaining it. On the other hand, peaks tend to be non-synchronous and more dispersed, giving them a more rounded appearance. This is the reason for the convention of measuring cycle period from low to low.

Figure 1.13 shows three harmonic and synchronised sine waves. The diamonds in the lower part of the diagram represent the location of the troughs and the triangles in the upper part represent the location of the peaks. As you can see, the distribution of the diamonds is more uniform.

Although the market consists of a much larger set of cycles and the picture is more complex, we see the same thing. Figure 1.14 shows a monthly bar chart of the FTSE 100 between 1984 and 2010. Apart from two apparent anomalies in 1987 and 1994, the tops are rounded and the bottoms are sharp.

Figure 1.13: Harmonic waves in phase showing synchronisation of troughs and dispersion of peaks

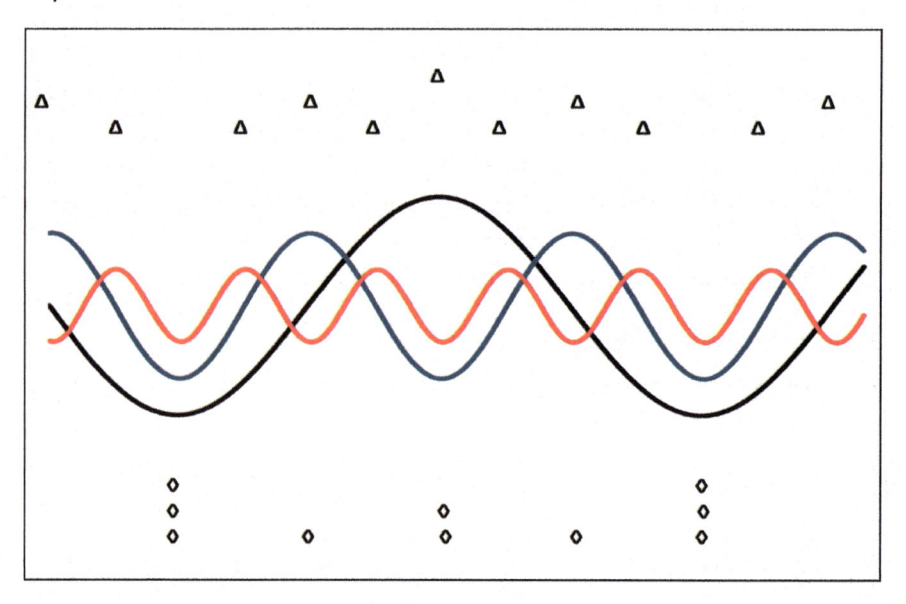

Figure 1.14: FTSE 100 showing tendency for sharp bottoms and rounded tops (Data: Yahoo)

Implications

Synchronicity means that the troughs of longer waves will coincide with the troughs of all of their shorter harmonic neighbours. For example, the time location of an 80-week low will be the same as that of a 40-week low, a 20-week low, a ten-week low and so on down.

What it does not mean, however, is that a short cycle low also implies the presence of a longer cycle low. This makes sense of course, because in any time series short cycles will be more numerous than long cycles and mathematically, not every short cycle trough can correspond to that of a longer cycle.

The usefulness of the phenomenon of synchronicity to cycle analysis should be apparent. Once a long cycle period trough has been identified, we have immediately identified the time location of all shorter cycle troughs. This will be all become a lot clearer when we start looking at actual techniques later in the book.

Behavioural explanation

The reason often given for rounded tops and sharp bottoms markets is as follows: hope dissipates slowly whereas fear, being a more powerful motivator, reaches a crescendo faster[9].

Most traders will be familiar with the feeling of wanting to hold out for a bit more profit, believing that the market has further to go up and getting more excited as trading profits grow. At the same time, new buyers attracted to higher prices continue to probe higher until gradually the weight of sell orders from more thoughtful traders makes itself felt. Eventually demand is exhausted and the emphasis shifts from the bid to the offer. Positive sentiment takes time to unwind.

On the other hand, once the herd stampedes, it is a brave soul who ignores the call. Traders at all time-frames up to the longest cycle in the approaching trough hurry to unload their positions until they are sold out. Because this happens fast, time on the chart seems to compress and the move into the low appears sharp and steep.

Fear in equal or even greater measure is also present on the other side of the lows as short sellers at all time-frames up to the longest cycle in the trough rush to cover their positions. This again has the effect of compressing time on the chart adding to the sharp appearance of the trough.

Cyclic motion

Cycles transporting energy

Before moving on to discuss the principles of *nominality* and *variation*, it is worth spending a moment thinking about the actual motion of cycles in markets.

A modern physicist might say something like *there are no things, only waves*. What is meant by this is that what we take for granted as solid matter is actually a complex web of electromagnetic waves or cycles. Thus, the chair you are sitting on is made of waves; this book is made of waves and so on. This all sounds a bit far removed from the practicalities of everyday life, but it does lead to another important property of cycles.

Waves are not things in their own right they simply transport energy through things[10]. When you flick the end of a skipping rope the transverse wave that runs along its length is only displacing the rope vertically, it is not actually moving it forward. Similarly, ocean swell is the energy of wind and tide rotating the sea upwards at a given point and then moving on, rather than the sea pouring from one place to another.

Thus wave energy in each case is transferred from point to adjacent point creating the illusion of forward movement. In the same way a film creates the impression of continuity, but is in fact just a series of separate images constantly remade.

Cycle energy in the market

Applying this analogy to market cycles forces the question, what medium is the wave energy passing through? The obvious answer is that it moves through prices, but more accurately it moves through the mood of the market participants.

The medium of mood

Traders' emotions

The ostensible driver of prices, supply and demand, is a different concept in freely traded financial markets than it is in, say, a market for bread or shoes. We buy (or short sell) in the markets planning to reverse the trade at some point in the future so that we can make money. In other words we hope for a positive outcome.

Alternatively, we sell a long position (or cover a short) because we have made money and we fear being stuck with something we cannot sell on at a favourable price. In other words we fear a negative outcome. In normal circumstances, this emotional content is largely absent (when purchasing bread for example).

It is the emotions of individual traders that persuade them to either buy or sell or stay out of the market. Of course traders do not live in isolation; they are members of society and as such they are subject to the overall mood of society. Even though price marks the progress of a cycle, the medium through which cyclic energy is transmitted is social mood.

History repeats

We know that mood changes over time. The 54-year Kondratieff cycle is sometimes thought to be the time it takes for one generation to forget the lessons learnt by the previous generation: how much different do you think social mood was after the Depression compared to at the top of tech bubble? How different was the mood of the times in the early 1960s to that of the 1980s, or the mood in March 2009 to the mood in January 2011? These long-term cyclical swings do not come out of nowhere – they build step by step and these steps are cyclical in nature.

This process of cyclical change is repeated at every timeframe right down to the daily level. The emotions on a trading desk over the course of an afternoon are no different to those over twenty days or twenty weeks. The Dutch trader buying and selling tulips in 1637 will have had a lot in common with a hedge fund manager trading asset-backed securities in 2006.

People's motivations remain the same, and the patterns caused by cyclic action we see in the price charts of the nineteenth century are broadly the same as they are now and, no doubt, as they will be in years to come.

The Nominal Model

Rather than there being an infinite number of different individual cycles in the price history, there appears to be a specific set. These share the characteristics of cycles described so far and yet they are separate. Hurst called this the *Nominal Model*.

- The longest cycle catalogued in the model is 54 years, the next shorter cycle is 18 years and the shortest at this degree of magnitude is nine years. For the purposes of Hurst cycle analysis, these are treated as very long-term trends.

- At the monthly level, a nine-year cycle divides into two 54-month cycles, which further divide into three 18-month cycles (usually labelled 80 weeks), which further divide into two nine-month cycles.
- The nine-month cycle is the equivalent to a 40-week cycle, which consists of two 20-week cycles, which subdivide further into two ten-week cycles.
- The 10-week cycle is labelled as an 80-day cycle on the daily chart and this breaks down into separate 40-day, 20-day and ten-day cycles.
- Naturally, cycles also exist longer than 54 years and shorter than ten days.

Table 1.3 is a summary of the Nominal Model in calendar days and trading days.

Table 1.3: Simplified Nominal Model showing calendar days and trading days[11]

Calendar Days

Years	Months	Weeks	Days
54			
18			
9			
	54		
	18	80 (560D)	
	9	40 (280D)	
		20 (140D)	
		10 (70D)	80
			40
			20
			10

Trading Days

Years	Months	Weeks	Days
54			
18			
9			
	54		
	18	80 (392D)	
	9	40 (196D)	
		20 (98D)	
		10 (49D)	56
			28
			14
			7

Calendar time and trading time

Cycles run in calendar time rather than in trading time. This seems counter intuitive and why it should be so is a good area for further research. We will consider some possible reasons in the last chapter, when we discuss the causes of cycles, but for now it is probably best just to accept it.

Hurst's Nominal Model is based on calendar time and not trading time, which presents a slight problem for anyone using a trading platform set up only to show trading days, which of course means pretty much everyone. The following conversion therefore needs to be made at the daily level:

- There are roughly 250 trading days in a 365-day calendar year. To convert calendar days to trading days, therefore, multiply by 0.7 (250/365).

- Conversely, to convert trading days into calendar days, divide by 0.7 (multiply by 1.42)
- Thus, the nominal 80-day cycle is 80 x 0.7, or 56 trading days
- The nominal 40-day cycle is 40 x 0.7, or 28 trading days
- The nominal 20-day cycle is 20 x 0.7, or 14 trading days, and so on

These numbers should be familiar to most technicians as the basis for the popular 55-day moving average; the 26-day standard setting for MACD; and the 14-day default settings for RSI, DMI and Stochastics.

Time gaps

Hurst's original daily charts showed time gaps for weekends and holidays, which means that there is some distortion when these are omitted and the bars are continuous. Obviously, because there are no week-long gaps in trading, this problem does not present itself on weekly charts. The problem on the intraday level is acute however, which is why you will need a modified trading platform to perform Hurst analysis at this timeframe. David Hickson's Sentient Trader – a superb automated Hurst cycles analysis system – does just this[12].

Figure 1.15 shows an example of the FTSE 100 with the first four gaps marked with X[13].

Figure 1.15: FTSE 100 bar chart 1 July–21 October 2010, with gaps for non-trading days

Alternative cycles

Arguably there are alternative cycle durations which recur in market price history: for example the ten-year decennial cycle; the four-year US Presidential cycle; the business cycle; seasonal cycles; the lunar cycle, and so on. These are all expressions of the Nominal Model and for clarity it is probably best to stick to Hurst's original nomenclature.

A cursory examination of two stock indices, the Dow Jones Industrial Average (DJIA) and the Japanese Topix, will show that Hurst's Nominal Model appears to be a fairly accurate representation of what is actually happening.

For the sake of brevity, we will only be considering the long cycles from 54 months to 54 years. However, as above, so below; the subdivisions continue all the way down to the shortest cycles. You will be exposed to numerous examples of shorter cycles over the course of the rest of the book.

Nominality in the DJIA and Topix

The charts that follow (Figures 1.16 to 1.23) are an attempt to isolate the long cycles of the Nominal Model in the DJIA from 1900 to 2010 as well as in Topix from 1949 to 2010. The technique used is a rough and ready version of Hurst's method of extracting cycles in market data; *phasing analysis*. This will be covered in detail in chapters four and five.

The rows of coloured diamonds in the lower part of each chart correspond to the approximate time location of troughs in the component cycles (54Y, 18Y, 9Y and 54M): the convention being, as you have learnt, to measure cycle periods between cycle lows rather than peaks.

Thus, the top row displays time locations of the nominal 54-year cycle troughs; the second row displays the nominal 18-year cycle troughs; the third row displays the nine year cycle; and the fourth row the shows the troughs of the 54-month cycle.

The Dow Jones Industrial Average: 1900 - 2010

Overview

Figure 1.16 shows the broad sweep of prices in the DJIA over the twentieth century and the first decade of the twenty-first century. The charts that follow will break the period into shorter sections. This is not intended to be the last word, and some analysts may disagree with the interpretation, but the purpose here is to illustrate the concept of nominality. Glance through the charts and check the results tabulated at the end.

Chapter 1 | The Properties Of Cycles

Figure 1.16: Dow Jones Industrial Average 1900-2010 (Data courtesy of www.wrenresearch.com.au)

For experts in economic cycles, it might look like liberties are being taken with the 54-year Kondratieff cycle (or K-Wave) placement in 1982. Kondratieff, a Russian economist, who first proposed this cycle, suggested that 1896 was the last low in the nineteenth century, which would make 1950 the following low. Since this puts the low right in the middle of one of the strongest rallies this century, it is a difficult case to make.

If any year is to be a contender for a Kondratieff low, then surely 1932 would be it. This would make 1878 the previous low, the beginning of the railway age. If we take a shortened cycle of 50 years from 1932, then 1982 was the most recent K-Wave trough. This corresponds to the start of a major bull market, the last in fact of the twentieth century, which culminated in the tech bubble of 2000.

One could argue therefore that if the current K-Wave is also running short at 50 years, then it topped in 2007. Assuming that even longer cycles underlying the K-Wave are not advancing, then as of 2010, we are three years into a multi-decade decline.

DJIA: 1900–1921

Figure 1.17 shows the DJIA from 1900 to 1921. Three clear 54M cycles (red diamonds) are apparent although the first cycle is shortened. Although it is not needed in this chart, the data has been detrended and the output is shown in the lower window. Detrending is simply a method of extracting underlying trend from the data so that the cycles show up more clearly. In this case it is a percentage based moving average convergence-divergence (MACD) line set at three and 12 years. We will talk a little more about the concept of detrending in chapter four.

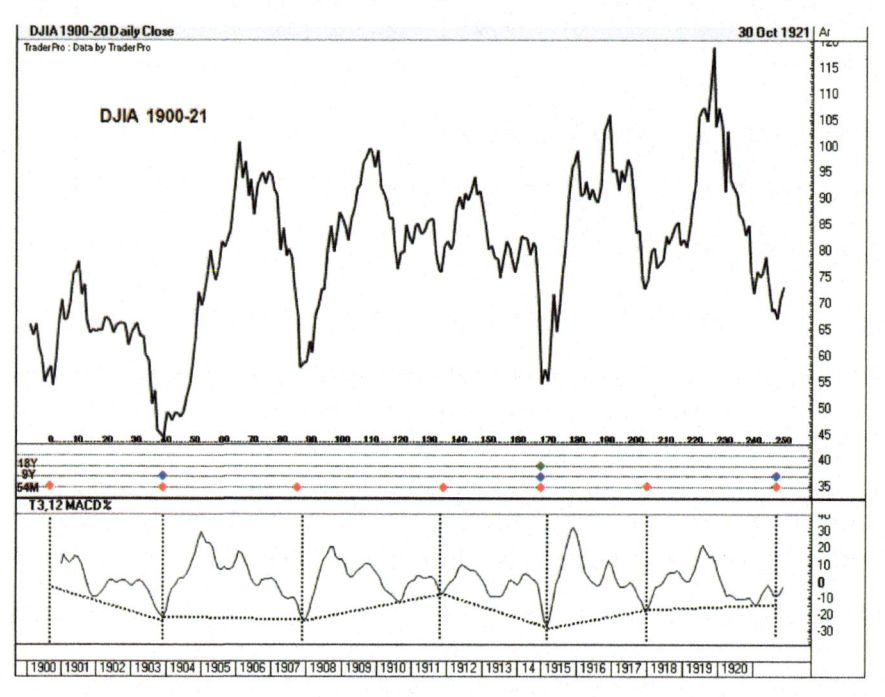

Figure 1.17: DJIA 1900–1921 (Data courtesy of www.wrenresearch.com.au)

DJIA: 1921-1942

Figure 1.18 shows the Dow between 1921 and 1942, notice that it is quite difficult to isolate cyclic movement in the sharp rally into the 1929 top. Picking out the cycles period by period is often straightforward but at other times some artistic licence is needed. That is just the nature of cycle research and we more or less have to live with it.

That said, the tools that will be introduced in later lessons will show that this element of subjectivity turns out to be less important than it at first seems. The detrending tool helps pick out the cycles in this period.

Here we see a clear 54M cycle (red diamond) emerging from the 1932 K-Wave low.

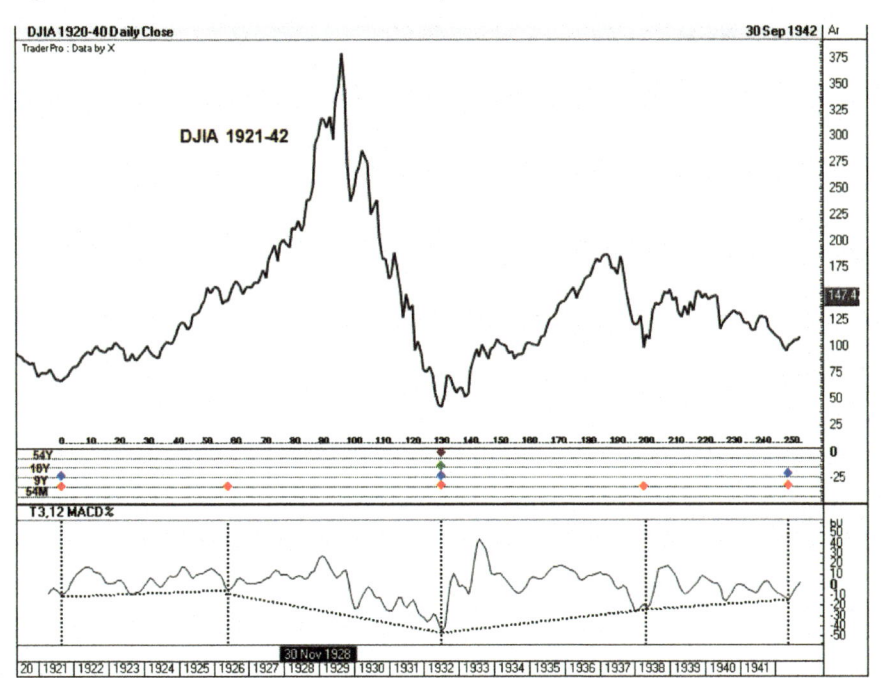

Figure 1.18: DJIA 1921-1942 (Data courtesy of www.wrenresearch.com.au)

DJIA: 1942–1962

Figure 1.19 shows the DJIA from 1942 to 1962. Although the last three cycles are regular and quite clear, at first glance, the 18-year low between grids 80 and 90 (in 1949) does not seem like much of a trough and the previous cycle is more or less non-existent.

This 20-year period represents the strongest bull market of the last century, both technically and in terms of fundamentals. This is an example of cycles being obscured by the interaction of other cycles and underlying trend.

Figure 1.19: DJIA 1942-1962 (Data courtesy of www.wrenresearch.com.au)

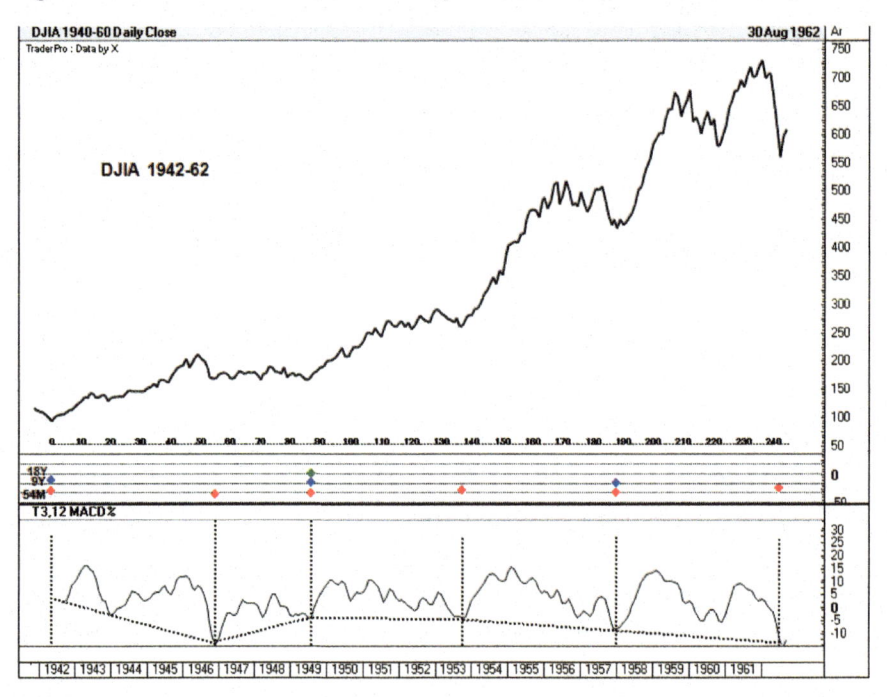

DJIA: 1961-1982

The period from 1961 to 1982 shown in Figure 1.20 can be viewed as a transition period between the long bull market of the previous 19 years and the final rally of the next 18 years into 2000.

The cycles show up clearly and regularly as the underlying long trend shifts sideways, performing much the same job as a flag or a pennant.[14]

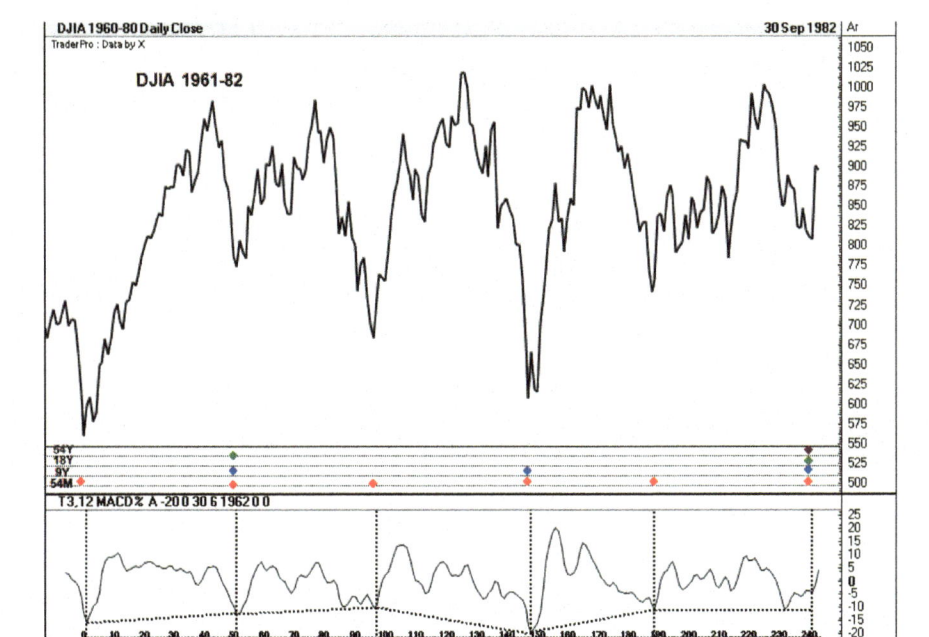

Figure 1.20: DJIA 1961-1982 (Data courtesy of www.wrenresearch.com.au)

DJIA: 1982-2002

Figure 1.21 shows the last push up from 1982 into 2000 and the first reaction decline into 2002. Once again the cycles are obscured by the strong underlying trend and some judgment is called for on a chart of this length. The detail would be considerably clearer at lower timeframes.

Figure 1.21: DJIA 1982-2002 (Data courtesy of www.wrenresearch.com.au)

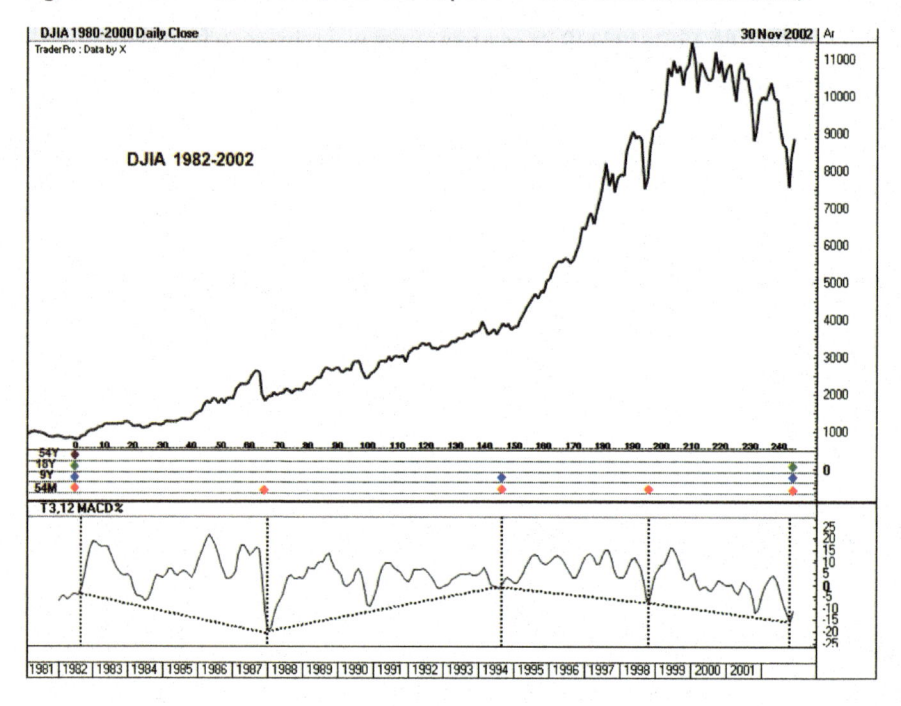

DJIA: 2002 - 2010

Figure 1.22 shows the eight years from 2002. The 54-month low at grid 38 is obscured by underlying trend and the nine year cycle looks to be running short at 77 months, however this is to be expected as the sharp sell-off out of 2007 compressed the cycle.

Figures 1.22: DJIA 2002-2010 (Data courtesy of www.wrenresearch.com.au)

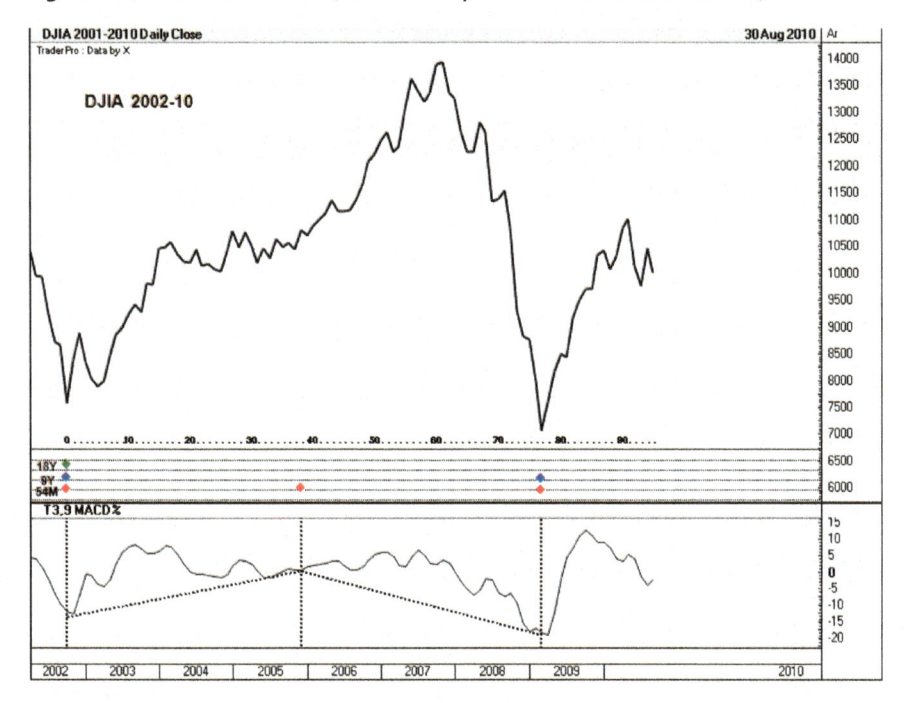

Table 1.4 is shows the data in spreadsheet form. The summary results are as follows:

- Nominal 54-month cycle: average period, 52.5 months
- Nominal nine-year cycle: average period, 9.1 years
- Nominal 18-year cycle: average period, 17.1 years
- Nominal 54-year cycle: average period, 50 years

Table 1.4: Dow Jones Industrial Average Periodicity 1903-2010

Month end	Close	54M	9Y	18Y	54Y
30/11/1903	44.32	0			
30/09/1907	67.71	46	92	92	
30/12/1914	54.57	83			
30/06/1921	68.45	78	161		
30/03/1926	140.45	57			
30/06/1932	42.83	75	132	293	
30/03/1938	98.94	69			
30/04/1942	95.34	49	118		
30/10/1946	169.15	54			
30/07/1949	175.91	33	87	205	
30/08/1953	261.21	49			
30/12/1957	435.68	52	101		
30/06/1962	561.27	54			
30/09/1966	774.21	51	105	206	
30/06/1970	683.52	45			
30/09/1974	607.86	51	96		
28/02/1978	742.11	41			
30/07/1982	808.59	53	94	190	601
30/11/1987	1833.54	64			
30/06/1994	3624.95	79	143		
30/08/1998	7539.06	50			
30/09/2002	7591.93	49	99	242	
30/10/2005	10440.07	37			
28/02/2009	7062.93	40	77		
Mean		52.5M	9.1Y	17.1Y	50Y

Nominality in Topix: 1949-2010

Figure 1.23 shows a chart of Topix over the period 1949 to 2010, with summary results and data given in Table 1.5.

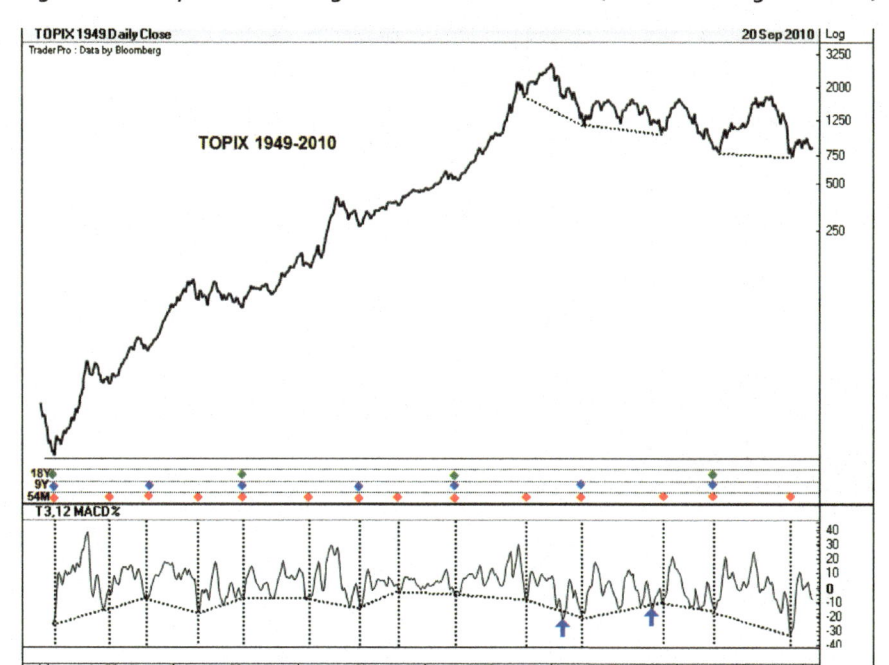

Figure 1.23: Tokyo Stock Exchange TOPIX Index 1949-2010 (Data: Bloomberg Finance LP)

- Nominal 54-month cycle: average period, 54.2 months
- Nominal nine-year cycle: average period, 8.8 years
- Nominal 18-year cycle: average period, 17.6 years

Table 1.5: TOPIX periodicity 1949-2010

Month End	Close	54M	9Y	18Y
20/05/1950	10.65	0	0	0
20/11/1954	27.24	54		
20/12/1957	44.06	37	91	
20/10/1962	86.23	58		
20/07/1965	82.4	33	91	182
20/12/1970	147.69	65		
20/11/1974	267.86	47	112	
20/10/1977	379.9	35		
20/08/1982	519.11	58	93	205
20/10/1987	1793.9	62		
20/08/1992	1163.77	58	120	
20/10/1998	1043.02	74		
20/04/2003	790.72	54	128	248
20/02/2009	739.53	70		
Mean		54.2	8.8	17.6

Variation

From the rough analyses of the DJIA and Topix it can be seen that the actual average periods over the data samples were very close to the expected nominal values. However, you will also have noticed that there were sometimes significant excursions from the mean.

In the DJIA data for the largest sample, the 54-month cycle, the maximum period is 83 months, whereas the minimum period is only 33 months. In the Topix data the maximum period in the 54-month sample is 74 months and the minimum period is 33 months.

The Nominal Model represents long-term averages of cycle periods and it is there to guide us. It does not mean that you can expect to see exactly the nominal cycle durations roll out on cue time after time. On the face of it, this variation may seem to make the forecasting of cycles a little suspect, but in fact it is much less of a problem than it seems, as will become apparent when we look at the causes of variation and how to predict it in later chapters.

Conclusion

Cycles in the market share the same physical quantities. Understanding basic terms like period, amplitude and phase, borrowed directly from physics, helps us to understand the nature of market cycles. We saw that price action in the market is a composite of a multiplicity of cycles (Principle of Summation) and that rather than being any old group of cycles, the market consists of a specific set of more or less uniform cycles (Principle of Nominality) and this is true for a very wide range of diverse instruments.

Long cycles tend to be of greater magnitude than short cycles and there is a proportional relationship between period and amplitude (Principle of Proportionality). It was also shown that there is a harmonic relationship of two and three between neighbouring cycles (Principle of Harmonicity) and that wherever possible troughs tend to converge (Principle of Synchronicity). However, we have also seen that the real world is not so neatly accommodated by these guidelines (Principle of Variation).

Hurst analysis is a system of tools: we do not just blindly rely on individual signals, but combine empirically derived techniques with sound underlying logic to build up evidence to forecast future cyclic action. The next chapter introduces the first basic tool in this system, the *Valid Trendline (VTL)*.

Endnotes

[2] For 'market' read any freely traded liquid financial market: equities, bonds, commodities, currencies, ETFs, etc.
[3] In physics the value would be 1 (0 to 1 or 0 to -1).
[4] This relationship tapers off approaching the upper limit.
[5] Diagram courtesy of Alexey Lyapin PhD, University College London, Department of Physics.
[6] Example courtesy of Christopher Willis PhD, Imperial College London, Department of Physics.
[7] Tony Plummer, *Forecasting Financial Markets* (Kogan Page, 2008).
[8] Thanks to Jessica Chan, Royal College of Music.
[9] The opposite tends to be true in commodities markets, where peaks represent fear.
[10] Although not all waves need a medium; for example, electro-magnetic radiation does not. Thanks to Alastair Dunn PhD, University College London (UCL).
[11] The actual periods Hurst proposed were: 77.9; 39; 19.5; 9.7; 5 weeks and 68.2; 34.1; 17; 8.5; 4.3 days. Because these are long-term averages and there is variation from the mean, the convention is to use the shorthand values of the simplified Nominal Model.

[12] See page 348 of this book and the website **www.sentienttrader.com** for more information on David Hickson's system.
[13] Also note that the original Hurst charts only show high, low and mid-price.
[14] This pattern is a sideways pause usually halfway along a fast up or down move and has the appearance of a flag flying at half-mast.

2 BASIC TOOLS I: VALID TRENDLINES

Trend and Trendlines

Introduction

We have seen that cycles in financial markets are governed by common physical laws and that price action is the result of cycles interacting. These cycles have properties which make them semi-predictable. Because cycles are fractal and therefore self-similar at all degrees of magnitude, very long cycles share the same properties as very short cycles. There appears to be a uniform nominal set of cycles in the market and these cycles are related to one another by a factor of two or three with their troughs tending to occur synchronously. On top of this we have seen that the length of each cycle is in proportion to its magnitude: simply put the more power driving the cycle up or down, the longer the duration of that cycle.

Cycles in diverse natural phenomena, including freely traded financial markets, are influenced by myriad forces causing variation from the norm. This complicates the picture somewhat but does not invalidate the underlying logic. Analysts and traders who understand the mechanics of cycles have a definite edge over those who do not, because they are able to see beneath the surface of the market and anticipate future price action.

It has been shown that price movement is the result of a multiplicity of different cycles which combine by addition. We have also seen that even when we use fixed inputs in a spreadsheet programme to create the cycles ourselves, it is still difficult to look at the resulting composite and recognise what components went towards generating it. This task is made even harder when looking at real market cycles because they are imperfect, and because underlying trend distorts the overall form. We can therefore only estimate and average the component cycles' period, phase and amplitude. Having said that, isolating the component cycles and gauging their respective influence on prices is the main thrust of Hurst analysis. It is here therefore that we need to start looking at the specific tools that allow us to do this.

The first tool we will study is the *Valid Trendline (VTL)*. This differs from the traditional trend line both in the way it is constructed and in the function it performs. Traditional trendlines can be inherently subjective and a poor gauge of real trend, whereas the VTL is based on an entirely different interpretation of trend and is a much more objective measure. We will therefore need to review traditional trendlines and discuss some of their limitations as well as familiarise ourselves with a new concept of trend, before going into the specifics of how to use VTLs and the rules that govern them.

This will be unfamiliar territory to many readers so there will be plenty of examples. It may also seem that there is a lot to remember and that unexpected effort is involved. Although this is usually the case when learning a new skill, more work does go into VTL analysis than it does with standard trendlines. On the other hand, the extra effort is well rewarded because the information VTLs yield has a great deal more practical utility.

At the end of this chapter you should have a grasp of the cyclic concept of trend and be able to start looking at the market in a completely new way. You should also be able to draw and interpret VTLs. VTLs are only one element in an entire system of tools and will be revisited again and again throughout the book. The more exposure and practice you have, the more proficient you will become and eventually you will be able to combine VTLs effortlessly with the other techniques that will be introduced later.

The Concept of Trendlines

Overview

Before considering trendlines, we need to look at the concept of trend. The most common definition holds that trend is the overall direction of the market: either up, down or sideways. However, this is quite loose since at any given time there are a multitude of different trends in prices and as often as not they going in different directions. Thinking in terms of net trend direction, although a useful guide, is too vague to be of practical use and difficult to establish using conventional tools.

Trends also vary in length: some last for years, others just minutes. Many market observers believe that if a trend has been going for a long time, it is more likely to continue than reverse. Others believe the opposite to be true and that an established trend is more likely to reverse than one that has just begun. A trend goes through different stages of growth and eventually ends. However, recognising precisely which stage prices are in at any moment is often quite difficult.

A common way to highlight trend is to draw trendlines on a chart. Trendlines can give a sense of order and even comfort, but the absence of clearly defined construction rules make them subjective and at times misleading.

Hurst's insight

Hurst's insight was that trends are simply a derivative of market cycles and that their direction, duration and strength are therefore a function of underlying component cycles. By reframing trend in terms of cyclic action, Hurst provided a more precise definition which allowed for the development of a new set of objective tools. First though, a quick review of traditional trendlines.

Traditional trendlines

The ostensible job of a trendline is to describe a trend. Trendlines are used to show trend direction, maturity, rate of change or duration. It is not always clear, however, exactly what is being measured and different analysts may have their own way to assign weight to different criteria. One of the main problems associated with traditional trendlines, therefore, is that they are non-standard and are vulnerable to subjectivity.

Figure 2.1 is a weekly chart of the S&P 500 Index showing several of the numerous recommended ways to draw trendlines.

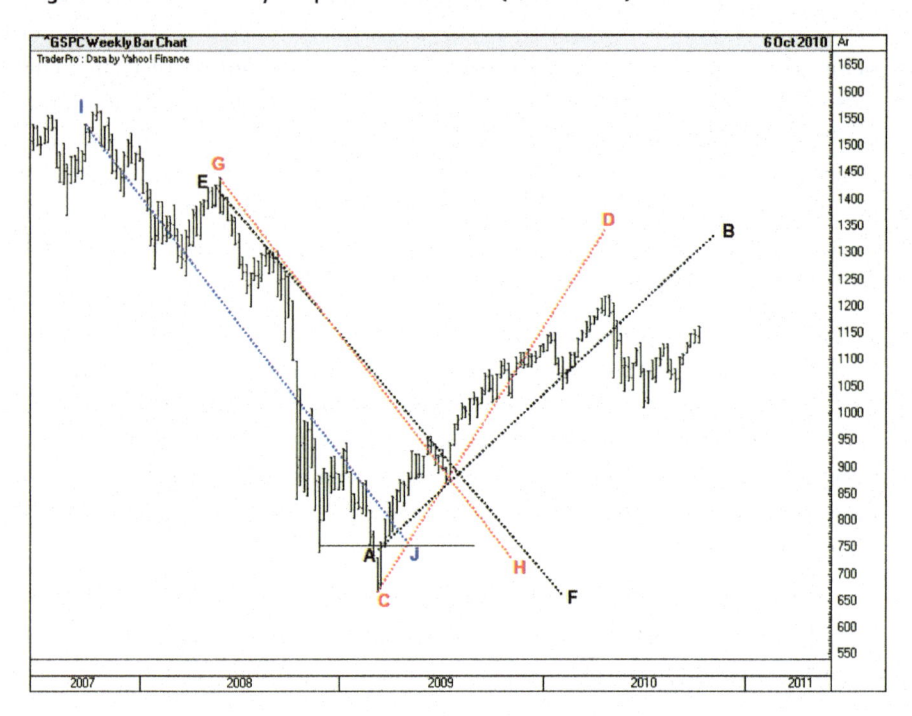

Figure 2.1: Different ways to position trendlines (Data: Yahoo)

Connecting price extremes

One of the most common ways to draw trendlines is to connect two extreme price levels and then project the connecting line into the future. For example, a downtrend line will start at an extreme high (an intraweek or intraday spike) and make the first touch at a subsequent lower extreme high, as in G to H in Figure 2.1. In the same way, an uptrend line will start at an extreme low and make the first touch at the next higher low, as in C to D. The job of the projected line is to provide clues about price movement in future time.

One question immediately arises however: how do we choose the second trendline touch point? Which subsequent lower high or higher low you use depends on your time horizon and the significance you attach to new price levels as they come along. In real time it is difficult to say with certainty that the next trend touch point is in place. What seems obvious in the middle of the chart is rarely clear at the right edge of the chart.

For example, when the big stock market reversal in March 2009 was recognised, analysts would have been drawing in, rubbing out and then redrawing trendlines as new data came through.

Using the close behind the spike

Another school of thought holds that it is fundamentally incorrect to use the price high or low as the starting point for a trendline, but rather the close just behind the spike should be used. A straight line is then drawn from this point to the next *appropriate* close, as in E to F in Figure 2.1.

The argument here is that high and low spikes signify market overshoots and a trendline connecting these points is not representative of real trend in the market[15]. This idea can even be taken a step further.

For example the entire bottom formation at A in Figure 2.1 could be viewed as a market overshoot implying that the trendline should start only when the bottom formation is firmly in place, thereby generating line A to B. Once again, however, the same judgment call is needed to choose the second touch point.

Internal trendlines

Some market analysts, recognising the inherent subjectivity of positioning trendlines between price highs or lows, believe that to be truly representative a trendline must be placed through the middle of the data, as in I to J. This is similar to a least-squares regression line. Although internal trendlines do a good job describing past trend, in real time they are difficult to draw objectively and therefore somewhat less compelling.

Other methodologies

The field of technical analysis encompasses a variety of systems each with their own rules and guidelines and each with their own definition of trendlines. Practitioners of Point and Figure, for example, believe that bar chart trendlines are basically spurious and that the 45° line on a three box reversal chart is the only objective way to draw a trendline[16].

Students of DeMark will argue that trend lines should be drawn from right to left and should not attempt to catch any more than two touch points[17]. Followers of Elliott Wave Principle meanwhile say that only trendlines enclosing impulse waves or zigzag corrections are valid[18].

Overall, therefore, there is little consensus on what constitutes a trendline. There are also few hard and fast rules on how to draw them.

Trend Direction

Multiple timeframes

Most traders and analysts acknowledge that there is more than one trend in force at any given moment and will refer to longer and shorter time horizons before making decisions in their preferred timeframe. For example, a trader who operates in a daily timeframe may look at a weekly chart to get his or her bearings and fine tune entry and exit on a 30-minute chart.

Long term and short term are relative concepts of course. Five up days in a multi-week downtrend could be viewed in one of two ways to a technically orientated hedge fund manager: it could either be dismissed as market noise or taken as a clue that underlying conditions were changing and used as a signal to cover a short position.

On the other hand, to a day trader, the same downward swing of prices over a few weeks would be viewed as a major bear market.

The ability to identify trends across multiple timeframes is an important skill that is often poorly served by traditional trendlines.

Identifying trend

Figure 2.2 is a daily bar chart of the S&P 500 Index between September 2009 and October 2010. Prices rise steeply between February and April and then drop back just as steeply over the following months into the chart low at the end of June. From early July prices rise again for six weeks, decline for the next month and then rally strongly into late October. It is clear that there are different trends starting and stopping one after another, but it is hard to say unequivocally if there is any connection between these price moves.

Chapter 2 | Basic Tools I: Valid Trendlines

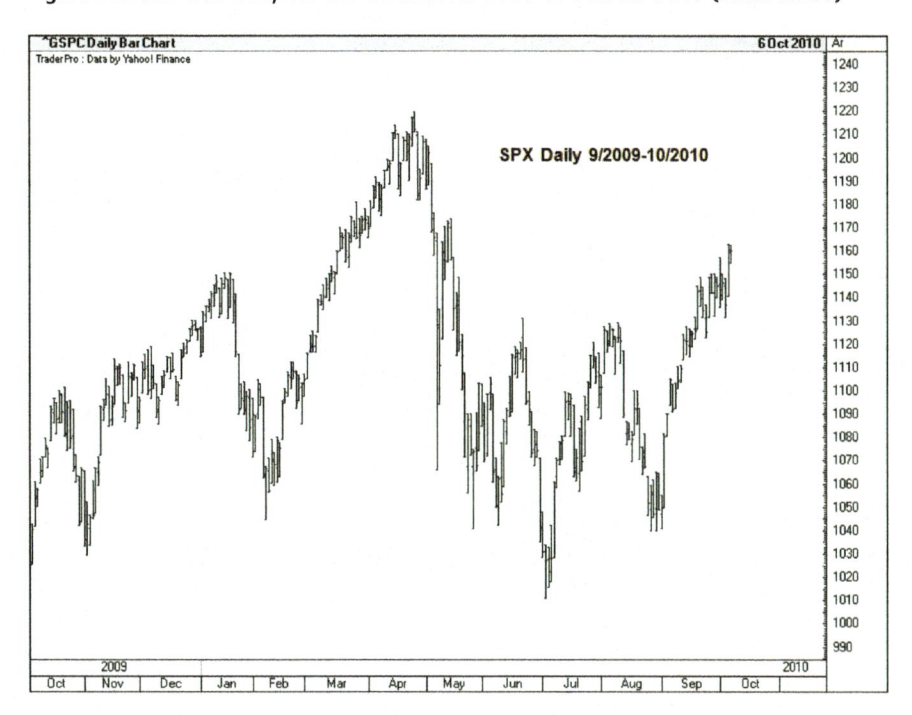

Figure 2.2: S&P 500 Daily bar chart December 2009 to October 2010 (Data: Yahoo)

Trend channels

To help get a sense of order, a typical starting point when looking at a price chart is to draw in trend channels. These are trendlines, either up or down, with a parallel drawn some distance away on the opposite side (called the return line).

Figure 2.3 is the same S&P 500 chart with two possible sets of channels added. The upper down sloping line connects the mid-April high and the second touch is the price high in early October. This point was chosen to highlight the breakout and could just as easily have been the late October high.

Figure 2.3: S&P 500 Daily bar chart February 2010 to October 2010 (Data: Yahoo)

A picture now seems to be emerging. It looks like the overall trend is down, but that more recently it may have turned up. This is fairly loose to be sure, but at least we might feel that we have some bearings now.

At this stage it is difficult to say whether prices, having moved up across the downtrend channel, have conclusively broken out and will continue upwards, or whether it is a false breakout which will result in prices being pushed back at the trend resistance line.[19]

A question of perspective

Still with the S&P500, but stepping back 12 months, Figure 2.4 shows the downtrend we were just looking at in a new light. Prices appear now to be moving down across a longer uptrend channel and if anything this new perspective seems to enhance the idea of an upside break and continuation as our eye now follows the trend up. Of course this is just a matter of personal judgment encouraged by the lines we have more or less arbitrarily put in.

Figure 2.4: S&P 500 Daily bar chart February 2009 to October 2010 (Data: Yahoo)

The longer view

Looking further back the context changes again. The weekly chart in Figure 2.5 shows that the March 2009 rally seems in fact to be part of a broader downtrend. It is now easier to imagine prices being pushed back and rejoining the downtrend at some point as our eye follows the projected trendline downwards.

We might also have noticed that the trend resistance line we were looking at in Figure 2.3 is in fact a continuation of a line that started in late 2007. In which case, it is easy to imagine that the line now has more authority and that the breakout could in fact be temporary.

Alternatively, we might believe that the line will act as strong support if prices come back to it and form a base for prices to work their way upwards. Again, it is a question of interpretation.

Figure 2.5: S&P 500 Weekly bar chart January 2005 to October 2010 (Data: Yahoo)

Going back further still, Figure 2.6 shows that the apparent downtrend from 2007 could in fact be part of a broader sideways consolidation arguably going back to 1997. Even so, the main sweep of prices since the mid-1970s still seems to be firmly up.

Overall then, it seems that there are trends within trends. It also seems that one's view can change completely depending on how much price action is actually being looked at. In many ways trendlines seem to show us what we want to see.

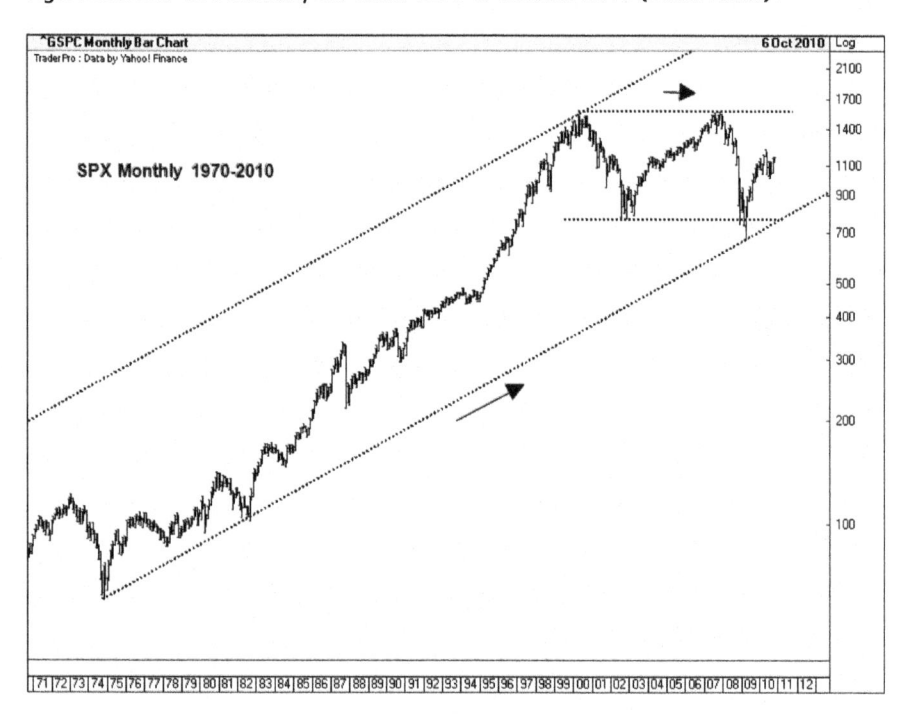

Figure 2.6: S&P 500 Monthly bar chart 1970 to October 2010 (Data: Yahoo)

Isolating net trend

The four preceding charts showed us that multiple, often conflicting, trends of different durations can co-exist and that their interpretation is often a matter of perspective.

Figure 2.7 is an attempt to summarise the various trends that were at work in the S&P in early October 2010. The grid in the top right corner indicates that there is an uptrend from 1974, a sideways trend from 1997, a downtrend from October 2007, an uptrend from March 2009, a downtrend from April 2010 and another uptrend from June 2010.

This information looks like it should be useful somehow, but it is not clear quite how one would go about using it. Even if we net the trends off and say that there are three up, one flat and two down, it still does not tell us much.

One thing that also seems to be missing is any reference to trend maturity. For example, how would our interpretation, if any, change if one of the ups became a down, or if all of the trends were down?

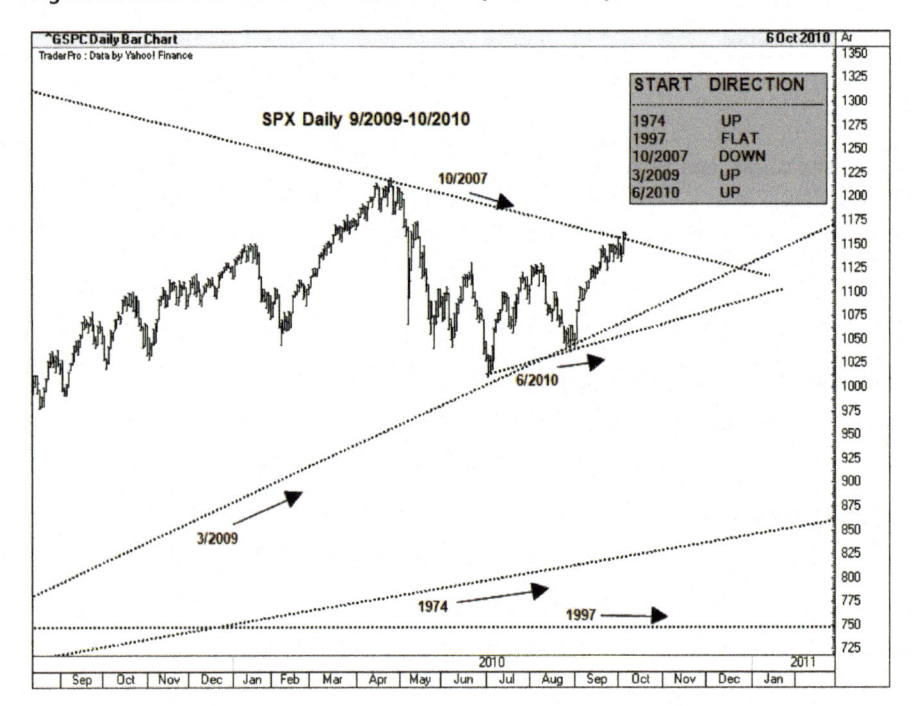

Figure 2.7: S&P 500 Trend Mix October 2010 (Data: Yahoo)

Trend Strength

Trend rate of change

One measure of trend strength is the price rate of change, which is indicated by the steepness of the trend and is the basis for momentum indicators. Figure 2.8 shows the S&P 500 from March 2009 to late October 2010 (please persevere with this somewhat busy chart). There are a number of different ways to portray trend strength[20] but here three colour-coded trend channels (red, green and blue) with dotted centre lines have been drawn in to highlight trend rate of change and trendline breaks.

Notice that the three channels rise at progressively shallower angles. The blue trend contains nearly all of the price action for 300 days, until it breaks conclusively at point (3). It is the longest trend but also the shallowest. The red trend is the steepest but only lasts 183 days breaking at (1). The rate of

Chapter 2 | Basic Tools I: Valid Trendlines

change of the green transition trend is somewhere in between and it breaks after 220 days at (2).

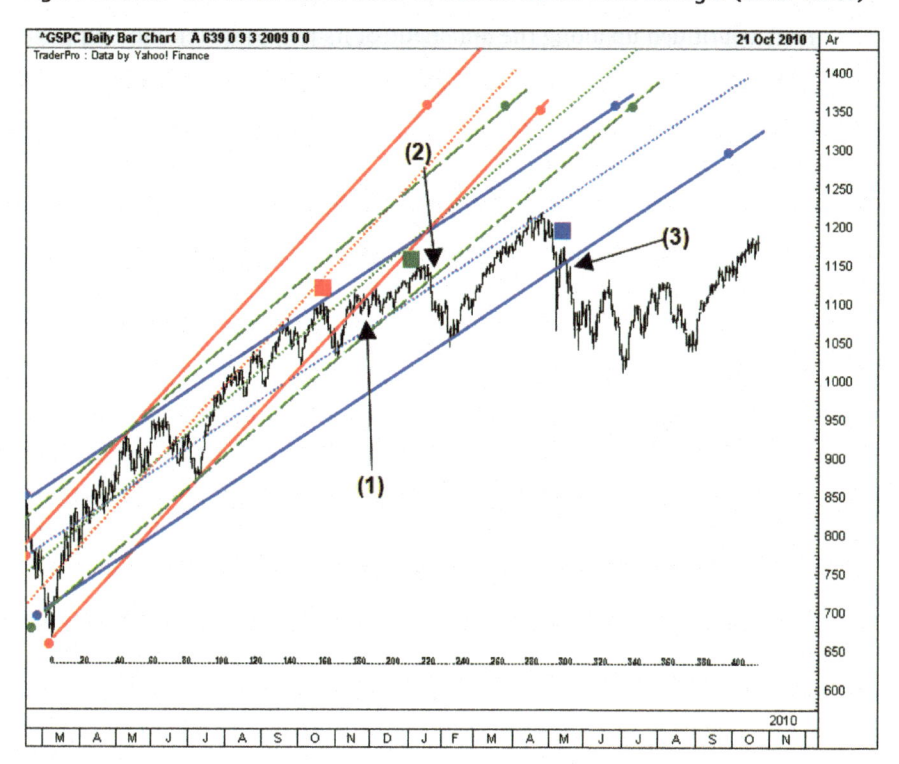

Figure 2.8: S&P 500 Index March 2009 to October 2010. Trend strength (Data: Yahoo)

Trendline breaks

When a trend finishes it will typically be marked by a trendline break and this is often used as a signal to exit a position. Trendline breaks, however, typically do not come out of nowhere. In an uptrend, as in this example, in each case price drops through the channel centre line and then fails to cross back up. This can be taken as advance notice that a downward break is about to occur.

The centre line failure and retest[21] in each channel has been marked by coloured squares and the actual trendline breaks occur shortly thereafter. However, there is a certain amount of subjectivity and arbitrariness involved here, which of course can lead to inconsistent trading results. Going through each signal in turn will help to illustrate this:

55

The red break at (1) would have been fine for very short term and nimble traders, but other short sellers would have been taken out of the trade on a tightish stop a month later. Long onlys on the other hand would have missed the chance to sell 100+ points higher. In fact, after the break, the red trend effectively continued up along the underside of its previous trendline support.

Similarly, trading the green break at (2) on the short side would have been another false start for anyone but short-term traders. In any case, the trade was losing money six weeks later.

The dramatic blue break in early May rebounded straight back into a trap before it really broke down, only to meander sideways off the lows for the next four months. The received wisdom here is that as the channels become shallower they are weakening and the third break is supposed to mark the big reversal. You can see that this did not happen.

Traditional trendlines have their uses as well as their limitations. They can bring a sense of order and they can help us get a fix on where prices are in the greater scheme of things. Arguably they are better than nothing. They seem to help identify trend direction and strength, although we do need to be specific about which trend we are looking at for this to have practical utility.

Furthermore, trendlines do not seem to be very effective at helping us judge the impact of other concurrent trends. Overall, results gained from using traditional trendlines can be inconsistent, not only because they are subjective and at times more or less arbitrary, but also because of a basic misconception about the nature of trend itself.

The Real Nature of Trend

Market commentators often tell us that they are either bullish or bearish. This is a vague way of expressing a belief about the future direction of trend. Often this belief is simply an extrapolation of past trend and it is common to find no specific mention of timeframe or target price.

An entirely different skill set is required to identify a future trend than is needed to recognise a past trend: although these skills are sometimes confused with one another. A tighter definition of trend is needed to overcome this.

The apparent mystery of trend

Trend, and by association trendlines, are sometimes regarded as mysterious phenomena. Recall the long DJIA chart in chapter one (Figure 1.16): an uptrend line joins the 1942 low to the 1982 low and an upper channel parallel line can be drawn so that it near enough connects the 1929 top and the 1966 top.

It is appealing to think that market participants are being drawn back to trend support and resistance over many years as if the market had some sort of memory for these key dates. In reality the explanation is more mundane. Trendlines are simply a graphical definition of underlying cycles.

Showing trend with sine waves

Figure 2.9 shows a sine wave bounded by two parallel horizontal lines, one connecting the tops, the other the bottoms. Figure 2.10 shows the same cycle tilted upwards and Figure 2.11 shows the same cycle tilted downwards. It is obvious what is happening here: a horizontal channel simply becomes what we think of as a trend channel when we change the angle. The trendline therefore owes its existence to the cycle troughs and peaks.

Let us say that the cycle period in the following three figures is 20 days and that trend is indicated in each case by the direction of the channel. We can therefore say that:

- The trend underlying the 20-day cycle in Figure 2.9 is flat
- The trend underlying the cycle in Figure 2.10 is up
- The trend underlying the cycle in Figure 2.11 is down

Taken a step further and recalling the discussion on summed cycles in chapter one, the underlying trend can be viewed simply as a section of a long cycle. If the section of the trend cycle is long enough relative to the time period on our chart, then it appears as a straight line.

Figure 2.9: Sine wave showing horizontal trend channel

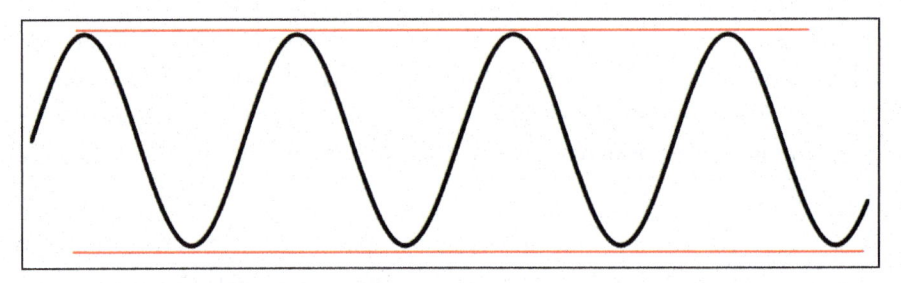

Figure 2.10: Sine wave showing uptrend channel

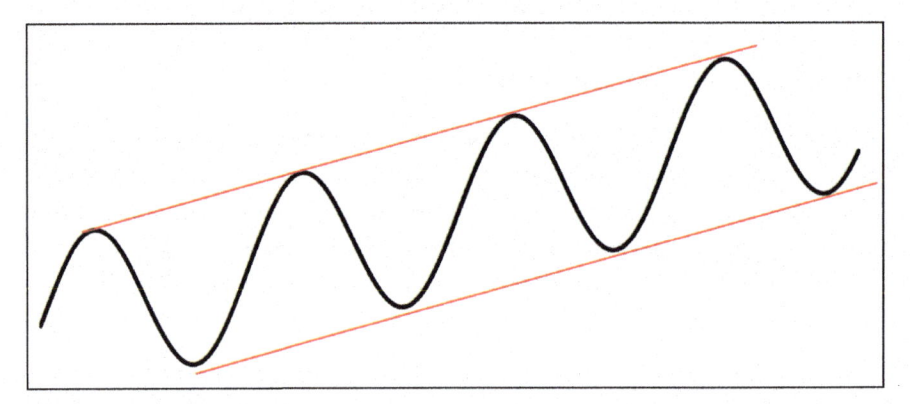

Figure 2.11: Sine wave showing downtrend channel

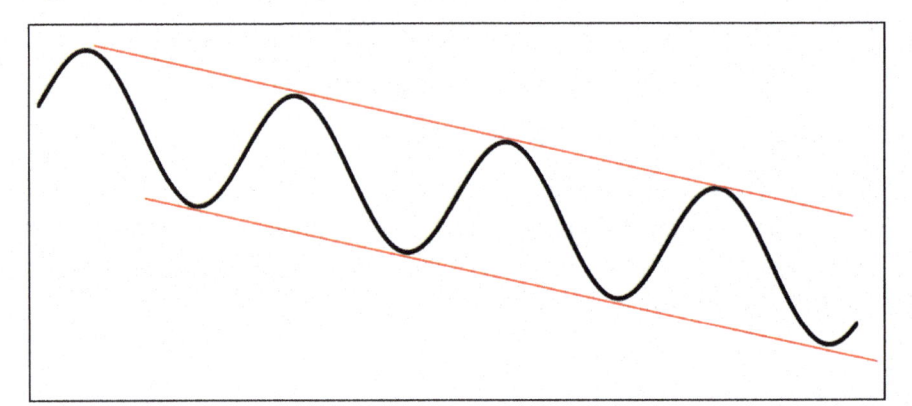

Trend underlying specific cycles

Trend therefore can be expressed more accurately as specific to a particular cycle. This can be illustrated in another way by recalling the composite cycle shown in Figure 1.4 in chapter one.

Figure 2.12 shows the same composite wave rescaled for clarity. Recall that this curve is the sum of the 156, 78, 18 and nine-day cycles. In other words the value of the composite cycle at each successive point along the time axis is the value of the 156-day cycle + 78 day + 18 day + 9 day + 5° trend.

- The up-sloping central line is the trend *underlying the longest component* – in this case the 156-day cycle. The composite cycle oscillates or mean reverts around this average as if it were an axis.

- In the same way, the line in Figure 2.13 shows the trend underlying the 40-day cycle, which is the 78-day cycle plus the trend (78 + 5° trend) and is the axis around which the 40-day cycle oscillates.

- Similarly, Figure 2.14 shows the trend underlying the 18-day cycle (156 + 78 + 5° trend) and Figure 2.15 is the trend underlying the nine-day cycle (156 + 78 + 18 + 5° trend).

Figure 2.12: Composite cycle (156, 78, 18, 9) showing the trend underlying the 156-day cycle

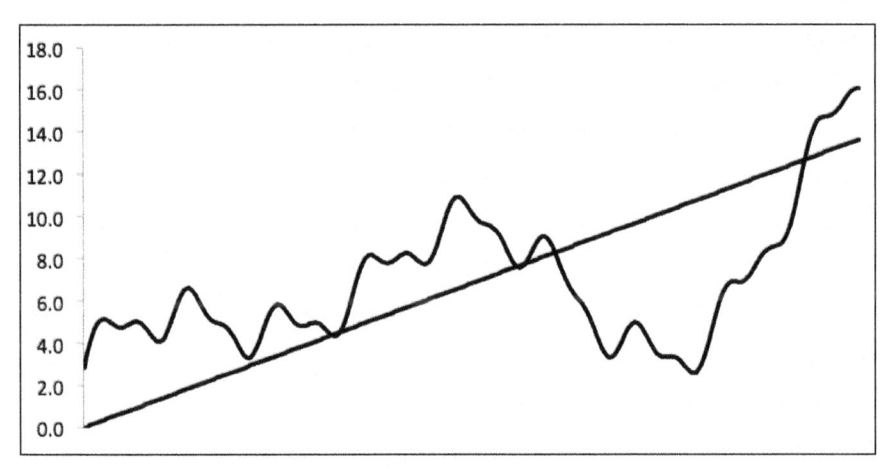

Figure 2.13: Trend underlying the 78-day cycle of the composite

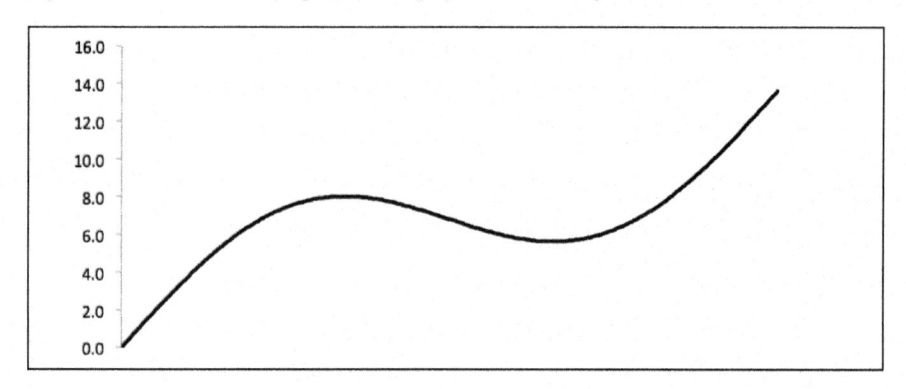

Figure 2.14: Trend underlying the 18-day cycle

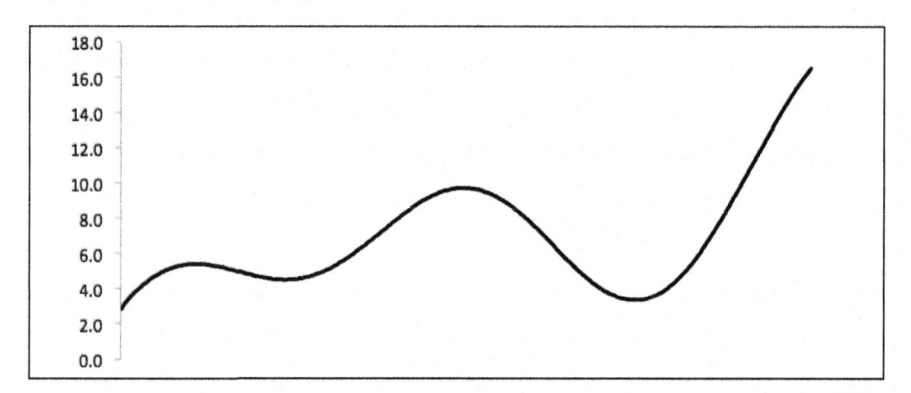

Figure 2.15: Trend underlying the nine-day cycle

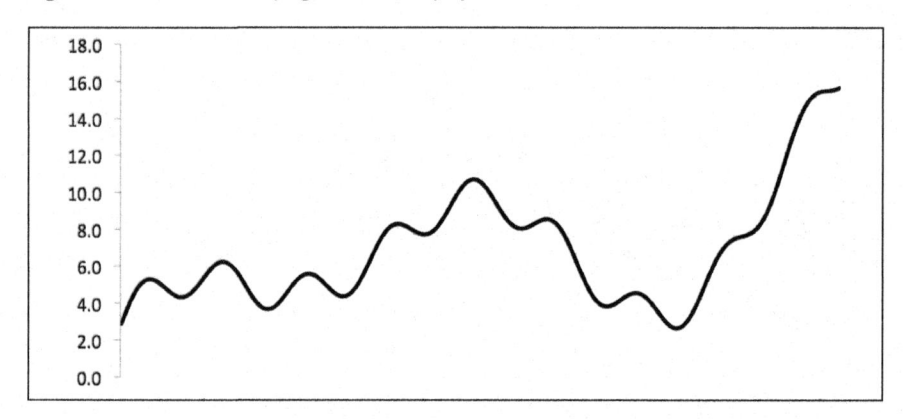

This is clearly a much more specific definition of trend, but it still remains to isolate the component cycles. The way we accomplish this is by using Hurst's Valid Trend Line (VTL).

The Valid Trendline (VTL)

Construction

The trendlines encountered so far would have been called arbitrary by Hurst. What differentiates Valid Trendlines is that they are derived from specific cycles and their construction follows specific rules, removing the need for subjective interpretation. In this sense, they are valid representations of underlying cyclic action.

The rules governing VTL construction and the way they are actually used might seem complicated at first, but once they make sense you will be able to draw them quickly and accurately and their meaning and effectiveness will become clear.

Once you properly understand the power of VTLs it is likely that you will be sceptical of traditionally-drawn trendlines forever more.

The rules

For a valid trendline to actually be valid, a number of construction rules need to be obeyed. For now just try to familiarise yourself with the rules and do not attempt to remember them word for word. We will be coming back to them in numerous real examples throughout the book. The rules are as follows:

- A valid *uptrend* line connects two consecutive troughs of a specific cycle.

- A valid *downtrend* line connects two consecutive peaks of specific cycle.

- If the VTL is crossed by prices between either of the two adjacent troughs or peaks, then the line is invalidated and cannot be used as a VTL.

- For a *downtrend* line, the trough of a cycle longer than the cycle associated with the VTL *must not* fall between the two consecutive peaks. For example, if the downtrend line is based on a 40-day cycle, then there cannot be an 80-day trough or that of a longer cycle falling between the two adjacent 40-day peaks.

- On the other hand, it is permitted for a peak of a cycle longer than the cycle associated with the VTL to occur between two consecutive lows. For example, if the uptrend line is based on a 40-day cycle, an intervening 80-day peak does *not* invalidate the line.

VTLs on composite charts

Let us now look at a composite chart that has been created from sine waves to allow us to get a better understanding of how VTLs are constructed and how the rules apply.

Figure 2.16 is a composite of a 40-day cycle[22], a 160-day and a 500-day. The 500-day represents underlying trend, the 160-day shows the intermediate swings and the 40-day represents the short-term oscillation.

- The two peaks connected by the red line, VTL A, are peaks of the 40-day cycle showing through on the composite. It is a *40-day valid downtrend line* because it is based on this cycle's peaks.

- The two peaks are consecutive and the trough of a longer cycle (in this case 160-day cycle or the 500-day cycle) does not fall in between them.

- The blue line, VTL B, connects two consecutive troughs of the 40-day cycle showing through in the composite and is therefore a 40-day valid uptrend line.

- As was demonstrated in Figures 2.9 to 2.11, the VTLs here are essentially horizontal lines drawn on the 40-day cycle, which is being tilted downwards in the case of VTL A and then upwards in the case of VTL B, by the action of the other two cycles.

Figure 2.16: VTL-downtrend (red), VTL-uptrend (blue)

Composite (500,160, 40)

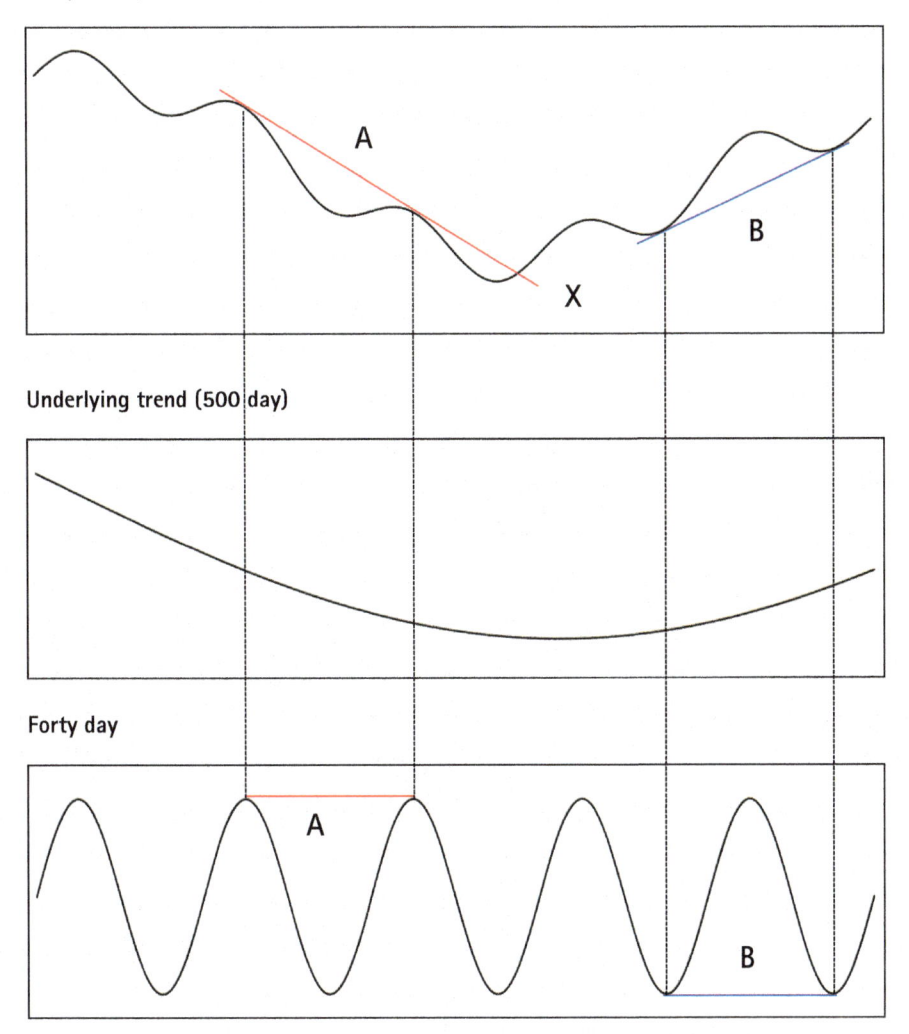

Underlying trend (500 day)

Forty day

160 day

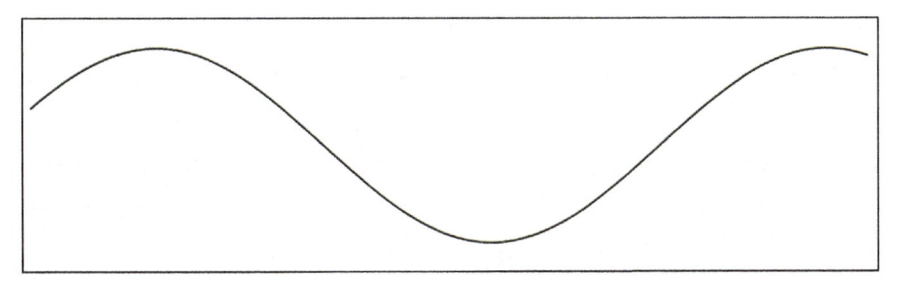

Figure 2.17 shows the same composite cycle, but with some minor modification to help illustrate the point.

Figure 2.17: Correct and incorrect VTLs
Composite (500, 150, 40)

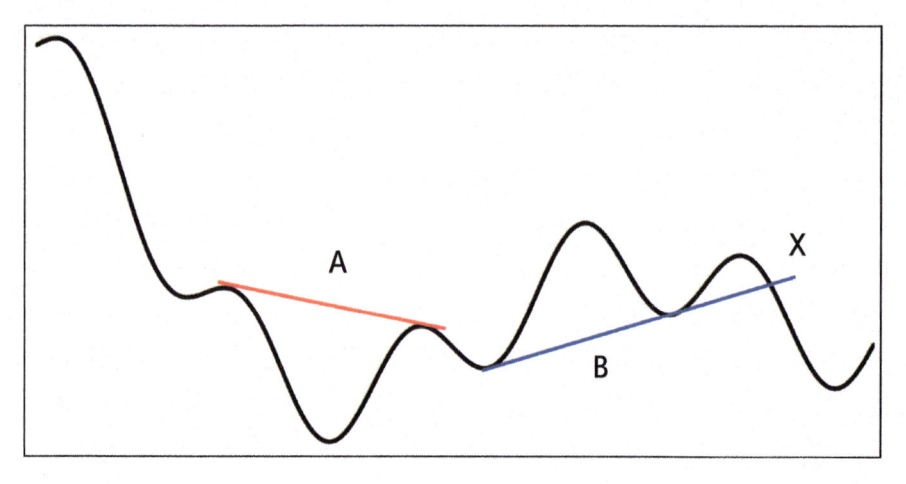

Underlying trend (500-day)

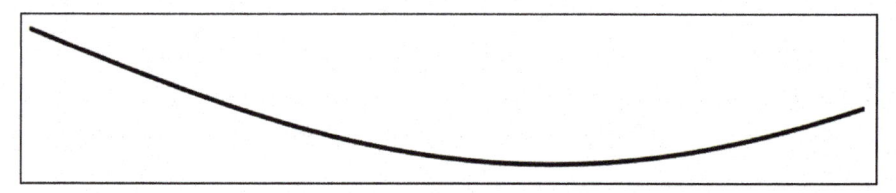

Forty-day

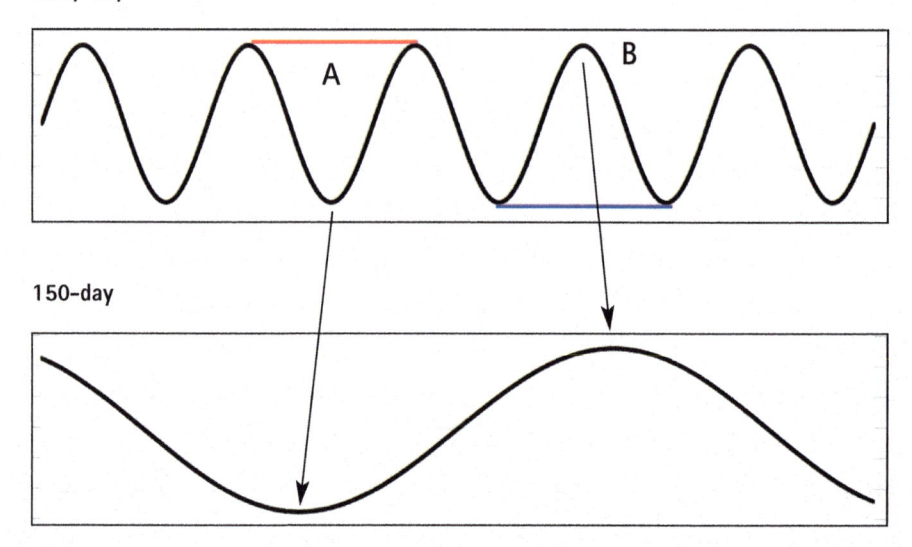

150-day

64

Although the red line A connects two consecutive 40-day peaks, it is *not* a VTL because the trough of the 150-day cycle (the next longer) falls in between the peaks. On the other hand, the blue line, VTL B, connects two consecutive 40-day troughs and although the 150-day peak is in between, no rule is broken because it is an uptrend line not a downtrend.

The Key Role Played by VTLs

Peak and trough identification

Recall Figures 2.12 to 2.15 which showed the trend underlying each component of a composite cycle. Each cycle oscillates around its trend and that trend is itself the sum of all longer cycles.

The 40-day cycle in Figure 2.16 oscillates around the 160-day cycle, which itself mean reverts to its next longer neighbour, the 500-day cycle. Therefore, the up and down movement of the 160-day cycle determines the overall direction of the 40-day cycle. When the 160-day cycle rounds its trough or peak and moves back in the opposite direction, any trendlines drawn between the peaks or the troughs of the 40-day cycle will necessarily be broken.

Thus, we see the red downtrend line A broken from below at point X as the composite comes out of the turn, which is the result of the 160-day cycle passing its trough. *This brings us to the key role played by a valid downtrend line: when the VTL is broken, the trough of the next longer cycle has been passed*, in this case the 160-day and looking at the bottom window we see that this has happened. Similarly, when a valid uptrend line is broken, it means that the peak of the next longer cycle has passed.

In Figure 2.17, the blue valid uptrend line B cuts the cycle at point X and if we look down to the bottom window, we see that in fact the 150-day cycle has peaked. Notice here that the 40-day cycle is in an uptrend, there have been two tests of the VTL but then there is a breakdown, caused by the 150-day cycle rolling over. This is a good example of how Hurst cycle analysis gives us the ability to look beneath the surface of price action and anticipate what will happen next.

How to draw VTLs

The purpose of a VTL is to identify peaks and troughs of component waves within the composite cycle. Let us run through one more time what was shown with the ideal cycles in Figures 2.16 and 2.17.

When a VTL is broken by prices the implication is that the longer cycle has turned. For a valid downtrend line, a break implies that the next longer cycle has turned *up* and that a *trough* of this cycle has been passed. For example, a 20-day down VTL break implies that the 40-day cycle has bottomed; a 40-day down VTL break implies that the 80-day cycle has bottomed, and so forth.

Furthermore, this reversal will have happened within the time span of the longer cycle period counting back from the break. So for the 20-day down VTL, a break means the 40-day cycle trough is likely to have occurred within 40 days back from the break.

For a valid uptrend line, a break implies that the next longer cycle has turned *down* and that a *peak* of this cycle has been passed. For example, a 20-day up VTL break implies that the 40-day cycle has peaked; a 40-day up VTL break implies that the 80-day cycle has peaked, and so on.

As for the valid downtrend guideline, the turn is likely to be the high price within the time span of one longer cycle period back from the break. So for the 20-day up VTL, a break means the 40-day cycle peak occurred within 40 days back from the break.

You are probably wondering how you are expected to remember all of this. As long as you grasp the underlying concept, which is straightforward, with practice you will quickly become adept and using VTLs will become second nature.

Furthermore, it should be remembered that these are only strong guidelines. They are not rules set in stone and the VTL is only one of several tools used to help pick component cycles out of the composite. If you are already in the habit of analysing the market by looking at multiple timeframes, then you are halfway there. The fact that there is a structure at all and that it has a certain level of uniformity gives you at least a probabilistic framework of outcomes which helps stack the odds in your favour.

Valid uptrend lines

Figure 2.18 shows the chart of British Airways (BAY.L)[23] from 10 October 2008 to 10 July 2009. As you saw with the DJIA and Topix examples in chapter one, the coloured diamonds in the lower grid represent time locations of component cycle troughs. How and where to place these diamonds will be covered in a later chapter.

For now let us just concentrate on VTL construction: specifically Valid Uptrend lines. There are nine VTLs drawn in this chart and we will go through them one by one. The examination will be detailed so you will need to focus. When you eventually *get* VTLs, you will not need to pay this much attention. Because the text gets away from the charts in this chapter, for ease of reference they can be downloaded from:

www.vectisma.com/downloads/VTLs.

Figure 2.18: British Airways showing Valid Uptrend Lines (Data: Yahoo)

1. Blue VTL (1) is based on the first 23.3-day cycle. This is the average length of the nominal 28-trading-day cycle – which is therefore running short at the current time (July 2009, the end of the data).

- VTL (1) is valid because it is pointing upwards and connects higher lows.
- It joins two *consecutive* price troughs of the 23.3 day cycle, shown by the blue diamonds placed at 0 and 12.

- There are no price crosses *between* these two adjacent lows.
- The first price cross from above is at grid 28. The next longer cycle is 46.5 days (nominal 56D cycle). Looking back 46 days from the break to find a price high tells us that the peak at grid 22 is the only candidate for the 46.5-day cycle peak. It is therefore marked with a red carat.[24]

2. Blue VTL (2) is based on the third 23.3-day cycle in the data.
- It is valid because it points upwards and two consecutive lows of this cycle, marked by blue diamonds at grids 29 and 54, are connected.
- There are no price crosses between the lows and the eventual price cross at grid 60 indicates that the next longer cycle, again the 46.4-day, has peaked.
- Looking back 46 days we find that the only candidate is the price high at grid 58, and so this is marked by a red carat.
- This 46.4-day peak also corresponds to that of the first 93-day cycle (20 week), which has troughs marked by olive diamonds at 0 and 78.
- Both cycle peaks thus identified by the blue VTLs are shifted to the right of centre, which is what we expect to see when the underlying trend is up. This is an example of *peak translation* and will be explained in chapter five.

3. Blue VTL (3) is once again based on the 23.3-day cycle, this time it is the seventh in the series and connects consecutive lows at grids 136 and 163.
- The line is pointing up and it connects two adjacent lows of the 23.3-day cycle.
- There is no intervening price cross to invalidate it.
- The break at grid 165 indicates that the next longer cycle, the second 46.4-day of the second 93-day cycle, has peaked – marked by the carat at grid 142.
- The price high is within the required 46-day time span back from the break.

4. Red VTL (4) is based on the first 46.5-day cycle (nominal 56 trading days) of the first 93-day cycle.
- The two consecutive troughs of this cycle are marked by red diamonds at 0 and 29.
- The line points upwards and there are no intervening price breaks.

- The price cross at 73 implies that the next longer cycle (the 93-day, 20-week) peaked at grid 58 and has been marked with an olive carat.

5. Red VTL (5) is based on the third 46.5-day cycle and connects adjacent cycle troughs marked by red diamonds at 78 and 136.

- There are no intervening price crosses and the break at 163 implies that the 93-day cycle peaked in the last 93 days.

- The price high at grid 122 is therefore the 93-day cycle peak and is marked with an olive carat.

6. Green VTL (6) is based on the ninth 11.7-day cycle.

- Adjacent troughs at 78 and 94 are connected.

- The next longer cycle is the 23.3-day and the price break at 99 implies that the 23.3-day cycle (the fifth in the series) peaked at grid 84. This has been marked with a blue carat.

7. Green VTL (7) is based on the eleventh 11.7-day cycle.

- Consecutive troughs at 104 and 118 are connected and the next longer cycle is the 23.3-day cycle.

- The price break at 136 implies that the 23.3-day cycle (the fifth in the series) peaked at grid 122, which is the highest point 23 days back from the break.

8. Try to summarise Green VTL (8) yourself.

9. Olive VTL (9) is an uptrend line based on the 93-day (20-week) cycle.

- Consecutive troughs at 0 and 80 are connected and the next longer cycle is the 40W cycle.

- The price break at 183 implies that the 40W cycle peaked at grid 60, marked by the purple carat.

Average cycle periods

The numbers on the right-hand side of the lower grid in Figure 2.18 represent average cycle periods of 188, 93, 46.5, 23.3 and 11.7 days. These are the current representations of the expected nominal cycles of: 40 week, 20 week, 80 day, 40 day and 20 day. This converts in trading days to 200D, 100D, 56D, 28D and 14D. To avoid confusion, from now on we will only refer to nominal cycles at the daily level in terms of trading days.

Table 2.1 is a spreadsheet showing the average cycle periods.

Table 2.1: Average cycle periods, British Airways – as of 20 July 2009

Nominal Period	20W	80D	40D	20D
Trading Days	100D	56D	28D	14D
Average Period	93	46.5	23.3	11.7
Number of Troughs	3	5	9	16
Periods	78	29	12	4
	108	49	17	8
		58	25	7
		50	24	10
			26	11
			32	14
			27	12
			23	12
				16
				10
				14
				18
				14
				13
				12

Valid downtrend lines

Figure 2.19 shows the same British Airways chart displaying Valid Downtrend lines. There are three shown in this chart and we will go through them individually.

Figure 2.19: British Airways showing Valid Downtrend Lines (Data: Yahoo)

10. Green VTL (1) is the valid downtrend line based on the seventh and eighth 11.7-day cycles, their troughs marked by green diamonds between grids 54 and 78.

- It is valid because it is pointing downwards; the line joins two *consecutive* price *highs* of the 11.7-day cycle. In other words the VTL connects two adjacent cycles of the same period.

- At no time *between* these two peaks does price cross up through the line.

- The trough of a longer-period cycle does not fall between the two peaks. A longer cycle trough in this case would be, for example, a blue diamond (the 23.3-day cycle) somewhere between 64 and 68.

- Price breaks up through the VTL at 82. The next longer cycle is 23.3 days and so looking back 23 days from the cross we should expect to see a price low representing the trough of the 23.3-day cycle, as indeed we do at grid 78.

71

11. Green VTL (2) is the valid downtrend line based on the fifteenth and sixteenth 11.7-day cycles in the series falling between grids 150 and 186.

- The VTL connects the peak of the first cycle at 166 (marked by a green carat) to that of the second cycle at 177 (marked by a second green carat).

- There is no intervening price break; the line slopes downwards and there is no trough of a longer cycle in between.

- The VTL is broken intraday at 187 and although prices drop to a new temporary low two bars later, this break terminates the VTL with the implication that the next longer cycle has bottomed (the 23.3-day in this case). The 23.3 day cycle low here is also part of a major nest of lows as the 40W cycle troughs.

12. Olive VTL (3) is the valid downtrend line based on the first and the second 93-day (20-week) cycles.

- The VTL connects the peak of the first cycle at grid 60 (marked by an olive carat) to that of the second adjacent cycle at grid 122 (marked by a second olive carat).

Prices do not break the VTL in-between the two peaks; the line is pointing downwards; and no trough of a longer cycle straddles the peaks, which in this case means there is no purple diamond (the 40-week cycle) between grids 60 and 122.

Invalid trendlines (non-VTLs)

You have been taught the rules of construction of valid trendlines and have had the chance to work through some examples. Because a good way to learn how to do something right is to know what it looks like when it is wrong, we will now look at some examples of incorrectly drawn VTLs – in other words, invalid trendlines.

Figure 2.20 shows the same British Airways chart, but this time with six incorrect VTLs drawn in.

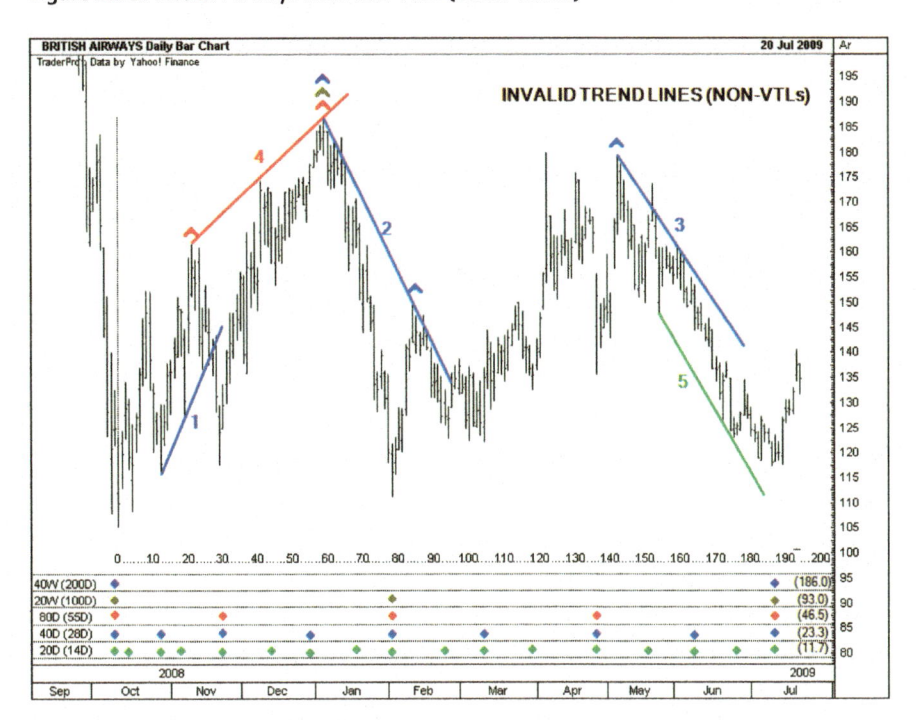

Figure 2.20: British Airways with non VTLs (Data: Yahoo)

- Blue uptrend line (1) is supposed to be a VTL line for the 23.3-day cycle. It points upwards and connects two adjacent diamonds, but these belong to two different cycles. The first belongs to the 23.3-day cycle and the second belongs to the 11.7-day cycle. This is not therefore a VTL.

- Blue downtrend line (2) is supposed to be a VTL for the 23.3-day cycle. It points downwards and connects two adjacent highs of the cycle, but these straddle at least one longer cycle trough, that of the 46.5-day (marked by the red diamond at 78). In addition to this, there is an intervening price cross at 65. Two rules have been broken and so this line is invalid.

- Blue downtrend line (3) is supposed to be a VTL for the 23-day cycle but it connects two different cycle peaks and the line is broken by price action at 152, thereby invalidating it.

- Red uptrend line (4) is pointing the wrong way. If peaks are connected the VTL must point down.

- Green downtrend line (5) is also pointing the wrong way. If troughs are connected, the VTL must point up.

Conclusion

VTLs are more objective than conventional trendlines because they follow specific rules. This means that they are far less open to interpretation. We have seen that there are different ways to draw traditional trendlines, which can lead to quite different interpretations. It was also shown that trendlines and trend channels can be misleading when used to measure trend strength or when signalling a change in trend.

There is never just one trend in operation and prices are always somewhere within a multiplicity of different, often conflicting, trends. Using traditional trendlines makes it difficult to extract the specific trend of interest and weigh up the influence of other trends.

The nature of trend is sometimes misunderstood as being either the result of collective memory or even as some sort of magical force. It is neither, but rather the result of underlying cycles interacting. Trend can only properly be expressed as underlying a specific cycle. The Valid Trendline is a natural extension of this concept. VTLs are not used in the same way as normal trendlines and their main purpose is to identify component cycles.

The rules governing VTL construction are straightforward. For valid uptrend lines, adjacent troughs of a specific cycle are connected and then extended. Where and when price intersects this line in the future, we can surmise that a peak of the next longer cycle occurred within one half-cycle back from the point of intersection.

For valid downtrend lines, adjacent peaks of a specific cycle are connected and then extended. Where and when price crosses the line in the future, we can surmise that a trough of the next longer cycle occurred within one half-cycle back from the point of intersection. In each case a price intersection between adjacent troughs or peaks is not permitted. And for the downtrend line, only a longer cycle trough may not fall between the two adjacent peaks that define the VTL.

You should now have a clearer understanding of the concept of real trend, the logic behind VTLs and how they are constructed. In the next chapter we are going to look at the second basic tool, the *FLD* or *displaced cycle*. Once you have mastered the use of both the VTL and FLD, you are a short step away from being able to conduct a full cycle analysis.

Endnotes

[15] Constance Brown, *Technical Analysis for the Trading Professional* (McGraw Hill, 1999).

[16] Point and Figure is a charting technique that, unlike other techniques, does not plot price against time. Instead it plots price against changes in direction by plotting a column of Xs as the price rises and a column of Os as the price falls. See Jeremy Du Plessis, *The Definitive Guide to Point and Figure* (Harriman House, 2005).

[17] DeMark Indicators™ are a suite of proprietary market timing tools that help identify the market's natural price rhythm and areas of trend exhaustion. See Thomas DeMark & Jason Perl, *DeMark Indicators* (Bloomberg Press, 2008).

[18] Elliott Wave proposes that market prices unfold in specific fractal patterns underpinned by investor psychology. See AJ Frost & Robert Prechter, *The Elliott Wave Principle* (New Classics Library, 2005).

[19] Resistance can be thought of as an imaginary level or sloping line that stops prices going further up and is the opposite of support, which stops prices going down.

[20] Other techniques could be momentum indicators such as RSI, ROC, DMI, MACD, Stochastics; certain price or Elliott Wave patterns; DeMark trend exhaustion signals; and so on.

[21] Retest means that prices break through a line in one direction, come back to the line from the other direction and fail to penetrate.

[22] Day is used here as convenient shorthand for any time unit.

[23] As of 21 January 2011 British Airways' merger with Spanish carrier Iberia took effect and BA delisted from the London Stock Exchange. The new holding company is International Consolidated Airlines Group SA (IAG.L)

[24] Carats (the hat image) represent peaks. Each separate actual cycle corresponding to a cycle within the Nominal Model is colour coded. VTLs and diamonds referencing the same cycle are therefore the same colour. This will be explained in more detail later.

3 BASIC TOOLS II: DISPLACED CYCLES – THE FLD

Introduction

In the previous chapter you were introduced to the idea of the Valid Trendline. You learnt that whereas conventional trendlines and channels provide *indirect* information about the action of underlying cycles, Valid Trendlines provide *direct* information about *specific* cycles. Because VTLs are based on individual cycles, by observing where that cycle crosses its VTL we can estimate the time location of reversals in the next longer cycle. This takes the concept of trendline breaks to the next level, because it provides us with actionable information not only about the validity of a break, but also about its magnitude. Furthermore, because there are fixed rules of construction, VTLs provide a higher level of objectivity. This not only helps increase conviction, but it also takes out a lot of the guesswork associated with conventional trendlines.

As you have seen, price action is the result of multiple cycles combining. The principal job of the VTL is to confirm reversals in specific cycle components. This is important information, but on its own cannot provide enough evidence to complete an analysis of the cyclic condition of an issue. It is also not enough to allow you to forecast future price action.

Hurst cycle analysis is an integrated system of tools and techniques and the best results are achieved when these are used together. The next tool we are going to study is Hurst's *Future Line of Demarcation*, or *FLD*. This indicator will be new to many market technicians, but the concept is straightforward and it is simple to construct. It also has a number of extremely useful properties.

An FLD is a replica cycle displaced by a fixed amount to the right of an original cycle: in other words phase shifted forward in time. This effectively creates two identical cycles on the chart, one offset from the other. How the base cycle and the displaced cycle interact yields actionable information.

In this chapter you will learn how FLDs are constructed as well as how to plot them on a chart. FLDs, like VTLs, can be used to isolate reversals in individual cycles. They can also be used to form estimates of the timing of future peaks and troughs. The principal role of the FLD, however, is to forecast the extent of potential price move. You will be shown not only how to use FLDs to project price targets, but also how to use this information to uncover the direction of underlying trend. Once you have understood the basics of individual cycle FLDs, we will move on to consider the role of multiple FLDs.

Each component cycle in composite price movement has its own FLD; plotted onto the chart multiple FLDs interact with one another in the same way as price cycles. The way FLDs combine with each other and the patterns they create tells us whether an imminent reversal is due or whether prices will consolidate at a certain level. You will be taught how to recognise the principal FLD patterns, the cascade and the pause zone, and shown how to interpret them.

By the end of this chapter you will know how to construct and plot single FLDs and be able to use them to identify reversals and project prices. You should also be able to tell the direction of underlying trend and interpret multiple FLD patterns. Once you know how to use VTLs and FLDs together, you will be ready to start isolating market cycles in a systematic way. This is the start of the fascinating and rewarding detective work that is Hurst Cycle Analysis.

Properties of the FLD

The mechanics of displaced cycles

One of the most original and useful indicators in the Hurst toolkit is the somewhat ponderously named Future Line of Demarcation (FLD). This is a line drawn in future time that precisely tracks a particular cycle, demarcating an imaginary forward boundary. In other words it is a duplicate cycle displaced to the right of the original.

The interaction of the price cycle and the displaced cycle provides us with valuable insight not only into the base cycle, but also into the overall cyclic condition of the market. Before getting into FLDs in actual price movement, let us examine the concept in ideal conditions.

Offset sine waves

Figure 3.1 shows two sine waves of the same period: let us say ten days. Cycle 2 is an exact replica of the original cycle (1), simply pushed forward by five days. The displaced cycle 2 is therefore a *half cycle out of phase* – it is in anti-phase – with the base cycle (1). The implications of this phase shifted relationship are as follows:

- The peak of the *base* cycle at point D corresponds to the trough of the *displaced* cycle at point B.

- The peak of the *displaced* cycle at point A corresponds to the trough of the *base* cycle at point C.

- As the *base* cycle rises, the *displaced* cycle falls. And as the *base* cycle falls, the *displaced* cycle rises.

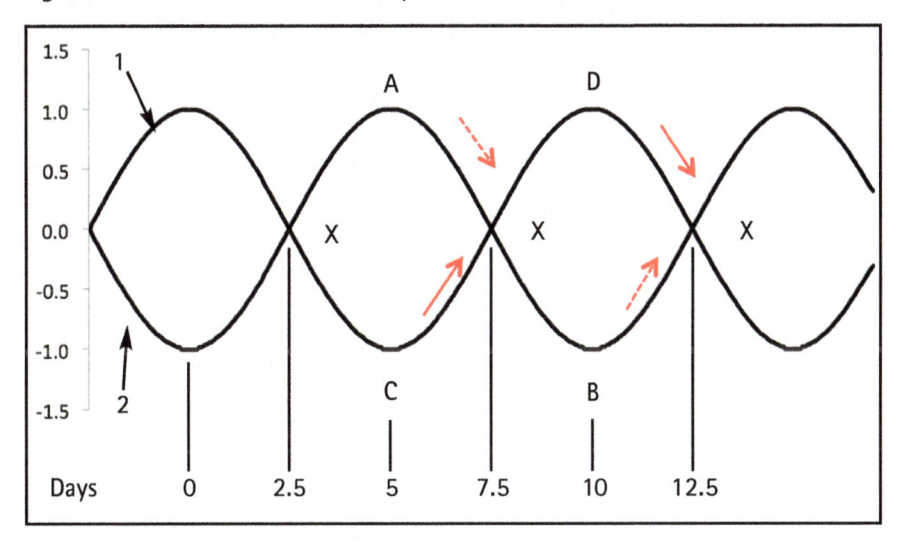

Figure 3.1: Sine wave with an offset replica

Trough and peak projection

Because the base cycle and the displaced cycle are moving in opposition, their paths must inevitably cross. These intersections are marked X and fall exactly halfway between the peak and trough of each cycle. At the point of intersection, therefore, we are able to say not only exactly how far the cycle has risen or fallen since its last reversal, but also how far it has yet to rise or fall before once again reversing.

The vertical distance from the trough at point C to the first intersection at point X is one unit (1 to 0). This is the same as the vertical distance from point X to the peak at point D (0 to +1). Thus, to work out the value of the next peak the vertical spread between the last trough and the intersection is added to the value at the intersection.

Similarly, to work out the value of the next trough, the vertical spread between the last peak and the intersection is simply subtracted from the value at the intersection.

Trough and peak location

In the same way, the intersection can be used to determine how far along in time the cycle is from its last peak or trough.

The time between adjacent troughs of the sine wave – the period – is ten days. The time from peak to trough and trough to peak is therefore half of this – five days. Because the intersection falls halfway between the peak and the trough of each cycle, we know that the last reversal must have occurred one quarter of a cycle back (2.5 days). We also know that the next reversal must occur after one more quarter cycle, i.e. in 2.5 days' time.

The simple device of overlaying a single out of phase sine wave and then observing the crossover points allows us to say exactly how far along the cycle is from its last peak or trough; how long it will take to reach its next peak or trough; and how much ground it will cover in between.

Clearly, information of this quality would be extremely helpful when looking at actual price movement. Although the real world is much less uniform, the concept of displaced cycles can be carried over to market cycles to great effect.

Calculating the FLD

As we have seen, to plot the displaced cycle (the FLD) a half period is simply added to the base cycle at each point in time, thereby describing the future path of the FLD. In Figure 3.1 the base cycle has a period of ten days and the displacement value is five days. This constant value is called the FLD number (FLDn).

The FLD number

For real market cycles, the FLDn is half of the average period of the cycle of interest, plus 1[25]. Thus, where P is the cycle period, the FLD number rounded up or down is given by:

```
FLDn = (P / 2) + 1
```

Refer back to the British Airways charts in the previous chapter. The average periods of four of the component cycles were calculated as: 11.7, 23.3, 46.5 and 92 days. Applying the FLD formula in each case gives:

- 11.7-day cycle, FLDn = (11.7 / 2) + 1 = 6.86, rounded up = 7
- 23.3-day cycle, FLDn = (23.3 / 2) + 1 = 12.65, rounded up = 13
- 46.5-day cycle, FLDn = (46.5 / 2) + 1 = 24.25, rounded down = 24
- 92-day cycle, FLDn = (92 / 2) + 1 = 47

Plotting the FLD

Many technical analysts blithely use indicators without really understanding how they are put together, mostly to the detriment of their analysis. Although a modern trading platform will run your indicators on command, the better you understand how they work the more skilful you will be in applying them.

Two examples

Simple FLD (1)

Figure 3.2 shows a simple example of an FLD plotted on the FTSE 100 up to 1 July 2010. Prices peaked on 22 June and then fell for the next eight sessions. The FLD runs parallel to prices off to the right. The grid numbers along the bottom of the chart represent each trading day. A blue dot has been added at the top of the chart just to help highlight the end of the data.

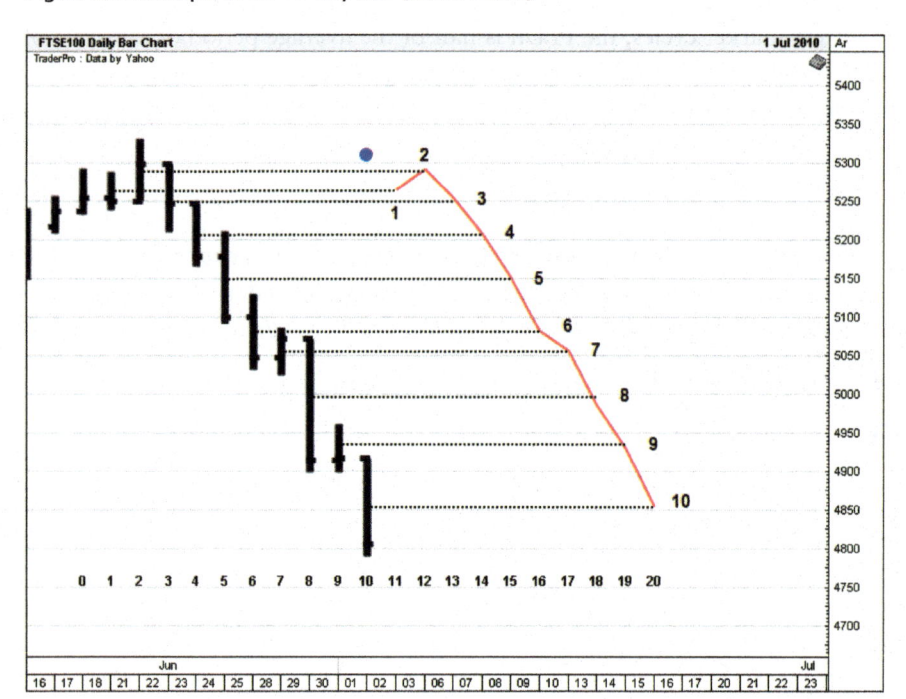

Figure 3.2: Example of an 18-day FLD (Data: Yahoo)

The FLD is based on an imaginary cycle with a period of 18 days and the calculation and projection runs as follows:

```
FLDn = (18 / 2) + 1 = 10
```

Starting at the first session – grid one – and finishing at the last session – grid 10 – the FLDn has been projected forward in time from the midpoint of each bar. These have been highlighted with horizontal lines.[26]

- The FLD begins plotting one bar past the last date, thus in this example the first bar at grid one projects the FLDn to give the first FLD value at grid 11.
- The second bar at grid two projects the FLDn to grid 12.
- The third bar at grid three projects to grid 13.
- And so on until the tenth bar at grid ten which projects the FLDn to grid 20, the last point on the FLD up to this time.

Complex FLD (2)

Figure 3.3 shows slightly more complex price action in the FTSE 100 up to 14 October 2010 with an FLD plotted. Price bottomed on 24 September and then rose in fits and starts over the next 15 sessions. The FLD tracks this move off to the right of prices.

This FLD is based on an imaginary cycle with a period of 31 days and the FLD calculation and projection runs as follows:

- FLDn = (31 / 2) + 1 = 16.5, which has been rounded down to 16.
- The FLDn is projected forward in time from the midpoint of each bar.
- The first bar at grid one projects the FLDn to grid 17, the FLD starting one bar past the last date.
- The second bar at grid two projects to grid 18.
- The third bar at grid three projects to grid 19.
- And so on up to the sixteenth bar at grid 16 which projects to grid 32, the last point on the FLD up to this time.

Figure 3.3: Example of a 31-day FLD (Data: Yahoo)

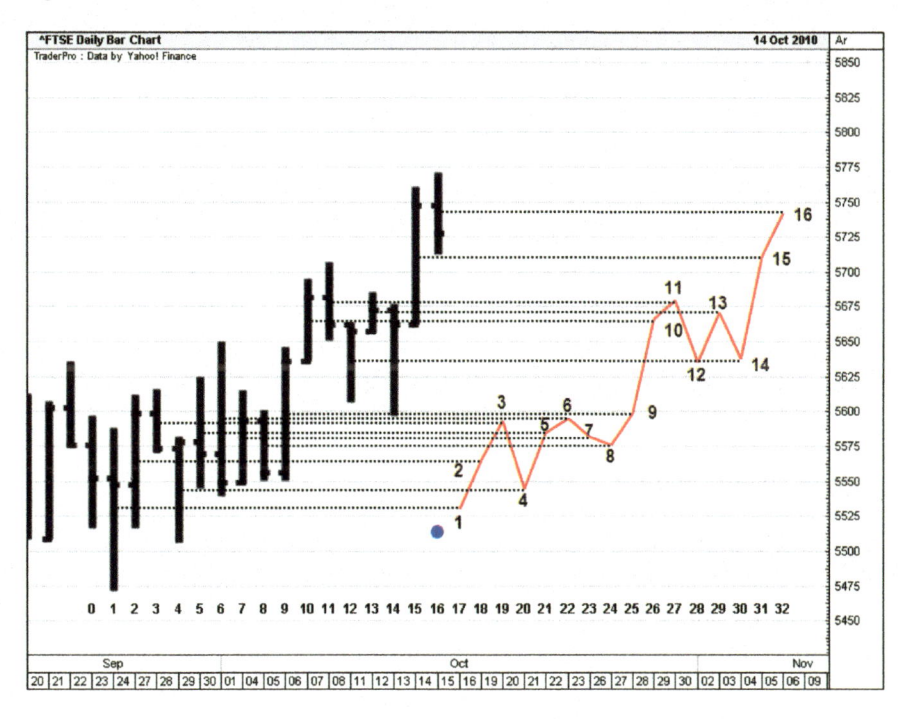

Coding the FLD

The preceding two examples illustrate how straightforward it is to construct and plot an FLD. Because Hurst developed his method of analysis before computers were widely available, the FLD was originally plotted by hand. While it is not a bad idea to do this a couple of times to get a better feel, it is impractical on an on-going basis. It is also unnecessary since the FLD can be programmed straight into your trading platform. The code is provided in Appendix 2 and you should load this into your system.[27]

You should now understand the thinking behind the FLD, know how it is calculated and plotted, as well as be able to run the code on your own platform. Now that most of the basics have been covered we can start looking at some real-life applications.

Applying FLDs

As you were shown in the offset sine waves example, FLDs can be used not only to identify past reversals but also to estimate the time location of future peaks and troughs. However, whereas individual sine waves are uniform and represent ideal conditions, market cycles are often far from uniform and are subject to myriad distorting forces.

That said, the same principles apply: when a price cycle forms a peak we can expect the FLD based on that cycle to form a trough; and when a price cycle forms a trough, we can expect the FLD to form a peak. The FLD number also tells us the magnitude of the reversal we should expect: the higher the FLDn, the bigger the reversal.

Also, because price and the FLD move opposite to one another, when prices are advancing we should expect to see the FLD declining; and vice versa, when prices are falling we expect to see the FLD rising.

Vedanta Resources example

Figure 3.4 shows FTSE 100 Diversified Miner, Vedanta Resources (VED.L), from February to September 2010. A red 70-day FLD has been plotted covering the entire chart. For ease of reference the FLD charts can be downloaded from **vectisma.com/downloads/FLDs**.

This is an example of an historical FLD and will be discussed later. For now though, look at the overall fluctuation of prices and note how the FLD exactly tracks price action in future time.

Two fairly regular cycles are apparent in the data and have been highlighted by semi-circles:

- The first cycle has a period of 72 trading days.
- The second cycle has a period of 69 trading days.
- The average period is therefore 70.5 trading days, equating to 103 calendar days.[28]
- The FLD number is given by: FLDn = (70.5 / 2) + 1 = 36.25, rounded down to 36 days.

Figure 3.4: 70.5-day FLD in Vedanta Resources (VED.L) February to September 2010 (Data: Yahoo)

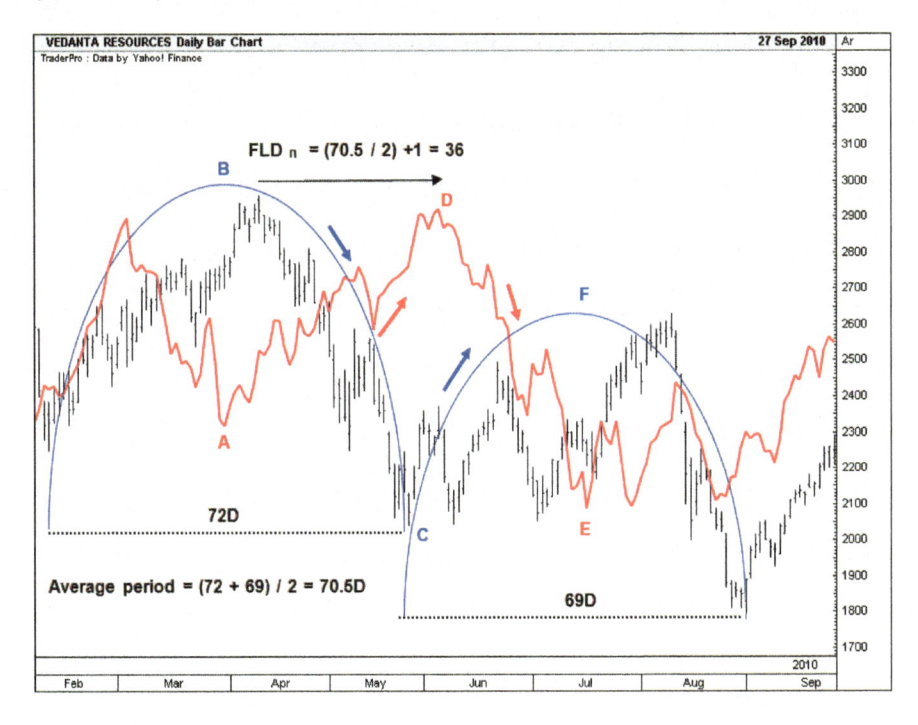

FLD-price interaction

You can see that point B, the peak of the semi-circle, corresponds to the FLD trough at point A, although the actual cycle peak is offset slightly to the right. Also, the FLD trough at point E corresponds to semi-circle peak at point F, but once again the actual peak is offset to the right.

If price troughs correspond to FLD peaks and vice versa, it therefore follows that when the FLD is headed up towards its next peak, the base cycle must be headed down towards its next trough.

Similarly, when the FLD is headed down towards its next trough the base cycle must be headed up towards its next peak. We have already seen how this works in the offset sine waves example and it is also the case in this chart.

Looking into future time

In Figure 3.4, FLD point A could have been plotted on the chart over a month earlier. When the first higher low in the FLD was then in place after point A, we could have tentatively assumed that the FLD had formed a trough and therefore that a peak in prices was likely around the same time, that is to say in late March or early April 2010.

As the FLD then tracked upwards, we could then have assumed that prices would be falling in this future time frame: that is to say from April onwards. We would also have known that the FLD would peak at point D in the first weeks of June. As it started heading down, we could have assumed that prices in this future time frame, from early June onwards, would therefore have been headed up.

As you can see from the chart, price and FLD have consistently moved in opposite directions, allowing us to forecast the general direction of prices well ahead of time in each case. This brings us to what happens when price and FLD intersect.

FLD-price intersection

The intersection of price and FLD can be used to identify cycle peaks and troughs in much the same way as price-VTL crosses can. You saw in the offset sine waves example how the intersection occurred one quarter of a cycle ahead of the last peak or trough.

In theory this means that when price and FLD intersect, the peak or trough of the cycle upon which the FLD is based (in Vedanta's case 70.5 days) should have occurred within the last 17.6 days (one quarter of a cycle back). Thus, when price crosses up through the FLD we will be looking for the price low within the last 17.6 days to be the *trough* of the 70D cycle. Conversely, if price crosses down through the FLD we will be looking for the price high within the last 17.6 days to be the *peak* of the 70D cycle.

Once we know that the peak or trough of a specific cycle – and therefore of a specific magnitude – has occurred and we know when this took place, then other things being equal we are in a good position to estimate the price and time location of the next trough or peak.

In actual markets, because of the influence of concurrent longer and shorter cycles, it is best to search for earlier peaks or troughs within the span of *one half cycle period* back from the cross, rather than the theoretical one quarter cycle. This gives you more wiggle room, but the message is the same.

Vedanta in real time

Identifying reversals

Figure 3.5 shows Vedanta as it would have appeared in real time in late April 2010. Look back at the long chart in Figure 3.4 to get your bearings: here we have just rounded the top of the first 72D cycle. The FLD intersection we are focusing on is the one at the end of the data.

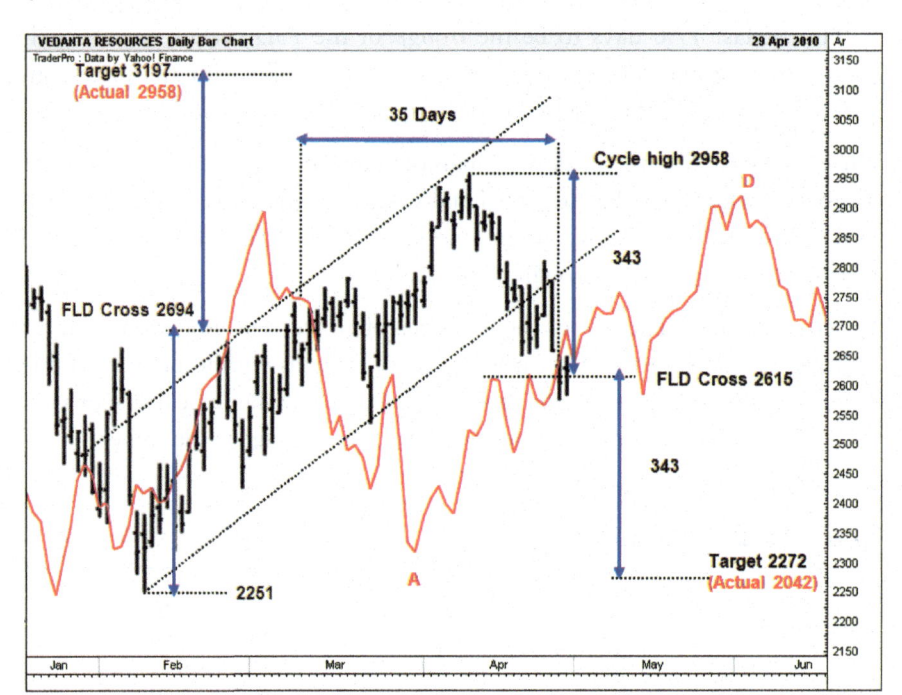

Figure 3.5: 70.5-day FLD downward cross in Vedanta Resources on 28 April 2010 (Data: Yahoo)

Prices advanced from the February low, peaked in early April and then dropped sharply back to the rising FLD.

- Price crossed down through the FLD at 2615 on 28 April. Measuring back one half cycle period (35 trading days) the price high within that time span is at 2958 on 12 April. This must therefore be the peak of the 70-day cycle.

- This is confirmed by the FLD trough at point A.

- Notice also that the lower trend channel support line was broken five sessions earlier. Because this is a 35D VTL – the approximate time between the February low and the first price touch in late March – its intersection confirms the earlier price high as the 70D cycle peak.

- At the time of the FLD intersection we would have been able to project 35 days ahead from the last peak (or 17 days from the intersection) to estimate when the next 70-day trough location was likely to occur. This trough would also be likely to correspond to the FLD peak at point D.

- Now glance back at Figure 3.4 again and see what actually happened. The cycle low came in more or less exactly on cue 30 days after the last cycle peak and directly below the FLD peak.

Projecting prices (1)

FLD-price intersections allow us to estimate the time location and magnitude of reversals, both in past and future time. This of course is extremely valuable in itself, but in fact the FLD intersection provides even more information: it allows us to forecast how far prices are likely to carry.

Recall from the sine waves example in Figure 3.1 that the vertical distance between the trough and the intersection was equal to the vertical distance between the intersection and the next peak; and vice versa, between the peak and the intersection, and the intersection and the next trough. At the point of intersection therefore we know we are exactly halfway up or down that particular cycle leg.

Refer back to Figure 3.5 again and look at the upward price cross of the FLD on 11 March. Applying what we learnt about projections on offset sine waves, let us see how it works on actual prices.

- The intersection is at 2694 and the most recent significant low (in February) is at 2251. The price difference therefore is 443 (2694 – 2251).

- Adding 443 to the intersection value of 2694 gives a projection of 3137. In this case, however, prices ended up topping out at 2958, falling short of the target by 179p.

- The second intersection on 28 April has price crossing down through the FLD. The 70-day cycle peak is 2958 and the cross is at 2615, giving a difference of 343.

- Applying the downwards price projection rule we simply deduct the difference from the intersection level which yields a target of 2272 (2615 – 343).

Now glance back at the full chart in Figure 3.4 to remind yourself what happened next. On 7 May, prices reached 2250 intraday and bounced hard; at this point the projection looked to have worked almost exactly. However, seven trading days later prices broke down and put in an intermediate lower low at 2042, overshooting the target by 230p (2272 – 2042).

Projecting prices (2)

Now let us go forward in time and look at the next example. Figure 3.6 shows Vedanta up to 9 July and we are looking at the second intersection at the end of data – for reference this is the third intersection on the original extended chart (Figure 3.4). Price crosses up through the FLD, projecting higher.

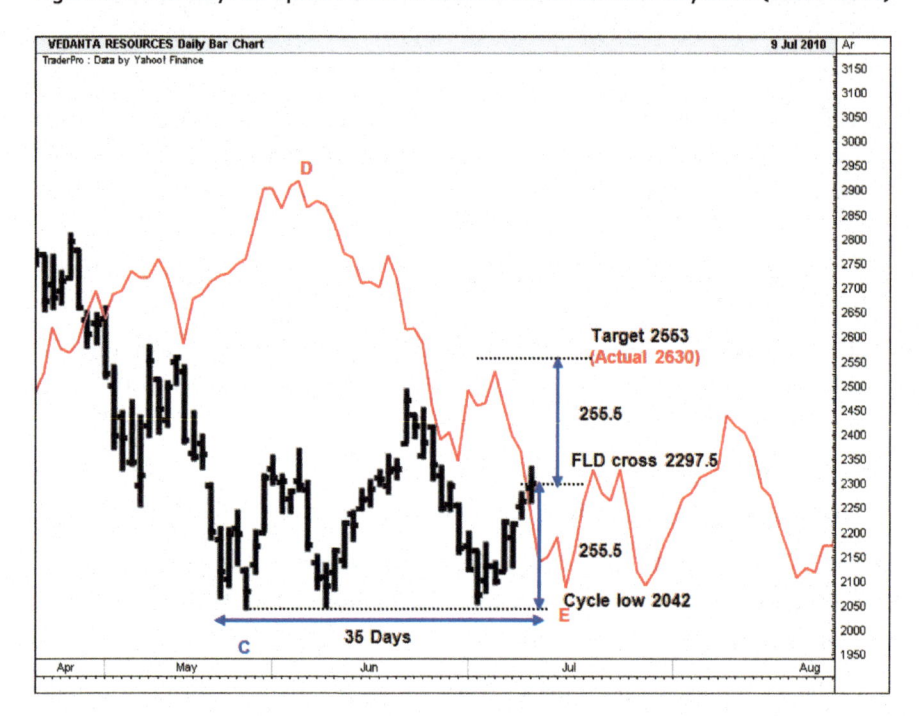

Figure 3.6: 70.5 day FLD upward cross in Vedanta Resources on 9 July 2010 (Data: Yahoo)

- Notice that the FLD cross occurs between two bars. The convention here is to take the mid-price of the bar immediately after the cross, in this case 2297.5.
- The price low within a time span of 35 days back from the intersection is 2042 at point C. The price difference therefore is 255.5 (2297.5 – 2042).
- This is added to the intersection value giving a target of 2553.
- Referring back to Figure 3.4 again we see that price topped out at 2630 overshooting the projected target by 77p.

FLD projections and underlying trend

Why projections fail

In neither of these examples did the achieved price match the FLD projected price: it was either undershot or surpassed. After the build-up given to the FLD projection technique this may seem like a disappointing result. However, it is not as bad as it seems.

Having a projection target that is derived from sound reasoning is better than not having one at all. For one thing it allows us to establish one half of a minimum reward-to risk ratio when entering a trade – something we will be covering in detail in a later chapter.

Whether prices end up hitting the projection target exactly, falling short or exceeding it, there is still valuable information to be extracted.

The reason FLD projections miss is the influence of underlying trend and trend, as you now know, is just shorthand for the sum of all longer cycles. Trend affects FLD projections in the following way:

- When trend is acting in the same direction as the projection, i.e. working with it, then the achieved price will overshoot the target price.

- When trend is acting in the opposite direction to the projection, i.e. working against it, then the achieved price will fall short of the target price.

For example, if a projection is made to the downside and the underlying trend is also down, then the achieved price will end up lower than the target price. If the projection is to the downside and the underlying trend is up, then the achieved price will end up higher than the target.

Conversely, if the projection is to the upside and the underlying trend is also up, then the achieved price will end up higher than the target price. If the projection is to the upside and the underlying trend is down, then the achieved price will end up lower than the target price. Table 3.1 is a summary of each of these combinations.

Table 3.1: FLD Projections summary

Projection	Underlying trend	Result	Price vs. Target	Trade profit
Downside	Down	Overshoot	Lower	Better short
Upside	Down	Undershoot	Lower	Worse long
Downside	Up	Undershoot	Higher	Worse short
Upside	Up	Overshoot	Higher	Better long

The following examples using offset sine waves will help to illustrate this idea. First, we will consider projections where there is no underlying trend and then we will see what happens when an uptrend and then a downtrend are present.

No trend component

Figure 3.7 shows a sine wave and its red displaced replica – FLD proxy. The sine wave fluctuates around a horizontal central axis indicating that there is no up or down trend component. Because the distorting influence of underlying trend is absent, each hypothetical FLD projection is met exactly. The intersection points occur halfway between peak and trough, giving: AB=BC and CD=DE.

Figure 3.7: Offset sine waves with no underlying trend

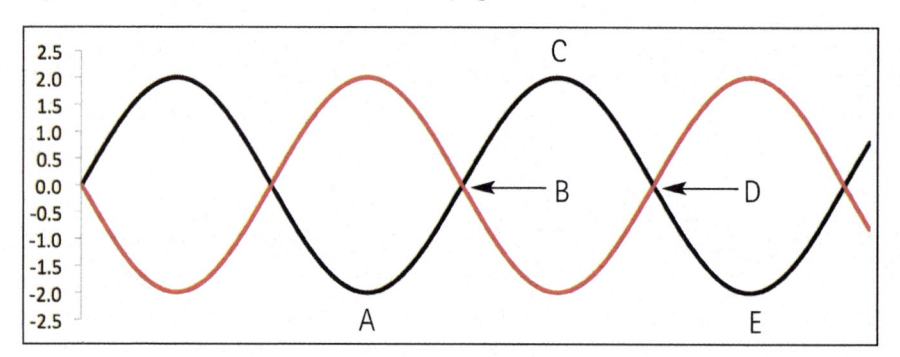

Addition of underlying trend

See what happens to the projections however when underlying trend is present. Figure 3.8 shows the same offset sine waves, but this time the central axis, instead of being a horizontal line, is the peak of a much longer cycle.

The solid black line is a composite of the long cycle and the original sine wave. The red line is a composite of the long cycle and the offset sine wave.

Notice that during the advance AB is greater than BC. Had a projection of AB been made at the intersection point B, it would have been undershot at point C because the underlying trend had rolled over. Similarly, during the decline CD is shorter than DE. Had a projection of CD been made at the intersection point D, it would have been overshot because the underlying trend had gone from being flat or slightly down to strongly down.

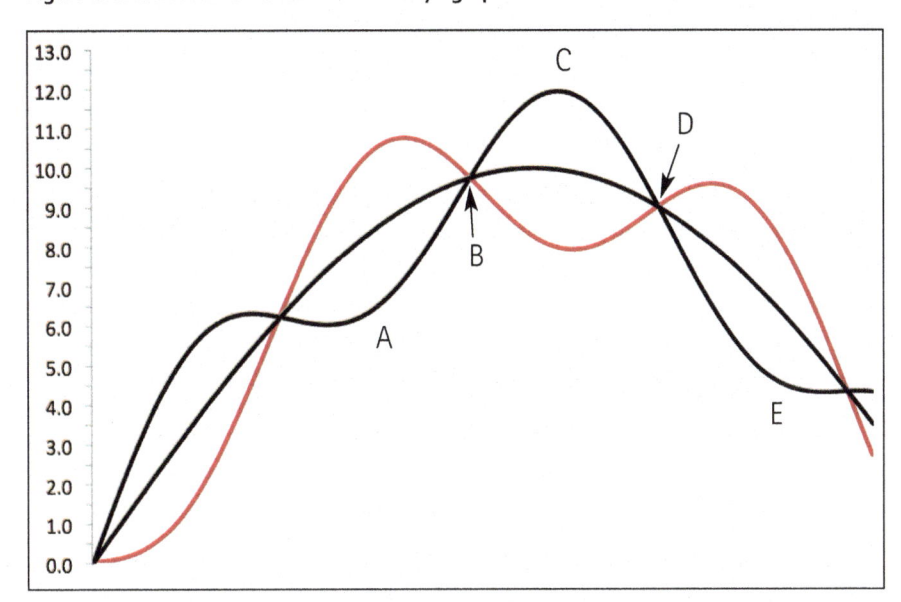

Figure 3.8: Offset sine waves with underlying uptrend and downtrend

You should by now have a better overall grasp of how FLDs are constructed. You should also be clear on how they can help locate turning points, provide guideline projections and allow us to observe the currents that run beneath the surface of the market.

So far the focus has been on individual FLDs. However, this is only part of the story. In fact more insight can be gained by looking at how multiple FLDs interact with one another and form patterns.

In the next section we will look at the two principal FLD patterns, the *cascade* and the *pause zone*, and learn how to interpret them.

FLD Combinations

Cascades and pause zones

We have already learnt that there are multiple cycles running through the market at any given time and that these cycles are governed by common principles. It is the interaction of these cycles that creates the composite cycle we see as price movement.

Each component cycle in the composite has its own FLD, which means that at any given time there must be multiple FLDs operating in the market as well. FLDs are simply duplicate cycles, so they must also conform to the same common principles of cyclicality. Because FLDs are cycles projected into future time, the patterns formed by multiple FLDs can be used to make forecasts about the future course of prices.

There are many FLD patterns but the two most important are the *cascade* and the *pause zone*. An ideal cascade occurs when prices are either advancing or declining steeply and FLDs are tightly stacked, evenly spaced and running parallel in the same direction. A pause zone is where, having run freely for a while, the FLDs start crossing. The guidelines are as follows:

- When prices are rising steeply FLDs will generally be arrayed below prices and will also be rising steeply: in this environment you should be looking closely for an imminent and sharp sell-off.

- When prices are falling steeply FLDs will generally be arrayed above prices and will also be falling steeply: in this environment you should be looking for an imminent and sharp rally.

- When FLDs have been running in parallel and then start crossing each other, then at that future time you should be looking for a consolidation rally or decline, or else an area of congestion. In other words the pause zone is likely to stop prices temporarily.

The tighter the FLD stack and the steeper the price move, the more powerful the signal and the more explosive is the subsequent price move out.

If the FLD stack is shallow, or if they wander about, criss-cross each other and are unevenly spaced, then the move out has less conviction. The following three examples from actual prices illustrate the concept. We will look at two high-conviction cascades, one rising and one falling, as well as a low-conviction cascade.

Rising cascade and pause zone

Figure 3.9 shows the Dow Jones Eurostoxx 50 advancing into 11 December 2007 with an array of FLDs rising in an evenly spaced, parallel stack below prices in near future time.

Figure 3.9: FLD rising cascade DJ Eurostoxx 50, 11 December 2007 (Data: Yahoo)

The FLDs have been colour coded[29] and numbered one to four. FLD number one, nearest prices (orange), is based on a seven-day cycle. FLD number two (green) is based on a 14-day cycle. FLD number three (blue) is based on a 28-day cycle and finally FLD number four (red) is based on a 56-day cycle.

The cycles are the trading day equivalents of daily cycles in the nominal set: 10, 20, 40 and 80 calendar days respectively. They have also been standardised for clarity and are not the actual average cycle periods in the data – although they are likely to be close. How to work out precise FLD periods will be covered when we look at phasing analysis in chapter four.

The pattern here suggests that a sharp downside reversal is imminent. As soon as the near FLDs break, set off a domino effect all the way down to the furthest FLD and possibly beyond. The criss-crossing of FLDs between 4300 and 4440 suggests that there will be some sort of rest or consolidation towards the end of December.

Through the rising cascade

Figure 3.10 shows what happened next. Prices broke through FLD 1 and projected down through FLD 2. The break of FLD 2 then projected down through FLD 3. The break in FLD 3 in turn then projected down through FLD 4. The cascade effect is simply the result of each FLD projection triggering the next. Eventually there are either no more FLDs through which to project or the gap between successive FLDs is too wide to cross.

Notice that as prices decline, the FLDs start to arrange themselves in a falling cascade indicating that at some point prices will be drawn back to the pattern and reverse through it, setting off an upside cascade. Notice also that prices are refreshed into late December in a short consolidation rally, as predicted by the pause zone.

Figure 3.10: Through the rising cascade DJ Eurostoxx 50, 18 January 2008 (Data: Yahoo)

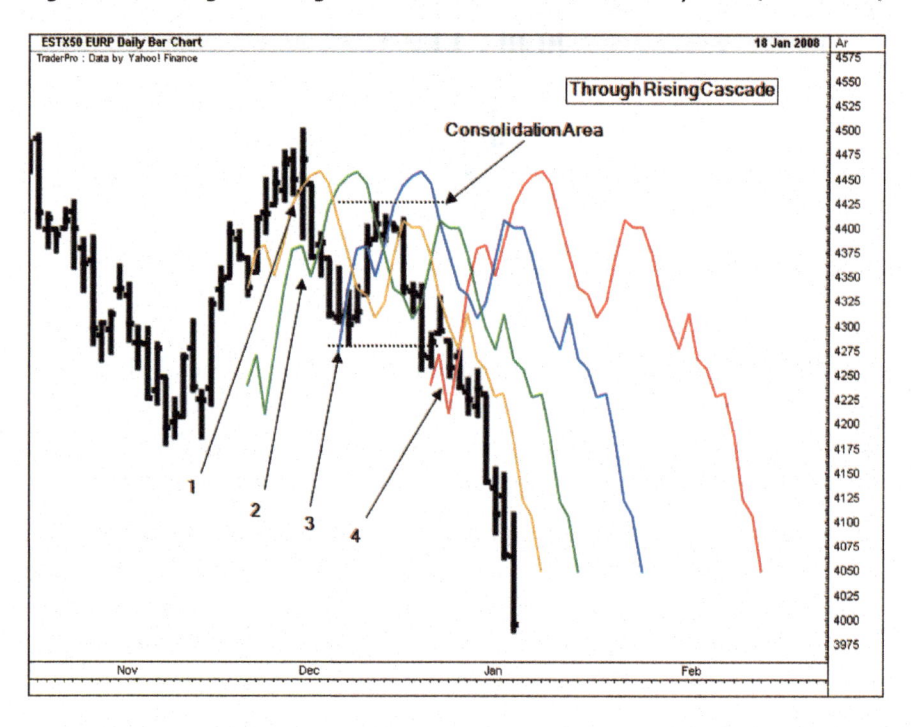

Falling cascade and pause zone

Figure 3.11 shows the Dow Jones Eurostoxx 50 declining into a price low on 14 June 2006 with an array of FLDs falling in an evenly spaced, parallel stack above prices in near future time.

Using the same colour scheme for each cycle we can see that a break of FLD 1 is likely to project through FLD 2 and so on through to FLD 4, signalling an imminent reversal and higher prices. Where the FLDs cross in the 3600-3700 range in mid-July, we are likely to see a consolidative pullback of some sort.

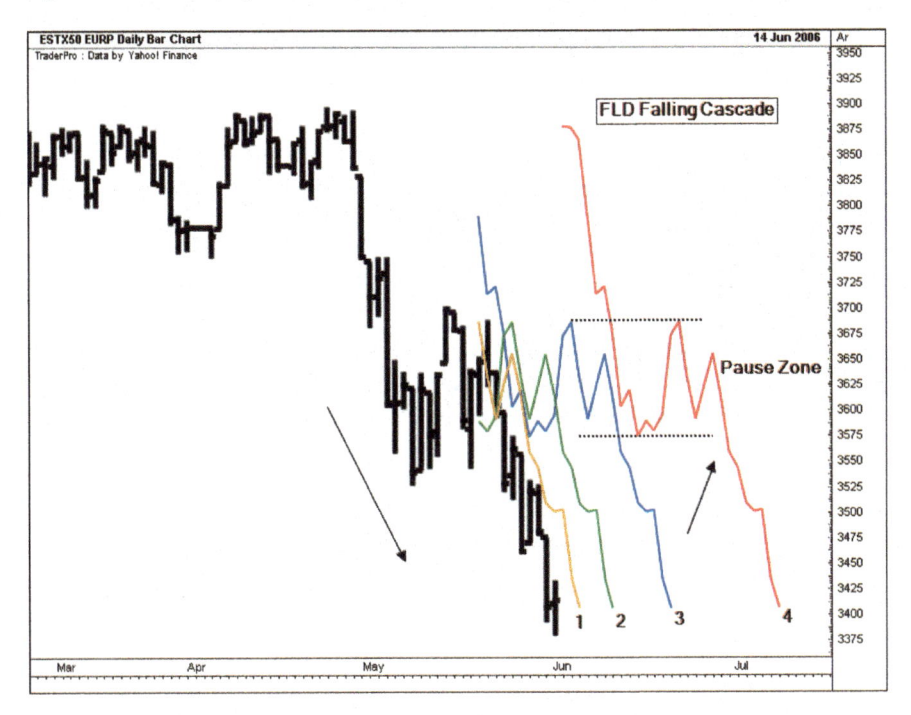

Figure 3.11: FLD falling cascade DJ Eurostoxx 50, 14 June 2006 (Data: Yahoo)

Through the falling cascade

Figure 3.12 shows what happened next. Prices broke through FLD 1 and projected up through FLD 2. The break of FLD 2 then projected up through FLD 3. The break in FLD 3 in turn projected up through FLD 4. Again each FLD projection is triggering the next.

Notice that prices enter a congestion area in July as predicted by the pause zone.

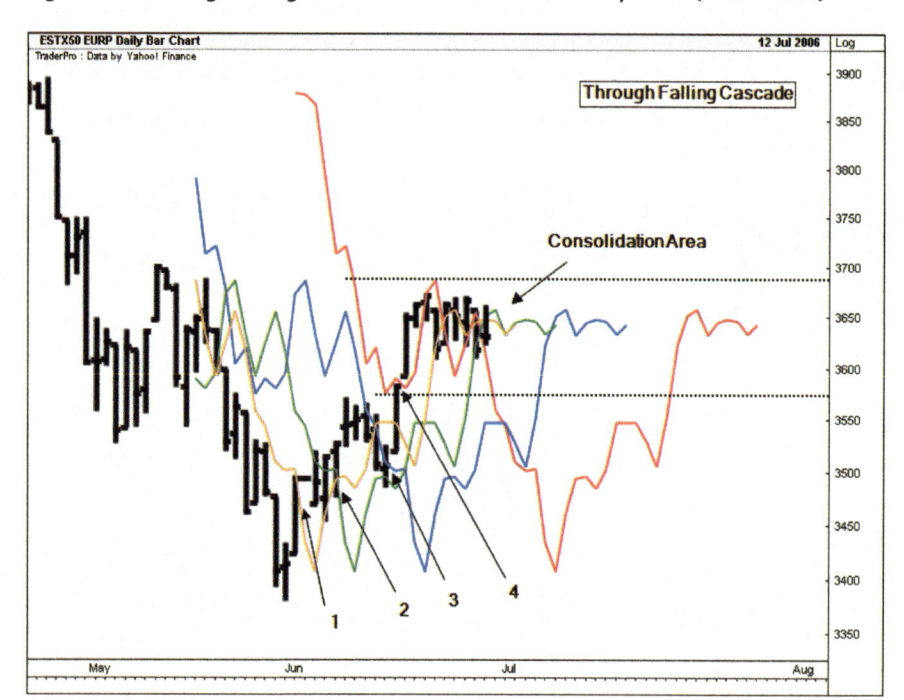

Figure 3.12: Through falling cascade DJ Eurostoxx 50, 12 July 2006 (Data: Yahoo)

Patterns of multiple FLDs, particularly the cascade and the pause zone, are powerful tools that can be used to warn of imminent reversals as well as to provide advance notice of when and where prices will halt.

You should now be able to recognise and interpret two key multiple FLD patterns. These crop up time and time again and we will be revisiting them throughout the book. There are many subtle nuances that have not been covered here that will reveal themselves as you gain more exposure and build experience.

Conclusion

Even though the FLD will have been a new idea to many readers, it should be clear by now that it is a powerful tool with multiple applications. Although you should know how to calculate the FLD number manually, for everyday trading and analysis you should load the code into your platform and plot FLDs automatically.

It was shown that when a replica cycle is added to a sine wave and phase shifted forward by a half period, we are able to measure exactly when cycle reversals are due to occur. It was also shown that when two identical phase-shifted sine waves cross, we are able to predict exactly the value of the next peak or trough.

In the market, this is equivalent to price crossing the FLD, either from above or below. We can use these crosses to help us gauge the magnitude of past reversals as well as estimate when future reversals are likely to happen. Additionally, we can use the difference in value between the intersection and the most recent cycle peak or trough to forecast how far prices are likely to carry.

Because there are multiple cycles interacting in the market, projections do not always exactly meet their targets. However, valuable information can still be extracted and FLD projection overshoots or undershoots provide us with a measure of underlying trend strength and direction.

Having grasped the basics of how to create and use single FLDs, we then looked at the more powerful concept of FLD combinations. The two FLD patterns discussed, cascades and pause zones, are used again and again in Hurst analysis. Cascades indicate that prices are due a sharp reversal and that we should start thinking about setting up a trade. Pause zones tell use when prices are likely to stall and that we should think about closing positions.

You have now been introduced to the two basic tools of Hurst analysis: the FLD and the VTL. You probably feel like putting them to work at once and feel free to do so, but do not expect any dramatic new outcomes because we are not quite there yet. Remember, Hurst analysis is an integrated system and to get the best results you need to not only master the tools but also learn how to use them together. It is a bit like studying the guitar: learning the chords is step one, but it is not until you can put them together seamlessly that you can strum a decent tune.

VTLs and FLDs are based on specific cycles within the composite and the next task is to learn how to isolate those components using Hurst's Phasing Analysis.

Phasing Analysis is part art, part science, and it will be a completely new concept to most. It will seem complicated and tricky at first, so you will need to concentrate and persevere. Later however, when you are an expert Hurst cycle analyst, you will wonder why you found it so difficult to begin with.

Endnotes

[25] The reason 1 is added will be made clear when we look at FLD price projections, but it is simply a device to ensure that when the FLD crosses price, it is a true cross. It is a bit like waiting an extra day to confirm a breakout signal. In fact, the usefulness of the FLD is more or less the same whether you add 1 or not.

[26] Although you can project the FLD from any point on the price bar (high, low, close, VWAP, etc.) the convention is to project from the midpoint (H + L) / 2.

[27] The code for the FLD – as well as all of the code used in this book – is provided in Updata's proprietary language as well as TradeStation's Easy Language. For users of other trading platforms, you will either need to translate the code yourself or contact the development team at your vendor. However, if there is enough interest, I will commission a developer in Metastock, CQG or Ninja to convert all of the code shown in the Appendices. I will charge a small fee for this to cover costs. Please email me on **cgrafton@vectisma.com** if you are interested.

[28] Remember the conversion from trading days to calendar days: 70.5 x (365.25 / 250) = 103. For trading days to calendar days multiply by (250 / 365.25).

[29] The colours used for each FLD are specific to cycle in the Nominal Model. Each cycle in the model is assigned its own colour and is carried over to VTLs and phasing analysis, which will be studied in chapter four. The complete table of colours and their programming numbers is provided in Appendix 2.

4 ISOLATING MARKET CYCLES I

Introduction

You have been introduced to the two basic tools of Hurst cycle analysis: the VTL and the FLD. You have learnt that VTLs connect cycle troughs or peaks and that their intersection with price provides information about recent reversals in specific cycles. You have also learnt how FLDs can help you make price projections and gauge trend direction.

In order to draw in VTLs you need to know where the cycles they correspond to start and finish. In order to plot FLDs, you need to know the average period of the cycle on which it is based. This brings us to the core element of Hurst's system: *phasing analysis*.

Phasing analysis is the method of isolating and then marking the time location of each component cycle trough in the composite data. This process provides us with the information required to calculate the average length of each cycle and tells us how far along they are at the end of the data. When these are both known, we are able to use VTLs and FLDs to estimate with a high degree of accuracy what is likely to happen next.

The Principle of Synchronicity tells us that cycles have a tendency to converge at troughs and form nests of lows. Cycle peaks on the other hand tend to be more dispersed. For this reason the convention is to measure period between troughs rather than peaks. You will be shown how to set up your system to enable you to mark these troughs in an organised manner and introduced to new tools and techniques that assist the process. One of these tools is the *cycle envelope*.

Cycle envelopes are sets of moving average bands calibrated to the dominant fluctuation of prices on the chart and set to enclose most of the price movement. Their purpose is to increase visibility and help initiate the phasing analysis. To understand how moving average bands emphasise cycles, you need to know how moving averages smooth data. You will be shown how this process works and how to apply moving average bands to the chart. We will also look at the concept of centred moving averages and examine why they are the preferred tool in cycle analysis.

Once your system is ready and you understand how to apply the tools, we will work through a detailed example of a phasing analysis on the weekly chart of a US security. This will be conducted in three stages, starting with the longest cycle and working down to the shortest. We will go through this exercise as thoroughly as possible explaining the decision-making process each step of the way. Phasing analysis will seem like hard work at first, but you need to remember that it gets easier the more times you do it.

When the analysis is complete and every cycle trough has been marked with a diamond, you will be shown how to assemble the raw data and use it to generate a phasing model. The status report within this model contains the information you will need to set up a trade.

By the end of this chapter you will know how to conduct a phasing analysis from start to finish and will be familiar with a range of new techniques. Phasing analysis is a bit of an art, so do not expect to become an expert overnight. It takes practice to become proficient and throughout the rest of the book you will be exposed to many more examples and case studies.

In the next chapter we will finish the phasing analysis that we are going to start here and look at two more techniques. By the end of it all you will be in a good position to start looking at setting up, running and exiting trades, which is the subject of the rest of the book.

Cycle Envelopes

Moving averages

Visualising data

Market prices are plotted as graphs because it is hard to get a sense for their movement just by looking at a column of figures – our brains do not work that way. Looking at a line, candle or bar chart immediately allows us to see how prices change over time and is of course the basis of technical analysis. Visibility can be enhanced further by applying a moving average (MA) to the data.

There are a number of different types of moving average[30] but they all perform more or less the same function: that of representing the value of a subset of prices in the data. One way to think of a moving average is to imagine a block of consecutive price bars moving across the chart: the width of the block being analogous to the moving average period. By focusing on a moving block of prices, the movement of individual bars is smoothed away giving us a clearer picture of overall price movement.

Although most traders will be used to moving averages, their application to cycle analysis is slightly different.

Centring the moving average

The convention in technical analysis is to line up the last value of the MA with the last signal, for example the closing price, at the end of the data. What this is actually doing, however, is artificially displacing the MA forward in time. This is useful, for example, in an MA price crossover system[31], but the alignment is specious.

The proper position for the MA value is not at the same time location as the last price, but rather in the middle of the subset of data that is being averaged.

For and against

One of main reasons traders do not like to have moving averages set up in this way is the time lag. For example, the last plotted value of a 55-day centred MA would be at the last date minus half of the MA period, leaving a gap of 27 days. This of course makes it useless for an MA price crossover system, because at the last date there is no MA.

Cycles analysts, on the other hand, like centred moving averages precisely because of the lag. If the MA is in the middle of the data then it more accurately highlights the movement of the cycle it has been calibrated to.

Figure 4.1 shows two simple moving averages plotted alongside one another: a conventional 15-day MA – shown in red – and a centred 15-day MA – shown in blue.

Figure 4.1: Comparison of conventional and centred moving average, Boeing (BA) daily (Data: Yahoo)

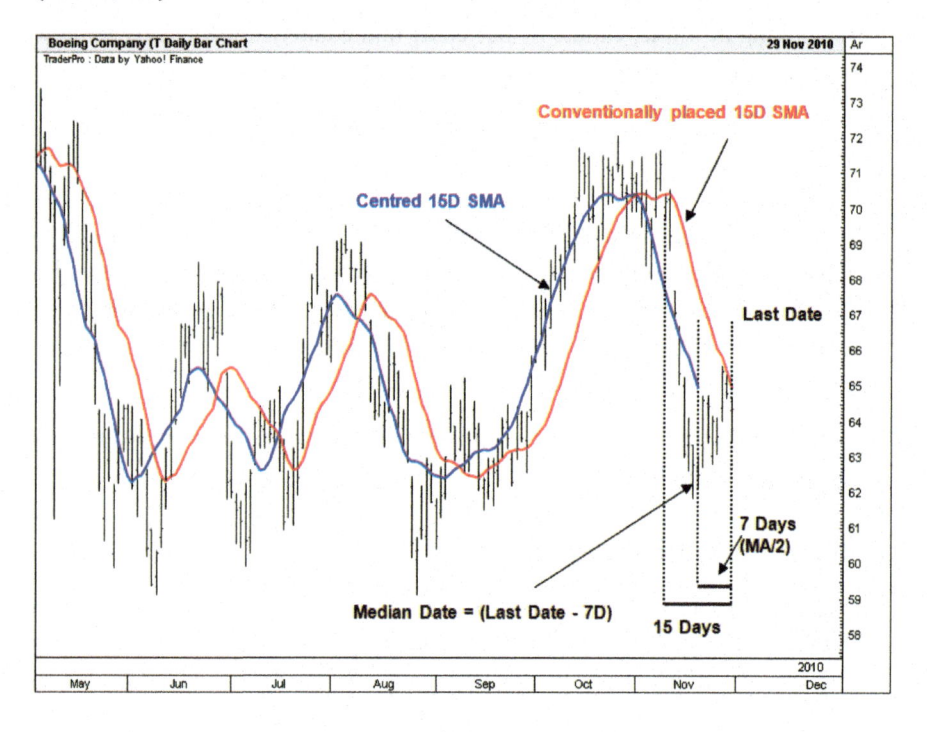

In phase versus out of phase

Although the averaging period is the same for both, the conventional MA stops plotting at the last date, whereas the centred MA stops seven days earlier. The longer the MA period, the longer the lag. For example, the data in this chart runs to the end of November. Were we looking at a 100-day centred MA here, it would have stopped plotting back in the summer.

Because the centred MA runs right up and down the middle of the price action, it accurately traces out the path of the cycle, more or less exactly picking out the time location of the peaks and troughs. In other words it is in phase with the cycle.

Chapter 4 | Isolating Market Cycles I

The conventional MA, meanwhile, is busy looking for crossovers and whatnot off to the right and calls the turns late, precisely because it is seven days out of phase.

The main function of all moving averages, including the centred MA, is to smooth out distracting market noise – or shorter cycles.

Moving averages as data filters

Moving averages work by allowing through the amplitude of cycle periods over a certain length and reducing or attenuating the amplitude of shorter cycles. The cut off level is determined by the length of the MA.

In digital signal processing this is called low pass filtering and as the name suggests it allows low-frequency (long-period) cycles to pass while cutting off high-frequency (short-period) cycles. This is exactly what a woofer in a loudspeaker does; it filters out high pitch sounds and emphasises the low frequency bass.

Smoothing

Table 4.1 shows closing prices as well as five-day moving average values over the last ten trading days of the previous Boeing chart.

Table 4.1: Boeing price data for the ten days to 29 November 2010 (Data: Yahoo)

Date	Close	5SMA	Excursion
29-Nov-10	333.90	336.34	-2.44
26-Nov-10	340.10	338.74	1.36
25-Nov-10	335.10	340.66	-5.56
24-Nov-10	333.80	344.18	-10.38
23-Nov-10	338.80	346.98	-8.18
22-Nov-10	345.90	348.26	-2.36
19-Nov-10	349.70	349.58	0.12
18-Nov-10	352.70	349.74	2.96
17-Nov-10	347.80	350.10	-2.30
16-Nov-10	345.20	352.42	-7.22
StdDev	6.88	5.46	4.34

The final column labelled *excursion* is the moving average value subtracted from the close. If you think of the MA as an axis and the close as fluctuating around this, then the excursion is just a measure of the extent of the fluctuation. Here the range is 12.74: varying from 10.38 below the MA to 2.36 above it. The moving average, therefore, is not showing these outlying movements.

Sine waves averaging out

This can be illustrated another way. Let us imagine that there is a five-day cycle in the data which is a perfect sine wave. During a full oscillation this sine wave rises above its central axis by exactly the same amount as it falls below it, which means that the average of each oscillation is zero. Put another way, there are as many positive values as there are negative values and they aggregate to zero.

If we now think of all of the cycles shorter than five days and imagine that they are also perfect sine waves, then exactly the same principle applies and the average of each of their oscillations is also zero. Thus, the amplitude of a five-day sine wave and all shorter sine waves is averaged or smoothed out by a five-day moving average.

Of course, cycles in the real prices are not perfect sine waves, which is why shorter cycles often show through to some extent. You can therefore think of the excursions shown in the table of data as being caused by the action of shorter cycles, which the moving average then eliminates.

On the other hand, because the short MA does not have the reach to average out anything longer than its own period, the longer cycles are able to show through at full strength.

Attenuation of amplitude

One of the by-products of smoothed data is that the amplitude is reduced or attenuated. Without the addition of the excursions from the mean, the range of travel of the cycle is less. You can see this of course by simply looking at the chart, but also by comparing the standard deviation of the closing price line (6.88) to that of the MA line (5.46). In other words, the closing price cycle amplitude is 126% of the MA cycle's amplitude.

Detrending data

By plotting the path of the excursions from the mean shown in Table 4.1, we can see the shorter cycles the moving average has left behind. Hurst called this the Inverse Moving Average and it is a method of detrending data: in other words, stripping out the longer cycles.

A word of caution here is needed. Because we are using centred moving averages the MA value needs to be subtracted from the price in the *middle of the data* being averaged rather than at the last date. If you do not do this, the output of the indicator that follows will be distorted.

Detrended data is best plotted as a histogram. The central axis is the zero line where the close and the moving average have the same value. Negative and positive data shows up more clearly using a histogram and it is easier to compare magnitudes.

Figure 4.2 shows the Boeing chart with a 14-day centred MA applied to prices and an Inverse Moving Average histogram in the lower window. This is just the MA subtracted from the close seven bars previously. The histogram and the bars have been colour coded in the same way for emphasis.[32]

Figure 4.2: Detrending a 14-day moving average to isolate shorter components (Data: Yahoo)

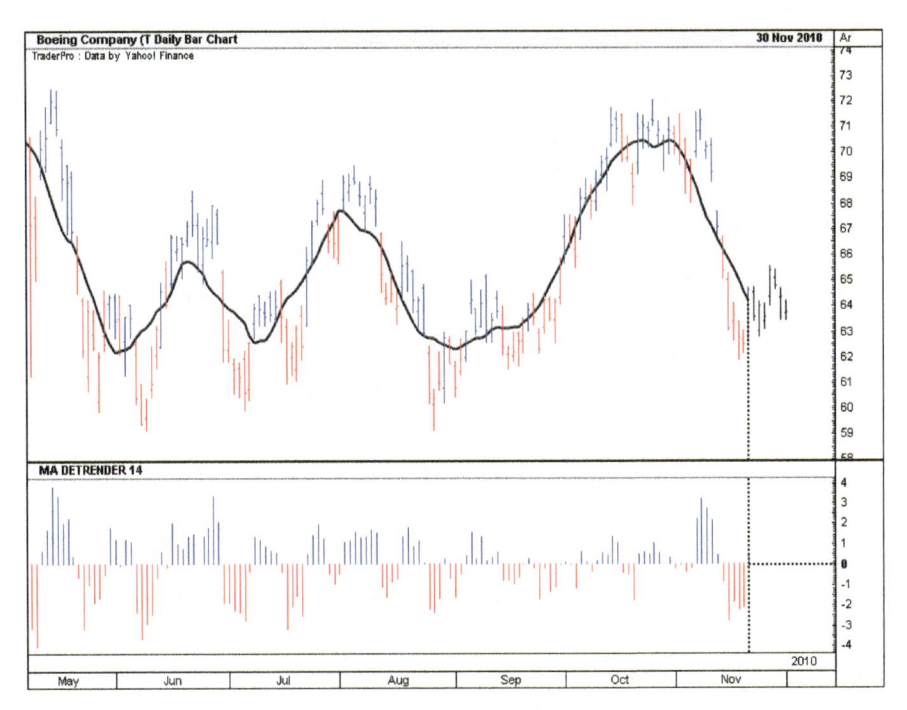

Using moving averages to highlight cycles

Figure 4.3 shows Boeing from September 1998 to July 2003. This is an almost picture perfect 54-month cycle showing its three harmonic 18-month (80-week) components.

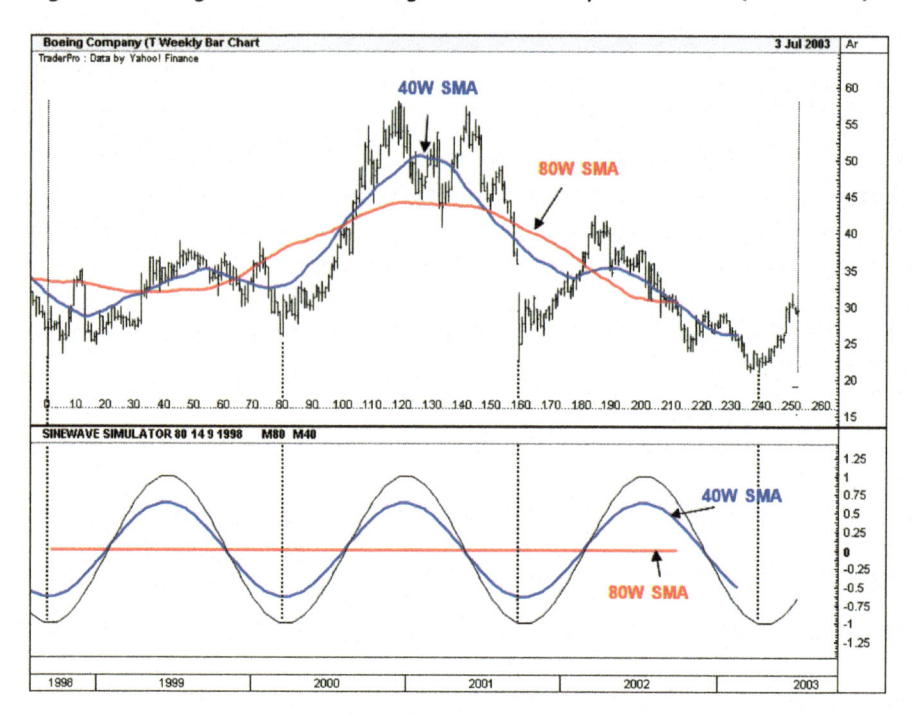

Figure 4.3: Boeing 1998-2003, showing three 80-week cycles with MAs (Data: Yahoo)

The lower window shows an 80-week sine wave in phase with the price cycle. Two centred moving averages, an 80-week and a 40-week, have been applied to both the sine wave and the price chart. Notice that the red 80W sine wave MA has been completely averaged out to a straight line and that the amplitude of the blue 40W sine wave MA has been attenuated.

In the price chart, although the red 80-week MA is not a straight line because longer cycles absent in the sine wave are showing through, it fails to pick out the major fluctuations in the chart. On the other hand, despite the fact that the blue 40-week MA has been attenuated, it does manage to pick out the turns of the longer cycle.

Constructing moving average bands

Having seen how moving averages can be used to emphasise cycles, we can now go a step further and create a set of moving average bands. This is simply an upper and lower curvilinear line plotted to run parallel to the MA. The MA period is calibrated to highlight a cycle of interest and the bandwidth is set to capture most of the price movement.

In this way the bands provide yet another level of visibility and are the basis of the Cycle Envelope (Hurst's Dominancy Envelope) used to help identify cycles in phasing analysis. Figure 4.4 shows a 40-week cycle envelope applied to the same Boeing chart.

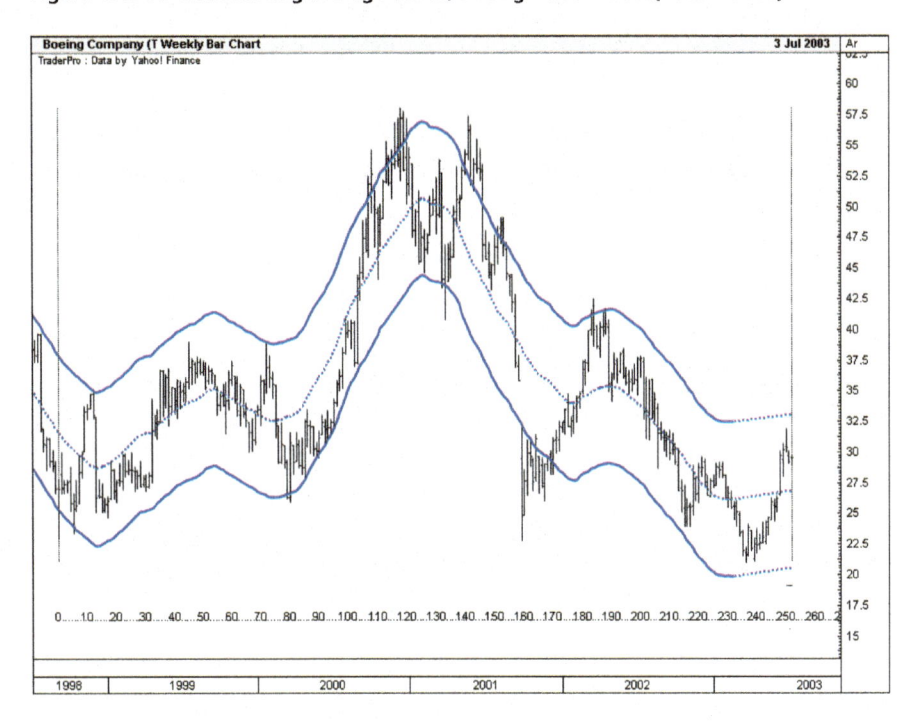

Figure 4.4: 40-week moving average bands, Boeing 1998-2003 (Data: Yahoo)

Bandwidth

The vertical distance between the bands – or width – remains constant throughout and should capture most of the price movement. Here it is $12.50 which is just over 20% of the high-low price range of the chart, although this will vary from issue to issue. Occasionally prices briefly penetrate the bands, but this is to be expected.

Gauging the bandwidth by eye can be a bit hit or miss, but it is possible to roughly measure the amplitude of the major swings against the y-axis and then halve the figure to set the bands. It usually takes a few attempts to get them just right.

Alternatively, you can use the code provided in Appendix 4. This automatically sets the bandwidth by calculating the maximum deviation within the high-low range and then adding and subtracting from a centred MA. It occasionally needs a little tweaking, but this is easy enough to do.

MA period

The period of the centred MA needs to be calibrated to capture the major fluctuation of the price movement across the chart. As we have seen, if the MA is the same length as the cycle responsible for this fluctuation it will not pick out the reversals. And if it is too short it will show every twist and turn. There are no hard and fast rules about setting the MA period, but as a rule of thumb between one quarter and half the length of the dominant cycle tends to work well.

You can set the MA period visually by measuring the distance between obvious troughs of the dominant fluctuation against the row of numbers[33] running along the bottom of the chart.

Notice that with the MA set to 40 weeks the cycle envelope turns up at grid numbers 12, 80, 180 and 230 and turns down at 50, 130 and 190, highlighting the associated troughs and peaks of the 80-week cycle. The average time between the spaces is 71.6 weeks, near enough the nominal 80-week cycle period.

Extrapolating the centred MA and bands

The centreline and upper and lower bands have been extrapolated as straight dotted lines from their last values up to the end of the data, filling in what would otherwise be an empty range due to the centring of the moving average.

Although the projections are straight lines and intervening price action is lost up to the last date, it is better than nothing and is a workable visual aid. Some analysts (including Hurst himself)[34] have tried to accurately project the cycle envelope past the last date. In order to do this, however, you need to programme in all of your assumptions on the cyclic condition of the chart. This can be done, although it requires some pretty fancy coding, but it is dangerous. You will end up relying on a set of lines that really have very little authority.

Multiple envelopes

Having plotted a 40-week cycle envelope to pick out the dominant fluctuation, there is nothing to stop us placing this in an 80-week cycle envelope as well. You can carry on doing this for as many shorter or longer cycles as you see fit.

Figure 4.5 shows the 40-week cycle envelopes embedded within the 80-week cycle envelope.

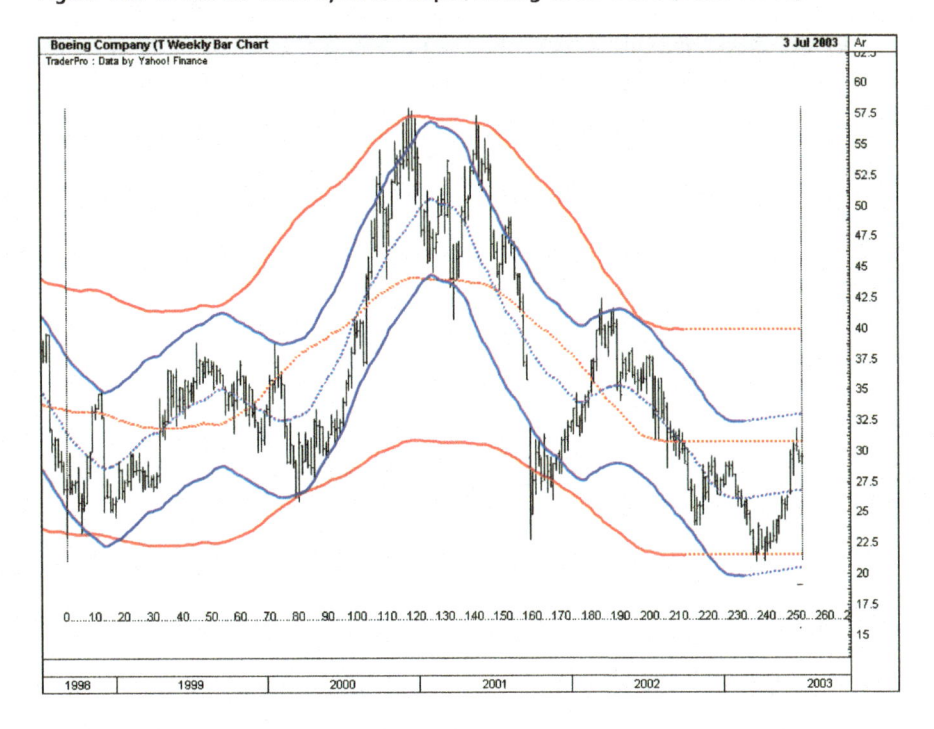

Figure 4.5: 40 and 80-week cycle envelopes, Boeing 1998-2003 (Data: Yahoo)

Phasing Analysis Set Up

Phasing analysis is the process of identifying component cycles by marking the time location of their troughs with diamond images at the bottom of the chart. The primary function of phasing analysis is to mark the troughs of each cycle within the composite wave and tick them off against the Nominal Model.

The average time between adjacent troughs is then calculated and used first to derive FLDs and secondly to estimate the time locations of future cycle troughs. The phase of each cycle is calculated using the position of the last known trough, the average period and the last date on the chart. From this information we can tell whether the cycle is topping, bottoming, going up or down or wwhether it is overdue. At the end of the phasing analysis a spreadsheet called the Phasing Model is generated. This contains the data and statistics derived from the analysis.

Preparation

Before conducting a phasing analysis certain preparation is needed. In the following pages we are going to conduct a real phasing analysis step by step. We are going to cover a lot of ground and there will be a lot of detail. To help you understand what is going on, we need to run through a start-up checklist of tools, codes[35] and techniques.

This might seem time consuming at first, but once it's done, it's done, and you will be ready to start. Figure 4.6 shows the same Boeing weekly chart set up for a phasing analysis.

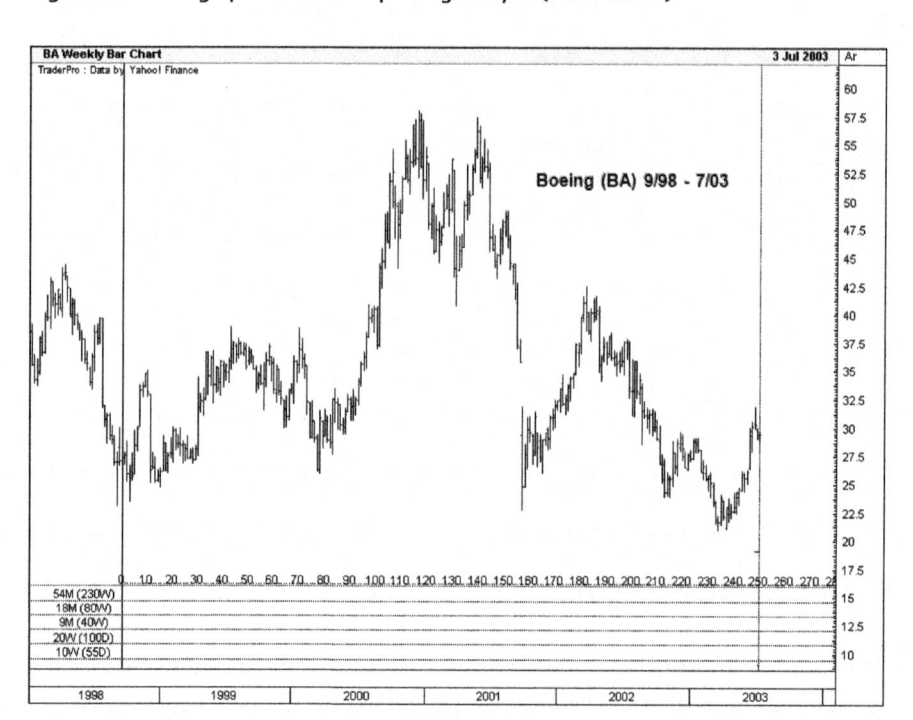

Figure 4.6: Setting up the chart for phasing analysis (Data: Yahoo)

We will be referring to this in the following text. Because the text gets away from many of the charts that follow they can all be downloaded from the website and printed off for ease of reference.[36]

Analysis timeframe

Arithmetic scale

To get started you need to choose a financial instrument: preferably one with a bit of up and down price movement. How to screen for suitable issues will be covered at length in the next chapter. You then need to set the scale of the chart to *arithmetic*. You can use semi-log scale but it requires a different set up and it can distort the analysis[37]. In any case, this is rarely necessary since 300 bars is usually the upper limit for Hurst analysis and semi-log is only really used with longer time frames.

Amount of data

Analysis normally begins on a weekly chart and then shifts down to the daily timeframe. Your trading software should have a default setting for the amount of data shown on the screen and it is probably best to set this at about 300 bars. This gives you a good panorama to start with and then all you need to do is manually adjust the chart to show the correct analysis range – normally no more than 200-250 bars. Hurst's rule of thumb was that the chart should display *at least* one and a half turns of the dominant cycle, i.e. the one that is responsible for most obvious fluctuation on the chart.

To judge the correct time span, glance down at the date range and look back approximately one calendar year on a daily chart or five years on a weekly chart. Alternatively use an equidistant cycle finder tool[38]. Start at the last date and drag it back the required amount of time, this will draw two vertical lines framing the analysis range.

Choosing a start date

The exact choice of start date is not that important, but it can be helpful to start from an obvious low somewhere near the beginning of the analysis range, i.e. about 200 bars back from the end of the data. Make a note of the start date you choose because it is a manual input for the set up code.

Referring to Figure 4.6 the chart defaulted to 300 bars and the equidistant cycle finder was placed at the last date and dragged back 250 bars to define the time span. The chart was then adjusted to show only this amount of data on the screen.

The obvious trough in mid-September 1998 was chosen as the start date, although it could equally have been the next major cycle trough in March 2000.

Diamonds grid

The grid in the lower part of the chart is where the phasing diamonds are placed and the row of sequential numbers along the bottom of the chart serves as a proxy for date. You will find it much easier to locate cycle troughs and project future cycles with grid numbers than dates.

Separate rows

Each row represents a different cycle in the nominal set. On a weekly chart the rows from top to bottom are for nominal cycle periods: 54M, 18M, 9M, 20W and 10W. On a daily chart the rows are: 20W, 80D, 40D, 20D and 10D (with their trading day equivalents added in parenthesis). These figures are shown in the bottom left corner of the grid. The actual average periods corresponding to the Nominal Model are calculated at the end of the phasing analysis and placed in the appropriate rows on the right hand side of the grid.

Diamonds are placed in the row corresponding to the cycle being analysed directly below the cycle trough that has been identified. Proceeding from longest cycle to shortest cycle, eventually every cycle trough is accounted for and the entire grid is filled with diamonds: fewer at the top marking the longer cycles and more at the bottom marking the shorter cycles.

Diamonds

Most charting software has a drawing tools function within which there should be a choice of different images. Find the diamond image, left click your cursor on it and simply drag it to the desired position. You can do this any number of times.

Colours

In a final full phasing analysis, the diamonds are colour coded according to the specific cycle they represent: in exactly the same schema as the FLDs and VTLs to prevent confusion. You will find, however, that it is better do a rough first draft using a single colour (say black) and then convert the analysis into a final colour-coded version when you are satisfied that all of the diamonds are correctly placed.

The reasons for this are as follows: firstly, it is an unnecessary extra effort to keep switching colours during placement. Secondly, the final placement is best left to a programme which positions the diamonds precisely; colours them according to the cycle they represent; automatically places possible future diamonds (actually dots); and inserts text boxes with the actual average periods and status analysis.

Although a two-stage approach might sound burdensome, it only takes a couple of extra minutes. If you are producing charts for clients, you will definitely want to do it this way. You will also find it easier to save your work and update the analysis later.

You can of course just print out a chart, grab a pen, draw the diamonds in by hand and do all of the calculations on paper. There is nothing wrong with this approach: it is fast, but it can be messy, your desk will be covered in sheets of paper and you will have to start again when you want to update your analysis.

Measuring cycle periods

Original methods

In his original work, which was written before the age of personal computing, Hurst recommended cutting out strips of paper and moving them around the chart to measure cycle periods of interest. This technique works so feel free to try it; however, the fun may wear off after the first few attempts.

Another rough and ready method recommended by Hurst is to hold your fingers apart and use them to measure distances on the chart rather like callipers. The technique is to spread the little finger and thumb to measure the largest distances; the thumb and index finger for shorter distances; the index finger and forefinger for even shorter distances and so on.

Try it. It works surprisingly well; it is very fast; and it is an excellent way to screen out issues that you do not think are ready for analysis.

Horizontal line tool

If, as is likely, you are analysing your charts on a computer screen, then best practice is to use a movable horizontal line (HL) as a measuring strip. Pretty much all charting software has this feature. Use the numbers in the diamonds grid to measure off a horizontal line the width of the cycle period you are interested in.

If you think that the cycle period of interest is 40 weeks, draw a horizontal line 40 bars wide and use this as a measure. Some cycles will be slightly longer and some will be shorter, but do not change the length of the line. Move the line to different positions on the chart and look for price lows within or just outside the line's range. It might sound a bit subjective, but it works and it is easy to do. As we work through the phasing analysis to follow, this will become clear.

In all of the charts that follow the horizontal lines have been left on the chart. They have also been numbered to show the order in which the measurements were made. A solid red line signifies a clear-cut measurement from a firm diamond position. A dashed red line is more tentative, and shows a measurement point with no firm diamonds, but where you think there could be.

The multiple lines and numbers are for demonstration purposes and in a real analysis you would only need to use one line to move around and at the end it would be erased.

The work involved

To the newcomer phasing analysis will seem arduous and complicated. Furthermore, any proper description of the process has to be excruciatingly detailed making it seem a lot harder than it actually is. There is no easy way around this because it is hard work and it cannot be described with a few superficial phrases.

If you feel like giving up and going back to the less effective techniques of standard technical analysis, recall the words of the American inventor Thomas Edison: "Opportunity is missed by most people because it is dressed in overalls and looks like work."

There will be plenty of chance to practice phasing analysis throughout the book and the more times you see an analysis done and the more times you do one yourself the more proficient you will become. That is just the way it is, so persevere.

How long should an analysis take?

To give you a benchmark, a good Hurst analyst should be able to do a full phasing analysis on both a weekly and a daily chart; work out the implications of all outstanding FLDs; establish entry levels, stops and targets using VTLs; and produce a Phasing Model in well under an hour.

If this still sounds like a long time, ask an equity analyst at an investment bank how long it takes them to write an initiation report. The good news is that once you have completed the analysis, much less effort is required to keep it current.

Conducting a Phasing Analysis

Initiation – the 54-month and 18-month cycles

The 54-month cycle

Phasing analysis starts on the weekly chart[39] and the first diamonds are placed at the most obvious troughs of *the longest cycle* that can fit on the chart. The longest cycle on a weekly chart will likely be all or part of the nominal 54-month (230-week) and the closest shorter neighbour will be the nominal 18-month (80-week) – remember that the harmonic relationship here is three rather than the usual two.

Figure 4.7 is the same weekly chart of Boeing with the diamond grid and a 40-week cycle envelope added. A semi-circle has also been drawn in to emphasise the purported 54-month cycle.

Figure 4.7: Phasing analysis of the 54-month cycle, Boeing 1998-2003 (Data: Yahoo)

The first task is to look for obvious lows in the 54-month cycle. These appear to be at either end of the chart at 237 and 0; thus they are separated by 230 weeks, which is exactly 54 months. However, if you look closely at each potential trough, you can that it is difficult to make a precise choice. In cases like this, as there are a number of minor price lows in the general vicinity, instead of placing a diamond you will place a question mark or an X and come back to it later.

When the exact position of a cycle trough is uncertain, it is standard practice to defer placement of a diamond. An example of this is where there is a mini double or triple bottom, but typically these are resolved as the shorter cycles are phased and the picture becomes clearer.

The 18-month cycle

No diamonds were placed in the top 54M, and we have decided to come back to the problem areas later. We should now continue the analysis of the next shorter cycle.

Figure 4.8 shows the attempted phasing analysis of the 18M cycle. The first thing we look out for are lows in the fluctuation of the cycle envelope. Because it was set up with a period of 40W, we know that it should be sensitive enough to pick out the peaks and troughs of the 80W (18M) cycle.

Figure 4.8: Phasing analysis of the 18-month cycle, Boeing 1998-2003 (Data: Yahoo)

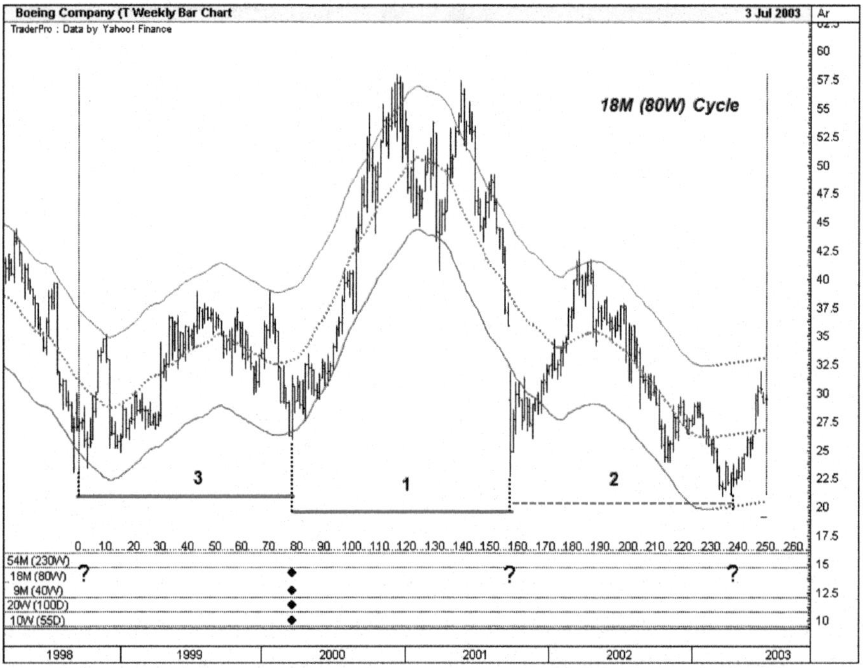

There are cycle envelope lows between 10 and 20, near 80, near 175 and between 225 and 230. However, only the envelope low around 80 unequivocally corresponds to a price low. We can therefore go ahead and place a diamond in the 18M row at 78.

Filling down

By the Principle of Synchronicity we can assume that all cycles shorter than 18 months also bottomed here. We can therefore place a diamond in each of the rows directly beneath this first 18M placement. Whenever you make a firm diamond placement, it is good practice to fill down straightaway.

Exploring for cycle lows

As we continue through the analysis of the 18M cycle, you will need to continually refer back to Figure 4.8 – or better still the print out from the website.

To start with we measure out a horizontal measuring line set at 80 bars wide. This is the distance between the two obvious lows in the dominant fluctuation and corresponds to the 80W nominal cycle.

First attempted placement

A diamond has already been placed at 78 so we can use that as our starting point. Position the horizontal line so that the left edge is at 78 and search for any obvious lows within the range of or just longer than the line (HL 1) to the right.

There is a price low at 157, the bottom of the crash sell off, and this seems like an obvious second diamond placement. However, it may in fact not be and is likely to be offset to the right.

The concept of offset cycle troughs will be covered in more detail in a later chapter, but for now the orthodox cycle low is not always in exactly the same place as the actual price low, since underlying downtrend tends to push the actual price low to the right. In which case, we could just as easily place the next 18M diamond at 165. For now then we will pass and put a question mark instead of a diamond and we will come back to it later.

Second attempted placement

Since the 18M cycle trough must be either at 157 or 165, we can go ahead and position the left edge of the line somewhere in between and search for the next 18M low off to the right (HL 2).

As we already found in the 54M cycle phasing analysis, an obvious contender seems to be the chart low at 237. However, there is a mini double bottom here and it is not clear exactly which price low should be chosen. Ultimately, it is fairly academic, but just to be rigorous we decide to come back to it later.

Third attempted placement

Going back to the diamond placement at 78 we now place the right edge of the horizontal line at the price low and search to the left (HL 3). The price low at 0 jumps out as a contender, as it did in the 54M sweep, but once again we see the ambiguous mini double bottom and decide to leave it for later.

Summary

After the first attempted phasing analysis of the 18M cycle, only one diamond has been placed and there are three maybes. That might not seem much of a result, but at least a foothold has been gained. Although this may have seemed a bit long winded, it would have taken an experienced Hurst analyst about 30 seconds to get this far.

Continuation – the nine-month and 20-week cycles

The nine-month cycle

Since there is nothing further to be done for now in either the 54M or the 18M rows, we drop down to the nine-month (40-week) cycle. This is the longest cycle contained within the envelope.

Figure 4.9 shows an attempted phasing analysis of the 9M cycle. The horizontal line measuring tool has been set to 40 weeks and the starting point has been chosen as the firm diamond placement inherited from the 18M analysis at 78.

Chapter 4 | Isolating Market Cycles I

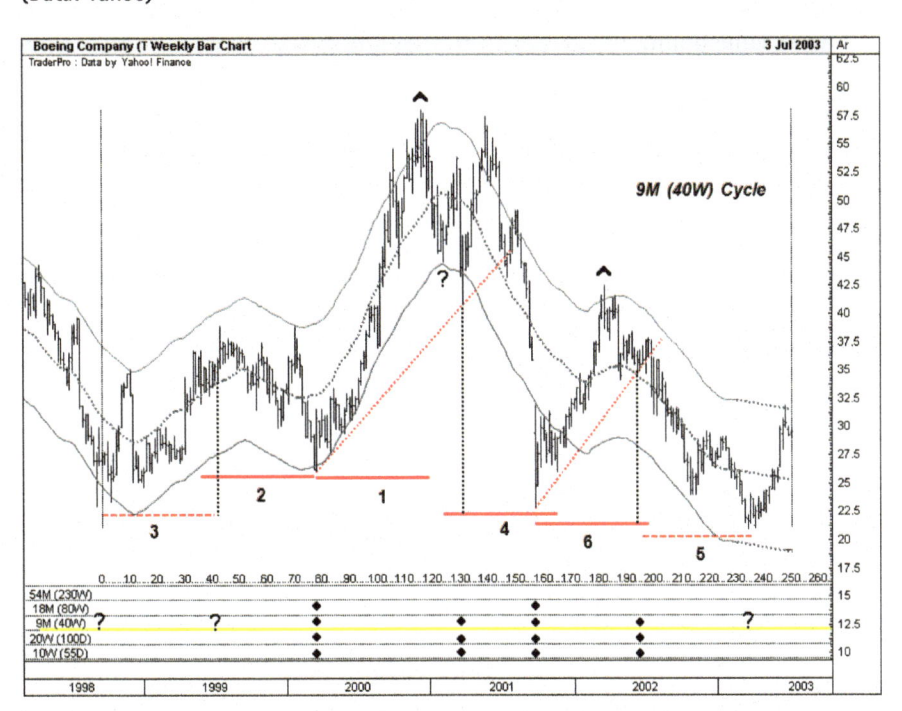

Figure 4.9: Phasing analysis of the nine-month (40-week) cycle, Boeing 1998-2003 (Data: Yahoo)

First attempted placement

Placing the left edge of the horizontal line at 78 and searching to the right (HL 1) we come across two adjacent lows, one at 124 and one at 131. These are outside the range of our horizontal line, but this is to be expected sometimes because of the Principle of Variation.

We have to choose one over the other at some point and our thinking would go something like this: the price at 131 to the right is lower and therefore the more viable candidate, but it is a long way out. On the other hand, if we end up choosing 124 to the left then we have to try to explain away the lower low at 131.

The clue here is to be found in the subdivisions of the shorter cycles. These will be labelled properly when we phase the 20W cycle, but for now notice that the cycle dropping between 131 to the sharp low at 157 has two clear subdivisions which we can assume are 20W cycles.

Therefore, were we to choose the low at 124, we would be left with one extra and unaccounted for cycle. In other words, the harmonic relationship would break down. The price low at 131 is therefore the stronger candidate and we can go ahead and place a diamond in the 9M row here as well as in the rows below at same point.

Second and third attempted placements

Placing the right edge of the line at 78 and searching left (HL 2) puts us into an area of ambiguity where it is very difficult to pick out a clear trough. We leave this for later and place a question mark.

Switching the left edge of the line to grid 0 and searching right into the same area (HL 3) does not help much. Since we cannot be sure, we pass on this placement as well placing a question mark.

Fourth attempted placement

Returning to the first placement made in this row and placing the left edge of the line at 131, we now search to the right (HL 4). Once again neither the sharp low at 157 nor its immediate neighbour at 165 can be chosen unequivocally, so we will need to come back to them.

Fifth attempted placement

Instead of exploring immediately to the right of the 157-165 area we decide to come back in from the far right of the chart, which seems a little more clear cut. Placing the right edge of the line at 240 we are looking back for a potential cycle low somewhere around 200 (HL 5).

If we choose the low on the right at 194 and then search right towards the end of the data, we can see two subdivisions which themselves break down into a further two subdivisions (the 20W and 10W cycles).

This satisfies harmonicity and does not leave any unaccounted for cycles. If we chose the low at 188 we would be left with an extra cycle and the 2:1 harmonic relationship would be broken. At this point the low at 194 seems to be the better choice, but we still need confirmation. To help illustrate the point Figure 4.10 shows these subdivisions in more detail. Study the diagram and count out the harmonic subdivisions: 0-i-ii-1 and 1-i- ii-2.

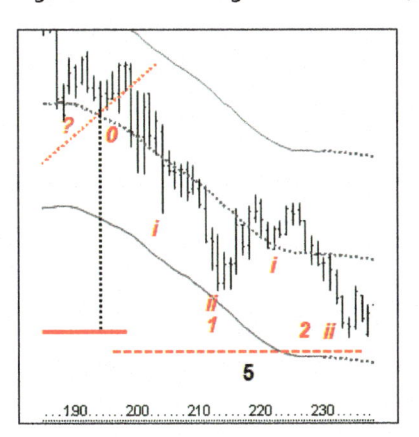

Figure 4.10: Detail of grids 190 to 240 (Data: Yahoo)

Sixth attempted placement

Using the same approach in the opposite direction, we place the right edge of the line at the 194 lows and search to the left, back into the previous area of ambiguity 157-165. This again provides us with two clear subdivisions, which can further be broken down two apiece.

Again, choosing the low at 188 means that one sub-division would be missing, breaking the harmonic relationship. The evidence therefore favours 194, so we can go ahead and place a 9M diamond there and fill in the diamonds in the two rows below.

Figure 4.11 shows the detail of the search to the left of 194. Study the diagram and count out the harmonic subdivisions: 0-i-ii-1 and 1-i-ii-2.

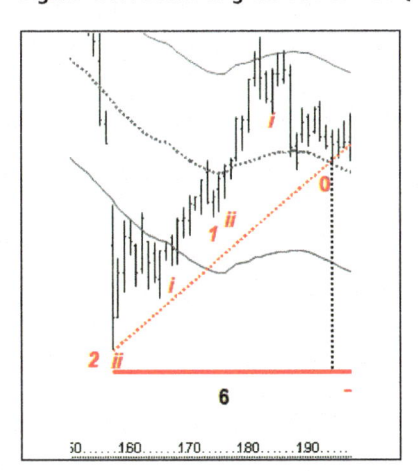

Figure 4.11: Detail of grids 151 to 194 (Data: Yahoo)

Seventh attempted placement

Since a placement has been made at 194 and since we have observed four harmonic subdivisions going back to the big low at 157, we can place the next 9M diamond with confidence at 157. Remember that 157 was also earmarked as a potential 18-month cycle trough earlier on, so as well as filling in the diamonds in the lower rows we can also place a missing diamond in the 18M row.

Summary

This is as far as we can go for now in the 9M row. Three new 9M diamonds have been placed at 131, 157 and 194 and one previously ambiguous 18M diamond has been cleared up at 157. Before moving on to analyse the 20-week cycle, you may have noticed two VTLs drawn in red on the chart.

The first VTL connects adjacent 9M lows at 78 and 131 and the break indicates that the price high marked with a carat at 116 is the peak of the second or middle 18-month cycle.

The second VTL connects adjacent 9M lows at 157 and 194 and the break here indicates that the price high at 181 is the peak of the third 18-month cycle.

The 20-week cycle

Figure 4.12 shows an attempted phasing analysis for the 20W cycle. As we drop down into the lower rows you may find it hard to visually line up the price low of interest and the diamond position in the grid, especially if the lows are situated towards the top of the chart.

To assist you here, either use the crosshairs tool that should be loaded into your platform at its maximum setting (that is to say with the vertical and horizontal lines reaching across the whole screen) or go for the low-tech solution and rest a flat bottomed ruler at the lower edge of your screen and slide it backwards and forwards.

Chapter 4 | Isolating Market Cycles I

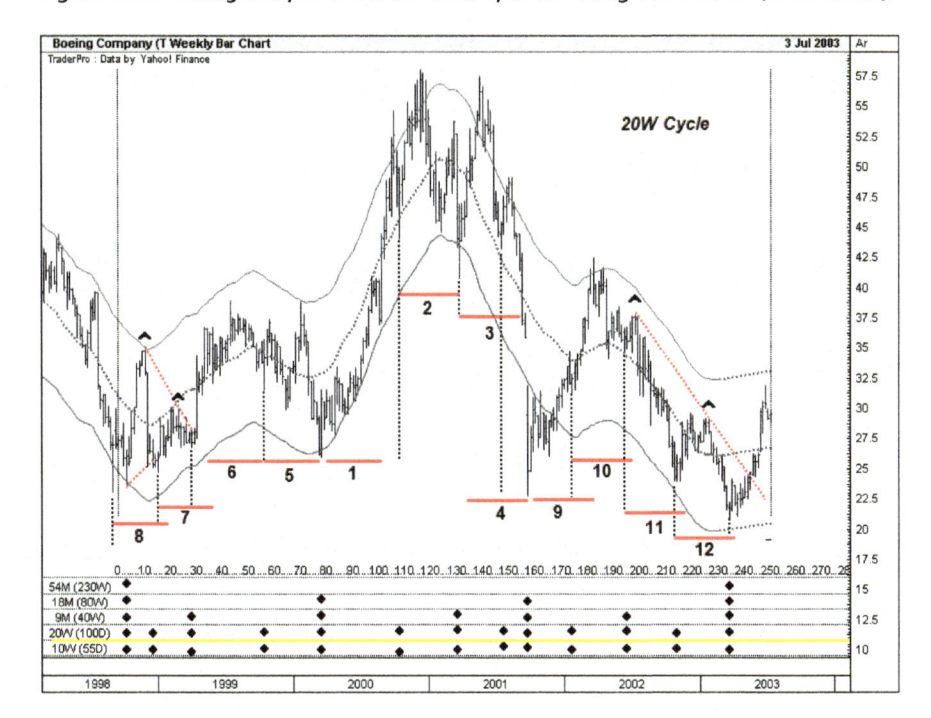

Figure 4.12: Phasing analysis of the 20-week cycle in Boeing 1998-2003 (Data: Yahoo)

First and second attempted placements

Set the width of the horizontal line at 20 bars and position the left edge at 78 (HL 1). Searching to the right throws up two possibilities: the lows at 100 and 108. We are dropped into a slightly ambiguous area and an immediate decision cannot be made.

We therefore switch the line around so that the right edge is at the 9M low at 131. Searching to the left (HL 2) highlights two clear fluctuations between 131 and 108; in terms of harmonics 108 is the preferred candidate. We can place a diamond in the 20W row at this time location and fill in the row below.

Third attempted placement

Now placing the left edge of the line at 131 low and exploring to the right we come straight up to the big low at 157 (HL 3). Since 131 and 157 are adjacent troughs of the 9M cycle, there needs to be a 20W cycle trough in-between. Clearly this would mean two very short 20W cycles, but variation allows for this and in any case there has been an extremely sharp sell-off which tends to dramatically compress cycle periods.

A 20W diamond must be placed somewhere in the middle of 131 and 157, or we will have one cycle trough unaccounted for. We therefore decide to place a 20W diamond at the 147 low. However unfeasibly short the cycle seems to be, harmonicity has been satisfied and it is an acceptable placement.

Fourth attempted placement

Switching back to the left-hand side of the chart now and exploring to the left of 78 (HL 5) there are two very clear ten-week cycles and a clear 20W cycle trough at 56. We can place a diamond in the 20W row here and one below.

Fifth attempted placement

Placing the right edge of the line at 56 and searching further to left (HL 6) there is another obvious low at 29. The intervening cyclic action is a bit confused but a placement has nowhere else to go in this area, so we go ahead and put a diamond at 29 and one below.

Because there is a 40W diamond at 78 and a 20W diamond at 56, the 20-week trough at 29 must also be a 40-week trough so we can place a diamond in the 9M row as well clearing up the earlier question mark.

Sixth attempted placement

Searching to the left from the latest 20W diamond at 29 (HL 7 and HL 8) there are two fluctuations before we get back to the start at 3. It is a safe bet that these are the 20-week waves, because there is really nothing else they can be.

We know that 3 is a major nest of lows which contains a 40W cycle low and we know that 29 is a 40W cycle low. There have to be two 20W cycles in between by harmonicity, which means we can confidently place 20W diamonds at 15 and 3. The cycles are being compressed because we are just coming out of a major trough.

Seventh attempted placement

Grid 3 marks the starting point for the analysis and you will remember that this was where we had a question mark for the first 54-month cycle trough. We can now safely place a diamond in the 54M row and by Synchronicity further diamonds in the 18M, 9M and 10W rows.

Notice the VTLs drawn between the lows at 3 and 29. The break of the 20W upward VTL indicates that the first 9M cycle peak is situated at 10. And the break of the downward VTL connecting the two adjacent 20W peaks confirms the low at 29 as the 9M cycle trough. It is never a bad idea to cross check your diamond placements against VTL intersections.

Final placements

All that remains is to place the last remaining 20W diamonds at the right edge of the chart. The most likely position for another 20W diamond in this area is the minor low at 174 (in-between HL 9 and HL 10).

Searching to the right of 194 (HL 11 and HL 12) throws up an unambiguous trough at 212, where we can place another 20W diamond with the final 20W diamond at 233.

The downward VTL joining the peaks of these last two 20W cycles is broken at 245, suggesting that 233 is also the 9M cycle trough. Since we also need to see an 18-month cycle trough here (two 9M cycles in one 18M cycle) we can go ahead and fill in the 18M row and by extension the second 54M cycle trough, which had also been left open since the beginning of the analysis.

Summary

The phasing analysis for the 20-week cycle is now complete and new diamonds have been placed at: 3, 15, 56, 108, 147, 174, 212 and 233.

Completion

The ten-week cycle

The real work is now over, you will be pleased to hear, and phasing the shortest cycle is often just a case of looking for a suitable low somewhere around the midpoint of two adjacent 20W diamonds. Instead of going through the whole chart again, we will just concentrate on the last section from 157 to 250.

Figure 4.13 is the phasing analysis for the ten-week cycle over this last section of data. A second cycle envelope has been embedded within the 40W envelope to highlight price movement. The centred MA was set to ten weeks to capture the fluctuation of the 20-week cycle.

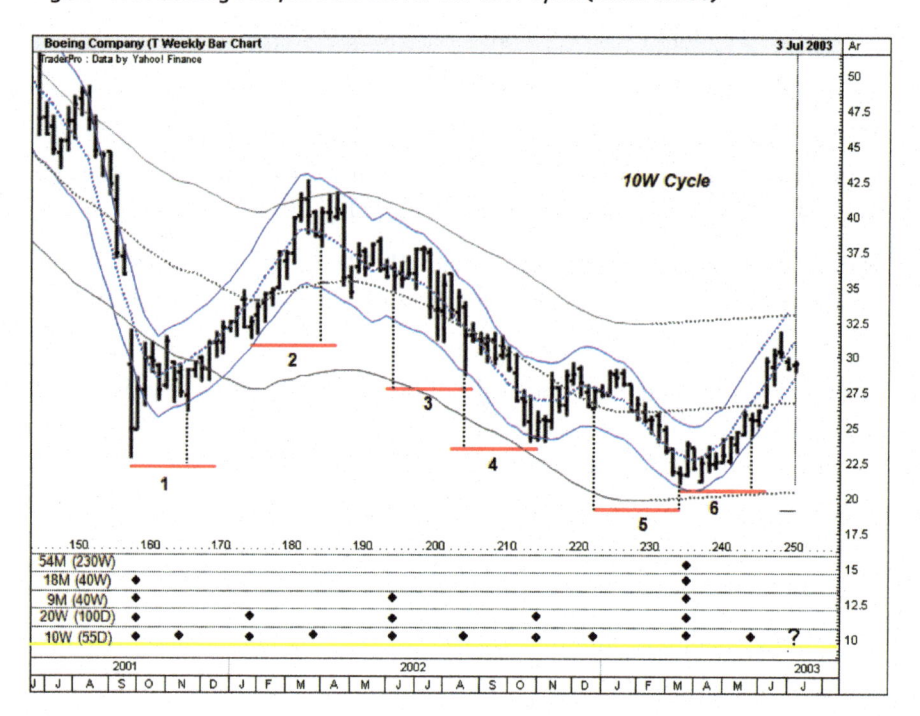

Figure 4.13: Phasing analysis abstract for the 10W cycle (Data: Yahoo)

First placement

Setting the horizontal line to a width of ten bars we start by placing the left edge of the line at 157 and search right (HL 1). The midpoint between the two adjacent 20W diamonds here is at 165 and there is a minor low at this point, so we can place a diamond here in the 10W row.

Second placement

Searching now to the right of the next 20W low (HL 2) the midpoint between this and the next 20W diamond is 184, which corresponds to a minor low in the upper area of the cycle. We can place a 10W diamond here as well.

Third placement

Searching to the right of the nine-month nest of lows at 194 (HL 3), the midpoint between this and the next 20W diamond is 203. This is confirmed by looking back from the low as well (HL 4). There is a clear low at 204 so we can place a diamond here.

Fourth and fifth placements

Exploring back from the 54-month nest of lows at 233 (HL 5), the midpoint is 222, which is exactly where we see a dip in the cycle. We can therefore place another diamond here.

The very last diamond is just past the nest of lows at 233 and is the minor low found to the right (HL 6) at 244.

That completes the first draft phasing analysis of Boeing on the weekly chart. Take a breather and then go back through the analysis making sure you understand how the diamond positions were chosen in each case. Just to reiterate, even though this may have seemed like torture, once you get the hang of it phasing analysis is easy! Persevere, it is well worth the effort and even though it may not seem like it now, sooner or later your ability to analyse price data will take a quantum leap forward.

The phasing model

Statistics

Having completed a full phasing analysis it now remains to put the raw data – the numbers corresponding to each phasing diamond – into the phasing model spreadsheet. This will then calculate the average periods of each cycle, the estimated time locations of near future cycle lows and the phase of each cycle at the last date. A status report will also be generated.

Average cycle period

The average period of each row can be worked out manually by counting up the number of diamonds, subtracting one to get the number of intervening gaps and then dividing into the number of the last diamond. However, the phasing model will do this automatically.

Diamond placements were made at the following time locations (with the number of individual diamonds in each row in brackets):

- 54M – 3, 233 (2)
- 18M – 3, 78, 157, 233 (4)
- 9M – 3, 29, 78, 131, 157, 194, 233 (7)
- 20W – 3, 15, 29, 56, 78, 108, 131, 147, 157, 174, 194, 212, 233 (13)
- 10W – 3, 10, 15, 21, 29, 42, 56, 65, 78, 91, 108, 118, 131, 140, 147, 152, 157, 165, 174, 184, 194, 204, 212, 222, 233, 244 (26)

The number of bars between each diamond is:

- 54M – 230
- 18M – 75, 79, 76
- 9M – 26, 49, 53, 26, 37, 39
- 20W –12, 14, 27, 22, 30, 23, 16, 10, 17, 20, 18, 21
- 10W – 7, 5, 6, 8, 13, 14, 9, 13, 13, 17, 10, 13, 9, 7, 5, 5, 8, 9, 10, 10, 10, 8, 11, 11

Giving average periods over the range of the chart as:

- 54M – 230 weeks
- 18M – 76.7 weeks
- 9M – 38.3 weeks
- 20W – 19.2 weeks
- 10W – 9.6 weeks

Next future trough

The next future cycle low is just the average period added to the grid number of the last diamond. The last time location for cycles 54M, 18M, 9M and 20W is 233. The last time location for the 10W cycle is 244. Giving future time locations of (rounded up or down):

- 54M - 233 + 230 = 463
- 18M - 233 + 76.7 = 310
- 9M - 233 + 38.3 = 271
- 20W - 233 + 19.2 = 252
- 10W - 9.6 + 244 = 254

This is the reason we run the numbers beyond the end of the data and leave a gap at the right edge of the chart.

Cycle status

The phase of each cycle is the amount of time that has passed since the last trough at the end of the price data. Apart from the ten-week cycle whose last low is at 244, all of the other cycles bottomed at 233. The end of the data is at 250, so the phase for the 54M, 18M, 9M and 20W cycles is 17 weeks and the phase for the 10W cycle is 11 weeks.

We can combine this information with the average period to determine the status of each cycle:

- 54M – the average period is 230 weeks and prices are 17 weeks along from the last 54-month cycle low, which means that the cycle is at the very beginning of its advance. The status is *bottoming/up*.

- 18M – the average period is 76.7 weeks and prices are 17 weeks along from the last 18-month cycle low, which means that the cycle is going up. Theoretically the estimated halfway mark is 38 weeks along – although translation could shift the peak to the right or left – so the 18M cycle here is about halfway between trough and peak. This is the fastest part of the move and the status is *up*.

- 9M – the average period is 38.3 weeks and prices are 17 weeks along from the last nine-month cycle low, implying that the cycle is slowing down. The theoretical estimated halfway point is 19 weeks along, meaning that prices are about two weeks away from a peak. The status is *topping*.

- 20W – the average period is 19.2 weeks and prices are 17 weeks along from the last 20W cycle low, which means that the 20W cycle here is just over two weeks from its next low. The status is *bottoming*.

- 10W – the average period is 9.6 weeks and prices are 11 weeks along from the last 10W cycle low, implying that it is late. There is a minor low at grid 250, but it is difficult to be sure that this is the next 10W low until more price bars have passed. The status is *overdue*.

Preparing the model

When a draft phasing analysis has been completed, open a phasing model template in Excel[40], then name and save it.

Figure 4.14 is an abstract of the model for the analysis that has just been carried out. The cells are mostly self-explanatory and where they might not be have been labelled. The model calculates all of the statistics and generates the code to create the final version of the phasing analysis. This entire process is explained in the website download.

Apart from entering the analysis date, ticker and issue name, the only thing you need to do (and indeed are allowed by the spreadsheet to do) is enter the numbers of all the diamonds you have placed. This is literally a two-minute job.

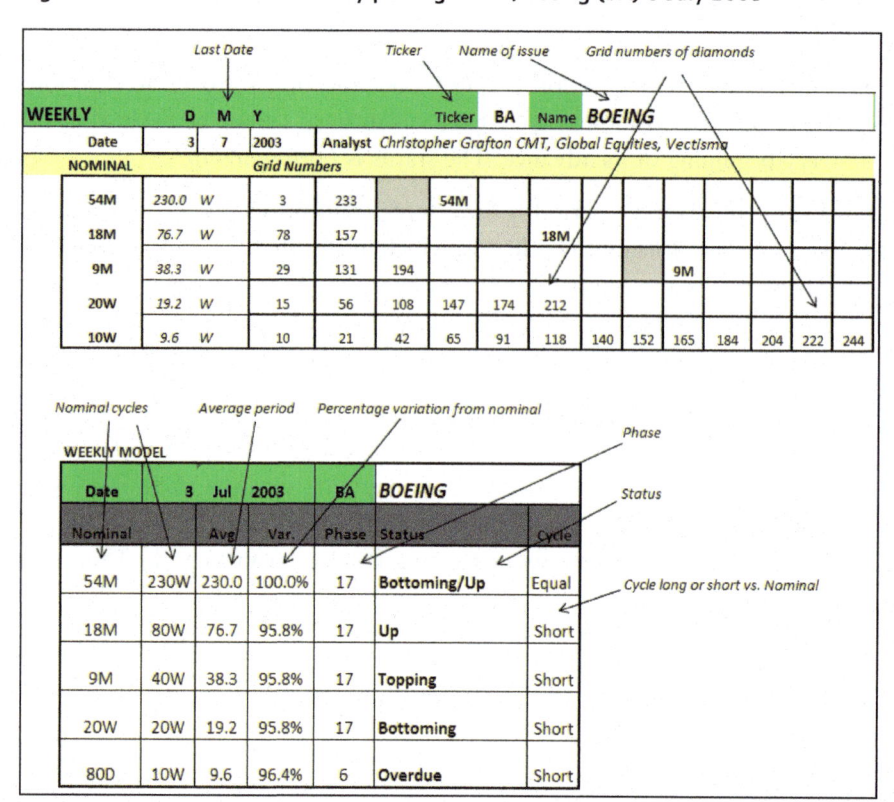

Figure 4.14 – Abstract from weekly phasing model, Boeing (BA) 3 July 2003

WEEKLY	D	M	Y		Ticker	BA	Name	BOEING				
Date	3	7	2003	Analyst Christopher Grafton CMT, Global Equities, Vectismo								
NOMINAL			Grid Numbers									
54M	230.0	W	3	233		54M						
18M	76.7	W	78	157			18M					
9M	38.3	W	29	131	194			9M				
20W	19.2	W	15	56	108	147	174	212				
10W	9.6	W	10	21	42	65	91	118	140	152	165	184	204	222	244

WEEKLY MODEL

Date	3	Jul	2003	BA	BOEING	
Nominal	Avg	Var.	Phase	Status		Cycle
54M	230W	230.0	100.0%	17	Bottoming/Up	Equal
18M	80W	76.7	95.8%	17	Up	Short
9M	40W	38.3	95.8%	17	Topping	Short
20W	20W	19.2	95.8%	17	Bottoming	Short
80D	10W	9.6	96.4%	6	Overdue	Short

You are free to enter numbers into the spreadsheet as you go along, but it is not advisable. Diamond positions get revised and you may forget to update the model. It can also be also confusing to skip back and forth from the model to the chart.

The best way to pinpoint the diamonds and their grid numbers is to use the crosshairs tool set at maximum (i.e. the horizontal and vertical lines spanning the whole screen). Then from left to right check them off and fill in the sheet: start with the long cycles and work your way down to the shortest.

You do not need to input every number. Once the model has been given the number for a longer period diamond is in place, it automatically fills in all of the shorter cycles (the effect of synchronicity repeatedly mentioned during the analysis).

Thus, in this example, once you had entered 3 and 233 for the 54M row, these numbers would automatically be entered in all of the shorter cycles as well. This means there is no need to enter 3 or 233 again.

Going down to the 18M row there are only two new numbers to enter, 78 and 157, which automatically fill in to the 10W level. Going down to the 9M row you only need to enter three new numbers, 29, 131 and 194 and so on. The trick is to look at the final version of the draft and pick out the diamonds between the longer cycles in each row and just count them. It takes a little bit of practice, but not much. If you double count, the statistics will be out of kilter and your results will be a mess.

Running the code

The final step takes under a minute. On sheet two of the model you will see a column of text and figures, this is the code needed to create the final version. The code itself (as well as full instructions on how to run it) can be found in Appendix 6.

Finished version

Figure 4.15 shows the final version of the phasing analysis with a text box displaying the status information of each cycle. FLDs, VTLs and the cycle envelope have all been omitted for clarity, although they would normally be displayed.[41]

The average period of each cycle rounded down is shown in the bottom right corner of the grid. The red dots are future trough positions and the short intervening horizontal line is their probable range either side. Recall that some of the gaps between diamonds were larger than others, which needs to be reflected in the future trough estimates. Hurst recommended using the cycle period maxima and minima to define the range, but the model calculates standard deviation instead. Thus the line either side of the red dot is one mean period plus and minus one standard deviation.

This concludes part one of using isolate cycles. The next chapter will examine another tool, the *Periodogram*, and finish the phasing analysis of Boeing on the daily chart.

Figure 4.15 – Phasing analysis final version, Boeing weekly bar chart, 1998-2003 (Data: Yahoo)

Conclusion

You will remember from chapter one how we added cycles together to create a composite curve. Even when you know the exact dimensions of the cycles being summed, however, and even if they are all perfect sine waves, it is difficult to tell from the composite curve what the original components were.

One of the ways we can isolate cyclic motion on a chart is to enclose the price movement in a suitable length cycle envelope. The moving average component smooths the data and if the moving average has been centred it will pick out the cycle's reversals.

The cycle envelope is a useful visual aid, but it is also quite a rudimentary tool and you should not ask too much of it. For example, just because the bands have been faithfully tracing out all of the twists and turns in prices up to the end of the data, it does not mean that they can be extrapolated and used as a road map of the future. It is a nice idea and it has been tried, but it is unreliable.

Phasing analysis will have been an entirely new technique to most readers. It seems like a lot of effort, but it gets easier and it is an excellent way to extract cyclic information from price data. Ultimately the whole purpose of phasing analysis is to help us decide where to enter a trade, how to then manage it and when to exit. You only need to analyse issues that are ready to trade, so the extra time taken when you do conduct a phasing analysis is time well spent if you can manage risk and make above average profits in less time.

You should now have a reasonable idea of how to conduct a phasing analysis and you should know how to set your system up, run the code and fill in the Phasing Model. The next chapter will be more of the same on the Boeing daily chart, but with a couple of new ideas thrown in.

Endnotes

[30] Exponential, Geometric, Triangular, Weighted, Adaptive, Wilder, Indexia, to name just a few. All have their own construction methods and properties. A good overview can be found in Kirkpatrick & Dahlquist, *Technical Analysis* (FT Press, 2007).

[31] In a moving average crossover system price crossing up through an MA is taken as a signal that the trend has turned up and that you should buy; whereas price crossing down through the MA is taken as a signal that the trend has turned down and that you should sell. It should also be noted that MA systems test very poorly. If only it were that simple.

[32] The code for the Inverse Moving Average can be found in Appendix 3.

[33] The code for the Cycle Envelope can be found in Appendix 4.

[34] Brain Millard, *Channels and Cycles* (Traders Press, 1999); J.M. Hurst, *The Profit Magic of Stock Transaction Timing* (Traders Press, 2000).

[35] All of the phasing analysis set-up code is provided in Appendix 5.

[36] vectisma.com/downloads/phasinganalysis

[37] Using arithmetic scale over very long time periods has the effect of reducing the movement of the earlier data making it difficult to analyse. This effect is not noticeable up to 250 bars.

[38] This simply draws a vertical line at one date and allows you to drag the line to another date to show the time difference in between. Most trading software has this tool preloaded.

[39] Although Hurst actually recommended starting analysis of an index (DJIA, FTSE etc.) on a monthly chart.

[40] The template can be downloaded from
vectisma.com/downloads/phasingmodel

[41] The final diamond placement code can be found in Appendix 6.

5 ISOLATING MARKET CYCLES II

Introduction

In the last chapter the technique of phasing analysis as a way of isolating cycles in price data was introduced. A detailed analysis was conducted on a weekly chart of Boeing and most of the main points were covered. You now know how to set up your screen, apply the cycle envelope, place diamonds and generate a phasing model. You also know how to initiate the analysis at the longest cycle using the cycle envelope, continue down phasing the intermediate and shorter cycles, and then finish the analysis with the shortest cycle.

You had the chance to look at some ambiguous situations, learnt how to use the principle of harmonicity to your advantage and came across the idea of delaying placement. You also saw that although the principle of variation caused some cycles to depart from their expected average lengths, there was often a logical explanation: compression into troughs for example. Clearly it is not possible in one book to cover every situation that is hard to analyse, but you will be introduced to a few more in this chapter and eventually you will start seeing the same patterns crop up and start knowing what to look for.

Finally you were shown how to use the phasing model and status report, which summarise the results of the analysis, calculating average cycle length, phase and direction of each of the component cycles in the data. This is the information you will be using when it comes to setting up and entering new positions.

If you are a longer-term investment manager running a large fund, the weekly chart may be as far as you need to go. For most traders, however, more detail is needed. Once the big picture is known from the weekly phasing analysis, we need to drop down to the daily chart and continue. Phasing analysis at the daily level is identical except that the labelling is slightly different. Other than that, it just picks up where the weekly analysis left off, typically focusing on the last 40-50 bars on the weekly chart.

The goal of the daily phasing analysis is the same: to produce a fully phased chart, account for all of the cycle troughs and fill out a cycle status report. The information gained at this stage can then be combined with that of the weekly analysis. When both weekly and daily analyses are complete, you will know where prices are headed in the broader scheme of things and you will also have a very good idea of how they are going to get there in the shorter term.

In this chapter we will carry on with a step-by-step analysis of Boeing on the daily chart which should help add to your growing understanding. Before we do this, we will take a quick look at another of Hurst's original tools, the *Periodogram*. Essentially this is an engineering tool applied to market analysis to assist with cycle identification. It is likely to be an entirely new concept to many readers and, without going into too much of the mathematics, which is a little forbidding, you will be shown how it works. We will also consider a next-generation version, the *Discrete Fourier Transform (DFT)* which you may find more practical for everyday use. To wrap up, we will discuss the idea of peak translation and you will be shown how to identify underlying trend direction by observing the displacement of cycle peaks.

By the end of the chapter you will have been through two full phasing analyses and should be starting to get the hang of things. You will have seen how the weekly and daily analyses fit together; you will have experienced a few more difficult phasing situations and seen how to solve them; and finally you will have a few more tricks up your sleeve: in the shape of the DFT and peak translation analysis. All of this is required preparation for when we start looking at setting up and entering trades in the next chapter.

Spectral Analysis

The periodogram

Isolating cycles mathematically

Hurst's original charts display a Periodogram[42] in their lower window. This is the output of a mathematical operation called spectral analysis which is the process of finding the frequency components of a signal by defining its cycles in terms of sine and cosine functions. The Periodogram is displayed as a histogram (bar chart) and a strong signal indicates the presence of a specific cycle in the data. In theory, the purpose of the Periodogram is to aid phasing analysis.

Figure 5.1 shows four sine waves in their respective phases. The periods from top to bottom are 80, 40, 20 and 10 and the respective amplitudes are 8, 6, 4 and 2. The cycles have been summed with an uptrend component to create the composite cycle shown at the bottom of the chart. The lower window shows a mini-phasing analysis giving the relative time location of each cycle low.

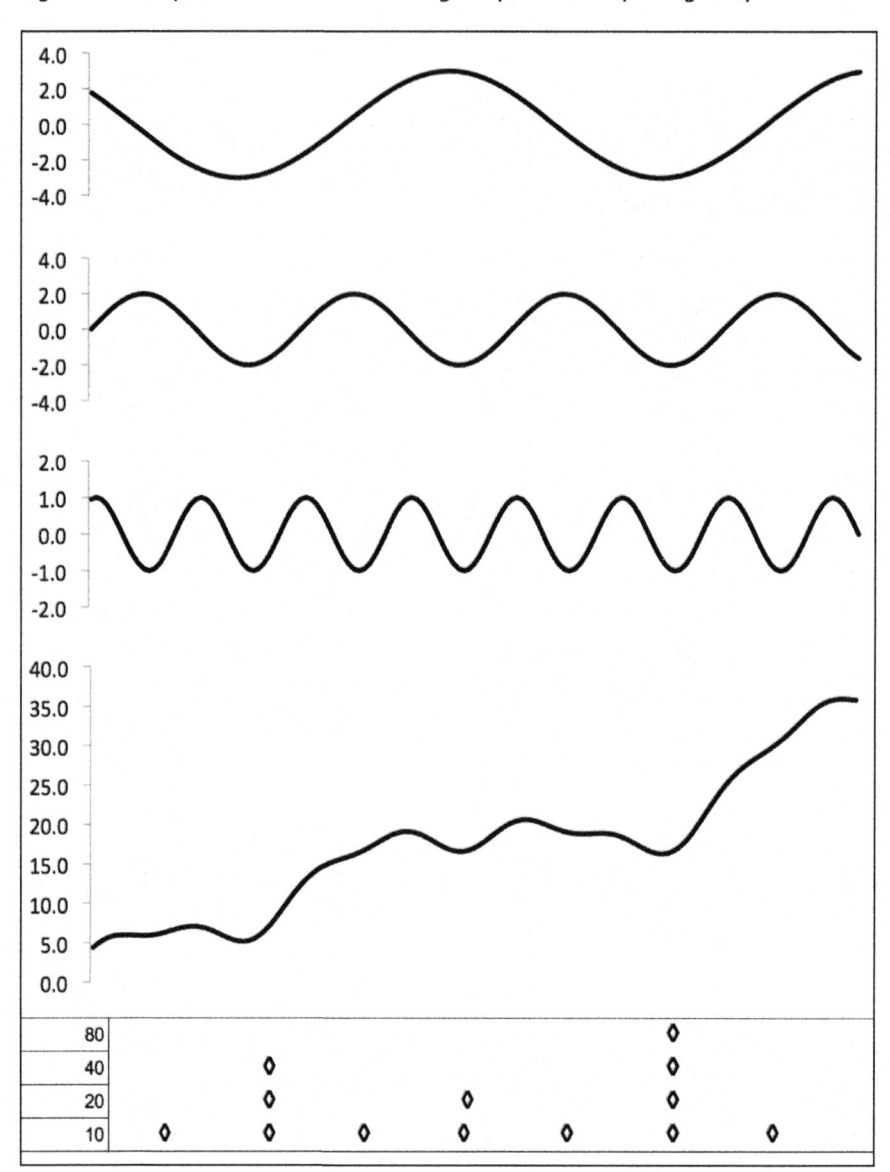

Figure 5.1: Composite of sine waves showing components and phasing analysis

Periodogram interpretation

As we have seen, it can be difficult to isolate the component cycles in a composite wave even when we know what they are supposed to be. Figure 5.2 is a Periodogram display of the previous composite of sine waves.

Chapter 5 | Isolating Market Cycles II

The histogram spikes at 2, 10, 14 and 16 represent power signals. This tells us that cycles corresponding to these *x*-axis values have the strongest amplitudes. In other words, the Periodogram has scanned through a spectrum of harmonic frequencies and picked out four dominant cycles.

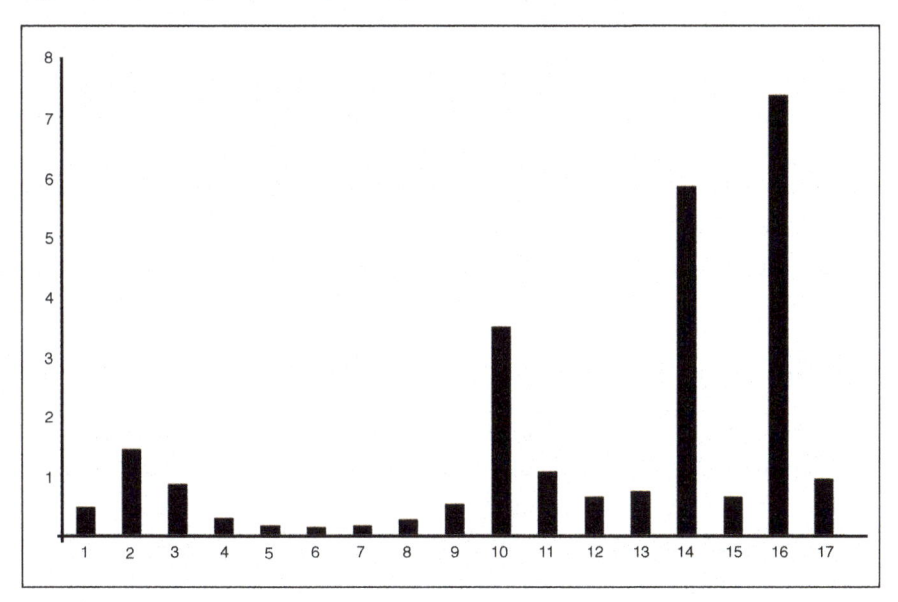

Figure 5.2: Periodogram of composite cycle

Table 5.1 is an abstract of the spreadsheet[43] used to calculate the Periodogram and the results are summarised below. A range of cycle periods (T) is shown – together with their *x*-axis values – corresponding to a preselected spectrum of frequencies (1/T). The Amplitude (A) value is muted until an actual cycle is found, where it then peaks in proportion to the cycle's period.

Table 5.1: Periodogram key data

X	1	2	3	4	5	6	7	8	9	10	11	12	13	14	15	16	17
T	9.2	9.8	10.4	11.1	12	13	14.2	15.6	17.3	19.5	22.3	26	31.2	39	52	78	156
A	0.5	1.4	0.8	0.3	0.1	0.1	0.1	0.2	0.5	3.5	1	0.6	0.7	5.8	0.6	7.4	0.9

- Grid 2 shows an amplitude spike of 1.4 corresponding to a cycle period of 9.8

- Grid 10 shows a spike of 3.5 corresponding to a period of 19.5

- Grid 14 shows a spike of 5.8 corresponding to a period of 39
- Grid 16 shows a spike at 7.4 corresponding to a period of 78

The Periodogram therefore has decomposed the original cycle components and reproduced them in graphical form. We can now see that the sine wave composite is made up of four components with periods of roughly 10, 20, 40 and 80. We also have an approximation of their respective amplitudes.

It is beyond the scope of this chapter to go into the mathematics of the Periodogram, but it is a type of Fourier Transform and plenty has been written on the subject[44]. Spectral analysis is a clever concept and seems to promise much, but there are some limitations when it comes to market data. Market waveform synthesis is nearly impossible because there is nearly a triple infinity of possible component wave parameters (amplitude, period, and phase).

Spectral analysis of market data

Prior to conducting a full phasing analysis, Hurst recommended first comparing the cycles highlighted by the Periodogram to those in the Nominal Model. The resulting Initial Cyclic Model would then be used to get the analysis started and later confirm its conclusions. This two-stage approach was the basis of the original methodology, but there are some practical problems. Although the Periodogram performs well on combinations of sine waves, it is less reliable on market data, which of course is less uniform and more noisy.

Figure 5.3 is the daily chart of Boeing for the 12 months up to 3 July 2003, showing a completed phasing analysis. This is a continuation of the weekly analysis described in the previous chapter and we will be going through it in detail in a moment. For now though, let us see how spectral analysis might have helped. The phasing analysis has identified average cycle periods of 97, 48, 24, 12 and 6 days. These correspond to cycles in the Nominal Model of 20 weeks and 80, 40, 20 and ten days respectively.

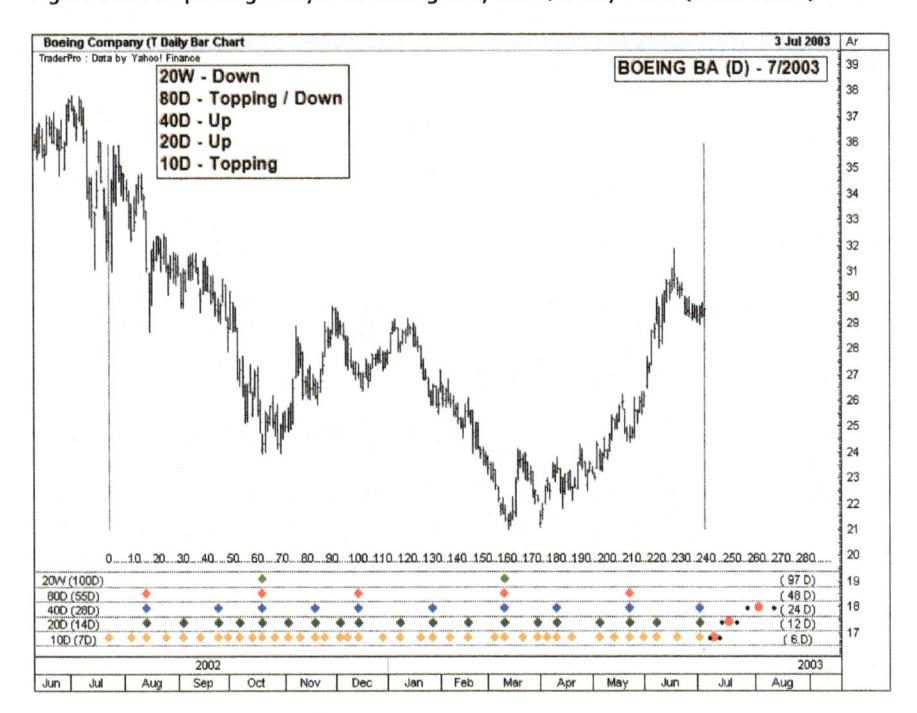

Figure 5.3: Full phasing analysis of Boeing daily chart, 3 July 2003 (Data: Yahoo)

Figure 5.4 shows a spreadsheet generated Periodogram of the same price data. The *x*-axis represents actual cycle periods from 12 to 234 days. The first thing to notice is that the output here is more ambiguous than it was for the composite sine waves. In spectral analysis terms, the resolution is low. The peaks are less clearly defined and it is difficult to say with certainty what the dominant cycles are.

There seems to be a spike at 13 and another at 26, although this could be a matter of interpretation. On the other hand the spikes at 47 and 117 appear to be clearer. The Periodogram may therefore be telling us that it has identified cycles with periods of approximately 13, 26, 47 and 117 days in the data. And although this more or less corresponds to the phasing analysis, some artistic licence has been used and we cannot be completely sure.

Hurst was an engineer by training and probably would have liked the idea that engineering spectral analysis could be directly applied to financial markets. The unfortunate truth is that the Periodogram does not test very well on real market data.

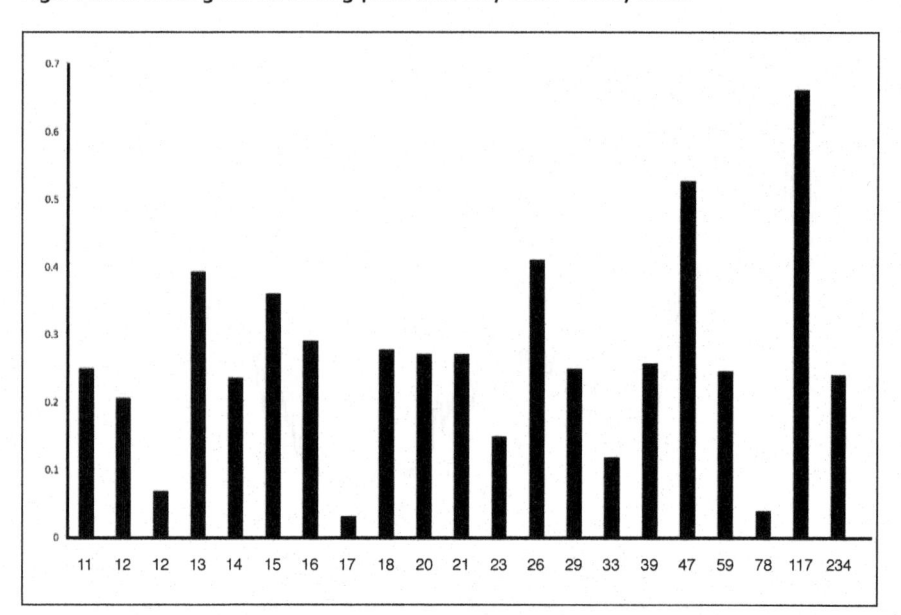

Figure 5.4: Periodogram on Boeing price data July 2002 to July 2003

Discrete fourier transform

An accurate phasing analysis can be conducted without a Periodogram, but if you really want to apply spectral analysis then you are better off using John Ehlers' Discrete Fourier Transform (DFT)[45]. This is a next-generation Periodogram and in many ways is more robust than Hurst's original. However, it too has its drawbacks.

John Ehlers is a retired engineer and probably the world's leading expert on the application of digital signal processing techniques in market analysis. He is the author of numerous books and the MESA programme[46].

The underlying mathematics of the DFT is similar to the Periodogram, but there are some fundamental differences. The first is the output, which is displayed as a corona chart rather than a histogram. Figure 5.5 shows the Boeing daily chart with DFT applied. This DFT uses Ehlers' nonlinear transform to enhance visual resolution.

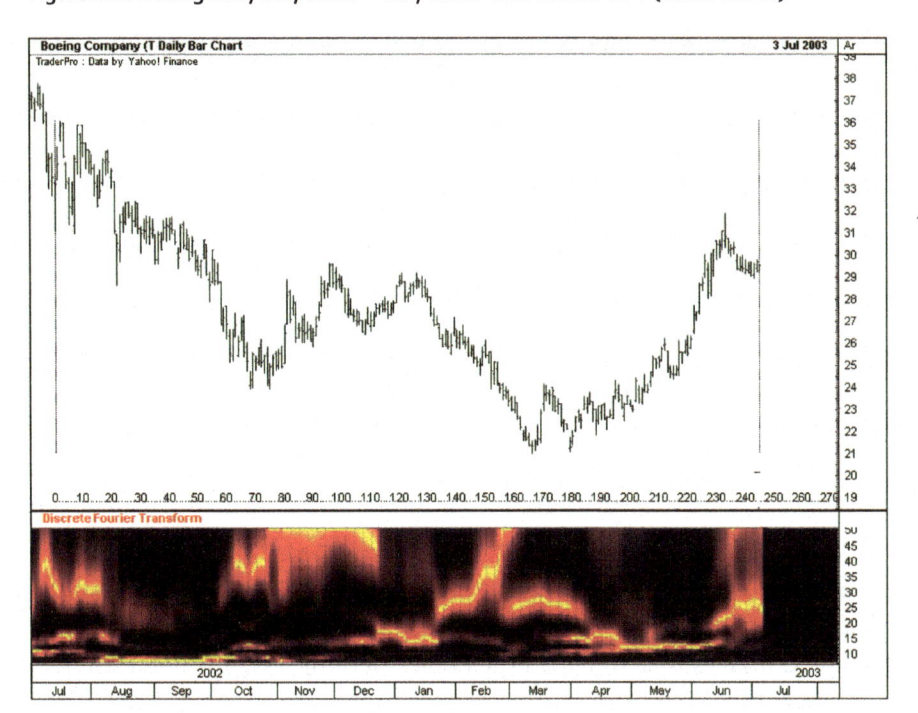

Figure 5.5: Boeing daily July 2002 – July 2003 with Ehlers' DFT (Data: Yahoo)

Corona charts

The corona chart or heat map will be unfamiliar to some readers, but it is quite straightforward. Instead of being represented by the height of a histogram bar, cycle amplitude is converted into colours. These range from very hot (bright yellow) to very cold (black) through shades of red, orange and yellow. When a clear cycle has been found in the data, a power signal is given by a bright yellow line with little aura. This is the Periodogram equivalent to a very tall bar.

The analysis at any given time is conducted over the last 50 bars rather than over the entire chart and the heat map is synchronised with the dates on the chart. Cycle periods are displayed on the *y*-axis and the range is 8 to 50 bars. Anything greater than 50 is considered by DFT to be a trend segment and therefore non-cyclical. For example, in the Boeing corona chart as prices begin trending down strongly in January and February 2003, the DFT heat map starts climbing into its trend range.

DFT plus and minus

Unlike Hurst's Periodogram, Ehlers' DFT does not attempt to identify all of the cycles in the data, but only highlights the dominant trading cycle. At the end of the price data on the Boeing chart the strong yellow line at 25 suggests that the period of the trading cycle at this time is 25 days. No other cycles are highlighted, but harmonicity would imply other cycles at 12.5, 50, 100, which is in fact exactly what the phasing analysis suggested. Also, in Hurst analysis a cycle with a period longer than 50 is still part of a cycle and not a trend.

John Ehlers himself admits that Fourier Transforms are actually of limited use in market analysis, mainly because the display simply shows the measured spectrum – no more, no less – and the result is poor resolution. This is why he developed the next-generation MESA suite of tools, which you are encouraged to take a look at. At the time of writing, the MESA tools can only be used with TradeStation.

You may find that applying the DFT study to each chart when scanning through multiple charts slows you down considerably. Because the code is complex, it takes time to reload each time. Nevertheless, it is not a bad idea when you have chosen an issue to analyse to quickly throw up a DFT chart and take a reading. More often than not the y-axis value of corona at the last date will give you a good indication of what to look out for when you phase the chart. Remove the study before you start your phasing analysis though.

Phasing Analysis – Daily Chart

Initiation and continuation

It is now time to continue the phasing analysis of Boeing at the next lower timeframe. Figure 5.6 shows the detail of the phasing analysis for the last 50 bars of the weekly chart. This now becomes the time span for the daily chart – approximately 250 days.

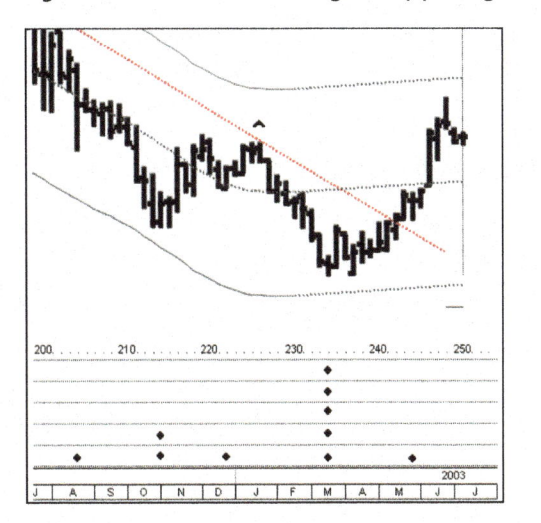

Figure 5.6: Abstract from Boeing weekly phasing analysis (Data: Yahoo)

The first thing to do is set up your screen to show 250 bars and apply the diamonds grid code. This is slightly different from the weekly version inasmuch as the cycles are labelled differently.

When this is done, manually transfer the diamond placements from the weekly chart to the daily chart. This is just a case of matching up the dates. Bear in mind though that the weekly bar is the price range from Monday to Friday and that the actual low of the week could have fallen on any day in-between. For example the nest of lows at grid 233 – the week ending 14 March 2003 – corresponds to the actual daily low of 12 March.

It is a good idea here to remind yourself of the cycle status on the weekly chart. This provides the context for your daily analysis. The 20-week cycle is down, the nine-month cycle is topping, the 18-month cycle is up and the 54-month is bottoming/up. The underlying trend is also up. We therefore know that any meaningful trading opportunity is likely to be on the long side of the market as soon as the next nine-month low is in place.

The 20-week cycle

We open the phasing analysis, as usual, with the longest cycle: in this case the 20-week. Figure 5.7 shows the Boeing chart with 250 days of price data up to the last date, 3 July 2003.

There is an obvious fluctuation in the middle of the chart and the time between the two lows looks to be about 90 bars. This is the dominant cycle and to enhance visibility on the chart we enclose it in a cycle envelope with a centred MA period of 45 days.

Figure 5.7: Phasing analysis of 20W cycle Boeing, July 2002–July 2003 (Data: Yahoo)

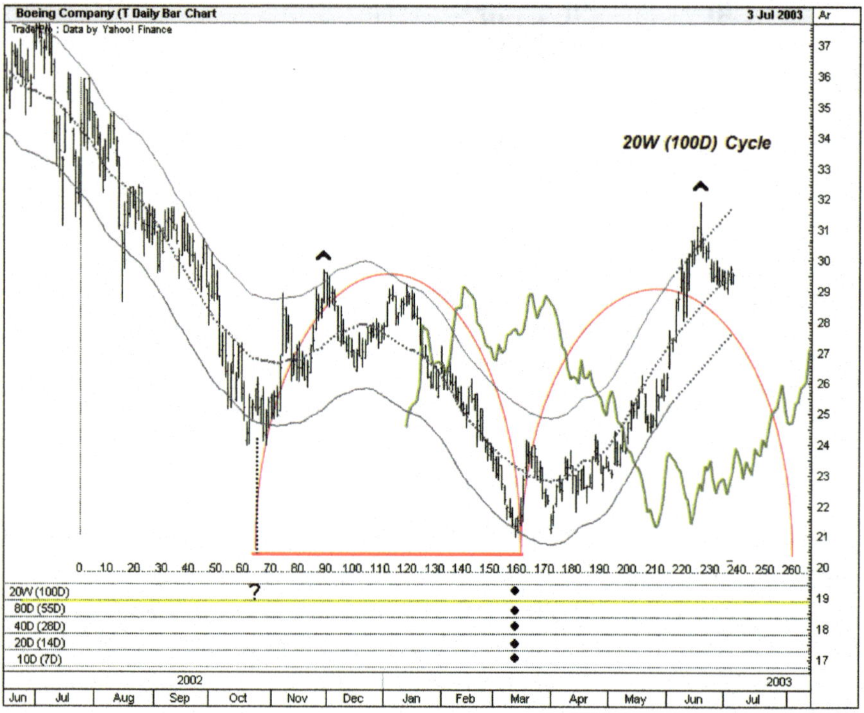

First placement

Twenty weeks is 140 calendar days and 98 trading days. The weekly cycles were running short at about 96% of the nominal average and this shortening effect carries over to the daily chart. We are therefore looking for a 20W cycle with a period of about 94 trading days.

This equates to the distance between the two obvious lows in the cycle envelope and will be the length of our first horizontal line (HL) measuring strip.

The chart low at 159 corresponds to the nest of lows on the weekly chart at 233 (14 March 2003). We can therefore go ahead and place a 20W diamond here and by synchronicity diamonds at the same time location in each of the rows below.

Second attempted placement

With the right edge of the horizontal line at 159 exploring to the left we come to the first cycle envelope low. This corresponds to 212 on the weekly chart where a 20W diamond was placed.

On the daily chart, however, there are two price lows here forcing us to choose between 62 and 68. There is not enough information to make this choice yet, so we delay placement of the 20W diamond expecting a later resolution.

Notes

We can further emphasise the 20W cycle by drawing in two semi-circles of roughly 100-day diameters. This is the equivalent of using a horizontal line measure and puts another possible 20W low around 260.

Recall from the weekly status analysis that at the end of the data (3 July 2003) the 20W cycle was 17 weeks along from its last trough and the status was therefore *down*. The second semi-circle confirms that we might be seeing this here.

A 20W FLD has been plotted showing a downward price cross at 200 (the olive coloured line on the chart starting around 120). This confirms that the cycle low at 159 is also that of the 40-week cycle, again confirming what we knew from the weekly phasing analysis. Notice also that the FLD has recently bottomed and has since been rising, pointing to a 20W cycle peak and subsequent decline in the same timeframe.

Summary

Although only one diamond has been placed at 159, there is nothing more to be done for now, so we can drop down to the next row.

The 80-day cycle

Although this is actually the nominal ten-week cycle, on a daily chart the convention is to label it as 80 days. Converting this from calendar days gives 55 trading days. The cycles are running slightly short so we set the measuring line to 50.

Figure 5.8 shows the attempted phasing analysis for the 80D (55D) cycle.

Figure 5.8: Phasing analysis of the 80D cycle (Data: Yahoo)

First attempted placement

We can add to our confidence that there is a nest of lows containing the 55D cycle around 60 by plotting an historical FLD. The cycle low is confirmed by an upward cross of the red 27D FLD at 80. You can run FLDs across the chart using the code, Hurst's two fingers method or, when you get good, simply do it by eye.

We can therefore use 60 as a rough starting point to explore to the left for an adjacent 55D cycle low. Placing the right edge of the horizontal line in this area (HL1) we notice a sharp price low at 15. This is about the right distance away for a 55D low and it corresponds to the 10W low at 204 on the weekly chart (14 August 2002). We can go ahead and place a 55D diamond here.

Second attempted placement

Switching across to the 20W nest of lows at 159 and exploring to the right (HL2) reveals a price low at 209. The intervening price action is choppy and the cycles are unclear, however this price low is exactly the right distance out and it corresponds to the weekly chart 10W diamond at 244 (23 May 2003). Another 55D diamond can be placed here.

Third attempted placement

Moving on, we now place the right edge of our measuring line at 159 (HL3) and look back. There is a clear price low at 100 which is another possible candidate. However, automatically placing a diamond here forces us to stretch out one cycle and compress another (measured by HL4).

This distortion caused by variation may well be valid, but it is safer to leave a question mark for now and come back to it when we phase the shorter cycles.

Summary

No more can be done in the 55D row for now. There are two new diamonds at 15 and 209 and two question marks. We now drop down to the next shorter cycle.

The 40-day cycle

Figure 5.12 shows the attempted phasing analysis of the 40-day cycle (28 trading days). The horizontal line is set at 25 bars.

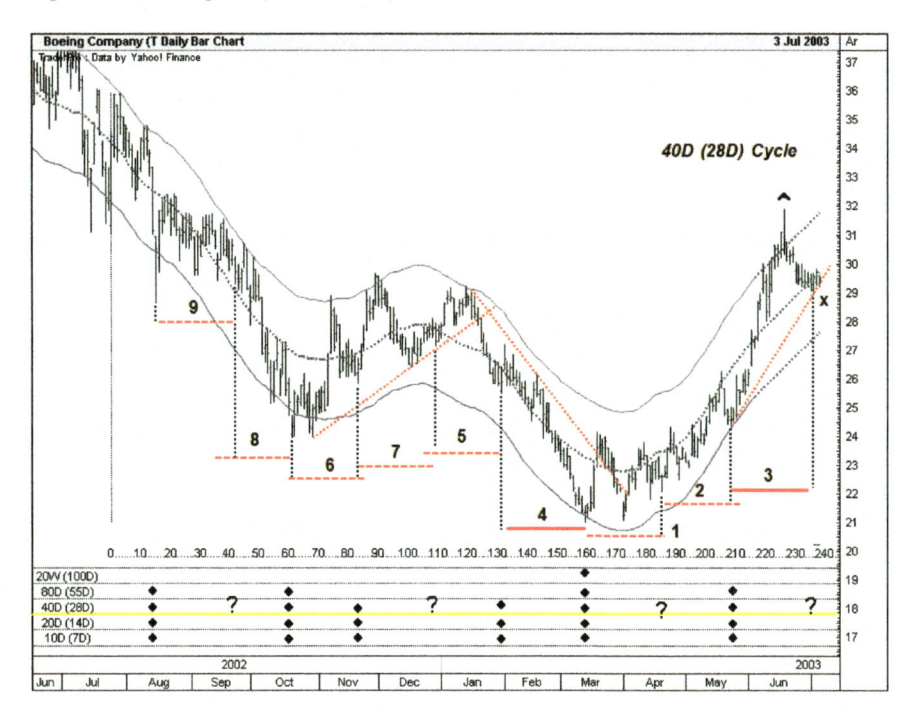

Figure 5.9: Phasing analysis of 40D cycle (Data: Yahoo)

First attempted placement

We decide to start at 159 and the first search is to the right (HL1). Since the next 55D low is at 209, we would expect to see a 28D low about halfway between. However, since nothing obvious jumps out at us, we switch the measuring line around and look back from 209 to see if this makes things any clearer (HL2). It does not so we place a question mark midway at 180.

Second attempted placement

Exploring to the right of 209 (HL3) reveals a price low around 240. However, this is right at the edge of the chart and we would need to see another higher low to be sure. We leave it for now.

Third attempted placement

Exploring to the left of the nest of lows at 159 (HL4) suggests a likely candidate for a 28D cycle low at 130. A strong downtrend swamps the cyclic form, but the two adjacent lows are clear and approximately the right distance apart. Additionally there is an obvious harmonic subdivision halfway along. We can therefore place a diamond at 130.

Fourth attempted placement

Searching left from 130 (HL5) is the low we overlooked before at 100. Again this is a bit far out, but a distinct cycle is formed. It is probably safe to place a 28D diamond here and by extension we have also resolved a 55D cycle low.

Fifth attempted placement

Exploring left from 100 (HL6) we see that although the possible 28D cycle is compressed – as often happens at the end of sharp short cover rally – its form is very clear. A diamond can be placed at 83.

Sixth attempted placement

Exploring left again from 83 (HL7) drops us into the nest of lows around 60 and we have to decide whether we choose the nearest price low at 69 or the one at 62. Because there is a clear subdivision in the cycle after 62, the next higher low, this might lead us to believe it is the first 14D cycle in this 28D cycle.

This would also resolve the previous question marks for the 55D and 20W cycles so we go ahead and place diamonds in these two rows as well. The 55D and 20W rows are now fully phased.

Seventh attempted placement

The area between the 28D diamond at 15 and 62 is difficult to read so it gets a question mark and we leave the 28D cycle for now and drop down to next row.

Summary

The 28D cycle phasing analysis has three remaining areas of ambiguity, which we expect to resolve later. Notice also that two VTLs have been drawn in. What do they tell you?

The 20-day cycle

Figure 5.10 shows the phasing analysis for the 20-day (14-trading day) cycle. Print the figure off from the website and go through this analysis yourself and see if you agree with the diamond placements. Take a ruler and pencil and draw in all VTLs. Use the two-finger technique to trace out all major FLDs.

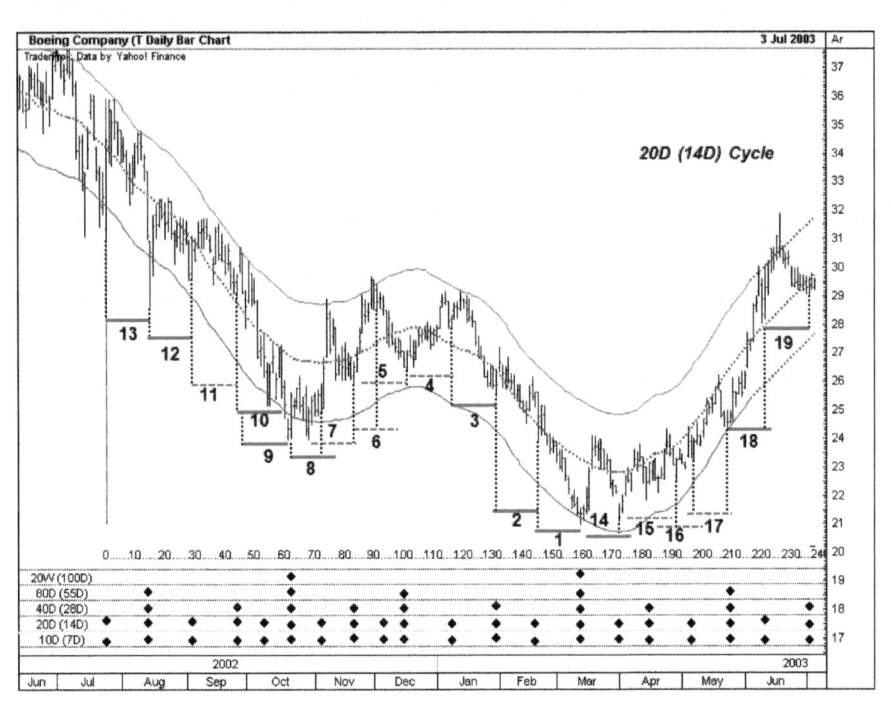

Figure 5.10: Phasing analysis of 20D cycle (Data: Yahoo)

The daily phasing model

Table 5.2 shows the status report for the completed phasing analysis corresponding to the full phased chart in Figure 5.3 shown at the beginning of the chapter. You should be able to see from these results that it is too soon to go long.

Table 5.2: Detail from the daily phasing model

Date: 3 July 2003				Boeing (BA)		
Nominal	Avg		Var.	Phase	Status	Cycle
20W	100D	97	97%	81	Down	Short
80D	55D	48.5	88%	31	Topping / Down	Short
40D	28D	24.7	88%	3	Up	Short
20D	14D	12.5	89%	3	Up	Short
10D	7D	5.6	80%	3	Topping	Short

The subject of set up, entries and trading cycles will be covered in the next chapter but for now it is enough to know that the principal cycles are headed down. In terms of timing, we are still 16 days away from a 97-day cycle low and 17 days away from a 48-day cycle low. You will also remember from the weekly chart that the 40-week cycle is in the process of topping.

In the real world therefore you would tuck this report away and take another look in a fortnight's time. There is no real need to work out the exact time locations of the ten-day cycle as it is more or less a case of filling in the gaps. However, it is essential that all of the troughs of the other cycles are accounted for. If they are not, your averages will be incorrect.

Using the phasing model

Incidentally, it is not an absolute requirement to use the spreadsheet model as you can work out the average cycle periods, phase and status by hand. Furthermore, in the next chapter we will look at ways of speeding things up a bit. Having said that, it is a small step to enter the data and a neat, colour-coded analysis with all of the statistics in place looks good, can be saved and is easily brought up to date. Best practice, therefore, is to use the model.

The last subject we are going to briefly cover is peak translation and the role it plays in helping to reveal underlying trend.

Peak Translation

Right translation

We often find that a cycle peak is either pushed to the right or pulled back to the left of centre. This can be highlighted by drawing a semicircle between the two adjacent troughs of the cycle. This phenomenon is known as *right translation* and is caused by an underlying uptrend.

Figure 5.11 shows the advance in the S&P500 from early 2003 to late 2007. Diamonds have been placed to mark the troughs of a roughly 40-week cycle and the intervening peaks at the bottom of the chart have been marked with red carats. The trend is up across the chart and each new low is higher than the last. Notice that in each cycle the peak has been pushed to the right. Notice also that the cycle downswings are a lot sharper and tend to take less time than the upswings, shown by red carats positioned to the far right between the black diamonds.

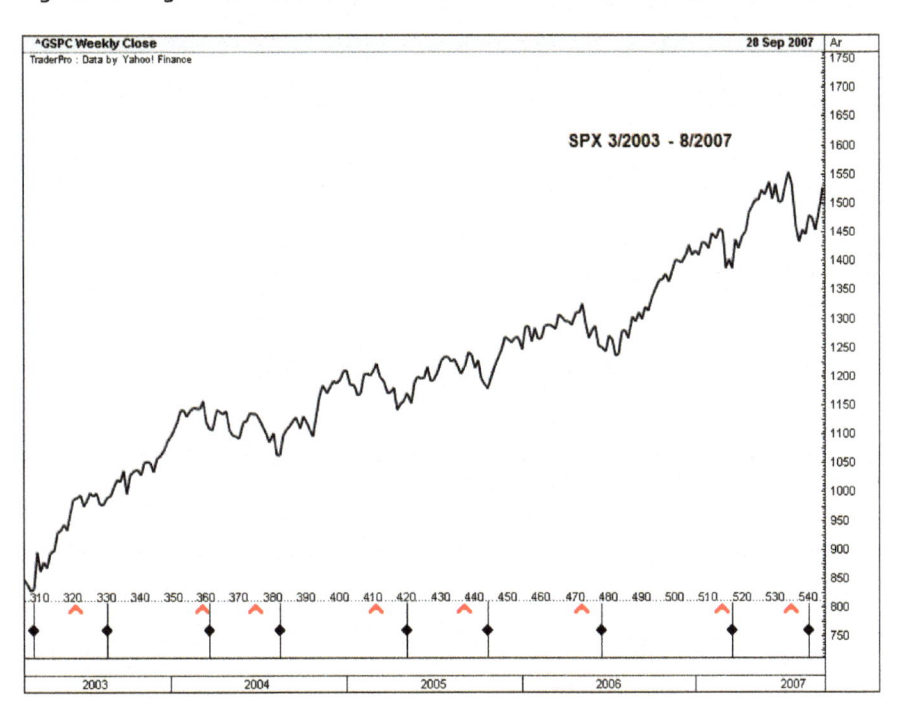

Figure 5.11: Right translation in the S&P 500, 2003–2007, advance (Data: Yahoo)

The uptrend is transmitted to each 40-week cycle which elongates the upswings and delays the topping out process. The downswing out of the peak is then compressed having little time to develop before the cycle low is due and uptrend reasserts itself.

Left translation

Figure 5.12 shows the S&P 500's decline from early 2000 to late 2003 highlighting the effects of left translation. Notice that the average 40-week cycle period is now running shorter at 30 weeks and that the peaks are being displaced to the left of centre, shown by the red carats being pulled to the left.

Figure 5.12: Left translation in the S&P 500, 2000–2003, decline (Data: Yahoo)

The peaks are being pulled back because the underlying trend is down. Here the downtrend is transmitted to the shorter cycles and the topping out process in each case happens quickly. The upswing into the peak is compressed and has little time to develop before the downtrend reasserts itself. The downswing is then stretched out effectively pushing the second trough forward. Notice also that there is less peak dispersion in the downtrend as prices move away quickly and cleanly from the peaks.

Conclusion

You have now worked through a full phasing analysis of one stock and are ready to move on to actual trade set up and entry. You have been introduced to a couple of spectral analysis tools: Hurst's original Periodogram and Ehlers' DFT. Whether you end up using them is up to you. If you choose not to, your ability to isolate cycles using phasing analysis will not be materially affected. You have also been introduced to the idea of peak translation. We will be looking at this again in later chapters. For now, it is enough to know that it is a very useful tool that can significantly assist your analysis.

In the next chapter we will study how to enter a trade on the long side using cycle analysis. It is here that all of the techniques you have learned so far, FLDs, VTLs, peak translation, cycle envelope and phasing analysis will finally start to come together.

Endnotes

[42] The term Periodogram was conceived by physicist Arthur Schuster (1851-1934) and originally referred to an estimate of spectral density for light waves.

[43] The Periodogram calculation has been recreated from Hurst's original notes and the spreadsheet can be downloaded from:
www.vectisma.com/downloads/periodogram

[44] Cherubini et al, *Fourier Transforms in Finance* (Wiley, 2009). Also visit **www.mathworks.com** which provides a range of scientific tools under the Matlab brand.

[45] The code is provided in Visual Basic for Updata and Easy Language for TradeStation in Appendix 7.

[46] The Maximum Entropy Spectrum Analysis (MESA) algorithm makes a high resolution estimate of the entire range of potential cycles and extracts the dominant trading cycle. This allows MESA indicators to be adapted to market conditions. John Ehlers (**www.mesasoftware.com**).

6 SELECTION, SET UP AND ENTRY

Introduction

In the last two chapters the process of phasing analysis was covered in detail and you should now be comfortable with the basics and be able to conduct a straightforward analysis without too much trouble. You should be able to identify component cycles within the composite as well as calculate their average period, phase and status. You should also be able to use the results of the phasing analysis to construct accurate VTLs and FLDs as well as project future cycle lows.

The reason we need accurate VTLs is to help us pick out turns in the cycles and the primary purpose of the FLDs is to project prices. Both of these functions are vital when it comes to planning a new trade and in this chapter we will review both of these tools and learn how to start putting it all together.

Because a full phasing analysis takes a while to complete, we need to be sure that the issue we are interested in is worth expending time and effort on. For this reason you need to know how to select those issues that are capable of giving the best possible return with an acceptable level of risk. You will learn how to screen a long list of securities to bring it down to more manageable proportions, thereby enabling you to focus only on those issues that are likely to meet your performance criteria.

Liquidity is obviously an important primary filter for many traders, but equally important is relative volatility. This is a measure of how active a security is compared to the rest of the market and is central to the concept of yield or performance over time. Because Hurst cycle analysis is principally a short to intermediate-term trading methodology with a strong bias towards playing reversals, the focus tends to be on securities that offer the largest percentage gain in the shortest possible time.

Once a list of liquid and volatile names has been generated, their charts need to be examined one by one to identify the best opportunities. You will learn a two-stage method of scanning charts, which will allow you to quickly pick out major cycles, estimate when they are likely to reverse and how far they are likely to run as well as ascertain the direction of underlying trend. When this information has been assembled you will be able to set up the entry with confidence.

Before entering a trade you need to have not only an estimate for how far the move will go, but you also need to know how much you are prepared to risk if things do not work out as expected. You have already learnt how to use FLDs to project prices and we will be using this technique to set targets. Additionally, the concept of the trading cycle will be introduced. This is the longest cycle in the composite that will carry prices directly to the target. You will learn how to identify the trading cycle ahead of time and how to use it to help plan the trade. You will also learn how to select stop loss levels intelligently to manage capital risk and provide the best reward-to-risk ratio per trade.

Once the potential trade has been framed by a stop loss and a target, all that remains is to choose a trigger to alert you as to the imminence of an entry and then a signal for you to place the order. This is commonly a price cross of a VTL. At this stage you will be introduced to the idea of trade risk which, unlike capital risk, refers to the probability of the trade being stopped out. Trade risk is a function of how quickly you enter a trade after a reversal and you will see that often it is better to wait rather than act immediately.

The set up and entry for short selling is broadly the same as it is for buy orders, but there are some special considerations you need to be aware of. For instance, tops form differently and this tends to increase trade risk. We will look at some of the guidelines for short selling and explain the differences in approach.

By the end of the chapter you should be able to turn a long list of securities into a shortlist, scan them for suitability and set up a buy as well as a short sell order. How to then manage open positions and exit the trade will be discussed in a later chapter.

Creating a Shortlist

Profitable trades with acceptable risk do not present themselves all of the time and quite often you have to wait for the ideal set up. It pays to be patient, but of course you do not want your capital to be idle for too long between trades.

Because there are myriad securities to choose from, if one does not offer an immediate opportunity then you can look always for another. However, because it takes time and effort to conduct a full phasing analysis, it is best to focus only on issues that offer imminent trading opportunities likely to provide worthwhile gains. There is little point in dedicating an hour or more to an analysis that will not lead to anything, which is why you need a method of sorting out the best candidates.

Screening for tradable issues

The concept of filtering

In order to make your workload manageable, you need to be able to turn a large universe of stocks – or whatever you trade – into a viable shortlist. A reasonable goal might be a system that provides you with a minimum of ten names to have under analysis at any given time. Twenty is better although some traders can handle more.

Generally speaking, a concentrated portfolio brings better results, but it all depends on your capacity for work, how much time you have and the dictates of your investment strategy.

There are many ways to turn a longer list of names into a short list and most are beyond the scope of this book. Some analysts will screen for relative outperformance or underperformance within specific sectors. Others will look for stocks with strong earnings momentum or attractive valuations or whatever fundamental argument seems reasonable at the time.

Pre-conditions

Many traders use technical screenings to highlight issues that may be worth further examination. For example, they might look at overbought or oversold stocks with divergence patterns, reasoning that they are ready for a reversal. Or the key selection criteria might be a breakout above a certain level, for example a 52-week high, or a price cross of a moving average. As many studies as you can think of applying to a chart, there is a way of creating a screening tool.[47] Most charting software will allow you run any manner of filters at will.

There also needs to be sufficient liquidity – enough outstanding shares available to trade – for you to be able to take a meaningful position. In other words, you need to be able to enter and exit without fear of either moving the price against yourself or getting trapped if there is a sharp sell-off. And if you are looking to go short, you will also need to check with your prime broker that there is enough borrow in the name and that the fee is worth paying.

You can have the best set up in the world, but if you cannot put a sensible position on or cannot source the borrow, it is a non-starter.

Hurst analysis filters

Volatility and cyclicality

The principle filters used in Hurst cycle analysis are volatility and cyclicality. In order to be of interest an issue needs to fluctuate enough to make it a worthwhile trading vehicle and the cycles need to be readable.

If a stock moves up and down only very gradually, then you are not going to make much money from it. And if it does not show clear cycles, then you are not going to be able to analyse it properly and are more likely to make mistakes.

Trading reversals versus long-term investing

It is important to note here that Hurst analysis is primarily a trading methodology and the best performance results are to be had in the short to intermediate timeframe: say six weeks to three months. For this reason the 18-month cycle is usually the longest you will need to analyse. Anything longer is simply classified as underlying trend[48].

This does not mean to say that longer-term investors cannot apply Hurst's techniques successfully, because they can. A pension fund manager, for example, will mainly use the 18-month cycle to decide when the time is right to accumulate or distribute stock. However, he or she will also keep a weather eye on the 54-month cycle and even the nine-year cycle for longer range shifts.

On the other hand, building large holdings takes time and entries and exits will generally be informed by the action of the 10, 20 and 40-week (nine-month) cycles.

It should also be borne in mind that cycle analysis is mainly about trading out of reversals. Or more to the point, waiting to enter a trade when there is enough evidence to suggest that a reversal significant to your particular timeframe has just occurred.

It is not about playing breakouts or chasing momentum moves. Nor is it about building positions ahead of major inflexion points.

Volatility index

Volatility, or more accurately actual current volatility[49], is a measure of price activity over a specified time period back from and including the last date – what programmers refer to as the *lookback* period.

In statistical terms it is a measure of dispersion of returns over a period of time, normally expressed in terms of standard deviation from the mean. It is not to be confused with implied volatility used in option pricing models.

Volatility typically conjures up the idea of risk. Because the price of a security with high volatility can be spread over a wide range of values, it is considered to be more *risky* than a security that exhibits less dispersion, i.e. has low volatility.

Risk here refers to the increased probability that an adverse move will stop you out or cause you to suffer a loss. Having said that, for the purposes of cycle analysis volatility is a *good* thing. The more active a security is, the faster you can make trading profits. And the faster you make trading profits the sooner you can redeploy your capital.

Screening for volatility

After you have screened out low liquidity names, the next step is to filter out issues with low volatility. Each of Hurst's original charts displayed a Volatility Index (VI) value. This is simply a measure of a security's volatility relative to that of the overall market and as such allows comparisons between issues to be made. The higher the value of VI, the more active the issue is compared to the market and the more attractive it is as a trading vehicle.

The description of Hurst's volatility index and the more effective spin off that follows is a little involved, but it is worth going through the calculation to gain a better feel for the mechanics.

VI formula

In Hurst's original work the lookback period over which the Volatility Index was calculated equalled the period of the dominant cycle. It is possible to automate the calculation of this variable period, but it is complicated and involves some heavy coding. Furthermore, it is not entirely necessary. Most volatility measures in common usage use a fixed lookback period of 14 or 30 bars.

Although the one-size-fits-all approach is generally not ideal, our purpose here is simply to gain a quick general sense of relative activity in order to select those securities that are most likely to give us the best gains in the shortest time possible. For that reason a fixed lookback setting is acceptable.

For each bar within the lookback period the average price of the current bar is subtracted from the average price of the previous bar and the *absolute* difference is then expressed as a percentage of the average price of the *previous* bar. This is expressed as:

```
ABS [(H(0) + L(0))/2 - (H(1) + L(1))/2] / [(H(1 )+ L(1))/2] * 100
```

Where: H(0) is the high price of the current bar; H(1) is the high price of the previous bar; L(0) is the low price of the current bar; and L(1) is the low price of the previous bar.

For example, taking the last two bars of a specific stock, Rolls-Royce (RR.L) in the FTSE 100 Index on 7 January 2011. H(0) = 663, L(0) = 655, and H(1) = 671 and L(1) = 658.5, then the percentage change by this measure over the two sessions (CSec) would be given by:

```
CSec = ABS {(663 + 655)/ 2 - (671 + 658.5)/2} / (671 + 658.5)/2 * 100 = (659 - 664.75) / 664.75 * 100 = 0.86%
```

Each percentage change value over the lookback period is then added together and the sum is divided by the number of bars in the period (n). In other words, the average percentage change for the security over the period (VOLSec) is calculated. And since prices move forward in time, this average is in fact a simple moving average, implying that as new values come in the oldest values are dropped off.

```
VOLSec = ∑CSec / n
```

Average True Range (ATR)

Sharp-eyed readers may notice that Hurst's basic measure of volatility is not a million miles away from Welles Wilder's Average True Range (ATR)[50]. Wilder actually called ATR the Volatility Index and published the formula eight years after Hurst produced his original Cycles Course.

Although it is not known if Wilder was actually building upon Hurst's earlier ideas, the fact is that ATR is a next-generation volatility measure and for a number of reasons does a slightly better job than Hurst's VI.

Additionally, ATR is in common usage and is pre-programmed into many trading platforms, making it readily available.

ATR formula

Volatility is just a way of expressing range of price movement and the largest range of a security in one day is the distance between the high and the low. This information on its own does not tell us much and so it needs to be compared to something else.

As we have already seen, Hurst limited the calculation to the previous day's average price and while this works fine, it does not give the full picture. Wilder's approach on the other hand was to look for the maximum difference possible between the two sessions. This he referred to as the True Range. Thus, the price distance selected is the greatest value of:

- The absolute difference between the current bar high and the current bar low – ABS {H(0) – L(0)}

- The absolute difference between the previous bar close and the current bar high – ABS {C(1) – H(0)}

- The absolute difference between the previous bar close and the current bar low ABS {C(1) – L(0)}

Wilder's Volatility Index is then calculated as ATR (0) using the previous bar's volatility index ATR (1) and the current bar's True Range TR (0) over a 14-bar lookback period. The calculation is:

```
ATR (0) = 13 * ATR (1) + TR (0) / 14
```

Figure 6.1 shows the Rolls-Royce candlestick chart on 7 January 2011 comparing Hurst's VI and Wilder's ATR. The value for VI is 5.75, some 70% of the ATR which has a value of 8.

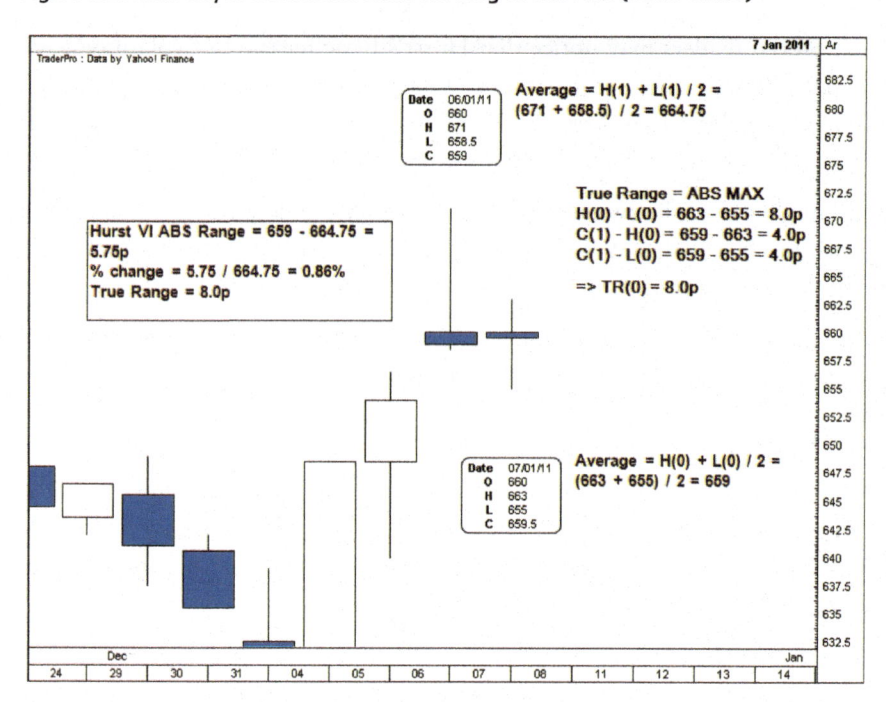

Figure 6.1: Rolls-Royce candlestick chart showing VI and ATR (Data: Yahoo!)

Relative Volatility (RV)

The last step in the Volatility Index / ATR calculation is to divide the security's ATR by the ATR of an index. The calculation for the ATR of the index is exactly the same as that of the security, but of course it uses the index price values instead. This gives a measure of relative volatility which allows us to make the comparison between active and less active securities on our list.

Before we do this, however, one final adjustment needs to be made to ATR. Because True Range is expressed in price points we need to normalise it by converting into percentage terms in the same way as Hurst's VI.

There are several different ways you can do this, but the preferred method is to divide the 14-period ATR value by a 14-period simple moving average[51]. Thus the final formula for Relative Volatility becomes:

```
RV = (ATRSec (14) / SMASec (14)) / (ATRInd (14) /
SMAInd (14))
```

Where the calculation period for each component is 14 bars, ATRSec and SMASec are the ATR and the SMA respectively of the security; and ATRInd and SMAInd are the ATR and SMA of the index respectively.[52] It is then just a question of entering the value into the first list of liquid names and sorting the list by RV value from largest to smallest.

Weekly and daily RV

Table 6.1 shows the top and bottom five names first at the weekly level and then at the daily level on the DJIA Index as at 28 October 2005. Notice the correlation between the data in the two tables.

Of the top five weekly names three are also in the top five daily names and Alcoa, not shown, comes in at number six. Of the bottom five weekly names only Johnson & Johnson fails to make it into the daily; it ranks ninth from the bottom.

Table 6.1: RV and ATR values among DJIA members, 28 October 2005 (Data: Yahoo)

Weekly data

Ticker	Name	RV (W)	ATR (W)
DJI	DJIA Index		2.71
CAT	Caterpillar	2.07	5.61
AA	Alcoa	1.98	5.39
MCD	McDonald's	1.95	5.29
HPQ	Hewlett-Packard	1.92	5.22
MRK	Merck	1.84	5.00
PG	Procter & Gamble	1.16	3.14
JPM	JPMorgan	1.16	3.15
JNJ	Johnson & Johnson	1.14	3.09
KO	Coca-Cola	1.07	2.91
GE	General Electric	1.00	2.69

Daily data

Ticker	Name	RV (D)	ATR (D)
DJI	DJIA Index		
HPQ	Hewlett-Packard	1.73	3.05
CAT	Caterpillar	1.72	3.03
XOM	Exxon Mobil	1.52	2.68
MCD	McDonald's	1.49	2.63
HON	Honeywell	1.43	2.51
IBM	IBM	0.90	1.59
JPM	JPMorgan	0.89	1.57
PG	Procter & Gamble	0.84	1.47
GE	General Electric	0.82	1.44
KO	Coca-Cola	0.79	1.39

Beta

At first glance relative volatility looks a bit like Beta, which is a measure commonly used to describe a stock's returns relative to the overall market[53]. However, it is not the same. Beta already incorporates the correlation of returns between the issue and the market and therefore cannot be used as a measure of relative volatility.

Benchmarking

The standard benchmark Hurst used for stocks and commodities alike was the Dow Jones Industrial Average (DJIA). This is acceptable for US stocks, although you might like to consider using the broader S&P500 (SPX) instead. Outside of the US, it makes more sense to use the index specific to that region, for example FTSE 100 (UKX) for the UK, DJ Eurostoxx50 (STOXX50E) for Europe and Topix (TPX) for Japan and so on. If you are looking at global sectors, you should use one of the Dow Jones or FTSE specialist global indices as the denominator.

Limitations

Screening for relative volatility is just one system and is not a panacea. Sometimes you will screen out a low RV issue that is about to embark on a huge tradable move; and at other times high RV value issues will not deliver the expected results. Additionally, remember that volatility is backward looking and also in absolute terms low volatility is often a lead indicator of high volatility and it is not uncommon for a security that has been languishing in a narrow range to break out explosively.

Conversely, a security that has been very active often needs to calm down for a while before becoming active again. Furthermore, if liquidity is not an issue then other things being equal you are more likely to see bigger moves in low-priced small cap names than in the mega caps, which need huge amounts of value traded to swing them around.

Ultimately, however, you have to start somewhere and you are generally better off choosing high relative volatility names over those that are comparatively less active.

Yield

Another important concept related to volatility in Hurst's approach is yield. This is just another way of expressing percentage performance per unit of time. Simply put, the less time it takes for an issue to generate gains, the more attractive it is from a trading perspective.

To work out the value for yield you need to annualise the percentage gain over the duration of the trade. The way to do this is to divide the number of calendar days in a year by the number of days in the trade and multiply the quotient by the percentage gain. For example, a stock that moves 20% in 30 days annualises at (365 / 30) x 20, or 243%. A stock that achieves 20% in 20 days on the other hand annualises at (365 / 20) x 20, or 365%.

Clearly, if you can achieve your desired trading gains in less time then not only are you compounding your returns faster, but you are also freeing up your capital earlier to exploit new trading opportunities elsewhere. This is why it is good practice to choose trades that offer the best yield rather than simply the best percentage performance.

In order to make this choice, we need to be able to estimate how far a price move will go and how long it will take to get there. And this of course is the *raison d'etre* of cycle analysis.

Scanning Charts

Once you have in place a primary list of names that have made the cut in terms of liquidity and volatility, it is time to start looking at the charts. Most trading software will allow you to pull up a list of instruments and scroll through their charts one by one. If your platform does not have this function, think about changing vendors.

As usual, we start on the weekly chart and then drop down to the daily. The reviews are done in two stages: an Initial Scan (IS) is conducted to get the broad brush strokes; then if anything jumps off the chart as a likely contender, it passes on to a Final Scan (FS) where further evaluation is made. Any issues that look promising at this second stage are then subject to a full phasing analysis.

Depending on the length of your primary list, this whole process should not take more than an hour or two. The watchword here is speed. Normally this is a job you would do once a week.

Initial scan – weekly chart

The purpose of the Initial Scan is to provide a rough feel for the movement and cyclic state of the securities under examination and then to choose those securities that meet the criteria for tradability. The IS checklist is as follows:

1. *What is the estimated period of the longest obvious cycle* – namely what cycle is responsible for the major fluctuation on the chart?

2. *What roughly is its amplitude* – in other words what are the percentage price changes of the swings associated with this cycle?

3. *Is the trend underlying the longest cycle* – in other words the sum of all longer cycles at the time – *up or down*?

4. *What is the estimated period of the next shorter cycle* – that is to say the longest cycle contained within the longest cycle envelope?

5. *What roughly is the amplitude in percentage terms of this shorter cycle?*

6. *Has there been or is there likely to be soon a reversal in either the longest cycle or the next shorter cycle?*

7. *Roughly what is the status of these cycles* – are they topping, bottoming, headed up or headed down?

Estimating cycle periods

The stock with the highest relative volatility in the weekly data – Table 6.1 – and the second highest in the daily is US Construction Machinery major, Caterpillar (CAT). Figure 6.2 shows the first stage of the initial scan of CAT on the weekly chart.

This figure will be used for the cycle length scan as well as the amplitude scan. The chart has been marked for both, but our focus for now is the cycle envelope, the dotted horizontal lines and the semicircles.[54]

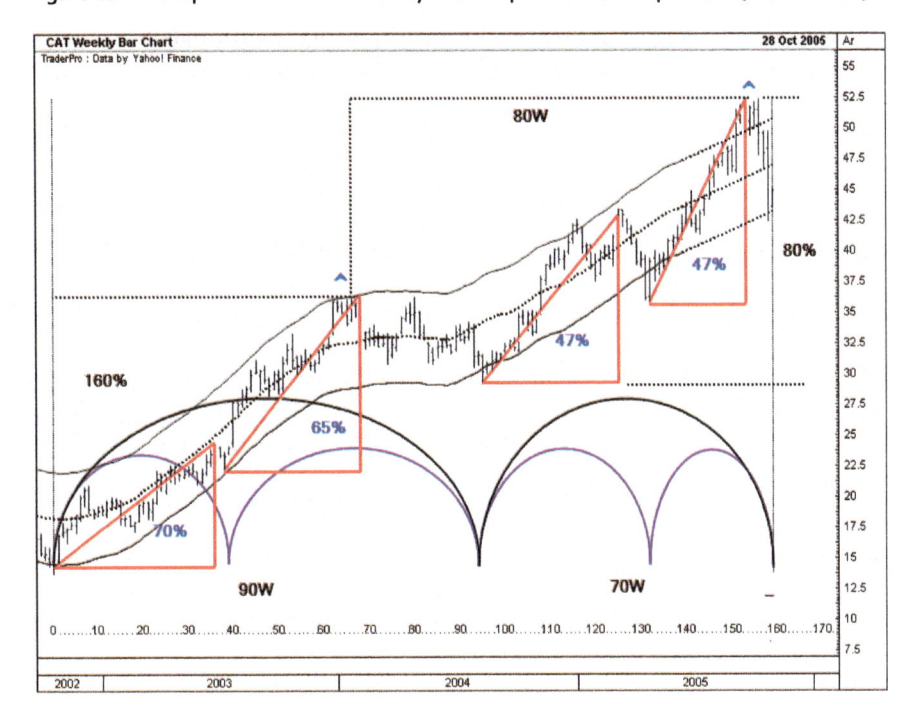

Figure 6.2: Caterpillar initial scan weekly chart – periods and amplitudes (Data: Yahoo)

Readability

What we are looking for here is readability. In other words: are the cycles clear or are they obscure and difficult to pick out? A glance at the chart shows a clear low at 0 and another unambiguous one around 90.

The longest cycle

Since the longest cycle on a weekly chart is usually the 18-month (80-week) and since the cycle between 0 and 90 is about the right length, we will assume that an 18M low is at 90. This looks to be the longest cycle the chart is capable of showing so a cycle envelope is constructed with a period of roughly half of this, namely 45 weeks.

The two lows in the envelope separated by 90 weeks more clearly highlight the 18M cycle. The next measurement can be taken from the flattened peak in the envelope around grid 70 and the high of the chart around grid 150, i.e. 80 weeks.

The final measurement is between the cycle envelope trough around grid 90 and the low price at the right edge of the chart at grid 160: 70 weeks. This may or may not be a cycle low of course, because it is right at the end of the data and there may be more to go. However, there is a very clear subdivision halfway along the cycle which satisfies harmonicity, which makes it a good contender for now for the next long cycle trough.[55] The average period of the longest cycle is therefore roughly (90 + 80 + 70) / 3 = 80 weeks, or 18 months.

Shorter cycles

Looking now at the fluctuations inside the cycle envelope, we have already observed an obvious shorter cycle low around grid 130 and there looks to be another minor shorter cycle low about halfway along the first 18M cycle around grid 40.

There appear to be four similar length cycles within the cycle envelope with an average length of about 40 weeks, which means it must be the nine-month cycle. In both cases the cycles were quite easy to pick out and correspond closely to the Nominal Model.

Tools

It is a good idea to keep a spreadsheet open while you do this and write in the rough values as you go along. This will make it easier to sort the data, give you a saved record for future watchlists and allow you to track relative volatility.

To help you make these rough measurements you can either draw in horizontal lines, employ Hurst's original technique of using spread fingers, draw in semi-circles as has been done here, or as you get better you can simply judge it visually. Basically, do whatever works, as long as it is fast.

DFT Check

In Hurst's original writings he recommended double checking these visual estimates with the Periodogram, for which read Discrete Fourier Transform, introduced in chapter five.

Feel free to do this, but remember that because the DFT is quite a heavy code, it will dramatically slow you down as it loads for each chart and your quick scan will turn into a very long and tiresome process. Furthermore, it is not really necessary.

Estimating cycle amplitudes

The upside percentage changes shown in Figure 6.2 are 160% for the first 18-month cycle and 80% for the second. The percentage changes for the four nine-month cycles from the beginning to the end of the data are 70%, 65%, 47% and 47%. You may want to print out this chart from the website to make it easier to refer back to.

What we are looking for here is percentage move per unit measurement on the actual chart itself, i.e. inches on the screen. A big run on a chart that fills the screen can be a 10% move or it can be a 50% move; obviously we are more interested in the latter.

The longest cycle

Starting with the 18M cycle the first low at grid 0 is about $14 and the first high around grid 70 is about $36. The difference is $22 and the percentage change is calculated by dividing the first value by the second value, in this case: (22 / 14) = 1.57. Multiply this by 100 to get roughly 160%.

Techniques

Again Hurst's method was to use spread fingers to measure off the distances between consecutive lows and highs (or vice versa for shorts). However you will probably find the cross hairs tool loaded into most charting software more practical. Simply place the cross hairs at the appropriate cycle inflexion point and read the price off the y-axis. This does not need to be done with a great deal of precision.

Volatility and amplitude

To give you a better idea of why the RV screen is such a good starting point, compare the performance of General Electric, the stock with the lowest relative volatility in the DJIA at this time, to Caterpillar.

GE took 68 weeks to rise 67% from the 11 October low to its first 18M cycle peak, an increase of 0.98% per week. Meanwhile Caterpillar took exactly the same time to reach its first 18-month cycle peak but increased by 162%, yielding 2.38% per week[56].

Summary

The initial scan should take an experienced cycle analyst under a minute to conduct.

At the end of this scan we have ascertained that the Caterpillar's 18M and 9M cycles are fairly uniform and clear and that the upswings of each of its nine-month cycles has averaged approximately 60%. So far so good: we now need to turn our attention to the longer-term trend component.

Estimating underlying trend

The principal method for establishing the direction of underlying trend is to use historical FLDs. In chapter three you learnt how to project target prices using FLDs. When price crosses through the FLD, the price difference between the last cycle low (or cycle high) to the point of intersection is then added to (or subtracted from in the case of short sales) the value of that intersection point to generate a theoretical target price.

Using FLD projections

You will also recall that these projections are not always exactly met and that the reason for this is the influence of the sum of all longer cycles – the trend. Recall that when underlying trend is in the same direction as the projection, the target tends to be overshot; and when underlying trend is in the opposite direction to the projection, the target tends to be undershot.

This can be reverse engineered to provide insight about trend direction, which we need before entering the trade.

Open or inactive

If an FLD projection has been made, but the target has not yet been met then the projection remains *open*. Conversely, if an FLD projection has been made and the target has been met then the projection is *inactive*.

For example, if you are looking to go long, but there is a big downside projection still open, then you need to either resolve any conflict in the analysis or wait before taking action.

Similarly, if you are about to go short but there is a big upside FLD projection still open, then you need to either make sure it has been neutralised or hold off making the trade until the downside target has been satisfied.

Normally, an FLD projection is neutralised or rendered inactive when prices eventually cross through it in the opposite direction, or there is an appropriate VTL break pointing to a reversal.

Using historical FLDs

A historical FLD is simply an FLD that has been plotted back into the past. For current projections we do not need the FLD to be plotted back very far at all. However, if we want to gauge underlying trend we need to see how price cycles and FLDs have interacted over the whole chart.

An FLD, as you have learnt, is just a price cycle displaced forward in time by one half of the period of the cycle it is based upon, i.e. by the FLD number. Hurst's two-fingers method, where the fingers are separated by the FLD number and run across the chart, was explained in chapter three.

You can also move a horizontal line the length of the FLD number around the chart to see where it intersects price. The best method, however, is to run the past FLD code provided in Appendix 2. Don't forget that you need to make the setback period long, say 200 bars+.

FLDs in action

Figure 6.3 shows the same weekly Caterpillar chart with historical FLDs for the 18M and 9M cycles plotted – the black and purple lines respectively. Certain points along the price path have been marked A to E, which we will examine one by one.

Point A

Using the cross-hairs tool we can see that the black 18M FLD has been crossed from below by prices at around $20. Recalling from our scan for amplitude that the cycle low is at $14, we have an upside projection of (20 – 14) + 20 = 26.

The next 18M cycle peak is at $36. The projection has been overshot by a wide margin and so the trend underlying the 18M cycle at this point must be up. This intersection also signifies that the price low at grid 0 is that of the 18M cycle trough.

Point B

The purple 9M FLD downward cross is at $33. The last peak is at $36 giving a downside projection of 33 - (36 – 33) = 30. This has been more or less met.

Had the target been overshot, we would have surmised that the underlying trend was flattening out. Since it has not been, we assume that it is still up. The cross here also marks the price high around grid 70 as the 18M cycle peak.

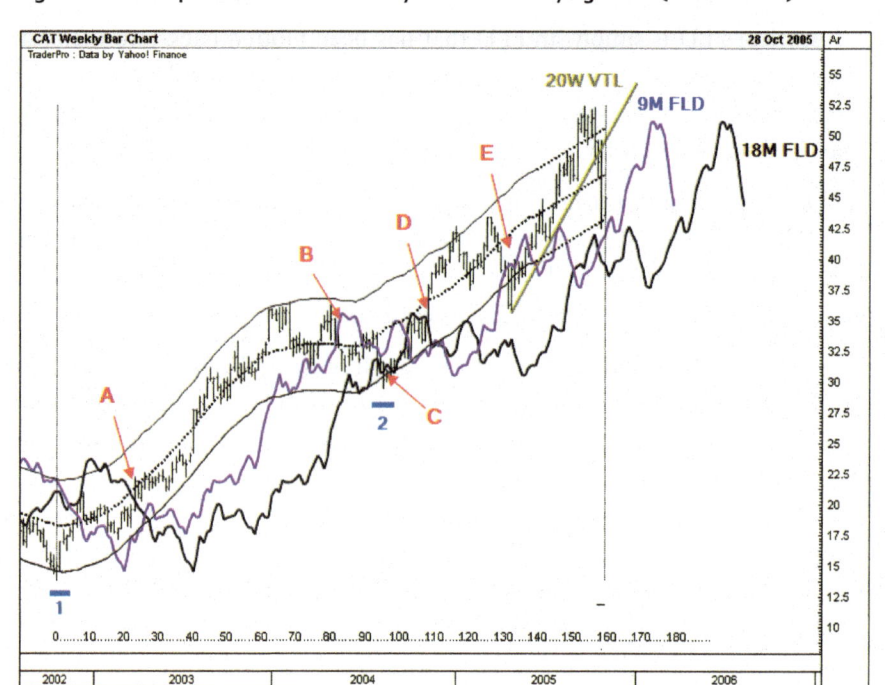

Figure 6.3: Caterpillar initial scan weekly chart – underlying trend (Data: Yahoo)

Point C

The 18M FLD has not been convincingly penetrated here and so no downside projection has been generated, strengthening the case for the uptrend.

Point D

The 18M FLD is crossed from below at a price of $35, the last cycle low is at $30, giving a projection of 40. The cycle tops out at $52, giving an even greater overshoot. The upward price cross of both FLDs confirms the recent low as that of both the 9M and 18M cycles.

Point E

The third 9M cycle tops out at around $43, the downward FLD cross is at $39 giving a downside projection to $35. This is more or less met/slightly undershot again leaving no open downside projection.

Notice also that the last price low is just above the 9M FLD. Were this to be broken to the downside then there would be a theoretical projection to $32. Before doing anything, therefore we need to be sure this does not happen.

Finally the two FLD projections past the end of the data are not forming an orthodox cascade pattern and as such, an imminent sell off is less likely. For one, the FLDs are too far apart and second there has been a cross just below the last date – in other words, they have not been running parallel for long enough.

Summary

At the end of the data, we could have sketched in the 20W VTL by eye and its downward cross means that the second 9M peak and therefore the 18M peak has passed. It is probably safe to say that at the grid 160 low, the trend is strongly up and since we are unlikely to see lower prices, the most recent low is probably that of the 18M cycle.

To summarise then: the cycles in the Caterpillar chart are clear; the price moves are meaningful; all upside projections have been overshot; there are no outstanding downside projections; a series of higher lows starting with points 1 and 2 have been put in; and all of the cycle peaks are translated to the right. We need to look at this stock in a bit more detail to make sure we are not missing anything.

Final scan – weekly chart

Although the description of the initial scan is quite involved, there is nothing here that you have not seen before. Do 20 initial scans one after another and, as long as you properly grasp the underlying concepts, you will be racing through them by the end.

Remember, we are looking for candidates worthy of further examination, nothing more. We are not trying to do a full phasing analysis, nor are we trying to produce a masterpiece presentation.

A good cycles analyst should be able to look at a chart for less than two minutes and, without putting a mark on it, ascertain whether it is good to go or not. This is the level of skill you should be aiming for.

In this case a fairly thorough initial scan has been carried out and we have extracted useful information. The purpose of the final scan is to make sure that there is no contradictory evidence and ascertain what the trading cycle is.

Working through the final scan

Figure 6.4 shows the results of the final scan on the Caterpillar weekly chart including an abbreviated phasing analysis, current FLDs and the recent downward VTL.

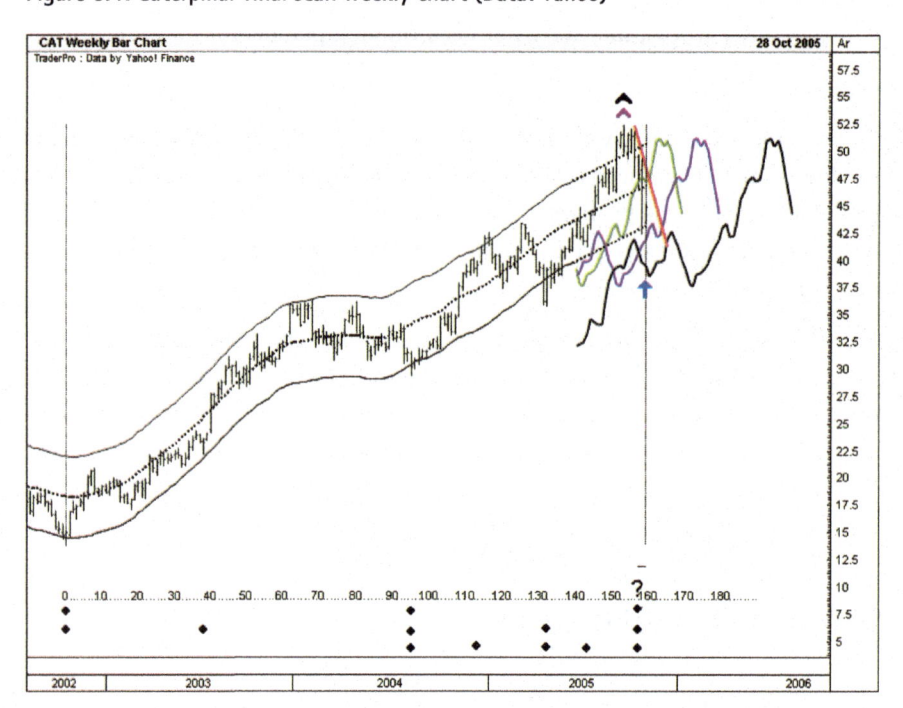

Figure 6.4: Caterpillar final scan weekly chart (Data: Yahoo)

Summary of action points

Rough phasing analysis

The troughs of the 80W, 40W as well as the most recent 20W cycle lows are marked with black diamonds. This enables us to draw VTLs, measure the average periods, plot FLDs and estimate the phase of each cycle. These values can be jotted down onto a rough calculation spreadsheet.

VTLs

VTLs should be checked for price crosses to confirm cycle troughs and peaks. We have already used the 20W VTL and have no further use for it. An as yet unquantified downward sloping VTL has been drawn in red connecting the last two price highs at the extreme right of the chart.

If prices cross up through this VTL this could be the signal that the 20W low is in place, although we will need to look at it in more detail on the daily chart to be sure. If the second 20W cycle trough is indeed in place then, because we are due a second 9M cycle low as well at this time, it follows that this will also be the 18M cycle nest of lows.

186

FLDs

Plotting the 80W, 40W and 20W FLDs at the last date we can draw the following conclusions: the 20W FLD intersects prices at $47. The cycle high is at $52 therefore the downside projection is $42, which is met more or less exactly.

Because we know that the trend is up, the 9M FLD is unlikely to be penetrated from above by price. Furthermore, because the 20W and 40W FLDs are crossing each other, we should expect a sideways congestion area at this time rather than a major decline, something we would see if a tightly stacked cascade was in place.

Conclusions

Having conducted both an initial as well as a final scan on the weekly chart we believe that the risk is to the upside and prices are now one week along a new 18-month cycle, highlighted by the blue arrow.

A price cross through the downward 10W VTL around $46 is all we need to confirm this. Figure 6.5 shows the detail towards the end of the weekly data.

Overall it looks like Caterpillar is a candidate for further analysis. We now need to drop down to the daily chart to confirm our assessment and if possible set up the entry.

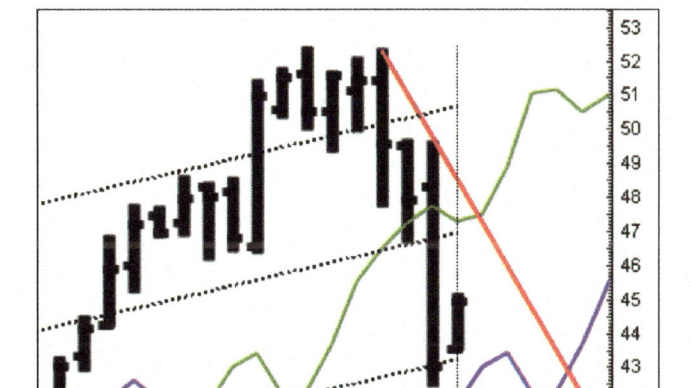

Figure 6.5: Detail of Caterpillar weekly chart, 28 October 2005 (Data: Yahoo)

Final scan – daily chart

Figure 6.6 shows the results Final Scan on the daily Caterpillar chart. The first thing that needs to be done is estimate the cycle periods and place diamonds at likely troughs. We do not need to fill in all of the harmonic gaps and we do not need to be all that precise. We need just enough information to be able to work out cycle phases, draw in the appropriate recent VTLs and calculate FLDs.

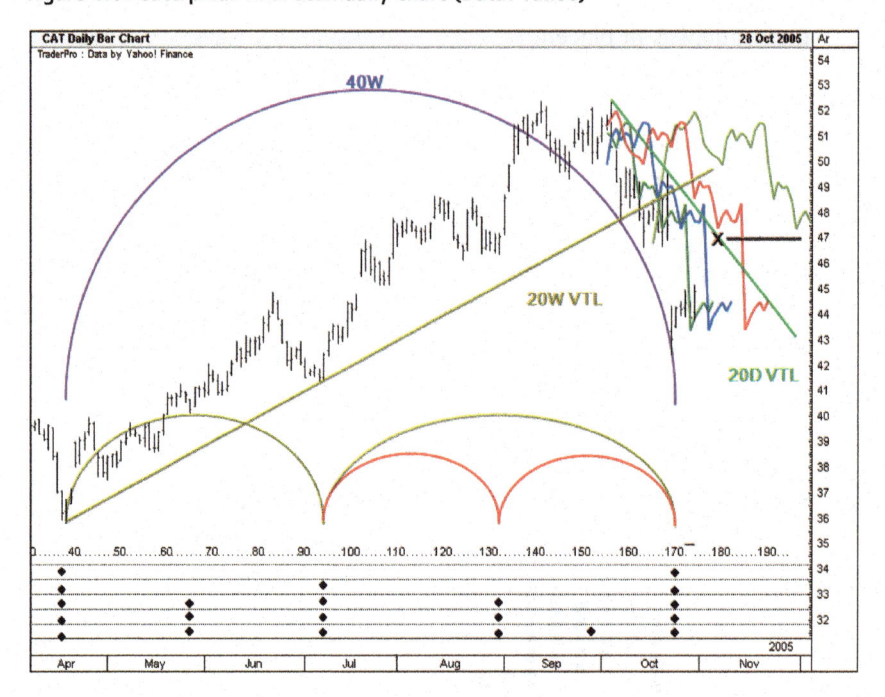

Figure 6.6: Caterpillar final scan daily chart (Data: Yahoo)

Overview

Our scan of the weekly chart led us to believe that the cycle from April to October 2005 is the nominal 9M (40-week) running short at about 180 calendar days. This has been highlighted on the daily chart with a purple semicircle. The 20-week and 10-week cycles have also been drawn in in olive and red respectively.

Remember we are doing a fast scan here and you will be tracing out the cycles and looking for VTL breaks visually and then placing diamonds. There is no need to actually place semi-circles on the chart.

Chapter 6 | Selection, Set Up And Entry

Average cycle periods

The nominal 80D cycle is 55 trading days and roughly measuring the spaces between the 55D cycle lows shows that this component is running short with an average length of 33 days.

All shorter cycles are therefore calculated off the 33D (80D nominal) cycle giving 17D for the 28-trading day (40D nominal cycle) and 8D for the 14-trading day (20D nominal cycle).

FLDs

FLDs are then calculated and drawn in at the right edge of the chart. We can immediately see that the FLDs are tightly packed and running parallel above prices in a cascade pattern. This is a good sign that a major reversal is about to take place.

The most recent price low is around $42 and we can roughly estimate that if prices do reverse then they should project through the near FLDs to the most distant (the olive 20W FLD) at around $50. This would give an upside projection of $58. Since we know that the underlying trend is up and that this projection will most likely be overshot, we can pencil in a conservative potential target of $60.

VTLs

The previously unquantified VTL drawn on the weekly chart looks to be that of the 14-trading day nominal cycle (eight trading actual period) on the daily. If prices break up through this VTL, then we know that the next longer cycle, the 28D nominal, has formed a trough.

Looking at the harmonic subdivisions over the entire 40W cycle we are still pretty certain that both the 55D cycle troughs are due. We can therefore assume that if this VTL breaks it will confirm that the 40W and therefore the 18M nest of lows is in place. A break of this VTL will therefore be our signal to go long.

Summary of IS and FS

Screening

To summarise what we have learnt so far: we started off by running a relative volatility scan on stocks within the Dow Jones Industrial Average, which would of course pass the liquidity test, and saw that Caterpillar showed the highest weekly value at 2.07 with a normalised 14-week ATR of 5.6%. It also had the second highest daily RV value at 1.72 with a normalised 14-day ATR of 3%. Clearly this stock was capable of delivering high percentage gains over less time than its peers and in fact the chart shows it rising in two 60-week upswings of 160% and then 80%.

Scanning

Scanning the chart we saw that the long cycles we would have been expecting to see, the 18M and 9M, were clear and easy to read. Taking very rough period estimates we were able to draw in FLDs which showed us that throughout the chart and right up to the most recent data, projections had been consistently overshot, a clear signal that the underlying trend was up.

A recent downward price cross of a 20W VTL told us that a 9M cycle had recently peaked and our period estimates and assessment of harmonic subdivisions told us that an 18M cycle nest of lows had potentially very recently formed.

At this stage we moved down to conduct a quick final scan of the daily chart and were able to confirm our findings on the weekly chart.

Potential set up

It was noted that the downward VTL drawn on the weekly chart was that of the nominal 14D (20 calendar days) cycle, running at about eight trading days and a price cross from below would confirm the 18M nest of lows and could be used as a trigger to enter the trade.

It was also estimated that an upward cross of the furthest FLD shown on the chart would project prices to around $60. We decide to look for an imminent long entry.

Entering the Trade

The set up

Once a primary list filtered for volatility has been screened and a two-stage scan on both the weekly and daily charts has been conducted, you should have a number of candidates that are ready to be traded.

It is good practice to carry out a full phasing analysis of the very best candidates once you have finished the final scan on the daily chart. This is to ensure that nothing has been missed and there is no contradictory evidence.

In the case of Caterpillar, there is probably enough evidence here to place a buy order as soon as the nearest downward VTL has been crossed.

Putting the pieces of the trading puzzle together well ahead of time allows you to remain dispassionate and to think clearly. You will find it a lot easier to weigh up the evidence for and against the trade sitting on the sidelines than you will when actually running a position. If you are unsure, or if the picture is muddled, then either search for more evidence, wait or move on to something else.[57]

There are a few more steps before actually placing the order. The first thing that needs to be worked out is whether this trade is the best use of our equity at the time. Having conducted a scan of the primary list, it is likely that a number of opportunities presented themselves. What we are looking for, however, are the trades that will allow us to make the most meaningful gains in the least amount of time. To make this assessment, we need to establish the trading cycle.

The trading cycle

There is normally one cycle responsible for taking prices most directly to the target and you should ascertain what this is for each security in your primary list during the initial scan phase. What you are looking for is good moves up or down in percentage terms, but with small counter moves (retracements). You can either use Hurst's low-tech finger measurements or you can apply the measure chart tool loaded into most, if not all, trading software.

Looking back at Figure 6.2, for example, you can see how the second 18M cycle on the chart, helped by the underlying uptrend, took prices from $29 to $52 in 60 weeks between August 2004 and September 2005. Although bottom to top this is an 80% move, halfway along there is an 18% retracement. Since not many traders can live with this sort of drawdown, the 18M cycle would have been a poor choice for a trading cycle in this case.

The 9M cycles that comprise the second 18M cycle, bottom to top, on the other hand, returned 47% each over 21 weeks. However, you would still have had to accept average pullbacks of 7%, which is still potentially outside the acceptable range.

Entered and exited appropriately the average performance of the four 20W cycles in this 18M set is 19.75% over 6.5 weeks (158% annualised) with the average drawdown only 3%. This is a much better ratio and the 20-week cycle, therefore, would have been the ideal choice for the trading cycle. In mountaineering the direct route to the summit is called the *directissima* and this is what we are looking to take in each trade.

Choosing the trading cycle

Hurst recommended passing on any trade that did not offer a direct route to a 20% gain. Some traders are happy with 15% while others think 20% is too little. You need to decide for yourself, but whatever you use, at least you are able to compare potential opportunities properly. After all, why would you choose to trade a security that offers you 10% over six weeks if another can give you 20% with the same risk?

Once you have chosen your trading cycle you need to stick to it. You should not switch up to the next longer cycle mid-trade if you think prices are going higher (or lower for shorts). For example, if you are long the 20W cycle and you think it will project further, then stay with it, do not suddenly switch your trade tracking analysis to the 9M cycle because you will invariably be shaken out. If the 20W cycle reverses mid-trade then it is a signal to exit. Managing open positions using cycle analysis will be covered in detail in a later chapter.

Establishing a percentage performance target before you enter a trade is an important first step, but we also need to know how much we are willing to lose if our analysis turns out to be wrong.

Capital risk

It is bad practice to enter a trade without first setting a stop. This is an order in the opposite direction to your trade which will force an exit if there is an adverse move causing a loss greater than you are willing to accept.

Even with a robust methodology like Hurst's, trading is still about evaluating a range of probable outcomes or, put another way, playing the odds. Sometimes your analysis will be wrong, in which case you will need to exit as soon as possible and re-appraise. Sometimes an unanticipated fundamental shock will rock you out of the trade. In all of these cases a stop will limit the damage to your trading equity.

Setting stops

Typically risk per trade is calculated as a percentage of available capital. Some traders think that 3% is acceptable, whereas others are willing to risk no more than 1% of total equity per position. It is beyond the remit of this book to provide an elaborate disquisition on money management and if you are not completely *au fait* with the principles of risk you should get yourself up to speed.[58] For our purposes here we are interested in risk versus reward in the trade itself. In other words, we need to be able to frame the trading opportunity in terms of potential gain as well as loss.

Imagine that you buy a stock at $50, which your analysis suggests will rise by 30% to $65. At the same time as you enter the buy order, you also place a sell order to be executed if the price drops to $45, an adverse move of 10%. Thus you are risking $5 to make $15. Or put another way, you are putting up $5 to see if your analysis is correct. The reward-to-risk ratio in this case is three to one (3:1) and it is rare that you will want to accept anything less. This of course provides another way to filter for trading candidates. A security may offer 20% upside, but if the nearest level you can protect the trade is 10% below your entry, then your risk reward is only 2:1. This is enough for some traders, especially at the intraday level but, combined with trading costs and slippage, eventually it will take its toll on your trading equity.

Once you have chosen your target price, stop loss level and minimum reward to risk (at least 3:1), the only remaining variable is the entry price. Hurst suggested putting together a table for each trade showing various reward-to-risk ratios and their associated entry prices. This is a way to help you choose the maximum price you are willing to pay (minimum price for short sales) in order to stay within your risk parameters and still make the trade worthwhile. This method can be useful when an entry trigger is activated and prices then move quickly away in the direction of your trade, but in general it is enough just to enter as soon as you can after the entry conditions are met.

The process of establishing entry conditions is intimately connected to another type of risk: that of trading risk. Whereas capital risk refers to the actual amount you will lose if you are stopped out, trading risk is the probability of price actually hitting the stop at all before achieving the price target. In other words, if trading risk is high, you are more likely to be stopped out than if it is low. Before we look at entry triggers and trading risk, however, let us quickly finish the evaluation of Caterpillar and see what it did post-analysis. This should help drive home some of the concepts that have just been introduced.

Review: Caterpillar set up and entry

Figure 6.7 shows the daily candle chart of CAT as at 10 March 2006, four and a bit months after the original analysis was completed when the decision was made to look for a long entry in the stock.

- Prices rose out of the suspected nest of lows on 21 October 2005 at $42.43 and went straight up, closing a nearly $3 gap and breaking the 20D VTL to the upside. Our analysis suggested that a break of this VTL would signal that all cycles up to and including the 18-month had bottomed and therefore that the recent lows were unlikely to be revisited for a long time. As such the next available price after the break, the following day's open at $47.30, was taken to enter the position.

- To protect the trade a safe stop-loss level would have been just below the recent suspected big cycle low, say at $42.40. However, the higher low four days later at $43.80 is the first full ten-day cycle in the new 18M cycle upswing and is chosen in preference.

- We had already seen recently in Caterpillar that the longest cycle capable of producing 20% moves with minimum drawdowns in the least time was the 20-week cycle. This is therefore taken as the trading cycle and the 20W FLD is used to project prices. The previous estimate was for a break at 50 projecting 58, but because the underlying trend is supportive we expect it to reach at least 60.

- The capital risk of the trade is the stop-loss level subtracted from the entry price (47.3 − 43.7) or $3.60 and this is maintained throughout the trade as a simple trailing stop. The potential reward of the trade is the entry price subtracted from the target (60 − 47.3) or $12.7. The reward-to-risk ratio is therefore 12.7 / 3.6 = 3.5:1.

- The trade ended up being stopped out 84 trading days (121 calendar days) after entry at $63 giving a 33.2% return − 100% annualised.

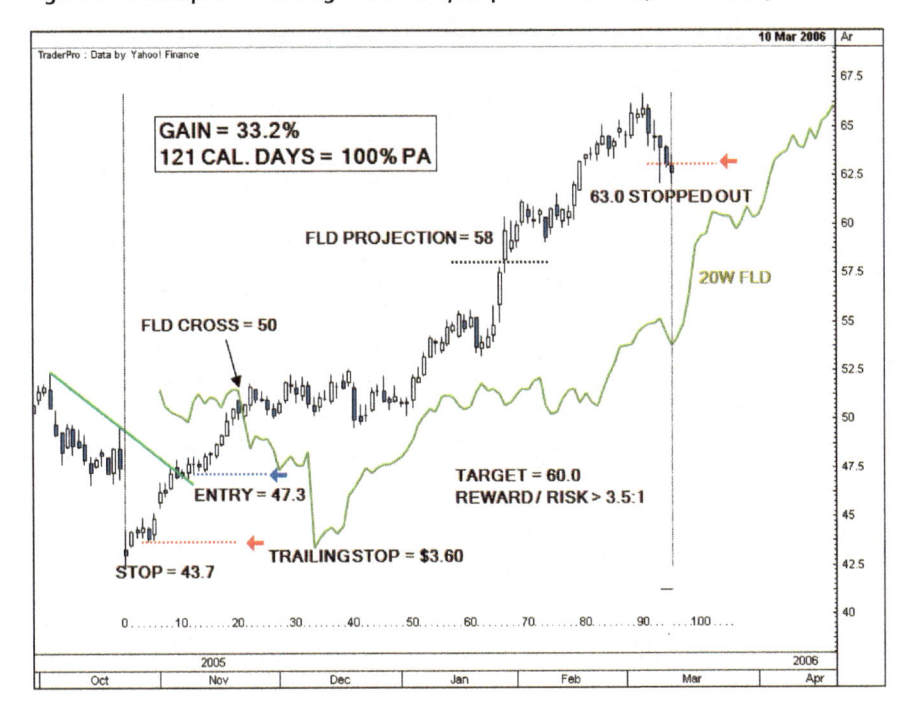

Figure 6.7: Caterpillar – trading the 20W cycle post VTL Break (Data: Yahoo)

Entry conditions

Trade risk

Although capital risk can be more or less exactly judged ahead of time[59], trade risk is less easily quantified. The rule of thumb, however, is that the closer your entry is to a cycle extreme, the higher is the probability that you will be stopped out.

In the case of a buy order this means that the further away from a cycle low you enter the position the more chance you have of staying in the trade. The same principle applies to short selling and cycle peaks, only more so, but this will be covered in a later chapter.

Nests of lows

One of the core principles in Hurst's methodology is to wait for confirmation before entering a trade, even if this means accepting lower absolute performance. All cycles are a composite of a set of shorter cycles and before the longest cycle in the composite can be said to have reversed all of the shorter components need to have reversed as well. If there is a very long component in a nest of lows, for example an 18-month cycle, then the price move out will be of a higher order of magnitude and worth trading. But, on the other hand, because the next shorter cycles have proportionally large amplitudes, the adverse price moves are likely to be significant. Unless you are prepared to accept very high capital risk, therefore, your trade risk will be very high.

You will remember from chapter one that the highest rate of change in any cycle occurs halfway between the peak and trough in either direction. Conversely the lowest overall rate of change is at the cycle turning points. You are therefore better off waiting for the cycle to get going than jumping in too early and needlessly tying up your trading equity. Remember also that the longer the cycle, the longer it takes to reverse.

Overall then, trade risk decreases as prices move away from the major cycle low – what Hurst called the edge band of the cycle envelope – and into the mid-band, after the first shorter cycles in the new move out have put in their lows.

VTL breaks

In chapter two it was shown that valid trendlines are just straightened out sections of curvilinear cycles. A cycle is driven around its turn by the next longer cycle and a break of its VTL means that the longer cycle has turned. Each cycle has a VTL associated with it and going into a nest of lows these slope downwards connecting adjacent peaks of the each individual cycle.

By simple geometry, the longer the cycle, the more time between peaks and the shallower the VTL. It therefore follows that as the cycles become progressively shorter going into the nest of lows, the VTLs become progressively steeper, until eventually all of the shorter components have bottomed and are ready to start up again. As each cycle reverses, these downward sloping VTLs are then crossed in an upwards direction, starting with the steepest and ending with the shallowest, which signifies that the trough of the longest component is behind us.

In this way, VTL breaks can be used as a trigger to alert you to the fact that a specific cycle low is in place and you can then track these breaks until you have reached the cycle you wish to trade.

Review: Telefonica set up and entry

In Caterpillar's case the buy order was entered immediately after the break of the 20D VTL and the set up and action signal were quite straightforward. The following example shows a longer more complex bottom where multiple VTLs are considered.

Figure 6.8 shows the chart of Spanish Telco major, Telefonica (TEF-MAC), in August 2002. The stock has fallen over 70% since its March 2000 high and is under observation because we think a major cycle low is due. A phasing analysis has been conducted and the view is that prices are currently in the second 9M cycle of the third 18M cycle of a 54M cycle. We believe that prices are a couple of months away from a major nest of lows that should see a sizeable and sustained reversal.

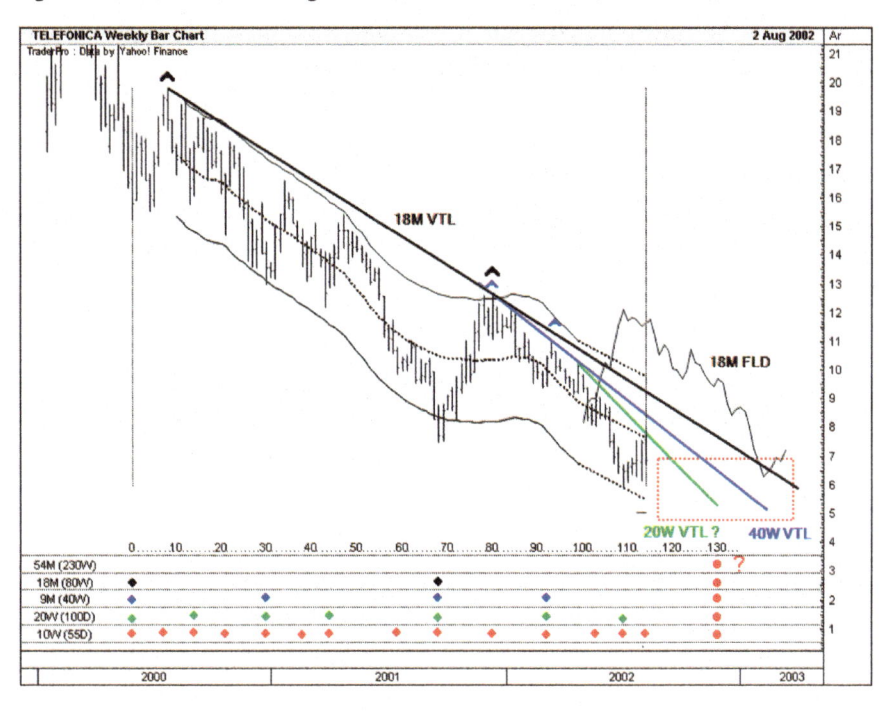

Figure 6.8: Telefonica declining into the 2002 nest of lows (Data: Yahoo)

Drawing the VTLs and FLD

Because the underlying trend is strongly down, the assumption is that the price high between €12 and €13 around grid 80 is the latest 18M peak translated to the left. An 18M VTL has been drawn in connecting it with the previous 18M peak at around grid 10. Extrapolating the line into the future, the deduction is that if we are right about the upcoming nest of lows, then a break of the VTL between €6 and €7 will put a 54M trough (the next longer cycle) somewhere around grid 130, i.e. in early October.

This information together with the cycle periods given by the diamonds you have been able to place so far, allows us to place red dots at grid 130 marking estimated time location for the future nest of lows.

An 18M FLD has also been plotted and can be seen to be running above prices. A clear FLD peak has formed around grid 110 suggesting that an 18M cycle is indeed due. Because the underlying trend is down, the assumption is that the price cycle low will be translated to the right and therefore offset from the FLD peak. It would not have been unreasonable to assume at this point that should the VTL break to the upside then so too would the FLD, enabling us to make an upside price projection well ahead of time. 40W and 20W VTLs have also been drawn in, although at this time we cannot be completely sure that the peaks are accurate. Nevertheless, their extensions help to pick out a high probability area for a bottom range, indicated by the red box.

Nest of lows and bottom range

Figure 6.9 shows Telefonica fast forwarded to March 2004. The sharp sell-off into grid 110 and the subsequent bounce was a false start for anyone looking to enter the 18M trading cycle. Had you jumped the gun here, anticipating the big reversal, you would have been stopped out 12 weeks later.

A month or so after the actual 54M nest of lows on 4 October 2002 (grid 123) the 17W and 31W VTLs (nominal 20W and 9M) were broken to the upside in quick succession. However, had this been taken as a second potential entry signal for the 18M trading cycle, once again it would either have been stopped out or been a wasted 20-week sideways move.

It was only after the break of the 18M (62W average period) VTL at grid 147 that prices started moving up with any consistency. At this point confirmation was finally given that the 54M nest of lows was in place and that the risk was to the upside. This would have been taken as an alert but as it is an edge band trade, the mid-band entry signal would have been given by the break of the very next 10W VTL. This produced a 56% move over the next 48 weeks, giving a yield of just over 60%.

To make a point, had you entered the position at the break of the 17W VTL, hung on through a 20% drawdown in December and exited at exactly the same place, your yield would have only been 43%. This of course takes no account of the opportunity cost involved.

Figure 6.9: Telefonica rounding the 2002 nest of lows (Data: Yahoo)

Short Selling

The techniques for long and short are broadly similar: you still need to screen for the best trading candidates, conduct a phasing analysis and calculate the cyclic status. And you still need to establish a price target, stop level and minimum reward-to-risk level before committing capital. Furthermore, the tools needed to do this, the VTL and FLD, are the same whichever side of the market you are on. However, there are some differences in the overall approach to short selling that that you need to be aware of.

We are going to work through two case studies in which all of the essential points of short selling using cycle analysis are covered. In these examples we will revisit the idea that market tops are qualitatively different from market bottoms and examine how that affects things like trade risk and trading discipline.

Two case studies

The following two case studies in US telecommunications major Verizon (VZ US) and the MSCI Spain exchange-traded fund (EWP) highlight the most important points. Largely it comes down to understanding that the shape of market tops tends to differ from that of market bottoms and that as a result trade risk is increased. This can be offset by ensuring that you only trade with the trend, by being aware of some of the peculiarities of short selling and by maintaining good trading discipline throughout.

Case Study 1– Verizon Communications

Figure 6.10 shows a 20-week price cycle and 51-day FLD in Verizon Communications from December 2005 to May 2006.

Trade when the trend is pointing down

If we were following this price move in real time, we would have been waiting for the cycle to confirm that it had reversed before looking for a short entry set up. The first principle in short selling – for anyone other than very nimble short-term traders – is to only enter positions when the trend underlying our trading cycle is down. For example, if our trading cycle is 20 weeks, then the direction of the sum of all longer components has to be confirmed to be down before the trade is entered.

At the time of the price high at grid 34 (just under $26) we would have known that the upside projection triggered by the 51D FLD (nominal 80-day cycle) cross at around $23 had been overshot. This was an indication that the underlying trend was up and that the environment was still unfavourable for short sellers.

Chapter 6 | Selection, Set Up And Entry

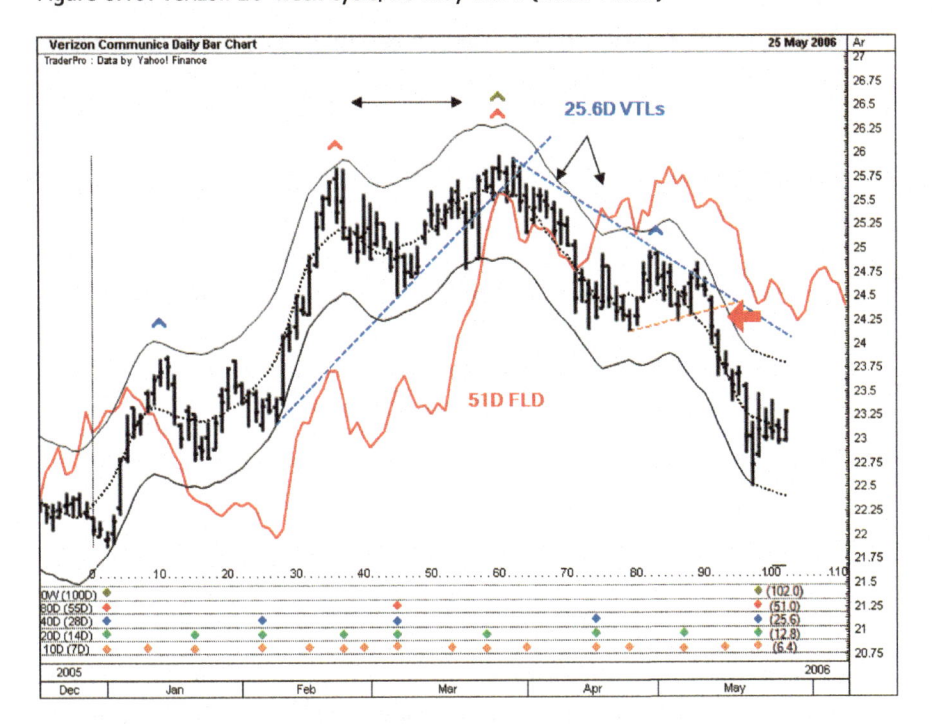

Figure 6.10: Verizon 20-week cycle, 25 May 2006 (Data: Yahoo)

Wait for confirmation

Prices decline from the price high at grid 34 but then recover and put in a second peak 26 weeks later at grid 60. However, it is only after the up sloping 25.6D VTL (nominal 40-day cycle) is conclusively crossed down by prices at around grid 63 that we can be sure that a 51D cycle peak is in place.

At this point it should be obvious that the first peak is translated to the right. Since we also know that the FLD upside projection was overshot and that to date a lower low has not been put in, there is nothing yet to suggest that prices have stopped advancing. We cannot even think about placing a short until we know that the 20W cycle has rolled over and the risk is to the downside.

Do not act on alert

It is only when price breaks down through the 51D FLD that we can be sure that a cycle high is in place. This also gives us our first lower low since grid 45 and is the evidence we have been looking for to show us that the 20W cycle has in fact reversed direction.

Furthermore, we now have a downside projection of around $23.40. However the FLD cross is an alert only; it should not be taken as an action signal. At this point the last thing we want to do is to start chasing the move down, because if we do we will almost certainly be stopped out with a loss.

Let mid-channel pause (MPC) complete

Quickly turn back to chapter one and look at the head and shoulders pattern of Figure 1.4. This composite wave was constructed simply by adding a long sine wave to a second shorter sine wave: the length of the short sine wave being just over a quarter of the length of the long one. Thus the overall shape of the composite is created by the long cycle and each of the shoulders is created by the countertrend action of shorter cycle.

Quarter cycle period rule

Thus, the upswing is interrupted halfway along by a brief price decline caused by the cycle one quarter of the length of the longest cycle showing through. Similarly, the downswing is interrupted halfway along by a brief price rally caused by the cycle one quarter of the length of the longest cycle showing through.

Going back to our Verizon example, the longest cycle here is the 20 week, which we know has rolled over and is now heading down. In this case, the cycle with one quarter the length of the 20W cycle is the 26.5D cycle. We therefore expect this cycle to peak halfway along the downward 20W cycle envelope (channel) and must wait for it to pass before attempting to enter on the short side. If we jump in too early, our stop will be hit.

Variation in MPC

Of course, mid-channel pauses can sometimes be exceedingly shallow or even imperceptible, for example when the downtrend is very strong and swamps the short components. On the other hand, sometimes MPCs can be very steep and rise right back up to near the previous high. How significant this countertrend rally will be can depend on a lot of subtle factors, but the most important as you will see is underlying trend. As your experience as a Hurst analyst grows your ability to spot nuances will increase and you should be able to predict the strength of the MPC with little difficulty.

Entry signal

The MPC kicks in and prices rally into the 26.5D cycle peak, causing the 20W cycle downswing to pause briefly. We now need to wait for confirmation that this peak is in place before entering a short position. In this case it is the downward price break of the 6.4D VTL (ten-day nominal cycle) – marked by the red arrow. This break will also leave behind it a price spike at grid 89 which can be connected to the last known 26.5D cycle peak at 62.

Considerations

Unsynchronised tops

You can see from this example that short selling requires patience. It is rarely a good idea to enter a short trade immediately after a long trade, because the cycle you were trading needs to roll over first and this not only takes time, but it often results in very choppy price action. Whereas cycle lows tend to synchronise creating sharp bottoms, tops tend to be more diffuse and peaks tend to occur consecutively rather than at the same time. The common reason given for this is that hope dissipates slowly and fear comes on quickly. There is a bit more to it than this, but for now the most important thing is to know that it tends to be so.

A case in point here is the triple top in the 26.5D cycle that formed between grids 75 and 90. Another is the double top that formed in the 26.5D cycle between grids 0 and 25.

Generally speaking, the longer the longest cycle in the top, the choppier it will be as the shorter cycles, each of them translating either left or right, put in their peaks. This is more common in equities than in commodities, where the greed-fear equation works in reverse. Tops in commodities represent the fear of high prices, and tend to be sharp.

Of course, while this is what we tend to see, it is not a universal law and you must stay alert for anomalies. Dramatic, steep reversals can and do take place, tops in equities can be sharp, MPCs can be non-existent and so on. Having said all that, an astute analyst can often tell ahead of time when things will deviate from the norm – the warning signs are there if you care to read them.

Increased trade risk

Because shorter cycles tend to peak one after another, gradually building the longer cycle top, the risk of being stopped out close to the level of the price high – in the cycle envelope edge band – is higher. In fact it is not normally until after the mid-channel pause has been passed that the best risk reward opportunities present themselves. This may seem like a long wait, but patience in short selling is often rewarded, whereas hastiness is usually punished severely.

Increased capital risk

Overall, therefore, trade risk is higher for short selling than it is on the long side. The reason countertrend rallies tend to be sharp is because short sellers are fearful and the reason they are fearful is because they know they can end up losing more than they put in. Here is how it works:

- I buy a stock at 100p with no stop and it drops to zero. I lose all of my money, but that is all: it cannot fall any further.

- I short at 100p with no stop and it rises to 300p. I lose all of money plus an extra 100p. In the first case, my loss is 100%, in the second it is 200%.

Of course, most traders would try not to let this happen, but it illustrates the point. Short sellers tend to cover fast because they do not want to be wiped out and in the rush for exits prices tend to rise very quickly.

Lower potential performance

Another point to remember is that short selling does not give you as much bang for buck, so to speak, per trade. For example:

- I enter a long trade at 80p and sell at 160p: my return is 100%.

- I enter a short trade at 160p and cover at 80p: my return is only 50%.

This is why it is doubly important to make sure that the instrument you wish to trade can actually provide you with meaningful returns.

Verizon here is a case in point. Even if you were able to enter a short position at the exact top of the mid-channel pause and were able to cover at the exact bottom, you still would have made less than 10%. Having said that, because sell offs at this late stage of a cycle tend to be fast, the increase in yield can sometimes make up for it.

Case Study 2 – MSCI Spain ETF

Figure 6.11 shows iShares MSCI Spain ETF weekly chart between March 2009 and June 2010. A full 18-month cycle (average period 66 weeks) is shown together with its FLD.

Figure 6.11: iShares Spain ETF (Data: Yahoo)

Underlying trend

Although there is very little right translation being displayed in the cycle, the underlying trend is definitely up. The upside projection generated by the FLD price cross at grid 12 has been overshot; and if the price low at the end of the data is indeed the cycle trough the downside projection of the FLD price cross at grid 55 has been undershot. Furthermore, the second trough of the 66-week cycle is some 30% higher than that of the first.

Mid-channel pauses

The mid-channel pause (MCP) during both the up-leg and the down-leg have been highlighted by blue arrows. In both cases these have been caused by the peak of the 16.5W (nominal 20W) cycle – one-quarter the length of the 66W cycle – showing through.

Notice that the first MCP is shallow as the uptrend swamps its individual components. The second MCP on the other hand, is steeper as the uptrend forces it up and outwards. Were the underlying trend during this leg down instead of up, then it would be very much harder to pick out. In fact this is one of the ways we anticipate the strength of a mid-channel pause.

Top formation

The long cycle peak forms over 18 weeks and as you can see any attempt to short at the highs would have been quickly stopped out.

The break of the 33W (nominal nine-month) VTL at grid 40 calls the 66W (18M) cycle high, but it is not until the first lower low is put in six weeks later that confirmation is given. The trade risk of putting on a short before this second signal would have been unacceptably high, although with perfect hindsight it looks as though it should have been obvious.

Alert and trading signal

Had we jumped in prematurely, we would have ended up shorting right into the mid-channel pause and the trade would have performed dismally over the next seven weeks. The correct action signal to enter the short trade therefore was immediately after the 28D VTL break. By this time we knew for certain that the 66W cycle had rolled over and was heading down and we knew for certain we had cleared the peaks of both the 33W and 16.5-weak cycles, leaving no further peaks below to stop out the trade.

Summary

Had this correct entry been taken after the 28D VTL break and then covered just above the low at $29, our trading performance would have been 30% in just eight weeks: a yield of 195%. However, from top to bottom the down-leg of the 66W cycle here dropped 42% over some 20 weeks. It may seem odd then that we were on the sidelines most of the time, but had we not been we would have seen our equity chewed up in capital loss not to mention the opportunity cost. In the end, we managed to pick up the best reward to risk trade in the entire move.

You may well ask if it always pays to abide by these somewhat conservative rules. Sometimes it is true that you will get caught out and miss the beginning of a big downside move.

Figure 6.12 shows Market Vectors Egypt ETF in mid-January 2010, the dramatic trend-channel break marking the beginning of the popular uprising against President Mubarak.

Unfortunately, its possible that no amount of analysis would have helped you get into this move. But having said that, even in an out of the blue sell off like this, we still see a mid-channel pause: had you used this as a short entry set up and had you leapt out of the trade at the bottom, then you would have made 15% in three sessions, equating to a yield of 365%.

Figure 6.12: Market Vectors Egypt ETF, 4 February 2011 (Data: Yahoo)

Conclusion

Of the many securities available to trade at any given time, not all of them are perfectly set up to provide a profitable trading opportunity. A complete analysis of the cyclic condition of a security takes time and effort and so you need to have a way of sorting the wheat from the chaff. The first consideration for many equity traders is liquidity, however once this hurdle has been crossed, equally important is the historical activity of the issue. The most attractive securities from a trading perspective tend to be those that are the most volatile.

Volatility is a measure of how well a security moves and you have now been introduced to Hurst's original Volatility Index, as well as the concept of Average True Range. For volatility to be useful as a screening tool it needs to be compared to the market as a whole, which is why we are more interested in relative volatility – or how well the issue moves relative to the index. Connected to the idea of volatility is the concept of yield and it was shown that rather than absolute performance, performance over time is a more valid measure. You should now be familiar with the simple task of annualising returns. This will provide you with a yardstick against which to compare potential candidates for trading. It will also show you where the best opportunity costs are.

Having converted a long primary list of securities into one that passes the liquidity, volatility and potential yield tests, the next step is see which issues offer the most straightforward analysis. The two-stage visual scanning approach allows you to confirm where the best gains are likely to come from as well as identify the imminent trading opportunities.

Once a security appears to be favourably set up for a trade, the next important step is to define the trade in terms of reward and risk. A quick review of FLDs showed their ability not only to uncover underlying trend, but also in setting price targets. The trading cycle concept was also introduced as a useful measure of potential performance.

Possibly more important than potential profit is potential loss and the importance of protecting your trading capital with stop losses was emphasised. Risk of loss was also compared with the probability that the trade would fail. Although trading risk is less is easy to measure objectively than capital risk, it is a concept you should be very familiar with unless you want to see the gradual erosion of your equity. Trades are more likely to fail if they are entered too close to nests of lows or at peaks, although intelligent use of VTLs will help show you when and where to enter the trade to minimise your trade risk and for the optimum reward-to-risk ratio.

As you have seen, the techniques for selling short are not vastly different to those used when going long. However, there are some peculiarities such as increased trade risk, which is a function of the altered nature of market tops. It is important when short selling, therefore, to maintain discipline and control risk more tightly.

Once you have entered a trade you need to ride it for maximum profit and the next chapter explores how to manage open positions using Hurst cycle analysis.

Endnotes

[47] If you are not sure where to start here, go to the Market Technicians Association website www.mta.org
[48] Hurst referred to this as $\sum L$ (sigma el), i.e. the sum of the long cycles.
[49] As opposed to actual historical volatility – for a set period from a past date; or actual future volatility – for a set period to a future date (for example option expiry).
[50] J. Welles Wilder, *New Concepts in Technical Trading Systems* (Trend Research, 1978).

[51] Recall that this is 14 trading days and therefore references 20 calendar days. As mentioned earlier in the text, volatility should ideally be geared to the length of the dominant cycle. However, because volatility will be picked up by any shorter cycles, 20 bars is an acceptable proxy. If relative volatility is high at 20 days, then it is not unreasonable to suppose it will be so for other cycles too.

[52] The code is provided in Appendix 8.

[53] Beta (β) is a measure of a stock's (s) returns relative to those of the index (i) it belongs to and is expressed by the formula: $\beta=Cov(Rs,Ri)/Var(Ri)$. If $\beta=0$ then the issue moves independently of the market; if $\beta=1$ then the issue's returns are in line with the market's, if $\beta=1.1$ then theoretically the issue moves 10% more than the market.

[54] For ease of reference the charts in this chapter can be downloaded from **vectisma.com/downloads/scans**.

[55] The reason the second 18M cycle is 20W shorter than the first is largely because of the two sharp sell offs between grids 126 and 130 and grids 150 and 160. This has the effect of truncating time, so to speak, and tends to shorten the cycle period.

[56] For argument's sake the assumption here is that CAT and GE's respective volatilities retained the same relationship in October 2002 as they did when the RV calculation was made in October 2005.

[57] Emotional control in trading is a big topic and beyond the scope of this book. Please refer to one of the best books written on the subject: *Trading in the Zone* by Mark Douglas (New York Institute of Finance, 2000).

[58] Most general technical analysis texts include a chapter on money management. Good discussions can also be found in Dr. Alexander Elder's *Come into My Trading Room* (Wiley, 2002) and *The Financial Spread Betting Handbook* by Malcolm Pryor (Harriman House, 2011).

[59] Once you have included transaction costs, capital risk can be higher than anticipated through slippage. This is the difference between the expected price and the executed price and applies to the entry as well as the stop. Slippage can be high in a fast market or where the stop falls within a gap – where price changes from one level to another with no trading in between.

7 MANAGING OPEN POSITIONS

Introduction

In the last chapter we looked at how to screen issues for relative volatility; how to scan them for readability and the likelihood of an imminent trade; and how to set up and enter a position. Having spent so much time screening, scanning and calculating entry, you cannot just forget about the trade and hope for the best once it has been placed.

Probably the most important thing to remember about managing open positions is that the better the preparation, the easier it is to manage the trade. You can be the best position manager in the world, but if you only choose pups and your entry technique is poor, then it will make little difference to your overall performance. In this chapter we are going to look at some more examples of set up and entry and then go on to study how to manage an open long position using all of the cyclic tools you have learnt so far.

The first case we are going to look at is all about when not to enter a trade. We will then study an example of an early entry that resulted in a poorly managed trade and finally we will look in detail at a well entered, well protected trade that was managed skilfully using cycle analysis.

When running an open position you need to continually ask yourself if the trade is on track or if you need to think about getting out. It is better to get out ahead of trouble and admit your error than hang on for grim life and allow losses to mount up. This of course means that you need to be able to judge when things are going well or if they have actually gone wrong.

You should now be familiar with the tools needed to accomplish this: the VTL and the FLD. As you will learn, their use is not restricted to phasing analysis and entry, but also to position management where they can be used to provide important, on-going feedback throughout the trade.

Trade management Hurst style is all about keeping your cyclic analysis current, building out your phasing model and revising your view if the evidence suggests you need to do so. Compared to many other methods out there, it may initially seem like yet another complicated brain-teaser and a lot of effort. However, like everything else in Hurst analysis, because it is unfamiliar it seems hard at first, but it all comes down to practice. The more times you manage positions using cycle analysis techniques, the more versatile and able you will become. Ultimately, of course, if you do not have a disciplined strategy based on sound principles, then you are just shooting in the dark.

Case Study – JPMorgan Chase 2002/2003

First attempt – August 2002

Figure 7.1 shows the weekly chart for JPMorgan Chase (JPM US) from mid-2000 to the summer of 2002. A phasing analysis has been conducted providing us with average periods for all of the expected cycles and allowing us to draw in the major VTLs and FLDs. The October 200 low around grid number 10 is being taken as the first 18-month cycle trough on the chart. The next lower price low at grid 103 in August 2002 is the right distance away – about 90 weeks – and there are two clear 40-week cycles intervening. This can therefore be tentatively labelled the next 18-month cycle trough.

The charts in this chapter can be downloaded for ease of reference from the site vectisma.com/downloads/openpositions.

Chapter 7 | Managing Open Positions

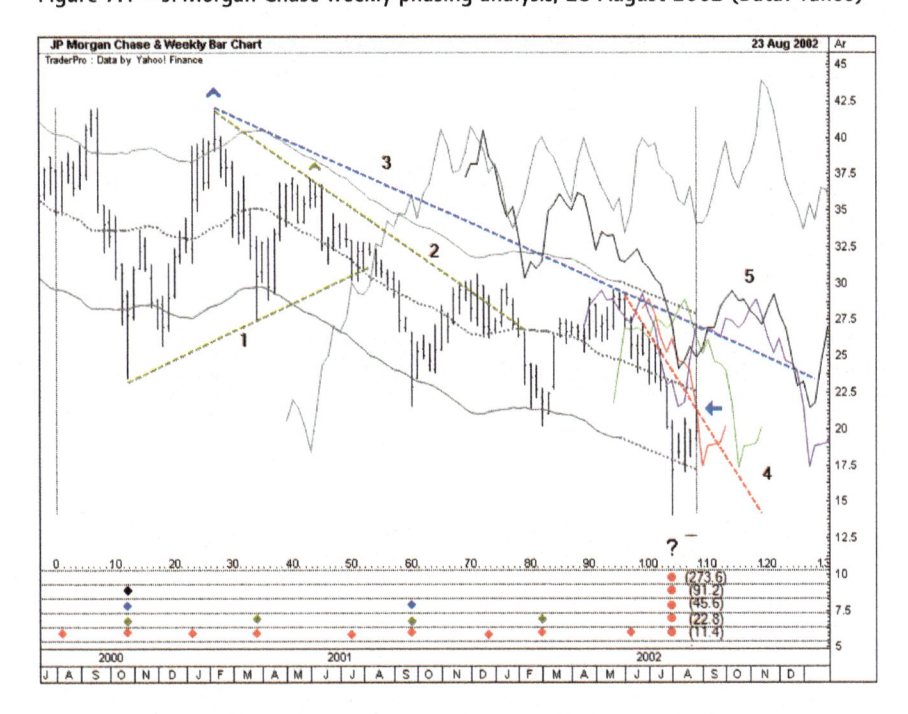

Figure 7.1 – JPMorgan Chase weekly phasing analysis, 23 August 2002 (Data: Yahoo)

Overview

Valid trendlines

The chart displays admirably clear harmonic cycles. The entire move consists of two nine-month waves which themselves subdivide into two 20-week waves. Two 20W VTLs have been drawn in:

- VTL (1) is broken down by price at $50, telling us that the price high between grids 20 and 30 is the nine-month cycle peak

- VTL (2) is broken up by price at $70 confirming the nine-month cycle low at grid 60

Trend component

A series of lower lows have formed telling us that the underlying trend is down. However, peak translation of the last two 20W cycles has shifted subtly to the right, indicating that the downtrend has flattened and potentially warning of an impending reversal.

215

An FLD of the longest cycle (54M, 273W) has been plotted and there is a price intersection at $31.5 (grid 50). The highest price within the last 18 months was $47.8 on 24 March 2000 (off screen) and this is assumed to be the last 54M high. The downside projection is therefore $15.2.[60] This was exceeded at the end of July 2001 (grid 104) emphasising that at this point the trend *is still down.*

Average cycle lengths

At 103 the average length of the cycles was calculated based upon the shortest fully phased cycle: the 10-week. The average period of the 10W cycle is 11.4W. The longer cycles up to the 18M are then calculated as harmonic multiples of two and the 54M is calculated as three times the 18M.[61] This is the preferred approach when the sample of longer cycles' diamonds is small.

Overall we can see that the cycles are currently running long at about 120% of the Nominal Model expectations.

Set up

Now, let us assume that we are looking at this chart on 30 August 2002 (110). There was a clear 20W cycle low just over 20 weeks ago and we have just witnessed a massive spike low. This therefore could easily be the next 20W low, which by harmonicity would also make it the low of the next 40W (9M) and 80W (18M). Before we dive in with buy orders, however, we need to look at the evidence carefully and get confirmation.

FLD projections

Prices have moved sharply up off the low towards the very end of the data and look to be just about to cross a 10W downward VTL (4). Furthermore, it looks like there is an FLD cascade lying just above and to the right of the last price. This is an alert that a major reversal could be about to take place. A break of the nearest FLD looks like it could easily trigger projections all the way through to the outlying 18M FLD at around $25. If there is a reversal and this does happen, then we immediately have an upside projection of $36.[62]

Action signal

We estimate that the VTL break would be around $20 and we prepare to drop down to the daily chart to stalk an entry. This is pretty exciting stuff at this point; we think we are about to correctly call an imminent major cycle trough with at least 80% upside! We might be wondering what could possibly go wrong. However, let us step back for a moment and coolly appraise what we are seeing.

Conflicting evidence

Trade risk

In the last chapter we talked about the concept of trade risk and you will recall that the highest probability of being stopped out is at the edge of the cycle envelope especially when this corresponds to a major nest of lows. Furthermore, the longer the longest cycle in that nest of lows, the higher the trade risk.

Long cycles do not turn on a sixpence: they take time to unfold. And in that time, other shorter cycles, which can be of significant magnitude, have to form their own troughs as they emerge from the bottom. The trade risk for this particular entry is therefore huge.

Capital risk

It is easy to get excited by the prospect of 80% upside, but the more salient question is: how are you going to protect this trade? The spike low is at $14 and placing a stop anywhere higher than this in these circumstances is just asking for trouble. So let us say we put a sell stop at $13.98.

Since we think the VTL break will be at $20, our stop will be over $6 lower than our entry. Our goal was to take $16 out of the trade, which gives us an adequate reward to risk ratio of 2.7:1, however if things go wrong – and they could very easily – we would be down 30%!

FLD Patterns

Suddenly the trade seems hasty and not a little imprudent. What else? Look at what the black 18M FLD is doing up and off to the right of the last price. It has topped and is headed down (marked 5 on the chart). We know from chapter three that price, therefore, should be forming an 18M cycle low at about the same time. The implication here is that the time location of the impending nest of lows is further to the right, i.e. yet to occur.

Furthermore, as we have seen, the 54M FLD price cross projection has overshot to the downside, indicating that the underlying down-trend is still in force, albeit possibly slowly turning up. Discretion being the better part of valour, we decide to hold off and see how things unfold from the safety of the sidelines.

Second attempt – October 2002

Figure 7.2 shows what happened next. Prices peaked though the VTL, held for two weeks and then dramatically collapsed – fortunately without taking us with it. Patience and prudence were thus rewarded and we were spared the drawdown. The eventual nest of lows was put in 15 weeks later at $11.99. Let us now examine a second attempt to enter JPM on the long side.

Figure 7.2: JPMorgan Chase second cycle low and recovery: late 2002-early 2003 (Data: Yahoo)

The phasing analysis has been updated and at the end of the data on 21 March 2003 everything except the 9M cycle – which is rolling over – is pointing up. Furthermore, prices have just penetrated the mid-band of the cycle envelope after a 5W VTL upside break. Potentially this confirms the last price low as the first 24.8-week cycle trough out of the nest of lows at grid 115.

Before we drop down to the daily chart and look at this set up in more detail, let us pause for a moment to look at an earlier trade that we could have easily taken: the one straight out of the big low.

Trading the rebound

Because we were too quick to call the previous spike down at the 18M nest of lows, we were very nearly hurt on the last trade. This would have been a clear case of emotion getting the better of sound judgment. When things get exciting – or scary – it is all too easy to develop tunnel vision and gloss over contradictory evidence. It can also lead to expensive unforced errors.

It is also easy to want to jump straight into the market after a near miss without properly re-evaluating cyclic conditions. In the last example, it seemed that everything pointed to you being right but you would have been early.

So having learnt your lesson, you may have been ready to have another crack at it. Of course, just because you are ready does not mean that the market is.

Entry

Let us now imagine that it is 11 October 2002. Figure 7.3 shows the detail of the upswing of the first 28.4W cycle and the recovery trade.

VTL alert and trigger

When the 52D (10W) VTL carried over from the weekly chart is broken by price, it confirms the nest of lows. However, it is a long way out.

A cross of the 13D day VTL (nominal 20D cycle), on the other hand, would carry the same message. And what is more it would provide a timely signal. In this instance a 6.5D (nominal 10D) VTL could not be drawn. However, it was possible to draw a VTL of the next shorter cycle: the 3.25D. This of course is far too sensitive to be used as a buy signal here, but its break does serve as an alert.

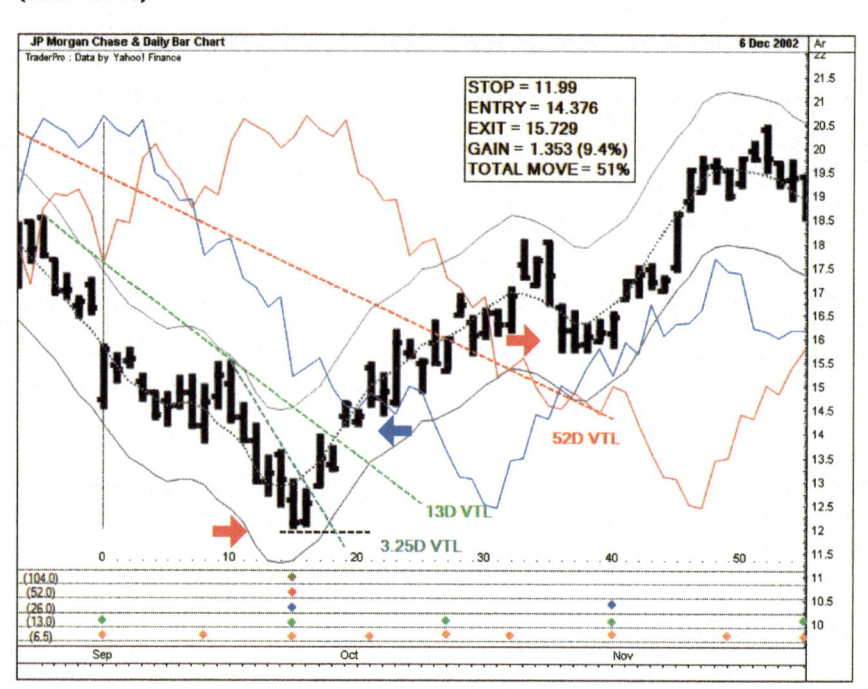

Figure 7.3 – JPMorgan Chase daily, September-December 2002: trading the recovery (Data: Yahoo)

If the 13D VTL goes then the 6.5D must have been broken, but more importantly the 26D cycle must have reversed. At this juncture, if this cycle has turned then so too must have the next longer 52D cycle. The 13D VTL is thus a proxy for the 10W VTL and its break is an ideal action signal.

The decision is therefore made to buy the open straight after the VTL cross. This would equate to $14, give or take. In the last chapter we talked about the importance of having everything set up *before* entering the trade.

Price target

Two FLDs (the 26D and the 52D) sit just above prices in a cascade pattern suggesting an imminent, sharp advance. The last price low is at $11.99 and we judge that price will cross the 26D FLD (blue line) at about $14, giving an upside target of $16.

A $2 advance is far from spectacular, but you reason that since the trend underlying the 26D cycle is up, you can expect the 26D peak to translate to the right. This should squeeze a bit more out of the trade, but more importantly, a break of this FLD projects through the 52D FLD (red line).

This would mean a target of at least $21. If you do end up entering at $14, then you are looking at a potential gain of 50%.

Trading and capital risk

If price drops below the recent low at $11.99 the implication would be that the cycle low has still not been seen and that your analysis was incorrect. This therefore seems like a good level to place a stop. An entry at $14 would give you just over $2 of capital risk versus $7 potential upside. This is a 3.5:1 reward-to-risk ratio, which is good.

If the trade fails, however, you stand to lose 14%, and although this is high, your thinking is that because this is a mid-band entry, the risk of the stop being hit is low. In any case, you have exceeded your basic trade selection criteria of 3:1 and 20% upside by a good margin. You feel confident.

Running the trade

On 15 October, price gaps up through the 13D VTL and since your order is to buy the next open, you are put into the trade at $14.376. This is higher than anticipated and at a stroke your initial capital risk has increased by nearly 20% to $2.386.

Nevertheless prices continue to advance and quickly cross up through the first 26D FLD putting you on track to hit the $16 target. Seven sessions later price gaps up through the 52D VTL confirming that the 20W nest of lows is in place. Three days later the 52D FLD is broken putting you on track for the $21 price target. So far so good: the trade is going well and you are making money.

On track

By 4 November (grid 33) prices have pushed all the way up to $18. In just 14 sessions you are up 25% and have nearly hit the second target. About now you are excited and looking ahead to see how much you can really make on this trade. Of course, at this stage, what you should really be doing is looking down to see how much of your gains you could give back if things go wrong.

Raising the stop

You realise that if prices retrace the move so far then you are exposed to a potential 33% loss, namely all of your gains plus your initial capital. You therefore decide to raise your stop. You might think that a decline of this magnitude is unlikely, but if you were wrong about the nest of the lows and this is just another rally in a downtrend, then it is easily possible.

Of course, in the event of a big sell off, the rational thing to do would be to capitulate as early as possible and limit the damage. But, without a strategy or a disciplined approach, there is no telling how you will behave when you are under fire. You might bail out quickly, or you might hold JPM in a death grip all the way down to your stop. For that matter, you might even decide to give the trade more breathing space and even lower your stop! Anything is possible in the heat of the moment when you do not have a coherent plan.

There are a few choices available to you on where to raise your stop to. However, let us say for argument's sake that you opt to use the initial spread: the entry level minus the stop level: $2.377.

Based upon the recent high of $18.115 and three sessions later, unfortunately, you are stopped out at $15.73. So, from having been up 25% at one point, you end up only taking 9.4% out of the trade. Factoring in, say, 10% slippage and trading commissions the real figure would be more like 8.5%.

Debrief

In retrospect it is easy to imagine that you would have jumped out right at the top: things often look blindingly obvious after the fact. Some traders find holding a profitable position, especially in a fast move, unbearably stressful and it is almost a relief for them to get out. For these traders sometimes it is enough just to have been right. Others are always looking for more and riding a move up for them is fun. It takes all sorts of course, but let us say that you are the second type: the punchy trader.

At the price high you would have been in an emotional, high-impact state looking for ever higher prices. You had called a big low after an earlier false start, the trade was on track ripping through FLDs all the way up, you had notched up 25% in 14 days and there was still an outstanding upside target $3 higher. Furthermore, there was even another outstanding 18M FLD target at $36!

You could not reasonably have entered any lower than you did and you could not reasonably have protected the trade any better at the start: except of course that your initial stop should have been placed below $11.99, rather than exactly at the low.

Avoidable Errors

In many ways, however, this was the wrong trade at the wrong time and it was poorly managed. There were a number of avoidable errors:

- The first mistake was that the trade was taken impatiently straight out of a major nest of lows. You would have at least wanted the first 20-week cycle to finish before looking to make an entry. So even though you got the mid-band entry right on the daily chart, you were still in an edge-band, high-trade-risk condition on the weekly.

- Secondly, you switched trading cycles up mid-trade breaking a Golden rule. The appropriate trading cycle here was 40 days, providing an initial target of $16. However, choosing this level would have offered only a 1:1 reward-to-risk ratio. Suddenly turning to the 80D trading cycle when you thought the higher target was possible ignored the fact that you might have to hold the trade through a 40D cycle low before the longer cycles had really turned up.

- Other than using a VTL break to get you in and FLDs to set your targets, at no point throughout the trade did you reassess the cyclic condition and update your phasing analysis.

- You were running too much capital risk throughout the trade and you did not adjust your stop to reflect new cyclic information coming in.

We could go on and of course the example is slightly exaggerated to make a point. The next example is a walk through how to manage a trade more skilfully using cycle analysis.

Third attempt - March 2003

Figure 7.4 is the daily chart showing the first 20-week cycle after the 11 October 2002 nest of lows. This is the same time period as the last 25 bars on the weekly chart shown in Figure 7.2. Take a moment to review that chart to get your bearings and help put the daily chart into its proper perspective.

Pre-trade checks

VTLs

Look at the chart and see if you agree with the diamond placements. Note that the second 54D cycle low at 60 is not the actual price low, but is displaced to the right, a concept to which we will be returning shortly. Notice also that the average periods at the bottom right of the chart have changed slightly to reflect the inclusion of the more recent price data.

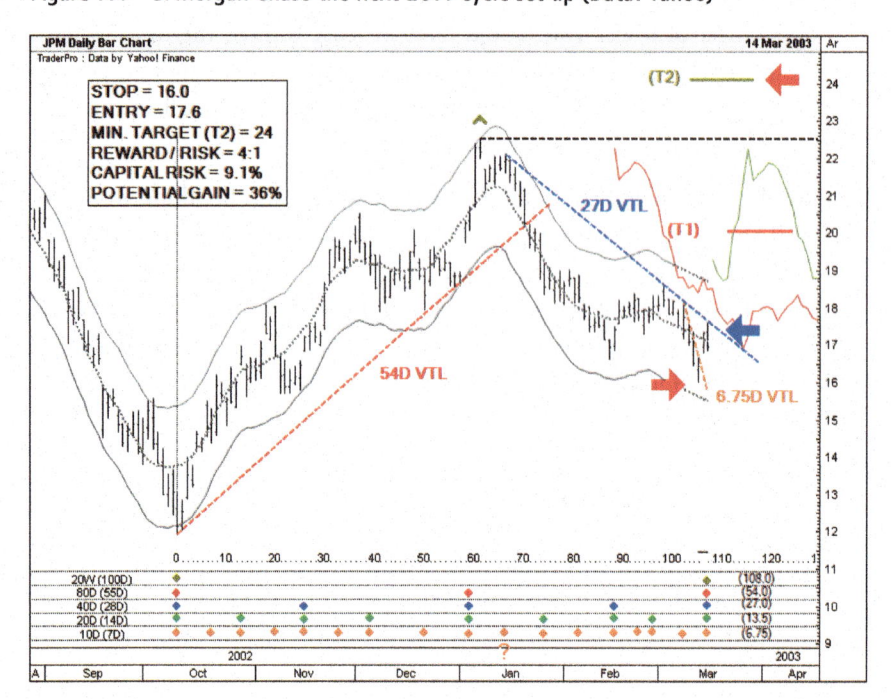

Figure 7.4 – JPMorgan Chase the next 20W cycle set up (Data: Yahoo)

54D and 6.75D VTLs

A 54D cycle (nominal 80D) VTL is crossed down by price at grid 70 implying that the recent cycle high is the 20W cycle peak. A 6.75D (nominal 10D) VTL has been drawn in at the right edge of the chart and was crossed up immediately after the ostensible nest of lows at 105. Furthermore, prices have also cleared the mid-line of the cycle envelope putting it into a lower trade risk environment. The implication at this point is that the 13.5D cycle low is in.

27D VTL

A 27D cycle (nominal 40D) downward VTL has also been drawn (blue dashed line) and is set to be crossed up by price just above $17. This will confirm that the price low at 105 is that of the 54D (10W) cycle. Since we are 105 days past the last definite 20W cycle low, this must also be the next 20W trough.

FLDs

A 54D FLD (red line) has been plotted and projects $20, the upward price cross having been estimated at $18.5 and the recent price low being $16. A

20W (108D) FLD (olive line) has also been plotted and an upward price cross is estimated at around $20, projecting $24.

The underlying trend is clearly up, indicated by the following observations: our analysis of the weekly chart; the strong right translation of the 20W peak on the daily chart; the higher adjacent lows of the 20W cycle.

This means that both projections are very likely to overshoot, probably by a good margin. It also reassures us that the 54D FLD projection will clear the 20W FLD triggering it for the higher projection.

Risk

If we enter the trade on the 27D VTL break at $17.60, and we place a sell stop at $16, then we are running $1.60 capital risk (9.1%).

Our minimum price target is $24, or $6.40 (36%) higher. Our reward-to-risk ratio is therefore 4:1. This is good and our basic trade selection criteria (+20% and 3:1) has been exceeded.

Trade risk

When price has crossed the 27D VTL and triggers our buy signal we will be in the mid-band of the cycle envelope not only on the daily chart but also on the weekly chart. We therefore think the probability of being stopped out is low.

Cycle status

A phasing analysis has been conducted up to the 14 March 2003, just ahead of the VTL break and potential trade entry. The average period for each cycle has been calculated based upon the ten-day cycle.

The status report taken from a complete phasing model is shown in Table 7.1. The weekly data has been taken from Figure 7.2. From this table you can see that the direction of every cycle – except the nine-month, which is topping – as well as the underlying trend is up.

Table 7.1: Phasing model JPMorgan Chase, 14 March 2003

Date 14 March 2003				JPMorgan Chase (JPM)	
Nominal		Avg	Var.	Phase	Status
Trend					Up
54M	230W	297.6W	124%	22W	Up
18M	80W	99.2W	124%	22W	Up
9M	40W	49.6W	124%	22W	Topping
20W	20W	24.8W	124%	2D	Up
80D	55D	54D	102%	2D	Up
40D	28D	27D	104%	2D	Up
20D	14D	13.5D	104%	2D	Up
10D	7D	6.75D	104%	2D	Up

If someone dropped this spreadsheet onto your desk, you would definitely want to look at the chart and think about buying as soon as possible. Normally you would wait for some of the shorter cycles to bottom first, but with such a strong uptrend these are likely to be swamped and exhibit very little pullback.

Everything is now in place to enter the trade: we have defined risk; we have set a target and an entry price; there is a legitimate action signal; and the near-term and long-term cyclic picture is in our favour.

The upswing of the previous 20W cycle from low to high was 86% – out of which we managed to take only 8.5%. We will therefore choose the 20W as our trading cycle. If conditions change, then we can always drop back down to a lower cycle

Managing the trade: the first leg

Figure 7.5 shows the first 13.5D cycle out of the nest of lows. The 27D VTL (blue dashed line) has been crossed along with the 13.5D FLD (green). Immediately afterwards the 54D FLD (red) is also crossed activating the $20 price projection.

Prices advance quickly, as we would expect with a set-up of this quality. A price high is attained just under the first target, which is followed by a consolidation lasting seven sessions. Prices then gap up out of the congestion range breaking $20.

Breakout and higher low

The breakout leaves behind a higher low and we can assume that this completes the first 13.5D cycle (the nominal 20D). So far the trade has started well and we raise our stop to just under the latest cycle low – at $18.8. Since this new stop is above the initial entry point, we are now running no capital risk.

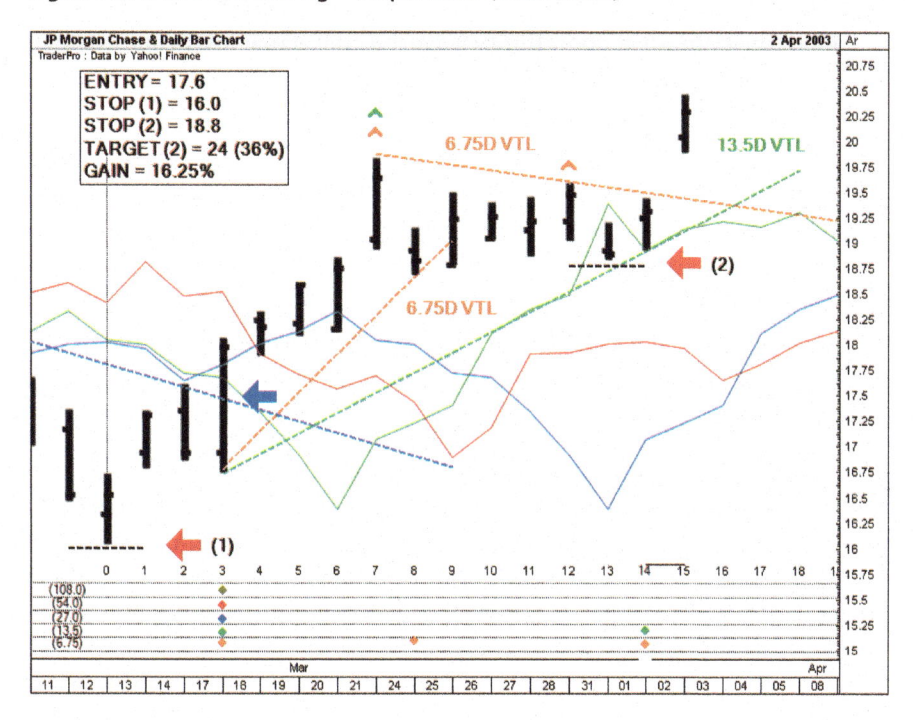

Figure 7.5: JPM trade: first leg – 2 April 2003 (Data: Yahoo)

Orthodox low versus actual low

Notice that the nest of lows at grid 3 has been shifted three bars to the right and is no longer the actual price low. If you look at Hurst's original charts you will often see that cycle lows are displaced right to the nearest higher low. At first glance this seems to be at odds with the Principle of Synchronicity, which tells us that all shorter cycle troughs should correspond to the long cycle trough. However, there is method here.

We have already seen how peaks are translated right or left depending on the direction of underlying trend. The same happens at cycle lows and troughs tend to be pushed to the right by a downtrend and pulled back to the left by an uptrend.

One reason to use the orthodox (displaced) low rather than the actual low is that it often allows you to draw in meaningful VTLs. For example, by moving the nest of lows to the right here, we are able to draw in a 6.75D VTL which then allows us to call the 13.5D peak at 7. Had we not done so, we would not have been able to connect the actual low with the first 6.75D low.

Some Hurst analysts adhere rigidly to the idea of displacing lows, while others are more relaxed. If an obvious VTL can be drawn by shifting the trough to the right, then do it. If not, leave it as the actual low. Your averages will not be dramatically affected.

VTLs and FLDs

As each new price bar comes in we draw tentative VTLs, which can then be confirmed or adjusted as new data reveals itself. By the time the 13.5D cycle breakout occurs we are able to draw in the 6.75D upward VTL from 3 to the next possible 6.75D cycle low at 8 – which confirms the cycle high – as well as a downward 6.75D VTL, the upside break of which calls the 13.5D low at 13. We are also able to draw in a 13.5D upward VTL which we will monitor for breaks going forward in the trade.

Note that the 13.5D (green) FLD forms a trough at 6 and a peak at 13. This was on the chart well before the trade was even entered and shows where the price cycle peak was likely to occur: namely around the same time as the FLD trough. Notice also that the price cycle peak is translated right of the FLD trough; confirmation, if you needed it, that the trend underlying the 13.5D cycle is up.

Trade monitoring

We have been able to use cycle analysis to confirm that the trade is currently on track and conforming to our expectations. And although we have been diligent, we have not been obsessive. Some traders like to monitor their trades all of the time, whereas others are more casual.

The first goal in a new trade should be to raise the stop as soon as possible and reduce or eliminate your capital risk. If you are hyper vigilant, however, you run the risk of becoming too busy and making unforced errors – like exiting the trade on a whim for example.

On the other hand if you are too relaxed, you can miss warning signs that market conditions are changing and that you should exit early. It is a balance that you just have to figure out for yourself.

Managing the trade: the second leg

When managing an open position, you need to be asking yourself: is the trade on track or has something changed? If something has changed where do I get out so that I limit my downside?

Without smothering the trade, or tying up your time needlessly, you need to keep an eye on cyclic conditions and confirm that they remain consistent with your analysis. If things are not going to plan, you need to have an exit strategy. Although this is the subject of another chapter, essentially it is all about maximising gains and minimising losses.

Figure 7.6 shows the trade to the end of its second leg up. After the breakout of the first leg up (the 13.5D cycle low), the first target of $20 was quickly exceeded. Prices continue to advance and a new higher low is put in at $20.54. This is nine bars after the last 13.75D cycle low, forcing the question: is this new low that of a long 10D cycle or a short 20D cycle?

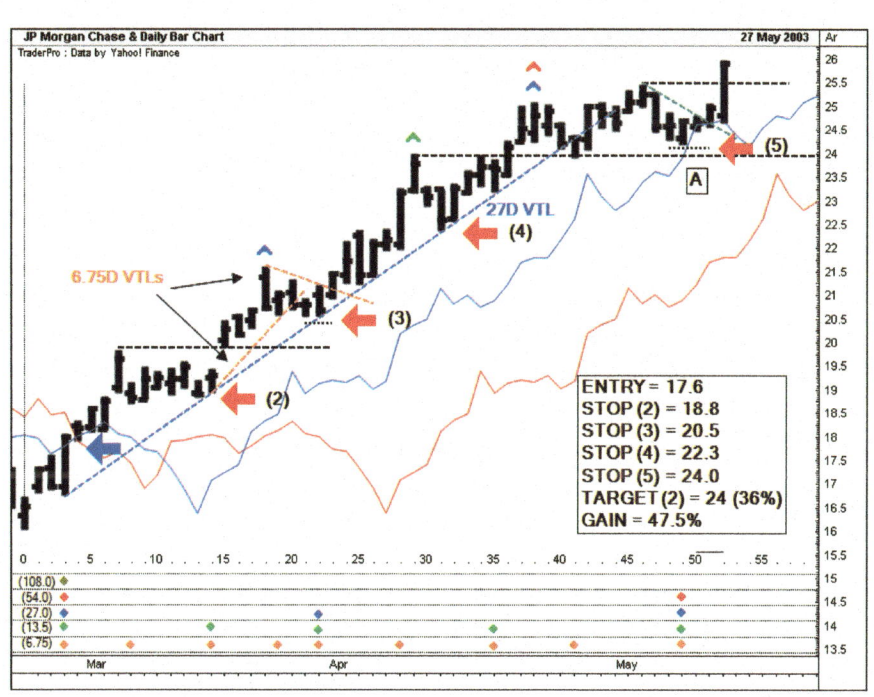

Figure 7.6: JPM trade: second leg – 27 May 2003 (Data: Yahoo)

The second 13.75-day cycle

The combination of a gap up earlier in the cycle, together with a sharp drop from the recent high, suggests that the cycle has probably been compressed. We therefore opt for 13.5D and provisionally place a green diamond at 22.

Two 6.75D VTLs have also been drawn in to pick out the cycle peak and trough. Furthermore, if the latest price low is a 13.5D cycle trough, then it is the second since the nest of lows and must be the 27D cycle low as well – albeit running short.

Once prices have pushed through the downward 6.75D VTL and a new minor high has been established we can raise our stop to just below the last cycle low, at $20.50. The evidence would suggest that we are now in the second 27D cycle of the first 54D cycle. The phasing analysis has been updated and our stop has been raised to a logical level protecting the lion's share of our gains.

The second 27-day cycle

Now that we have established the first 27D cycle low at 22, we can draw a VTL from the previous 27D trough within the nest of lows at 3. We can henceforth use this trendline to guide the trade up. When the VTL finally breaks, we will know that the most recent price high before the break is the 54D cycle peak. Since our trading cycle is 20 weeks, this will mark the end of the first upswing.

If the trend underlying the 20W cycle is still up, as we believe it will be, then the mid-cycle decline is likely to be shallow. The chances are we will not get shaken out of the trade, but we will need to stay alert. Also, because the uptrend is strong, the 54D peak is likely to be strongly translated to the right. It follows, therefore, that that the 54D cycle low will not be long coming. Our last stop (3) is placed at $20.50 and our upside target is $24, which we believe will be overshot.

First exit alert

Prices continue to put in higher lows and although the 27D VTL is broken at our $24 target, they then push higher. The break, however, is our first alert.

Price is still above the 27D FLD (blue line) but it is drawing near. The 27D FLD is also above and running parallel to the 54D FLD (red). The arrangement here is too spread out to be a classic cascade pattern, but it is a warning. If the resistance-support level (A) drawn through the most recent price low breaks, then we could easily see the 27D FLD go. And if that goes it will project down through the 54D FLD, giving an ultimate price projection of $20.

We therefore raise our stop to $22.3 (4) and watch. Price then puts in a higher low which we take to be the 54D cycle low. Once price breaks through the most recent high confirming the uptrend, we raise the stop again to $24 (5).

Managing the trade: the final leg

The last stop was placed at $24 and the 54D FLD target has been overshot. We assumed that this would be the case because of the influence of underlying trend.

From the weekly chart we know that there is still an outstanding 18M (91W) FLD upside projection of $36, but to achieve this we would need to switch up from a 20W trading cycle to a 40W, which we cannot do. If we want to go higher, then we need to exit this trade first and set up the next properly.

Exit signal

We know that we are now in the second 54D cycle of the second 20W cycle out of a big nest of lows back in October 2002. We also know that we will probably be forced out of the trade after this 20W cycle peaks. The signal for this is a break of the 54D upward VTL.

Since we now have two 54D cycle lows to connect, we draw this line in and extrapolate it forward. We estimate that if price was to cross down through this VTL, it would do so at around 28. This would therefore be taken as a signal to exit the trade for now.

Figure 7.7 shows the complete trade with the final leg annotated. Notice that a 13.5D upward VTL has also been drawn in at the right edge of the chart. The job of short VTLs at this stage is to stalk the exit. This is exactly the same process as using VTLs to enter the trade, but in reverse. In this example we have just run the trade right through the 54D VTL break.

In order to tighten up the exit, all you need to do is keep drawing in shorter upward sloping VTLs until finally the shortest is broken and the trade is exited. This will mean that you do not leave money on the table, so to speak. The method of covering shorts is identical to that of entering long positions.

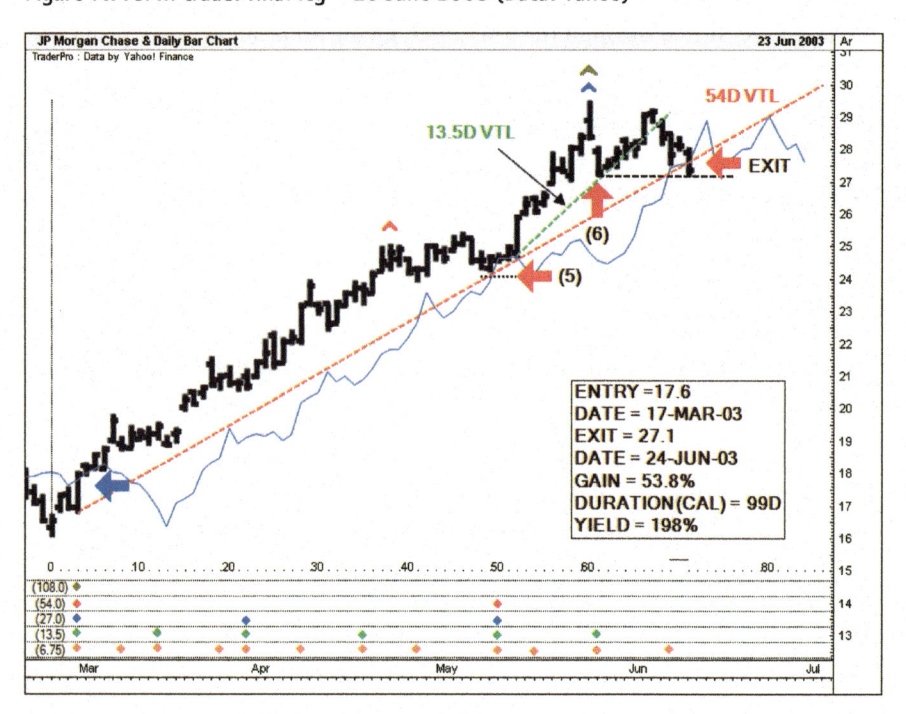

Figure 7.7: JPM trade: final leg – 26 June 2003 (Data: Yahoo)

Debrief

The trade was entered at $17.6 and we were stopped just below the last 20W cycle low at $27.1. This corresponded to a break in the 54D VTL, which signalled that the 20W cycle had peaked and would likely need to retrace before heading up again. The total duration of the trade was 99 calendar days and the total gain was 53.8%, giving an annual yield of 198%.

Through most of the trade we were running no capital risk and we were using cyclic tools to keep us on track, protect gains and consider exit points. Managing a trade like this takes more time and effort, but it is worth it. Another thing to remember is that the trade was well set up. Get that right and the rest usually follows. It is a bit like hiring a new trader. If you select only stars, then you do not need to micro-manage them into the ground to get results.

Figure 7.8 shows the trade in its wider context. The 18M cycle finally topped out at $36.47 on 5 March 2004. We ended up missing the last leg up of the trade, but that could have been avoided with a more sophisticated exit strategy.

Notice the 18M FLD which we drew in on the weekly chart way back in 2002. The estimate for an FLD cross at $25 was made even then giving us a $36 projection out of the big nest of lows just below $12 in October 2002. That it has been met so precisely over that time span alone should persuade you that Hurst analysis offers something that other systems do not.

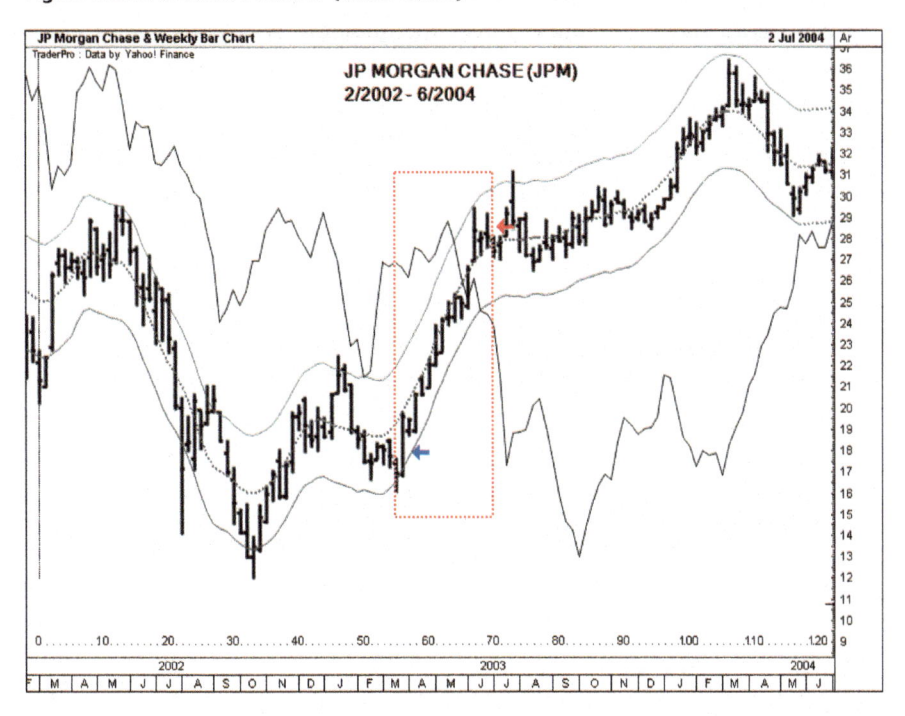

Figure 7.8: JPM trade overview (Data: Yahoo)

Had your investment strategy allowed you to take a 16% drawdown, you could have just stayed with the 18M cycle all the way to the highs. But bear in mind that your equity would have sat more or less idle for six months before prices eventually made the $36 peak. In fact had you stayed the course your yield for the whole period would only have been 104% versus the 198% made trading the 20W cycle.

Conclusion

You have seen that cycle analysis does not end with the set up and entry but is used throughout the trade. Tracking the trade using the tools you have learnt so far lets you know where you are at any given time, how much more upside there is and when you are wrong. However, the truth is that a correctly chosen moving average would have done just as good a job getting you in and out of the last trade. Which of course forces the question: why bother with Hurst analysis when you can just throw an MA onto the chart? You can buy when price crosses up through the MA and sell when it crosses down.

The last JPM example was a straightforward case to help you understand the concept of trade management using Hurst analysis more easily. A straight comparison with an MA price crossover system is therefore easier to make. What you will find, however, is that the simple MA price crossover system only works some of the time, i.e. when the market is trending. The rest of the time it is chewing your equity up with whipsaws. Hurst is a fully integrated system that uses multiple tools. It tells you when the odds are stacked in your favour and when they are against you. It gets you in early and out early. It allows you to compare one trade to another before you even commit capital. It takes work of course, but that is the business we are in.

You have now seen a few more examples of trade entry and have been reminded that you need to set the trade up properly before you get involved. If there is contradictory evidence, then eliminate it before you trade or move on. You have also been shown how to manage a trade by winging it and how to put in the work and get it right.

Endnotes

[60] 31.5. (47.8 - 31.5) = 15.2

[61] Count the number of spaces in-between 10W (red) diamonds = 9. Subtract the number of the first 10W diamond from number of last 10W diamond = (103 - 0). Divide the first value into second = 11.4.

[62] Spike low = 14. (25 - 14) + 25 = 36.

8 RSI AND ELLIOTT WAVE

Introduction

This chapter explores ways of combining two other technical methodologies with Hurst cycle analysis: momentum, in the shape of the Relative Strength Index (RSI) and Elliott Wave principle. While it is by no means an exhaustive treatment, you will see that these three disciplines have a lot in common and are mutually supportive. You will also be introduced to ideas that will help you significantly increase the speed and accuracy of your cycles work.

RSI is examined first and a summary of the basics is presented. You will learn how to work out the speed of a price move and see how this is applicable to cycle analysis. Momentum leads price and knowing where you are in the velocity and acceleration cycles will help you know when your analysis is on track or going astray. On its own, basic momentum has some drawbacks and we will consider these before going on look at how RSI is constructed and why it is a superior measure.

Many readers will have used RSI or at least be familiar with its use. We are going to look at some advanced concepts drawing on the work of a recognised authority in this area. You will be shown how to use these techniques to confirm cycle peaks and troughs, project future cycle legs and identify the direction of underlying trend.

Elliott Wave will be covered in as much detail as this book permits, but it is a big subject and so this discussion should be viewed as a primer. Nevertheless, it should quickly become apparent that cycle analysis and Elliott wave share many common characteristics and fit together well. A good

Elliottician will benefit from knowledge of Hurst's methods and a Hurst cycle analyst who knows the Wave principle will find his or her insight greatly enhanced. You will be introduced to the basic Elliott patterns and rules and their underlying logic will be examined.

One of the best ways to learn is to study real examples. Two case studies in Gold and the Euro will therefore be analysed using all three approaches: Hurst, RSI and Elliott. After quickly setting the scene in terms of news and fundamentals at the time of analysis, the cyclic state will be examined using Hurst's methods and the conclusions will be tested using RSI and Elliott Wave. Although the studies presented are mainly on the weekly chart, these techniques can be employed at any timeframe and for any freely traded financial instrument.

By the end of this chapter, you should understand how RSI works and be familiar with some more sophisticated techniques. You should be able to apply these to cycles and significantly sharpen up your analysis. As for Elliott Wave, it cannot be mastered in a few pages, but the following discussion should allow you to grasp the essentials and hopefully inspire you to take it further. Having said that, you should gain enough knowledge from this chapter to help you be able to recognise wave form and immediately identify underlying trend. You should also get a good sense for market rhythm and its benefit to cycle projections.

RSI and Elliott Wave – the Basics

RSI

The Relative Strength Index was developed by Welles Wilder back in the 1970s[63] and is a measure of momentum. Although, most readers should be familiar with RSI, not all will know how to get the most out of it. As an auxiliary tool in cycle analysis RSI can be invaluable and you owe it to yourself to master the techniques. We are going to look at how RSI is constructed and then consider some advanced techniques. Before we do so, however, let us quickly review the concept of momentum.

Momentum

Momentum in market analysis is velocity or rate of change of prices per unit of time. It should not be confused with momentum in physics – inertia – which is mass multiplied by velocity. A ten-day momentum indicator, for example, is simply the closing price[64] ten days ago – C(10) – subtracted from the close today – C(0) – given by:

```
M = C(0) - C (10)
```

or in percentage terms:

```
M% = 100 x (C(0) - C(10) / C(10)
```

Thus, if the price ten days ago is 100p and the price today is 120p, then the ten-day momentum is 20 or 2p per day (or normalised, 20% or 0.2% per day). A line drawn between these two prices will therefore point up.

Conversely, if the price ten days ago is 100 and the price today is 90, then the ten-day momentum is -10 or -1p per day. A line drawn between the two prices will therefore point down. The slope of the momentum line in either case is proportional to the speed of the price move. A horizontal line indicates zero velocity and it follows that the steeper the line, the faster the move.

First and second derivatives

You learnt in chapter one that the rate of change of a cycle is highest mid-way between peak and trough in either direction and slowest at the actual peak and trough. This is the same for *all* cycles regardless of their magnitude.

Figure 8.1 shows three ideal sine waves which, from top to bottom, describe: the basic price cycle; the momentum or velocity of the cycle; and the acceleration.[65] Velocity is defined as the first derivative of price and acceleration as the second derivative of price.

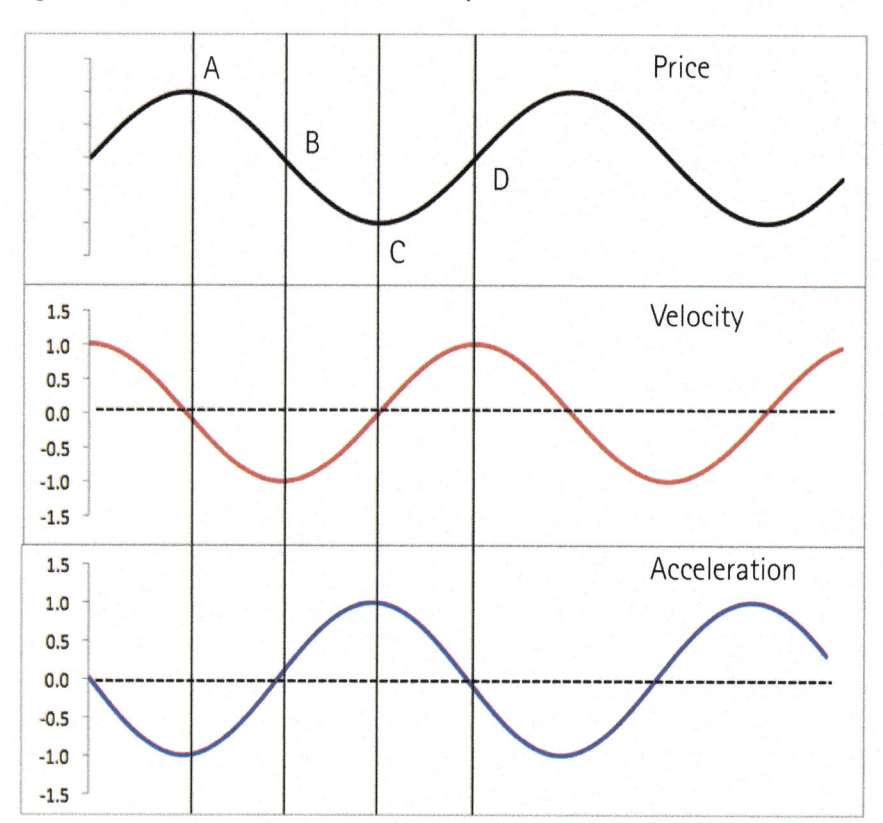

Figure 8.1: The first and second derivatives of price

- At point A the cycle is topping and the slope of the cycle is horizontal. Velocity is zero and acceleration is at its maximum (i.e. the furthest point below the dashed zero line).
- At point B the cycle is halfway down and the slope is steepest. Velocity is at its maximum (i.e. furthest away from the zero line) and acceleration is zero.
- At point C the process reverses, the cycle is bottoming and the slope is horizontal. Velocity is zero and acceleration is at its maximum (i.e. the furthest point above the dashed zero line).
- At point D the cycle is halfway up and the slope is again steepest. Velocity is at its maximum and acceleration is zero.

Also observe the phase relationship between these three sine waves. The velocity cycle is displaced one quarter of a cycle back and therefore leads the price cycle. Thus when momentum peaks, we know that theoretically the price high will occur one quarter cycle period later.

The acceleration cycle on the other hand is displaced back a full half cycle, which means that when acceleration peaks we know that the maximum velocity will be experienced one quarter cycle later. This of course is the basis for momentum of momentum (M²) indicators[66].

Wilder's adaptation

There are a number of problems associated with using momentum in its basic form. The first is the drop-off effect. As the most recent price data comes in, the first price falls out of the equation and the next price along becomes the first price, in much the same way as we see in simple moving averages. If the difference between these two signals is large, then the momentum reading is distorted. What is needed therefore is a more representative value for price change over the sample period, i.e. one that does not suffer from data drop off.

RSI formula

Wilder achieved this by comparing the total price gains of all of the up days in the calculation period to the total price declines of all of the down days. This relative strength value is then smoothed with a variation of the Exponential Moving Average: the Wilder MA[67]. The result is that the momentum calculation is more illustrative of the entire period and the problem of data distortion is solved. Thus, over a 14-day period relative strength (RS) is given by:

```
RS = average 14D up closes / average 14D down closes
```

The second problem is that when using a standard momentum indicator it is difficult to say how high is too high and how low is too low. In order to provide context and allow comparison, the signal needs to be normalised or converted into an index. The formula for the index of relative strength is therefore given by:

```
RSI = 100 - [100 / (1 + RS)]
```

Thus, RSI is bounded by a range of 0 to 100 (or if you like it is expressed as a percentage), which allows direct comparisons in RSI values to be made. For example if the RSI value is 50, you know that the average sum of price gains and losses over the period is balanced out. If RSI is at 70, then there has been a greater net price gain and positive momentum is high. If RSI is at 20, then there has been a greater net price decline and negative momentum is high.

Conventionally, RSI values above 70 are said to show an overbought market and RSI values below 30 are said to show an oversold market. Unfortunately this rather crude measure is inherently fallacious. We will be covering some more robust techniques using RSI shortly, however one last point needs to be looked at first and that is the calculation timeframe.

RSI period

Some analysts believe that the length of a momentum indicator – the calculation or lookback period – whether it is RSI, MACD, Stochastics or whatever, needs to be calibrated to the period of the cycle under observation. They argue that because market conditions change, a fixed length, one-size-fits-all approach is flawed. Thus, they argue, if you want to measure the momentum of, say, a 40-day cycle, the indicator needs to be set at half that period, or 20 days, to capture the full amplitude of the up and down swings. Others think that the length of the indicator should be no more than a quarter of the cycle, in this case ten days.

While it is true that variation affects the period and amplitude of cycles there is no particular need to constantly adapt your momentum indicators. It can be done, although automating it to, say, a spectral analysis tool is fiendishly difficult. It also misses a trick.

The common default setting for RSI is 14 periods, which was found to be optimum in Wilder's original testing. If you superimpose a 14D RSI onto, say, a 40D RSI you will find that although the long RSI is somewhat muted, the overall form is largely the same. The increased granularity of the 14 RSI, however, provides vital information about the shorter cycles. Because these are the components of the longer cycles, it is information that you do not want to throw away.

Thus, although the 14D RSI is less smooth than a longer RSI, the cycle information does not materially change and more useful detail is provided. This will become clearer when we look in detail at more advanced techniques.

Advanced techniques

RSI is often misused and its true potential is obscure to many traders and analysts. Most use RSI to simply look for overbought and oversold conditions or divergences. And mostly they misinterpret the signals they think they are being given. A leading authority on RSI is Andrew Cardwell[68], who has taken Wilder's original ideas to the next level and beyond. Cardwell has been working with RSI since 1978, originally doing everything by hand. He currently operates as a consultant.

Cardwell provided valuable advice for this chapter. Some of the methods he teaches, including; range rules, divergences and positive/negative reversal patterns for setting price objectives will be explained in some detail in the two case studies that we will cover in this chapter. Range Rules, for example, will be shown to be much more valuable in identifying the trend through the shift in RSI range. Divergences are just an overextension of the current move and actually signal a detour from the primary trend. You will find that these methods fit in extremely well with cycles work and help isolate trend change as well as forecast future price targets.

If you want to learn the basics of RSI, pick up Wilder's original work. If you are serious enough to want to really understand RSI, then Cardwell is your man.

Elliott Wave

Brief overview

The Wave principle discovered by R.N. Elliott in the 1930s is an approach to market analysis predicated on the idea that prices trend and reverse in observable patterns of growth and decay. These patterns are self-similar at all degrees of magnitude – fractal – and the same form and construction seen in price moves lasting decades can also be seen at the intraday level. As such Elliott Wave is an overarching description of market behaviour.

The world's premier exponent of Elliott Wave Theory is Robert Prechter CMT[69], who has been kind enough to allow the use of some of his teaching material. Although it is nowhere near as difficult as some people think, time and effort are required to master Elliott Wave. A solid understanding can be of great benefit to the Hurst analyst, as will be demonstrated in the case studies. Although a full and detailed description of all the patterns described by the Wave principle is beyond the scope of this book, the basic principles are straightforward enough.

Motive and corrective waves

For those unfamiliar with the Elliott Wave principle, it can seem arcane and complicated. However, it is not a convoluted theory plucked out of the air, but rather a description of how the market works based on observation. You need only know a handful of simple rules and guidelines to gain the basics. Once you have grasped their underlying logic, all that is then required is for you to hone your judgment. And that comes with exposure and practice.

The two basic wave modes described by the Wave principle are *motive* and *corrective*. Motive waves break down into five sub-waves and unfold in the same direction as the underlying trend (in Elliott terms the direction of the wave of next higher degree; in Hurst terms the sum of all longer cycles). Corrective waves, meanwhile, break down into three waves, or combinations thereof, and unfold in a counter-trend direction.

Impulses

The most frequently occurring motive wave is an impulse and as the name suggests it moves quickly and freely. It consists of three five-wave moves in the same direction as the overall move and two three-wave moves against (5-3-5-3-5). An impulse can either be going up or down, depending on the direction of the wave of next higher degree. Figure 8.2 shows the basic pattern.

Figure 8.2: The five subdivisions of an impulse motive wave[70]

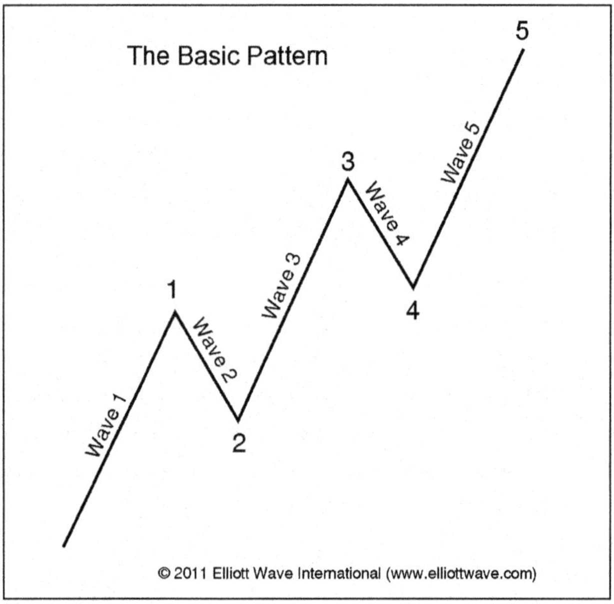

The rules governing impulse motive waves are as follows:
- Wave two cannot exceed the beginning of wave one. Thus in an uptrend, wave two cannot drop below the start of the move (above the start in a downtrend).

- Wave three cannot be the shortest wave, and although it does not need to be the longest, it often is.
- Wave four cannot enter the price territory of wave one: in other words there can be no overlap.

It makes sense to expect prices to flow more freely in the direction of underlying trend and more tentatively across the flow, as we have seen already in cycle analysis. This is why in an impulse move there is no overlap between waves four and one: there is too much pro-trend momentum. It is also why wave three cannot be the shortest.

Remember that in cycle terms wave three is halfway along the cycle, either up or down, and at the fastest part of the move. In fact it is not at all uncommon to see a continuation price gap in the middle of wave three. Prechter calls this the Point of Recognition, and it marks the point where the focus shifts away from the last trough (or peak) to the next peak (or trough), depending on which direction the cycle is going. In crude sentiment terms, in an uptrend this is where the crowd believes that the prices will go up forever; and in a downtrend it is where they believe they are doomed.

Corrective waves

There are number of different types of corrective waves and they take more skill to navigate. Except for triangles, there is always at least one five-wave impulse in the correction and the last leg always subdivides into five. Corrective waves can be described 5-3-5, 3-3-5 or 3-3-3-3-3, or any combination thereof. Although there can be structural differences, all corrective waves adhere to the basic three sub-wave form and all retrace the previous motive wave to a lesser or greater degree.

Figure 8.3 shows a common zigzag corrective wave and again this can either point up or down depending on the direction of the next wave higher. The other patterns include the Double and Triple Zigzag, Flat, Expanded Flat, Triangle and Combination, and are shown in Appendix 1.

Figure 8.3: A common corrective wave: the zigzag

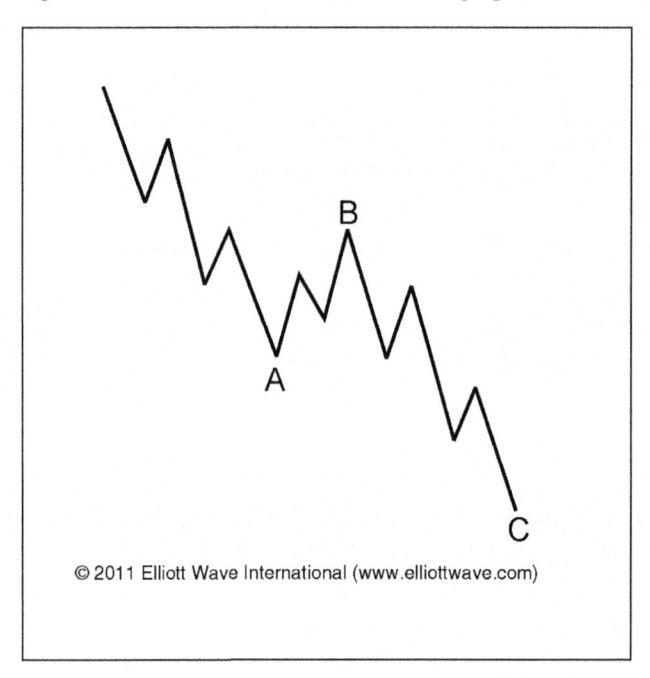

Because the direction of the next higher degree wave opposes the direction of the corrective wave, it is unable to develop into the full five waves. The counter trend force is also responsible for the overlap and generally more jagged appearance we tend to see in corrective waves. Although it is easier to identify and trade impulses, if any of the rules are broken, you immediately know the direction of underlying trend and that you are looking at a correction. This is extremely useful information to bring to your Hurst cycle analysis.

Markets move rhythmically and corrective waves tend to be proportional to the motive waves that spawned them. There are a number of guidelines on how far corrective waves should retrace and most are based upon so called Fibonacci ratios. Some of these will be described in the two case studies. Elliott targets corresponding to Hurst cycles targets should be taken as supporting evidence.

Plenty has already been written on the subject of Fibonacci and so the ideas will not be developed any further here, but Prechter is probably the best source. In brief, it is not uncommon to find that corrective waves retrace the preceding impulse move by 38%, 50%, 62% or 76%. Fibonacci ratios can also be applied to projections, often with better results and it is not uncommon to see the first leg of a move extending by 100%, 161% or 261%.

None of this is written in stone, but it is what we tend to see. The market is constantly seeking balance and as we have seen in Hurst, there is a strong theme of proportionality. Knowing what the higher probability outcomes are for corrections and extensions alike can be successfully applied to your Hurst cycle analysis.

Elliott Wave and cycles

The basic premise of Elliott Wave is that the market develops in a series of waves as part of a much, much longer five-wave pattern. The primitive structure being, as we have seen: three steps forward and two back. Each wave in the structure is related and one inexorably leads to the other. At any given time, therefore, the market is somewhere within this grand expansion and contraction, which Elliotticians regard as being primordial in nature. In fact Elliott's final publication in 1946 was rather ambitiously titled: *Nature's Law – The Secret of the Universe.*

Like Hurst analysis, the purpose of Elliott Wave is to locate price somewhere within a large set of interacting component cycles: from very short to very long. In this way a market analyst using either approach to navigate the market is rather like a sailor using latitude and longitude to cross an ocean.

It could well be that the natural laws of progress and regress governing markets are those discovered by Elliott rather than the slightly more mechanistic cycles approach. However, the two disciplines are by no means incompatible. Prechter has suggested that the Wave principle can probably explain the phenomenon of cyclic variation.

We have seen that average cycle periods tend to compress going into peaks or troughs. We have also seen how they tend to expand as the cycle gets under way. This is consistent with the form we see in impulse waves one, three and five: shorter durations in one and five – if there is equality – and longer in three. More research is needed here, but it is beyond the scope of this book for now.

Inherent consistency

Harmonicity can also be explained by looking at Elliott waves in sets. Figure 8.4 shows waves one and two: an impulse followed by a correction. A Hurst analyst would see one full cycle here with two harmonic subdivisions and each of these breaking down into a further two subdivisions. The higher lows would also suggest that the sum of all longer cycles, Hurst's $\sum L$, was up.

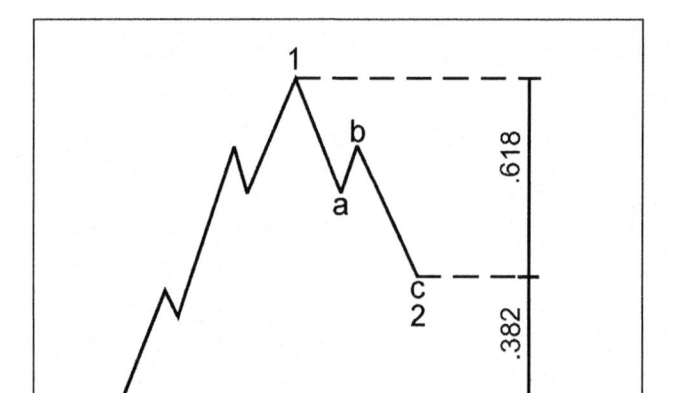

Figure 8.4: Full cycle with higher low showing common 62% retracement

Elliott Wave practitioners would identify eight cycles here counting the upswings and downswings separately: thus waves (1) and (2) consisting of waves 1, 2, 3, 4, 5, a, b, c. Hurst analysts on the other hand would group them together, thus: the first full cycle harmonic (1) + (2); the first cycle of the second harmonic being wave one through wave four; the second cycle of the second harmonic being wave four through (2) where it completes the full cycle.

Formulating market structure

The similarities in the two approaches can be also seen in the way that market structure is described. For example, a cycle analyst might say something like this: the market is currently one week along a seven-week cycle corresponding to the nominal ten-week, and is heading up. This is the first in a 15-week cycle, which is also advancing and this 15-week cycle is the second in a 30-week cycle which headed down. The 30-week cycle is the second in a 60-week cycle corresponding to the nominal 18-month and is also headed down. The underlying trend, which is to say the sum of all cycles longer than the 18-month, is bottoming.

Next time a client asks for your view on the market, say something like this and see if they suddenly remember an urgent meeting they need to attend. It's quite cumbersome and it is the reason it is better to just show a phased chart with a status guide.

An Elliottician on the other hand might say something along these lines: the market is currently in Minute wave three down of Minor wave A up of

Intermediate wave (Y) down of Primary degree wave four down of Cycle degree three up, and so on. It would even be possible to keep this going right down to micro degree to describe what happened in the last five minutes and right up to Grand Supercycle degree to show the move in the context of the last hundred years. It's a little less convoluted than Hurst, although it would still seem forbidding to the uninitiated.

In the two case studies that follow we will look at Gold and the Euro from the perspective of all three methodologies: Hurst cycle analysis, RSI studies and Elliott Wave. The usefulness of this multi-disciplinary approach should quickly become apparent. I am especially indebted to Jeffrey Kennedy[71] at Elliott Wave International for casting a critical eye over my Elliott labelling and for his tuition. Kennedy is an experienced Elliottician and a first class technical analyst and his advice is always worth listening to.

Case Study I: Gold, November 2008

On 17 March 2008 Gold very briefly pushed through what was considered an important psychological level of $1000, however it failed to hold and quickly retreated. This was the day after Bear Stearns was sold to JPMorgan Chase at $2 a share.

Some commentators regarded $1000 as ludicrously over-priced, but with the S&P 500 down 300 points from its October high others were making a fundamental bull case for Gold as an alternative asset class. Bernanke's *credit easing*, as it was known then, was also wheeled out as pro-inflationary and therefore viewed by some as a potential prop for Gold. However, the rally never came and by the time Lehman Brothers had filed for bankruptcy on 15 September, Gold had fallen a further $350.

The story was the same across every other major asset class and many were now staring into what they thought must be a low liquidity, disinflationary abyss. One popular view at the time was that Gold would keep falling. So let us see what insights a market analyst combining Hurst, RSI and Elliott would have gained.

Hurst analysis

Figure 8.5 shows a phasing analysis conducted on the weekly chart for Gold on 21 November 2008. The price low at grid 152 is a possible candidate for an 18-month and possibly even a 54-month cycle low, so diamonds have been tentatively placed.

All of the charts in this chapter can be downloaded from: vectisma.com/downloads/rsielliott.

The 18M cycle appears to be running short at approximately 60 weeks and an FLD corresponding to this period has been plotted. There is a price intersection of this 18M FLD at grid 140 which yields a downside projection of $680. This is met exactly at grid 152 implying that the underlying trend is flat. With no underlying downtrend and a 54-month cycle possibly having just started up, Gold appears to be set up for a long advance.

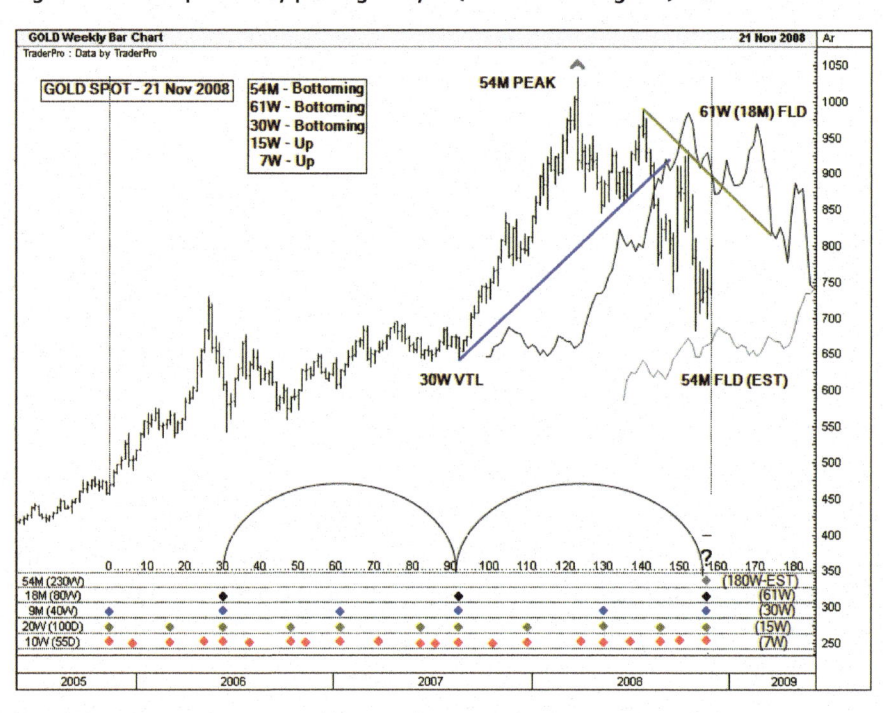

Figure 8.5: Gold spot weekly phasing analysis (Data: Bloomberg LLC)

Alternate view

On the other hand it could be the case that instead of having just completed a 54M cycle, prices have just entered the third and final 18M cycle of a 54M set. This would imply that the next 18M and 54M cycle low occurs some 60 weeks later and that would come in well below the recent trough. Additionally, an estimated 54M FLD is rising in future time just below the recent price action. Were this to be crossed by prices to the downside, a significantly lower price projection would be generated.

Only four weeks have passed since the price low at grid 152. A 10W VTL could have just been crossed (not shown), but since this would have been an edge-band alert right after a major nest of lows, the trade risk would have been too high to act upon. Ideally we would need to see a downward 20W VTL to break around the 800 level for confirmation that the 40W cycle (and by extension all longer cycles) was in place and that risk was firmly to the upside. At this point we could either drop down to the daily chart to gather more evidence or wait.

We could also switch our focus to cycle momentum to see if any further clues are being offered there.

RSI analysis

A weekly RSI analysis is shown in Figure 8.6. The RSI is set at 14 weeks and horizontal levels have been drawn in at 40, 50, 60 and 80. Two moving averages have also been applied to the RSI: a 9 SMA (red) and 45 EMA (blue). To help us build up the momentum picture, four of Cardwell's techniques are going to be shown: the Positive Reversal; Range Rules; Bearish Divergence and Bullish Divergence.

The first thing to notice in the chart is that the RSI cycle is leading the price cycle and is peaking and bottoming first. RSI is a measure of cycle speed and, as we saw in Figure 10.1, the RSI puts its highest reading when the price cycle is halfway up. By the time the price cycle peaks, RSI has already rolled over giving us the Bearish Divergence at point z. At the other end, as the price cycle approaches the ostensible trough, RSI starts turning up ahead of price giving us a Bullish Divergence signal.

Figure 8.6: Gold spot with weekly RSI (Data: Bloomberg LLC)

Positive Reversal

The first pattern we are going to look at is the Positive Reversal. This occurs when RSI declines and puts in a lower low, but at the same time prices decline into a higher low. This lower low of course is the basis for the intervening trendline. It indicates that the market is overextended to the downside and when the pattern completes, forewarns a reversal. In August 2007, RSI put in a low at 50 marked x, which corresponded to a price low at $657 – also marked x. Twelve months later a lower low in RSI occurred at 35 – marked y – but the corresponding price low at $787 was higher than the first by $130. The top of the pattern is the 18M price cycle high at $919 marked z.

The Positive Reversal tells us that at the second price low, downside momentum is unable to push prices any lower and that the cycle is effectively sold out and further downside is limited. It is also an indication therefore that the underlying trend is up, i.e. working against the move and that we can expect a price reversal with a magnitude proportional to the pattern as soon as momentum has fully unwound. This confirms the view that the price low at $682 could mark the 18M cycle nest of lows and can therefore be taken as supporting evidence for this view.

Typically a first RSI low does not signal the actual price low as there is usually enough built-in downside momentum to keep prices falling for a while longer. However, it does suggest that the end is at hand. When the price cycle does turn up, we should also be able to predict how far the first leg will advance by looking at the dimensions of the positive reversal pattern.

Projection formula

The greater the difference in closing price between x and y, and the higher the intervening cycle high z, the stronger the pattern. The following formula is used:

- The closing price associated with the higher RSI low (x) is subtracted from the closing price associated with the lower RSI low (y) and the difference is added to the intervening price high (z).

- Thus (y – x) + z, gives (787 – 657) + 919 = $1049.

Looking back to the cycle analysis it is clear that if prices did go as high as $1049 then they would have convincingly crossed up through the 18M FLD, let us say at around $950. This FLD cross would imply not only that the low at $682 was the trough of the next higher cycle – namely the 54-month – but also that a projection could be made to $1218[72]. Furthermore, once a positive reversal target has been cleared, it strongly tends to act as support for prices thereafter implying a new higher base to build upon. This level therefore can be expected to support the first cycle lows out of the big nest of lows.

RSI range rules

The positive reversal pattern's message is further strengthened by RSI's failure to break much below the 40 level. What we see here is RSI dropping through 40, but holding just beneath it. There are three successive tests lower but the downside break does not come. Because the third low is slightly higher than the first (36.28 versus 35.80) it suggests downside momentum is waning. RSI then breaks out above 40 giving an early signal that downside momentum may have unwound and that market conditions have changed, i.e. the 18M cycle has troughed.

RSI then goes on to clear not only the 40 level, but also the RSI 9 week SMA and a downtrend resistance line. Furthermore, at no point does the less sensitive and therefore more representative 9 SMA fall below 40. Taken together all of this is highly suggestive that the decline from the 2008 peak is exhausted.

Bull and bear ranges

There is a very strong tendency in an uptrend for RSI to find support at or in the vicinity of the 40 and the area between the 40-80 levels is referred to as the bull range. Thus, when the price cycle is advancing, retracements will not push RSI much below 40, but rallies will not push it much above 80. Conversely, when the price cycle is declining, corrective rallies will not push RSI much above 60, but neither will sell offs push RSI much below 20 (the lower extent of the 20-60 bear range).

In this case the inability of RSI to penetrate much below 40 and then to find support there indicates that the correction from the March 2008 high is just that: a correction, revealing the presence of an underlying uptrend. Had there been further downside pressure on prices, the RSI would have just carried on falling to the lower edge of the bear range.

Bearish Divergence

As Gold's weekly RSI overextended to just above 82 in early November 2007, price is given the blast off it needs for another leg higher. This is why it is dangerous to take the first RSI high as overbought, because it means exactly the opposite: it is a thrust that typically forces prices higher.

As we just discussed, however, once the price cycle starts heading into the peak RSI starts to fall back. Eventually the cycle runs out of steam and peaks. RSI then typically drops below 60 and refreshes ready for next push higher. It is not until RSI fails to retake the 60 level that we know that the price highs will not be revisited in that cycle. The sequence we often see therefore is: RSI peak, cycle peak, RSI divergence, followed by failure of the 60 level. When you see this, the cycle has peaked. Often this will correspond to a VTL break for additional confirmation.

Neutralising divergences

Another compelling reason to believe that the broader uptrend has not reversed is that the bearish divergence of March is negated by the positive reversal at point y. We then immediately see a double Bullish Divergence at the bottom of the move at the end of October. As prices continue to put in lower lows the RSI, as we have already seen, starts to put in higher lows just below the 40 level. This is exactly the same as Bearish Divergence at the top, just in reverse. The key thing to notice here is how tight these patterns are; no more than six bars wide. Generally speaking the tighter the pattern, the more powerful is the move out. Adding further conviction that a very strong move is building, is the fact that the cycle low here is supported at the same price level where it found resistance at the start of the pattern – highlighted by the blue horizontal (B).

Were prices going to push much lower, forcing us to reconsider our thesis that a 54M low was in place, we would not have seen this Bullish Divergence and we would have had to assume downside momentum was still building. Coming out of the actual cycle low, RSI and price start moving up together – i.e. they are said to be in gear – and the year-long positive reversal is now free to drive prices up to the first target.

The cycle analyst who knew RSI, therefore, would have had a lot more supporting evidence that the decline from March 2008 into the $682 price low in late October was a correction within a broader uptrend and that prices were in the process of reversing. This would have put him or her on the alert for a long-entry action signal.

Elliott Wave Analysis

Figure 8.7 is an Elliott wave analysis of the same weekly Gold chart. The March 2008 has been labelled wave three and the decline into the late October low has been labelled wave four – both of these waves are at primary degree[73]. If this count is correct and if wave four down is complete, then we are now looking for a final long leg up in a five-wave impulse wave at cycle degree.

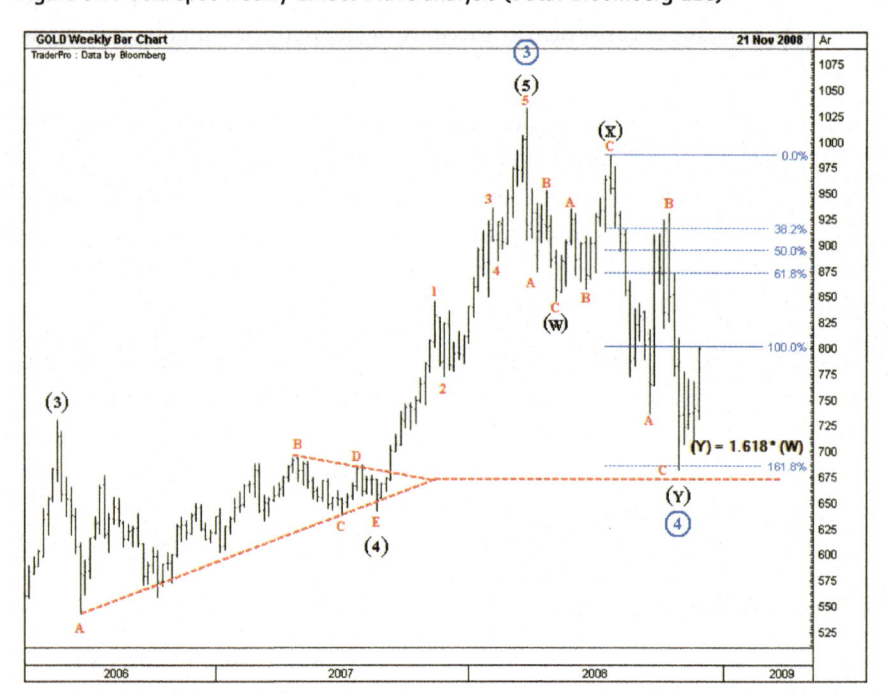

Figure 8.7: Gold spot weekly Elliott Wave analysis (Data: Bloomberg LLC)

Impulse wave

The termination of the triangle at intermediate degree labelled (4) corresponds to the last 18M trough at grid 90 on the cycle analysis chart. The subsequent advance then subdivides into five separate waves at minor degree (one below intermediate) – three up, two down – and respects Elliott's rules and guidelines[74]: wave two does not fall below the start of wave one; wave three is not the shortest; and wave four does not enter the price territory of wave one. Furthermore, the guideline of alternation is observed and we see wave two as being sharp whereas wave four is shallow. It is therefore a motive impulse wave, which means unequivocally that the direction of the next higher degree wave in this period is up.

Applying Elliott's rules and guidelines to an analysis of the daily chart would have made it possible to call the top quite precisely from around $900 – at the end of minor wave four. Cycle analysis on the other hand only confirmed this well after it had turned. The Elliottician who knew cycles therefore would have been able to identify this as the 18M peak and, therefore, even at this early stage, using Hurst analysis would have been able to estimate the next cycle low as being some 30 weeks away.

Corrective wave

Moving forward to the recent putative 18M cycle low, an Elliottician would have had no doubt whatsoever that the underlying trend was still up simply by looking at the way the price move down had unfolded. As we have seen, whereas impulse waves flow freely in the same direction as underlying trend, when the tide is in their favour so to speak, the opposite is true for corrective waves.

Zigzag

Prices here describe a WXY double zigzag and the movement is jagged and overlapping rather than free running. In Elliott terms, not only does it break the rules, but it also does not have the right look for an impulsive move. The final leg down (Y) deeply overlaps the first wave (X) and this can only happen in a corrective move where the underlying trend is in opposition. We therefore know that there has to be a resumption of the uptrend at some point. However, there is also a high probability that the correction has just ended.

Termination guideline

There is a guideline in Elliott Wave which states that a correction will often terminate within the range of the fourth wave of one lesser degree, in this case the symmetrical triangle at minor degree labelled (ABCDE). Non-Elliotticians sometimes scoff at these pronouncements, but there is logic behind it.

An impulse wave up develops a bit like this:

- The wave one bounce is the result of there being no one left to sell coupled with frantic short covering coming out of the cycle low.

- Wave two sees stale bulls unload their losing positions and pessimists shorting triumphantly.

- Wave three starts up when the lower low the pessimists were looking for does not come to pass and the great reload begins.

- Wave four is when the mood subtly shifts from: "What could possibly go wrong?" to "Where are the new buyers?"

- And finally wave five represents those new late buyers in action, the ones who swore they would get into the-move-that-will-never-end as soon as they got the chance.

The final round trip

The last group responsible for wave five is in aggregate the most speculative and they are usually wiped out when prices reverse. The round-trip from the end of wave four to the top of wave five and back again can be viewed as the removal of speculative froth. Once the final boom and bust cycle has completed, prices are normally back to where they started. This point is sometimes reached in one swift zigzag but sometimes it takes longer and meanders around as bullish sentiment is gradually unwound.

Drawing a horizontal line from the apex of the triangle around $670 would have therefore provided a high probability target for the end of the retracement (WXY). And indeed this is what we see; prices have bounced off it. This would be taken as further evidence that the nest of lows from the cycle analysis was in place.

Projection guideline

To add to the conviction that the correction is over, we can draw upon another useful Elliott insight. The final leg of a zigzag is very often either the same length as the first leg or a 1.618 – or less commonly 2.618 – Fibonacci multiple. Here we see the 1.618 extension come in almost exactly, giving yet more evidence that the bottom of the correction – namely the 18M low – is probably in place.

Overall then, the cycle analyst with an eye to Elliott would *know* that the underlying trend throughout this decline is up and that the cycle downswing from the 18M peak is very likely complete. Not only does the zigzag have the correct number of subdivisions, which themselves break down correctly according to Elliott rules and guidelines, but it also comes in exactly the projected target.

Gold conclusions

Both the RSI and the Elliott Wave analyses point to this last move down being a correction within a broader uptrend which supports the view that the 18-month nest of lows is already in place on 24 October at $682. This confirms what we strongly suspected from the cycle analysis and gives us added confidence that we can look to start building a long position, knowing not only that near-term risk is to the upside but also that the longer cycle is behind the trade.

Figure 8.8 shows what happened next: a downward 9M VTL was broken in February confirming the $682 price low (labelled circle four) as the 18M nest of lows – and by extension in this case – the 54M. In terms of Hurst, we are now advancing in the next 54M cycle and the status as at 17 December 2010 is up/topping. In Elliott terms it is possible that we are building intermediate wave one of primary degree five, up.

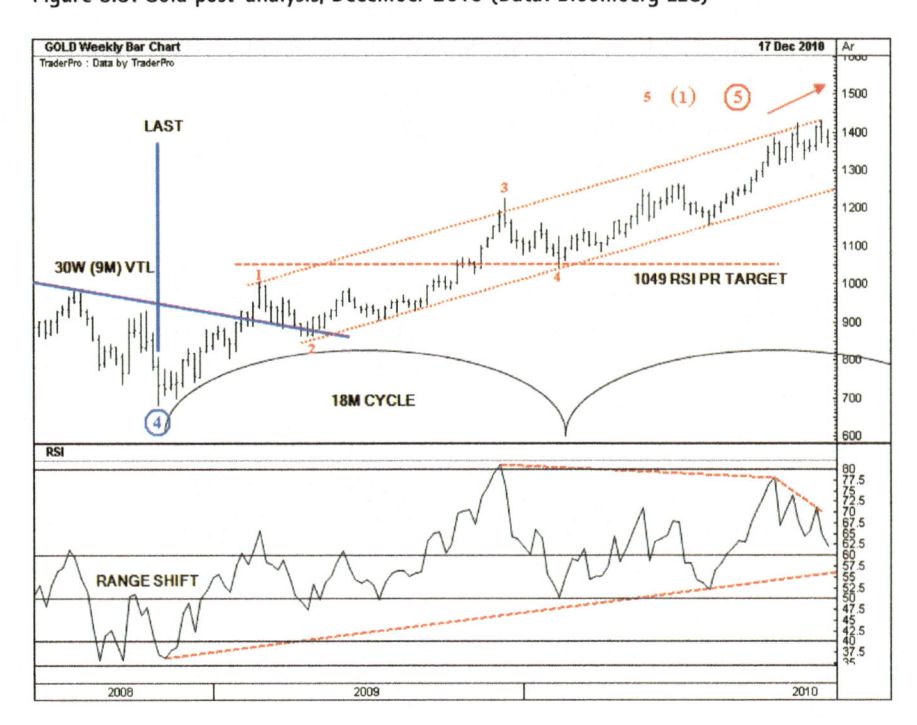

Figure 8.8: Gold post-analysis, December 2010 (Data: Bloomberg LLC)

Notice that the positive reversal target of $1049 was exceeded and then acted as support at minor wave four. Here RSI was also supported at 50, unable even to drop into the lower end of the bull range. Notice also that there is another short positive reversal pattern into minor wave two down, confirming upside momentum and wave two bounces of RSI 50. At some point, and it is too early to commit here, the next 54M cycle will peak. $1600 is a *tentative initial target* at which point there could be a significant retracement. Recall that a high probability termination area is wave four of one lesser degree, which *could* put prices right back around $1050 before the next major leg up.

Case Study II: Euro/USD, January 2010

Background

From the summer of 2008 through the dramatic sell-off in October/November 2008 (Lehman blew up in mid-September) the US dollar surged against all currencies in a classic flight to quality (government bonds also sky-rocketed).[75] Then there was a volatile counter-trend move in December, followed by a return to the 2008 highs for the USD in February. At that stage, the sell-off globally was complete. USD double bottomed and from March 2009 the risk trade rally that endured until the summer of 2011 started.

In 2009 the Euro almost regained all of its lost territory against the USD. A popular assumption in late 2008 was that the subprime crisis would be contained within the US and the damage would be restricted to the balance sheets of US investment banks; the argument being that the wider banking community, especially in Europe, would be immune. This was how market commentators were able to explain the year long 20% plus relative outperformance of the Euro against the US dollar from late autumn 2008.

In December 2009 however, this argument came under pressure as the world's main ratings agencies downgraded Greece's sovereign debt to junk status and cut the credit ratings of Portugal and Spain. If sovereign default was to be the next shoe to drop, so to speak, the question was: what impact would it have on those European banks with mountains of sovereign debt on their balance sheets? Was it also an indication that the subprime crisis has spread? And if so what would be the likely impact to the 16 countries that shared the Euro? Set against these worrisome scenarios, however, was yet another containability argument: Greece only accounted for 2-3% of EU GDP and was therefore peripheral. The fallout would be localised.

Throughout December the Euro experienced a vertiginous drop until it found support at the 200-day moving average just before Christmas Day. At this time the full scope of this next stage of the crisis was still unknown and the Eurozone/IMF €120bn three-year bailout was months away.

So, would the market shrug Greece off and continue upwards, or would it be pulverised? Let us then pick up the thread on 15 January 2010 and see what the charts tell us.

Hurst analysis

Figure 8.9 shows a phasing analysis conducted on the weekly chart for Euro-USD on 15 January 2010.

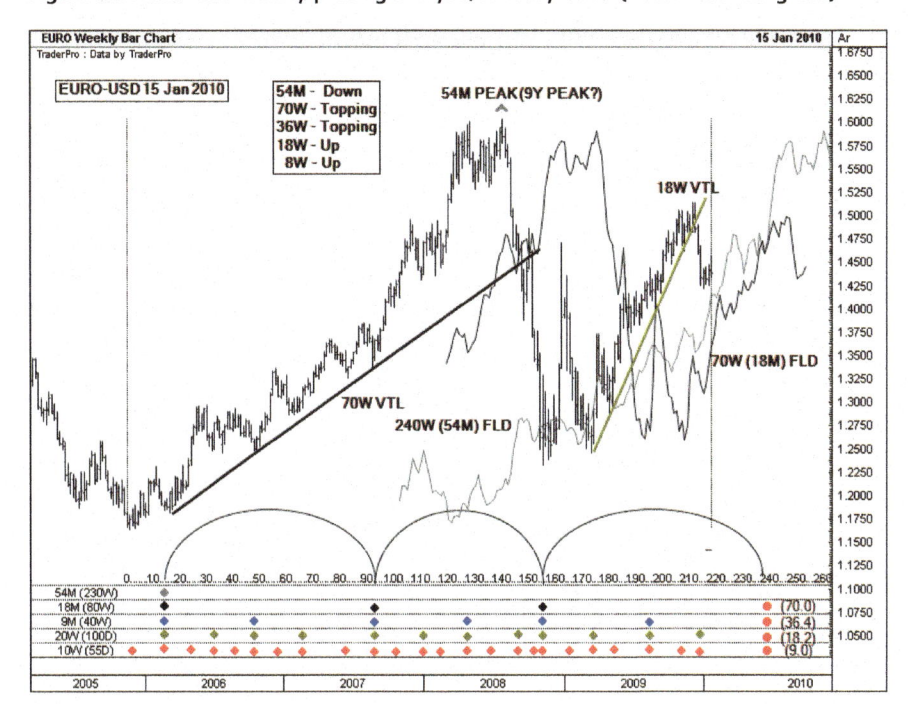

Figure 8.9: Euro-USD weekly phasing analysis, January 2010 (Data: Bloomberg LLC)

Cyclic status and VTLs

Prices look to be just over halfway along the third 18M cycle of a 54M cycle. The average length of the cycles is running short and at the last date the 54M cycle is down, the 70W and 36W (equivalent to 18M and 9M) are topping and the 18W and 8W cycles are up.

A 70W VTL was crossed by prices in September 2008, placing the 54M cycle peak at the price high of 1.6018 in late April. It is just possible that this is also a nine-year cycle peak strongly translated to the left.

Moving to the right of the chart, prices crossed down through an 18W VTL in early December 2009, indicating that the most recent nine-month cycle peaked at 1.5144 in late November. Because of cyclic distortion near the lows, it was not possible to draw an upward 36-week VTL in this case, but this peak is also presumed to be that of the 70-week cycle.

FLDs and underlying trend

A downward price cross of the 70W FLD at 1.45 in September 2008 projected 1.299, which was overshot. An upward price cross of the same FLD at 1.40 in early June 2009 projected 1.567 and this was undershot. The underlying trend was therefore down throughout this period. Since trend here is the action of the nine and 18-year cycles, it changes direction only very slowly. With no conflicting evidence, it is safe to assume that the underlying trend is still down at the end of the data in January 2010.

Sitting ominously just below the last price are both the 18M and 54M FLDs rising into future time. The implication here, therefore, is that prices will be falling in that same future time. If, as seems likely, a downward cross of the 70 week FLD does take place, then the projection is 1.285. However, because the trend is down this will probably be overshot and reach even lower. If this turns out to be the case then a lower low than the 18M nest of lows at grid 155 will have been put in and provide further evidence that the long trend is down.

It should also be noted that there is still an outstanding 54M (240) FLD downside projection. Price crossed down through this FLD at around 1.27. Since the 54M cycle peak was at 1.6, the target is 0.94, or sub-parity.

Conclusion

The risk is firmly to the downside. You would therefore be looking for an imminent entry signal to short the 30W cycle into the upcoming nest of lows.

Elliott Wave analysis

Figure 8.10 is an Elliott Wave analysis of the same weekly Euro chart. The 2008 high has been labelled five (circled) and is at primary degree, implying that at this point prices have completed the final stage of a significant advance. For the market to rebalance, therefore, a retracement of proportional magnitude is called for and indeed it appears to be underway.

Chapter 8 | RSI And Elliott Wave

Figure 8.10: Euro-USD weekly Elliott Wave analysis, January 2010 (Data: Bloomberg LLC)

Primary degree impulse move

Notice how freely the advance into primary wave five flows: minor waves one and four (in red) do not overlap and minor wave two does not drop below the start of wave one. Also notice that for this preferred count, wave five rather than wave three is the extended wave but, crucially, wave three is not the shortest.

Projecting targets

Referring back to the guidelines of termination, the horizontal line drawn in from minor wave four gave a high probability target for the end of the first leg of the correction around 1.25. This was met almost exactly and supported a double bottom which launched intermediate (B) up.

The second horizontal drawn in from intermediate (4) provides another lower target around 1.16. This is consistent with the cycle analysis, which suggested an 18M FLD projection of 1.285 – which in any case we think will be undershot – as well as an outstanding 54M FLD projection of 0.94, giving an average value of 1.11.

263

Primary degree retracement

Managing expectations

Sharp-eyed Elliotticians may notice something wrong with the count in the corrective wave down. It is being labelled (A), (B) at intermediate degree suggesting that prices may have just entered wave (C) of primary degree wave W down. We do not need to dwell too much on this point, but zigzags (and indeed other corrective structures) can also be expressed WYZ creating a so-called double zigzag. The message is the same, but the pro-trend subdivisions are themselves ABC zigzags. For those who are interested in further study, the intricacies of multiple corrections are fully explained in Prechter's work. For now it is enough to know that a downward retracement of the previous impulse wave is in progress.

The reason for this choice of labelling was explained by Jeff Kennedy at Elliott Wave International. Normally when a wave five ends, a whole new wave structure begins in the opposite direction starting 1, 2..., and so on. In this case, therefore, we would be building primary wave one down. Having just seen intermediate wave one down and possibly wave two up into the end of the data, we would be forced to consider the fact that we are just about to enter wave three down. Recalling that wave three is the most powerful move in the sequence, that would mean we are about to witness the beginning of the total annihilation of the Euro.

Now, while we should definitely be looking down, this is a big call and it would be prudent to step lightly. Since we are looking to confirm our Hurst analysis and since Hurst is predominantly a trading methodology, we do not need to try to be a hero and hit the ball out of the park.

Elliott Wave beginners are often too quick to call impulse moves and count 1s and 2s constantly on the look-out for the big wave trade in wave three. This is probably the main reason novice Elliotticians do not get results: they are always waiting for the big move that does not come.

There needs to be enough evidence in the data to support the call for primary wave one down and right now there is not. For example, primary wave five will be part of a much larger structure which, if understood completely, could force a rethink of this corrective move. The message here is do not try to overreach. As Kennedy points out, it is much better to have minimum expectations that are met than it is to have wild expectations that do not pan out. It is better to be conservative than have a big hole punched in your equity (for traders) or your reputation (for analysts).

We know that the market is consolidating 30% of the time[76] and as a general rule, when the correction breaks out of its channel, you will know which way the wind blows. Until then the safer bet here is to trade the correction down in stages.

So, we know we are in some sort of long-term corrective structure, the underlying trend has shifted down consistent with the 54M and probably the nine-year cycle rolling over and we have just seen a sharp counter-trend move up. Fundamentally inclined commentators might have said: it would be bad if sub-prime contagion takes hold in Europe, but this might not happen because Greece is really not big enough to matter. And anyway, look, we don't completely ignore technical analysis: prices are at the 200-day MA.

Hurst cycle analysis is less ambiguous and would say: the 18M cycle has just peaked and the trend is down, get ready to load up your shorts. Elliotticians might say: at the minimum a primary degree wave is pointing down and we are looking for an intermediate final (C) wave down right about now. We agree with the Hurst people.

Countertrend move up

Confirmation that the countertrend move up labelled (B) terminated at the end of November and is therefore likely to be the 18M cycle peak can be found on the daily chart. B waves are *always* three-wave affairs. Minor wave A up (red) is the short covering rally off the lows and minor wave B down is its retracement leaving one remaining leg, the C wave. Figure 8.11 shows the count up to the end of the data in mid-January 2010. The C wave in a zigzag correction *always* unfolds in five waves[77] and this is what we see here. It also comes in at a Fibonacci 76% retracement of the big move down from the 2008 highs. This is exactly what we would expect to see in a correction of this sort. Notice also that the 38%, 50% and 62% levels have also been respected serving as support and resistance throughout this correction. This is not magic, it is just the market conforming to its natural rhythm.

This confluence of indications is further supported by the overall form of the move: a species of rising wedge. Classical technical analysis tells us this pattern is highly predictive and very often results in a sharp sell-off.[78] As the downtrend leans on the pattern, the upswings are unable to really get going and we see a jagged, drawn out wave four, and the messy peak formation. This would have looked much more like a classic impulse move if the trend had been up instead of down. Instead it is another clue that a big break is coming.

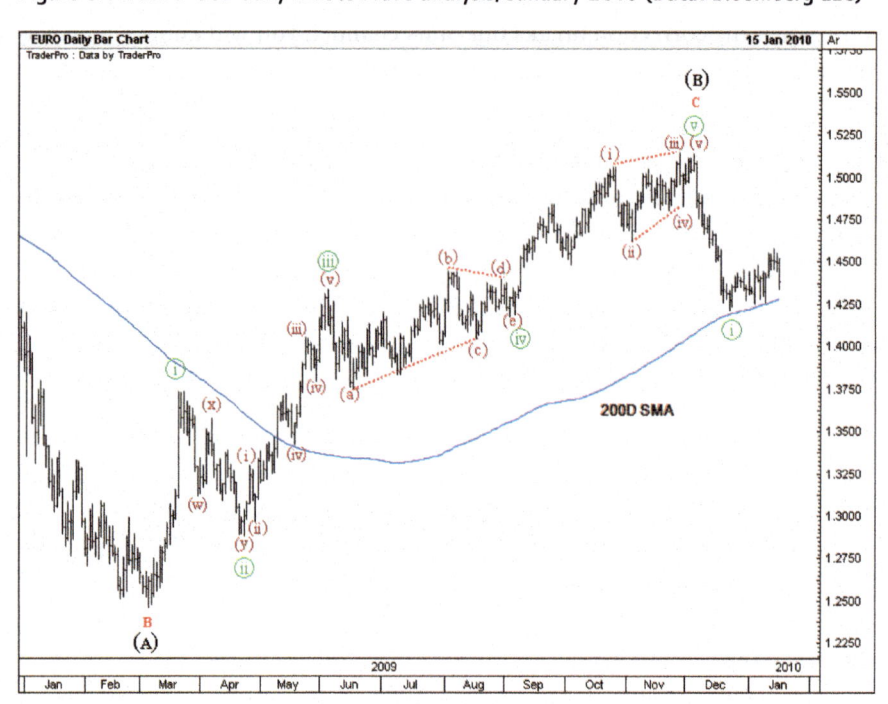

Figure 8.11: Euro-USD daily Elliott Wave analysis, January 2010 (Data: Bloomberg LLC)

RSI analysis

Figure 8.12 shows the RSI analysis of the Euro in the same period. Going into the big top we see RSI peaking in late November 2007. Multiple bearish divergences warn that price is overextended and a potential reversal is being signalled some 28 weeks beforehand. The 18M/54M cycle peak is finally confirmed when RSI first rolls over, drops below and then fails to retake the 60 level. This happens well ahead of any meaningful VTL breaks.

Negative reversal

We looked at the positive reversal pattern in the Gold case study. The reverse of this is the negative reversal. This occurs when RSI advances and makes higher highs, but at the same time prices decline putting in a lower close on the second RSI high. It indicates that the market is overbought rather than just overextended. Momentum is building but price does not follow and when the pattern completes, it is a signal that a downside reversal is due.

Chapter 8 | RSI And Elliott Wave

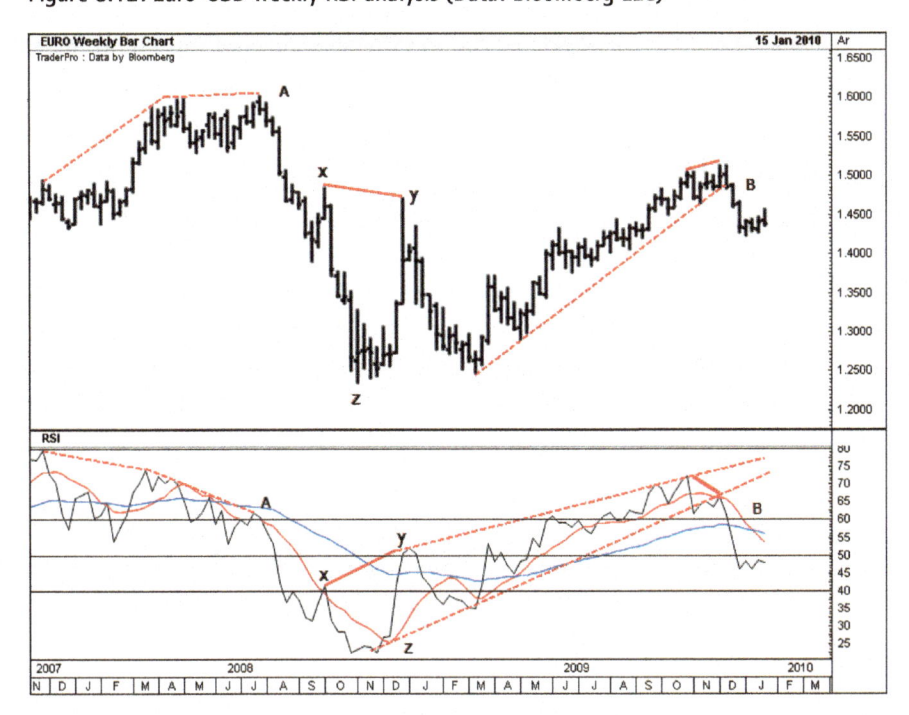

Figure 8.12: Euro-USD weekly RSI analysis (Data: Bloomberg LLC)

Here the pattern occurs between September and December 2008. The big spike up in price comes out of a deeply oversold RSI but fails to take out the previous high. As we have already seen with momentum spikes, the price cycle can carry on for some time afterwards, as it does here. So, once the signal has been given we need to store the information away and look for confirmation of an impending reversal as the move progresses.

Going into the cycle low, the first RSI peak at *x* corresponds to a close of 1.4607 on the price chart. RSI drops and then puts in a higher RSI at *y*, but the corresponding close is lower at 1.4208. The difference is then subtracted from the price low of the pattern at *z*, 1.2331.

Projection formula

As for the positive reversal, the greater the difference in closing price between *x* and *y*, and the lower the intervening cycle low *z*, the stronger the pattern. The following formula is used to project the first price target:

- The closing price associated with the higher RSI low (y) is subtracted from the closing price associated with the lower RSI low (x) and the difference is subtracted from the intervening price low (z).

- Thus z - (x - y) gives 1.2331 - (1.4607 - 1.4208) = 1.1932

This value closely corresponds to the FLD projection and the Elliott Wave termination guidelines and is confirmation that we should be looking down.

RSI rising wedge

The patterns we see in RSI are often amplifications of those we see in price. Here we see exactly the same rising wedge pattern, indicating that upside momentum is being leaned on by the action of the underlying trend, which is down. RSI is contained by an increasingly narrow range and eventually breaks down. There is a retest from below at point B, this fails and RSI then drops sharply, taking out the 60 level and the 45-week EMA before stabilising just below 50.

This would have been the signal that RSI had done what it needed to do, that upside momentum had completely unwound and that the negative reversal was now free to project its downside target. Notice also the very tight Bearish Divergence at B; this should be taken as a strong signal that the sell-off will be sharp and extended.

Euro conclusions

Figure 8.13 shows what happened next. Prices dropped nearly 18% over the next 104 days – yielding 63%.

At Minute degree i (circled) you could have been absolutely sure that prices were going to drop significantly. You had three sets of downside targets, and all the evidence you could have needed from Hurst, Elliott and RSI. Everything pointed to a sell off. Price then pulled away sharply at the wave ii high and dropped in a neat five wave sequence straight into the RSI Negative Reversal target at 1.19 and just through a 261% extension of wave i. It should be clear from the foregoing case studies that Hurst analysis is significantly enhanced by knowledge of Elliott Wave and RSI.

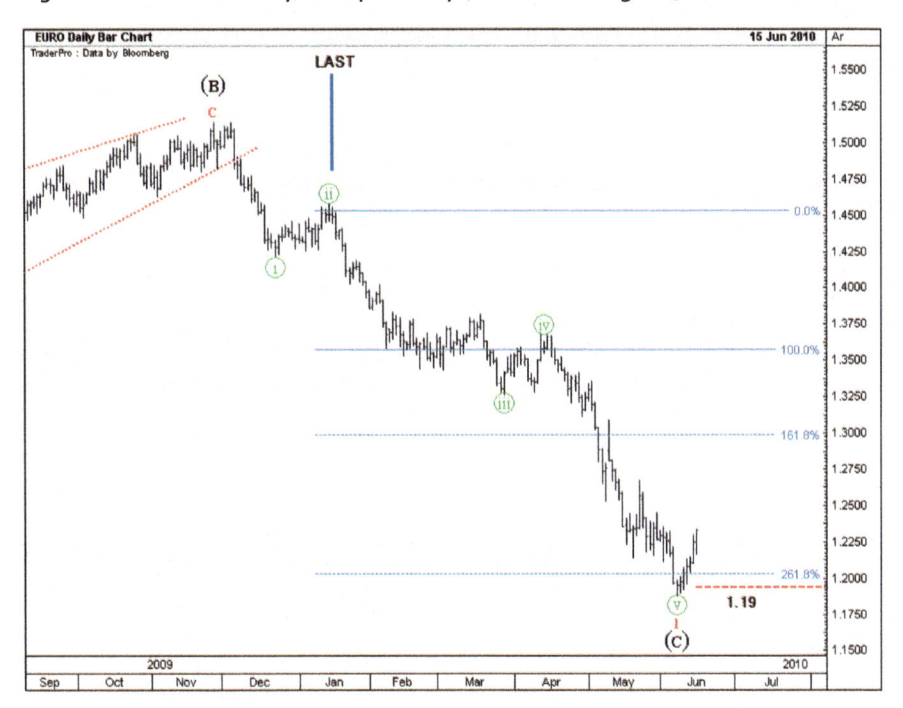

Figure 8.13: Euro-USD daily chart post entry (Data: Bloomberg LLC)

Conclusion

In this chapter you were introduced to two alternative approaches to market analysis: RSI and Elliott Wave. The discussion was by necessity superficial, but you should have taken a few key ideas away. Conclusions drawn from Hurst cycle analysis can be confirmed by judicious use of RSI and Elliott Wave. Not all alternative technical approaches are suitable, but these two are ideal. RSI is a true and representative measure of momentum and Elliott addresses market rhythm and structure. An understanding of both will help take your cycle analysis to the next level.

You have learnt how RSI works and have had a glimpse at some of its potential. It is a good habit to pull up an RSI chart before you run a cyclic analysis and see what conclusions can be drawn. This will provide you with immediate context and prevent fundamental errors. It will also narrow down the range of probable outcomes.

RSI is a proxy for price and everything that can be seen on a price chart can be replicated in RSI: chart, patterns, cycles, Elliott Wave, moving averages, second derivative indicators, and so on. However, because RSI leads price and often gives a cleaner signal, it often reveals a lot more. It is important of course to relate what you are seeing in RSI to the actual market. Not only because that is what you are buying and selling, but because it is the interaction of RSI and price that provides the insights.

The rules and some of the guidelines of Elliott Wave have been covered as well as the principal patterns. We have just scratched the surface here, but you should at least see the potential of combining this approach to market analysis with Hurst. Like RSI, you cannot expect to master the Wave principle in an afternoon. It requires diligent practice. Eventually, though, you will get the Elliott touch, everything will fall together and, if you are combining Elliott with Hurst, your cycles work will take off.

You have seen how Elliott and Hurst approach the same idea from slightly different angles. Both look at market structure, proportionality and rhythm and both acknowledge the immediate underlying driver: the mood of the crowd. Knowing where price is in Elliott terms can be applied directly to Hurst analysis and act as supporting evidence for a whole range of cyclic situations. Some of the most dramatic moves are seen when signals generated by Hurst, RSI and Elliott confirm one another.

There is plenty more that could be written on this combination approach and there are many connections that are yet to be made. We are limited by space and time here, but a future series of articles is being planned.

Endnotes

[63] Welles Wilder, *New Concepts in Technical Trading Systems* (Trend Research, 1978).
[64] Or any other price point: High, Low, Mid, etc.
[65] This concept is described well by Tony Plummer in *Forecasting Financial Markets* (Kogan Page, 2008) with whose kind permission it is reformulated here.
[66] An example of M^2 is RSI of RSI (RSI^2).
[67] Exponential Moving Average (EMA) changes the period (n) into a fraction and is given by $2 / (n + 1)$. Thus, the 14D EMA is $2 / (14 \text{ days} +1)$ or 13.3%. Wilder's average instead uses an EMA of 1/14 or 7.1%, which is equivalent to a smoother 27D calculation period.
[68] Andrew Cardwell, **www.cardwellrsiedge.com**.

[69] Robert Prechter is the President of Elliott Wave International, www.elliottwave.com
[70] All Elliott wave diagrams in the book were reproduced with the kind permission of Robert Prechter, Elliott Wave International.
[71] Jeffrey Kennedy is Chief Commodities Analyst at EWI and editor of their Futures Junctures Service. He has also put together a lot of excellent training material, which can be found at **www.elliottwave.com**.
[72] 950 + (950 − 682)
[73] Unlike Hurst analysis where we talk in terms of cycle periods, Elliott Wave refers to degrees. The degrees most commonly referred to are Cycle – roughly equivalent to Hurst's 18-year cycle, Primary, Intermediate, Minor and so on down to the lowest degree commonly referred to as Micro.
[74] The rules and guidelines are explained with detailed diagrams courtesy of Elliott Wave International in Appendix 1.
[75] Thanks to James Ferguson, Chief Strategist at Arbuthnot Securities in London for his input here.
[76] Edwards, Magee & Bassetti, *Technical Analysis of Stock Trends* (CRC Amacom, 2007).
[77] With the exception of triangles, this is true for all simple corrective waves.
[78] Thomas Bulkowski, *Encyclopaedia of Chart Patterns* (Wiley, 2005).

Conclusion

Summary

The basics

The concepts underlying Hurst's system of cycle analysis are straightforward. The basic premise is that price movement is a composite of multiple interacting cycles and regardless of financial instrument, market or timeframe, these cycles share common properties. They can all be described in terms of period, amplitude and phase; they repeat; a long cycle tends to produce a bigger price move than a short cycle; and at any given time a cycle is either: bottoming, going up, topping or going down. Furthermore, cycles combine by addition; they tend to be harmonically related; they tend to synchronise at lows and rather than there being an infinite variety there appears to be a definable set.

It is easy to take all of this for granted, but were these properties absent – for example if prices were just randomly distributed or if there was an infinite number of non-harmonic cycles – then price movement would look nothing like it does and cycle analysis would be next to impossible. The fact is, however, that these properties are present and therefore cycle analysis is not only possible, but it offers forecasting advantages over almost any other methodology.

Empirical roots

As for the legitimacy of the methodology, Hurst did not pluck it out of the air or make it up and nor is it the result of some rarefied but plausible theory that does not actually square with reality. An aerospace engineer by training, Hurst observed the market, ran over 30,000 hours of computer testing and then applied his knowledge of physics to create the model. At one point Hurst claimed that his method was 90% accurate and although this has not been verified, in the hands of a skilful analyst impressive results are possible.

Variation

Some analysts, unfamiliar with the core techniques of Hurst's system, are put off by cycles as a matter of principle because of their occasional irregularity and the apparent difficulty involved in isolating them in price data. For example, as we have seen, cycle length and magnitude tend to vary over time, which is why it is not enough just to throw a standardised cycle measurement tool onto your chart and expect it to pick out cycles into infinity. If that were possible, then Hurst's original course would have consisted of a couple of paragraphs. Having said that, variation can be anticipated: for example, we often observe that going into major nests of lows, time tends to compress and the cycles shorten. On the other hand, once a move is underway, cycle period tends to expand.

Price shocks

Sometimes price shocks can come seemingly out of nowhere and the cyclic picture can appear to change. When this happens, however, usually only amplitude is affected, leaving cycle period unaltered. The cycles then tend to quickly fall back into their long-term rhythm. In any case, to the skilled analyst those movements which take many market observers by surprise are often telegraphed well ahead of time.

Multiple timeframes

Hurst Cycle Analysis allows you to locate your position in the broader scheme of things much more effectively than just switching across multiple timeframes: for example, drawing trendlines on a weekly chart and then flipping over to the daily. Although many market technicians do not know how to approach this in a systematic way, most technical analysis techniques can be explained in terms of cycles.

Trendlines

Trend, as we have seen, is simply the action of underlying longer cycles and trendlines are an artificial device to describe them. However, because traditional trendlines are not based on specific cycles, they can be more or less arbitrary.

That does not mean they can never be used effectively, it is just that if you know what cycle is being described, as you do with the Valid Trendline, then the quality of the information with which you are provided is greater.

Moving averages

Moving averages are used to smooth out price action and are generally used to highlight trend. However, what they are really doing is highlighting cycles. The longer the moving average, the longer the cycle it represents.

However, because conventionally drawn moving averages are artificially displaced forward in time, they are not time-synchronised with cycle peaks and troughs and therefore do not depict the cycle accurately. Furthermore, the process of smoothing decreases the magnitude of the moving average's fluctuations. Thus, the longer the moving average, the less clearly it shows up cyclic movement.

FLDs

An FLD is similar to a conventional moving average, in that it takes an average price and displaces it forward in time. The difference, however, is that FLDs exactly trace out just under the full amplitude of the cycles they are based upon. Furthermore, because they do so well beyond the end of the data, they serve as a roadmap for future price action.

The underlying presumption here is that the original cycle exactly repeats in the future, which of course does not normally happen. However, by observing where the replica cycle intersects price in future time, all sorts of information about the future path of prices can be ascertained: projections can be made and underlying trend can be revealed. This information is unavailable to the analyst who is just using moving averages.

Support and resistance

Support and resistance levels are often used in technical analysis to determine where prices will stop, but again these levels are derived from underlying cyclic structure. Knowing what this structure is allows you to determine which levels will hold and which will be broken.

Exactly the same applies to traditional chart patterns. Knowing what combination of cycles formed the pattern in the first place gives you a big head start on other traders who are just following by rote. And since some of the very best trades come out of so-called failed patterns, this is good information to have.

Momentum

Similarly, momentum is just a proxy for the phase of the composite cycle. At peaks and troughs we can expect price rate of change to be low and in the middle we can expect it to be high. Momentum will give you a clue that something is changing, but it does not give you the whole story. It is all too easy to jump in early when a momentum signal is flashed up, but an understanding of cyclic conditions can keep you out of trouble. In fact, it does not matter how many sophisticated indicators you pile on top of each other; if you do not know where price is in the composite cycle, you are shooting in the dark.

Technical analysis

Most conventional technical analysis indicators are reactive: a price level breaks support or resistance or an MA; a momentum indicator signals overbought or oversold; sentiment is bullish or bearish; advancing issues are greater than declining issues; the 52 week high or low has been broached, and so on.

It is often then a case of trading on a signal generated by one or a combination of these indicators and then riding a trend until an opposite signal is given. With Hurst cycle analysis you are always one step ahead because you have in front of you a framework of probable outcomes. You know how far the move is likely to carry, how long it should take and you also know when you are wrong and why. Knowing what to expect also allows you to pick and choose what signals to take and what issues to trade. Trading a conventional indicator signal, getting stopped out, trying again and then seeing a paltry move will just erode your capital and leave you frustrated.

Putting the pieces together

The principal tools used in Hurst cycle analysis are the VTL and the FLD but in order to be able to deploy these correctly you need a complete picture of the cyclic status of the issue under observation. This is the job of phasing analysis and it provides you with all of the information you need to know about the current condition of the market. If you do not know the time locations of the component cycles in the composite, then you do not know where to draw your VTLs; you will not be able to tell the magnitude of cycle peaks and troughs; you will not know how far along prices are in each of the cycles at the last date and you will not be able to set up your action signals to enter or exit a trade. If you do not know the average length of the component cycles in the data you are looking at, then you will not be able to plot your FLDs, which means you will not be able to project future prices or interpret FLD patterns.

Of course it is more difficult to conduct a full cyclic analysis than it is to plot a moving average or pull up an indicator, but the effort is worth it if you are serious about consistently being able to put on trades with a high reward-to-risk ratio. Evidence takes time to collect and if you do not have a systematic method based upon sound reasoning then you run the risk of going into your trades half-cocked or allowing wishful thinking to overcome your judgment. In the words of Sherlock Holmes, "It is a capital mistake to theorise before one has data. Insensibly one begins to twist facts to suit theories, instead of theories to suit facts."[79]

The good news is that the more you practice Hurst analysis, the faster and more adept you will be and, as your skill grows, the more enjoyable the entire process will become. What is more you will see the market with new eyes as a market detective. In the same way that you would not expect to become an accomplished musician after a few days of practice with an instrument, you should not expect to master Hurst cycle analysis without proper study and application. You have now been presented with all of the tools you need to perform an analysis, you just need to practice.

The causes of cycles

Hurst did not elaborate on why market cycles exist, but thought it plausible that they were caused by some common external force.

Edward Dewey

One of the leading early thinkers on the causes of cycles was the economist Edward Dewey, who in 1931 was hired by President Hoover to find out the reason for the 1929 stock market crash and the Great Depression. The story goes that because Dewey was unable to get a satisfactory answer from the many economists he interviewed, he sought it outside mainstream economics. This inspired his life's work, the study of cycles, and led to the formation of the Foundation for the Study of Cycles in 1941, numerous studies and several books.[80]

What he and his researchers found over the years was that cycles exist in a vast array of seemingly unconnected natural phenomena from the stock market to animal populations and that many of these cycles not only appeared to share the same period, but were also in phase. His view was that everything could be explained in terms of cycles but what was left unsaid was why. Shortly before his death in 1978, when Dewey no longer had to fear having his research funding pulled, he wrote that the cause had to be extraterrestrial.

Extraterrestrial causes

The majority of investment managers and analysts reject the idea that planetary cycles acting on traders' emotions are the driving force behind the market. Nevertheless, research in this area is ongoing and many traders and fund managers do pay attention to the position of the planets, so it is worth looking at one of the theories.

Emotionality

The American financial philosopher P.Q. Wall wrote in the 1950s that: "The emotions of humanity rise and fall in patterns." These patterns show up in financial markets which are an extremely sensitive barometer of social mood. It is the collective emotion of market participants, either active or inactive, that governs the course of prices. This does not need to be the raging emotion of market extremes, but simply put a trader either feels hopeful that money can be made, or fearful that money will be lost.

It is not just speculative traders who are governed by emotion. An investment manager, who bases his or her decisions purely on fundamentals, is still driven by hope and fear: they want to make their bonuses, win accolades for outperforming a benchmark and keep their jobs. The valuation metrics of the companies they analyse are similarly determined by emotion: of the customers who can and want to buy their products and of the company management who decide to produce and sell them. For example, banks will not lend and people will not borrow if they are pessimistic about the ability to repay. Companies will only expand into new markets or take on new debt if they are optimistic about finding customers who can afford and are willing to buy their goods or services. Emotion suffuses the whole structure in one way or another.

Herding

Although individuals are capable of making rational decisions, large groups of people acting in unison are prone not to. Even analysts poring over company cash-flow statements every day do not live in a bubble and are affected by the mood of society at large, their peer group and the managers at the companies they speak to. Market technicians also take their cues from the rest of the market: from price action, volume and chart patterns, which all directly reflect the mood of society.

Some researchers believe that the herding instinct, which governs collective behaviour, is directed by a pre-rational or primitive part of the brain rather than the part which is responsible for rational thought. Because the collective mind is not conscious or self-aware, they argue, it is in tune with forces that govern all other natural phenomena. You could say that the collective mind is an instrument on which the rhythms of nature are being played. In other words, the language of the market is that of the pre-rational mind. One of the reasons so called esoteric systems such a Gann, Elliott or Hurst can be so compelling is that they reflect these underlying patterns most clearly.

Ionisation, serotonin and the magnetic flux

There are a variety of competing theories on the influence of the planets upon earthly cycles: some are well researched and seem to show statistically significant correlations with market action; others border on the charlatan and appear to have no forecasting track record whatsoever.

It is beyond the scope of this book and the ability of this author to evaluate the validity of every financial astrology market letter out there – and there are many – but to give you a flavour here is one theory explained to me by Bill Sarubbi, a former member of the Foundation for the Study of Cycles, who currently runs a market advisory service in Vienna. Sarubbi is an expert on market cycles and spent 14 years on Wall Street before running a $1bn technology fund in the Middle East. He believes that the underlying cycles in human emotions are caused to a large degree by fluctuations in levels of serotonin. Serotonin is a neurotransmitter found in our nervous systems and is responsible for our feelings of well-being. High levels of serotonin make us feel euphoric; low levels make us feel depressed.

Research has been done to suggest that atmospheric ionisation – in other words, electricity in the air – can strongly influence serotonin levels in humans and animals. Ionisation is the physical process of converting an atom or molecule into an ion by adding or removing charged particles. Increased positively-charged ions in the air make us feel depressed or lethargic, whereas increased negatively-charged ions make us feel alert and optimistic.

Studies have shown that certain winds, such as the Föhn, the Sirocco or the Mistral, which are strongly positively charged, cause higher than average instances of stress and anxiety. On the other hand, a negatively charged atmosphere, such as would be found by a waterfall, a lake or in mountain resorts leads to higher than usual feelings of vitality and happiness.

One of the causes of ionisation is electromagnetic radiation from the Sun – the solar wind. The Earth is protected from the solar wind by its magnetic field, but the solar wind is also responsible for the shape, density and fluctuations in the speed of the magnetic field. These changes can strongly affect the Earth's local space environment, causing radio interference and ionisation. Homing pigeons, for example, rely on tiny changes in their serotonin levels to navigate the Earth's magnetic field.

The Sun is not solid but plasma and just like the tides on Earth are directed by the Moon's gravitational pull, tides in the Sun's plasma are affected by the gravitational pull of the planets in the solar system; especially the two largest planets Jupiter and Saturn. The gravity of each planet combines with the others and as they describe their heliocentric orbits sometimes these combined gravitational fields – the gravitational vector – are stronger and sometimes they are weaker, depending on their relative positions. Thus the Sun's plasma changes shape cyclically, influencing the shape and density of its magnetic field, which in turn affects the intensity of the solar wind, which leads to fluctuations in ionisation on Earth, which affects mankind's serotonin levels, which causes the cyclicality in emotions that we read as market cycles... or so the theory goes.

It is not inconceivable that traders 100 years from now will look back on our present understanding of the markets in the same way as we look back upon medical handbooks from the Middle Ages. They may chuckle at how wrongheaded and archaic our approach was. Perhaps the 2111 version of Bloomberg will include gravity maps instead of market maps. It is interesting to think about what causes cycles in the market, but it is probably enough to understand that they are there and have the ability to read them. It is quite possible that knowing exactly where Jupiter and Saturn are in relation to the Sun at any given time will give you the jump on more Earth-bound traders. But then again, it might not. If you are interested, go ahead and try to find out.

I hope you have enjoyed reading the book. I enjoyed writing it.

Endnotes

[79] Sir Arthur Conan Doyle, *A Scandal in Bohemia* (1891).

[80] Edward Dewey & Edwin Dakin, *Cycles: The Science of Prediction* (Kessinger, 2010); Edward Dewey & Og Mandino, *Cycles: the Mysterious Forces that Trigger Events* (Hawthorn, 1971).

APPENDICES

Appendix 1: Elliott Wave Patterns

The following are the basic patterns described by the Elliott Wave Principle. Reproduced with kind permission from Robert Prechter, Elliott Wave International:

Figure A1.1 – Horizontal triangles

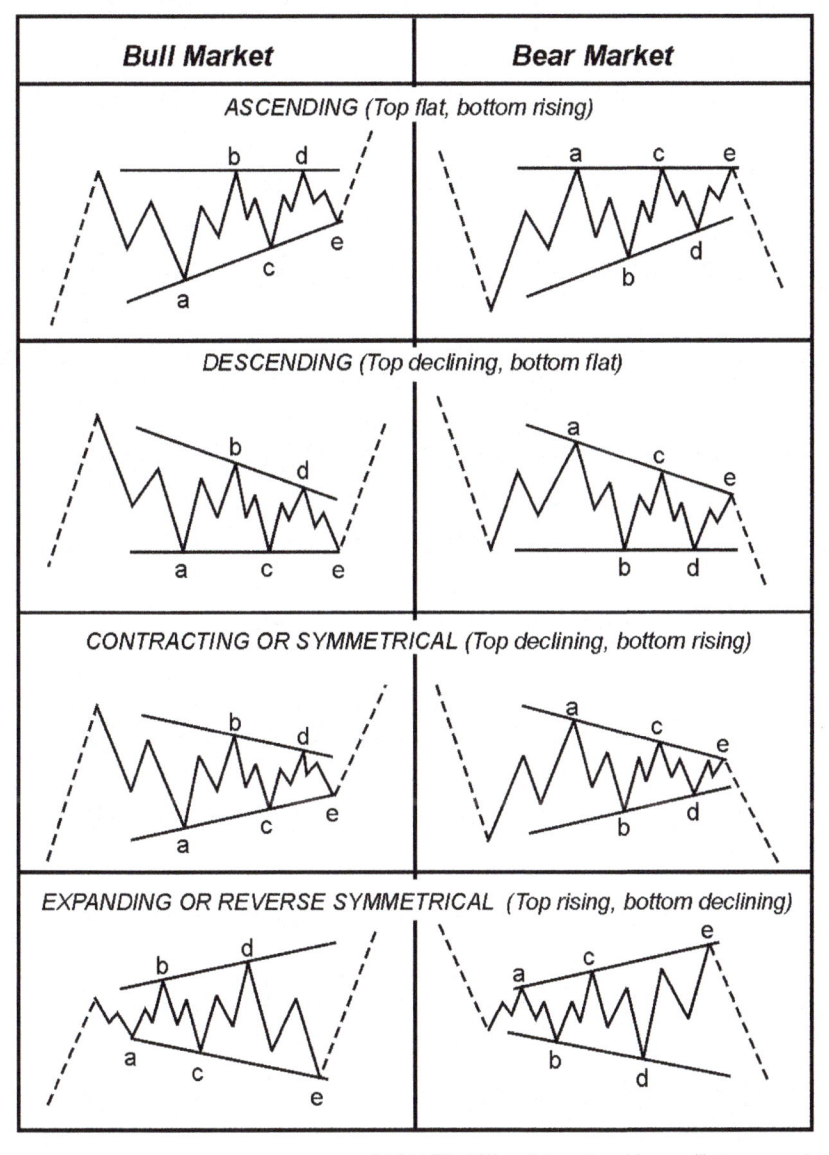

© 2011 Elliott Wave International (www.elliottwave.com)

Mastering Hurst Cycle Analysis | Christopher Grafton, CMT

Figure A1.2 – Bull and bear triangles

Bull Market

Bear Market

© 2011 Elliott Wave International (www.elliottwave.com)

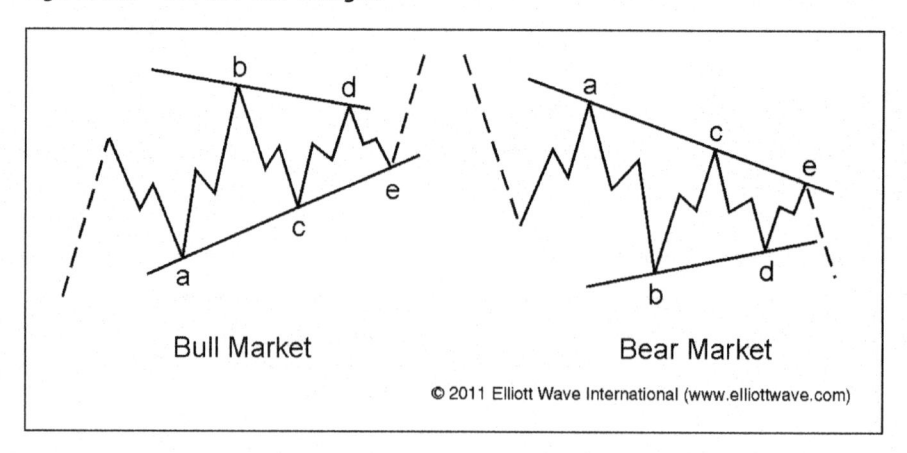

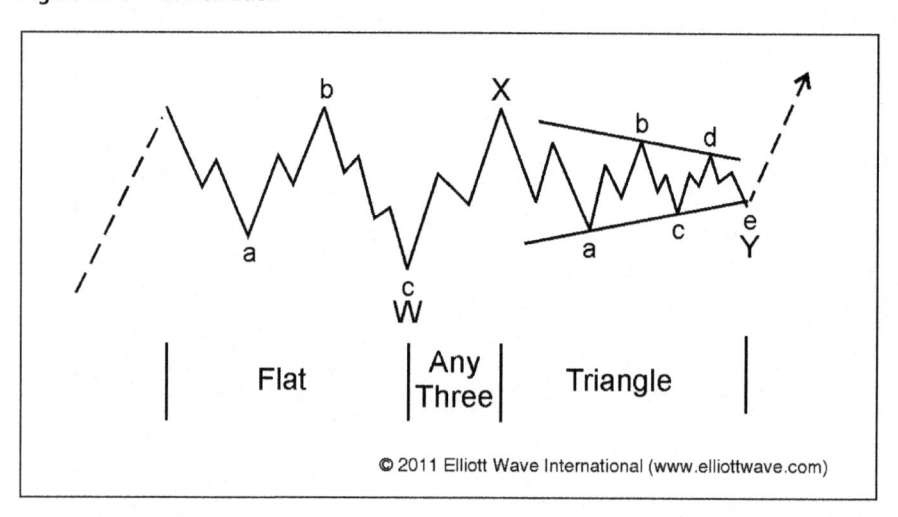

Figure A1.3 – Combination

Flat | Any Three | Triangle

© 2011 Elliott Wave International (www.elliottwave.com)

Appendices | Appendix 1: Elliott Wave Patterns

Figure A1.4 – Combination

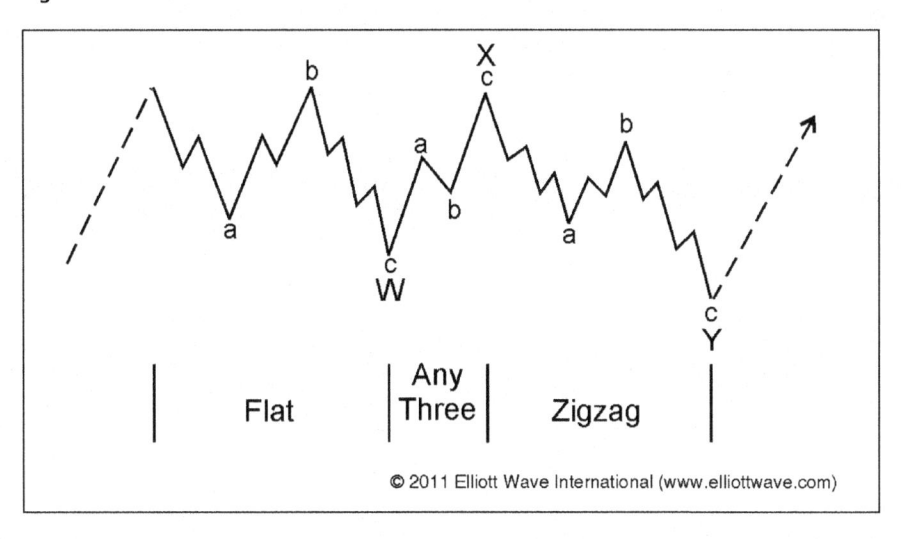

Figure A1.5 – Five-wave impulsive advance and channel

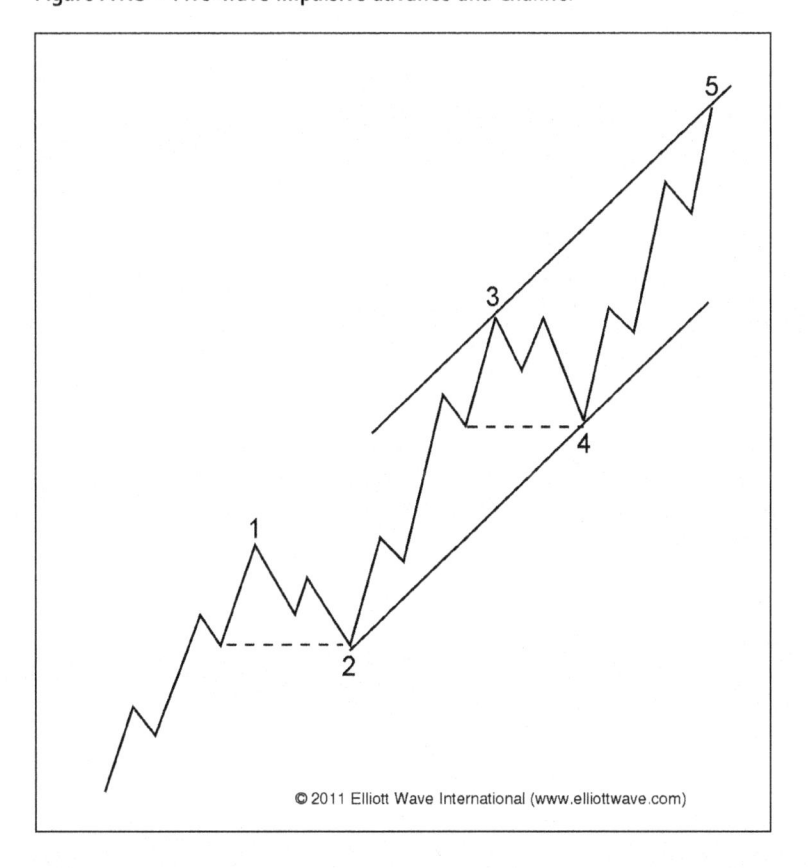

287

Figure A1.6 – 62% retracement (wave two)

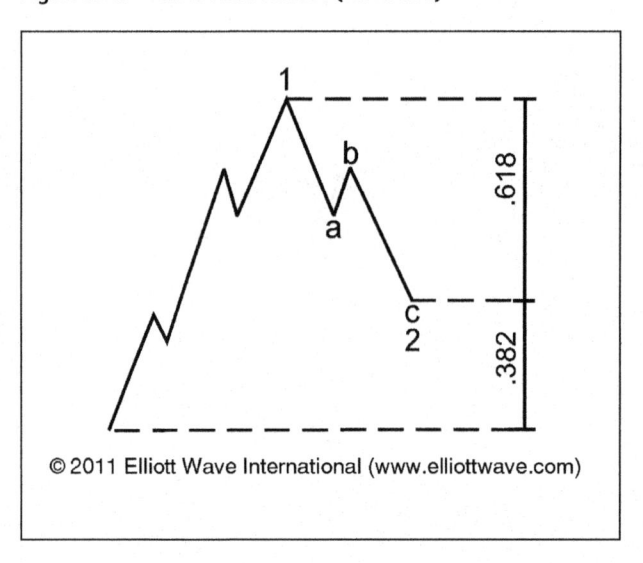

Figure A1.7 – 38% retracement (wave four)

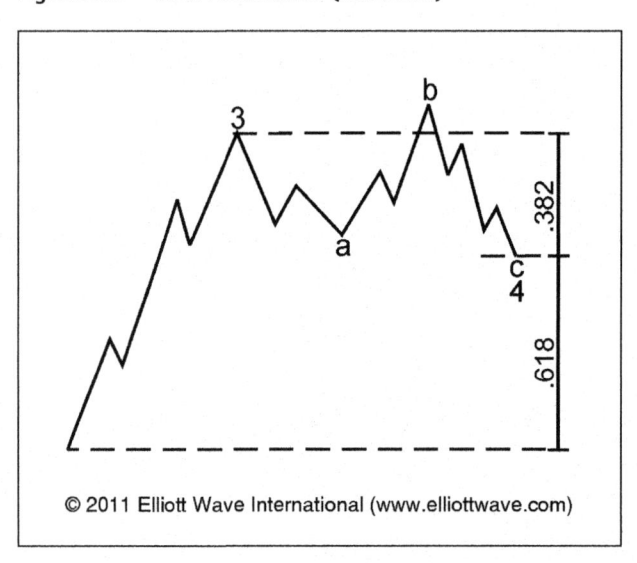

Appendices | Appendix 1: Elliott Wave Patterns

Figure A1.8 – First iteration – Motive and Corrective waves

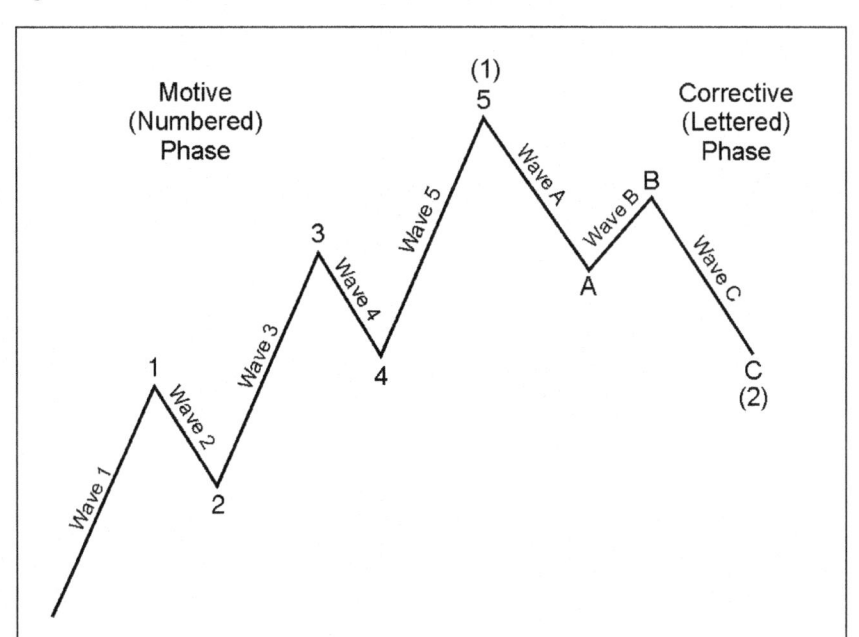

Figure A1.9 – Second iteration – Motive and Corrective waves further subdivided

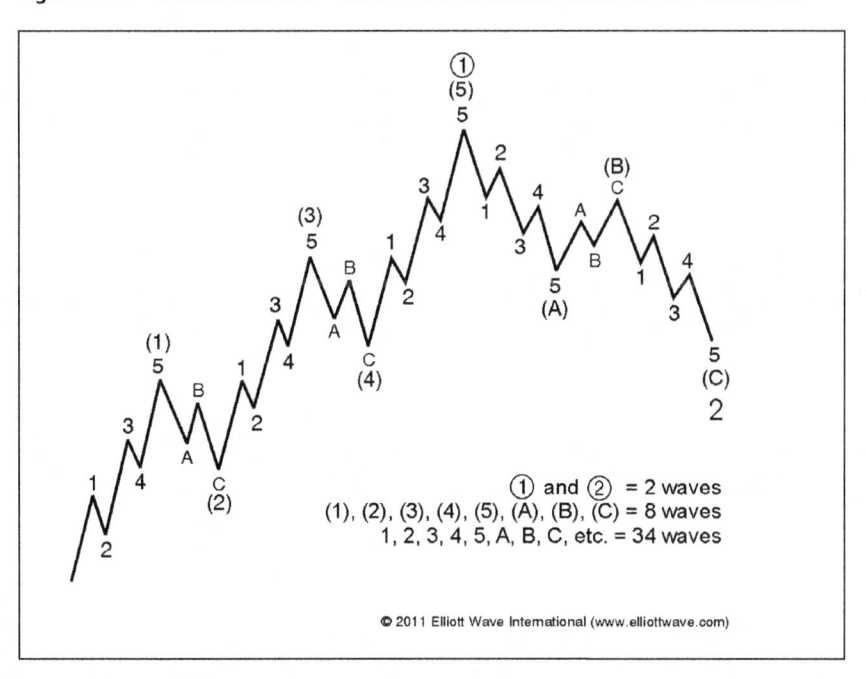

① and ② = 2 waves
(1), (2), (3), (4), (5), (A), (B), (C) = 8 waves
1, 2, 3, 4, 5, A, B, C, etc. = 34 waves

289

Figure A1.10 – Ending diagonal

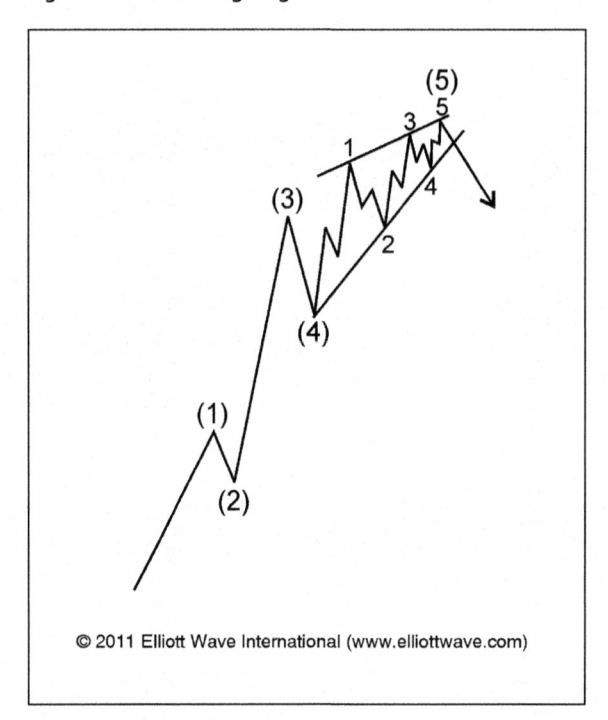

Appendices | Appendix 1: Elliott Wave Patterns

Figure A1.11 – Extensions

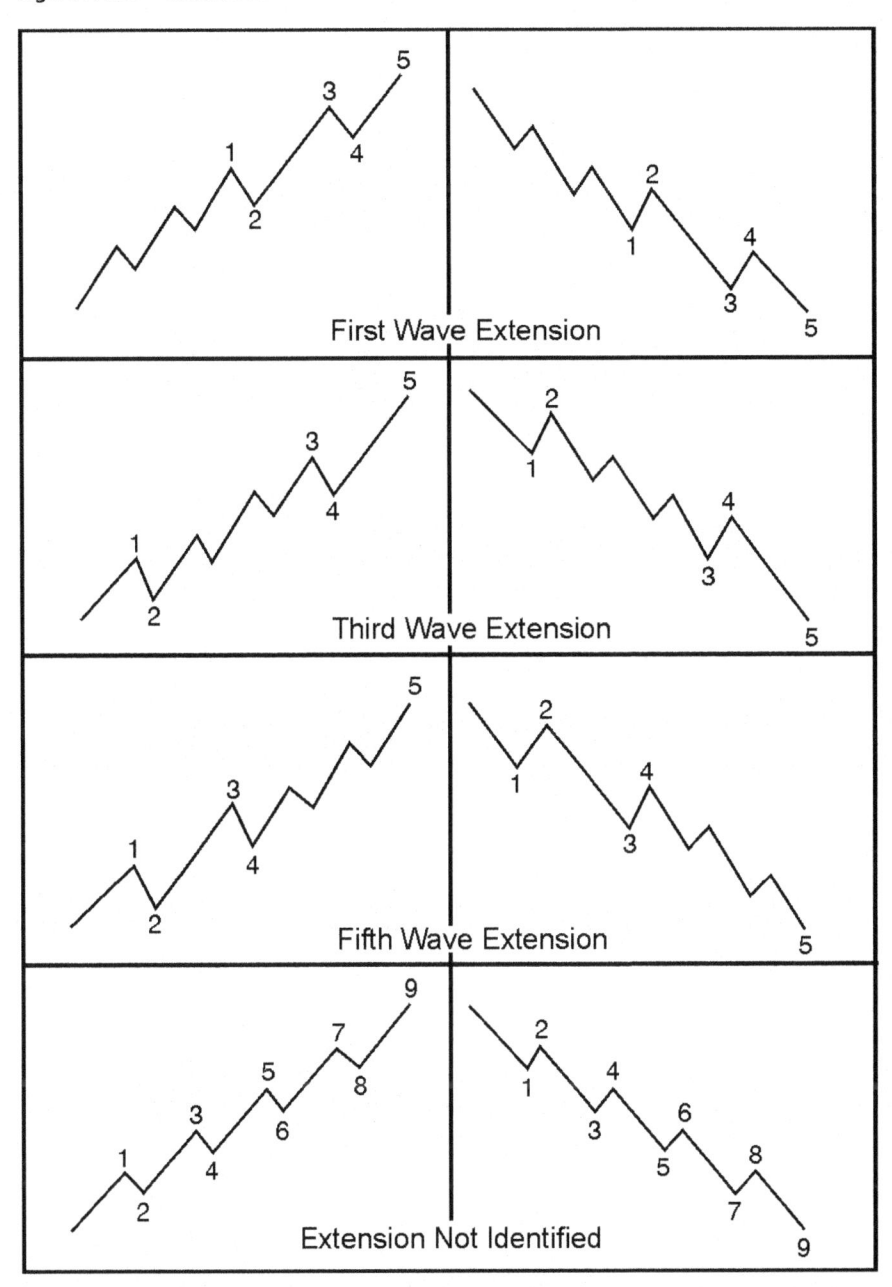

Figure A1.12 – Zigzag

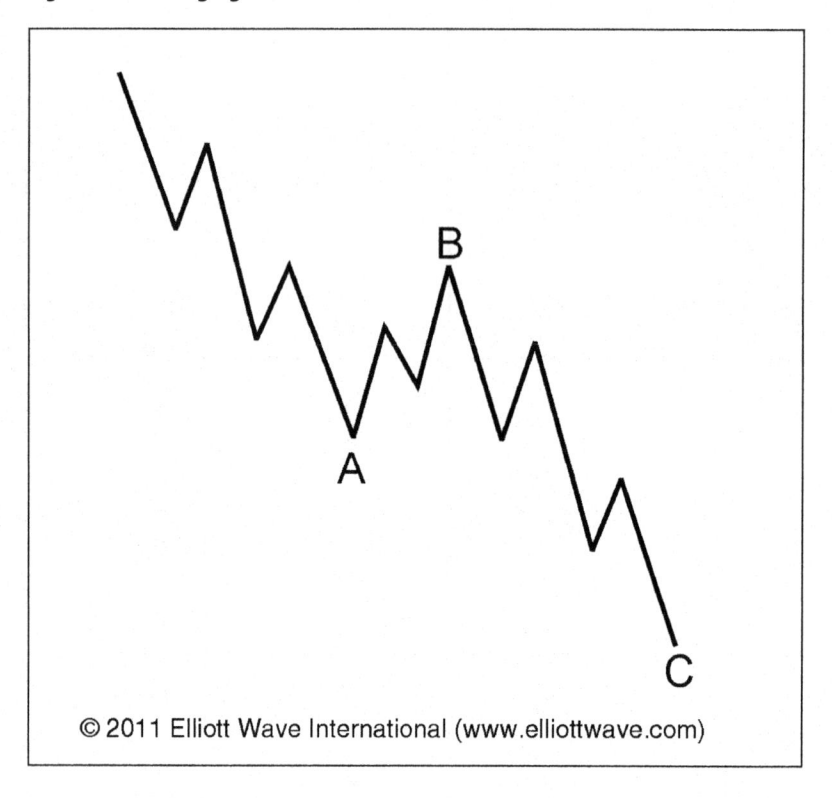

Figure A1.13 – Double zigzag

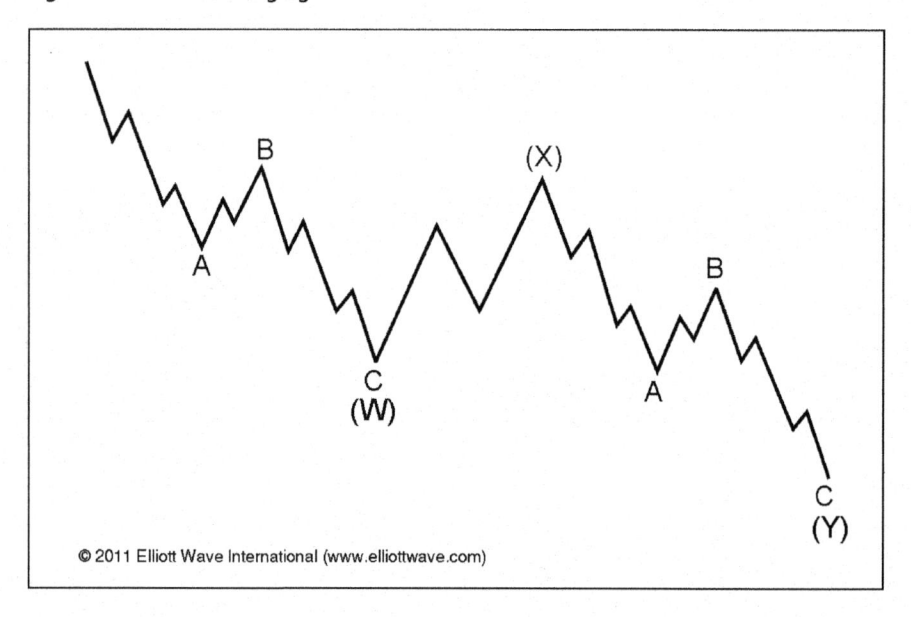

Appendices | **Appendix 1: Elliott Wave Patterns**

Figure A1.14 – Flat

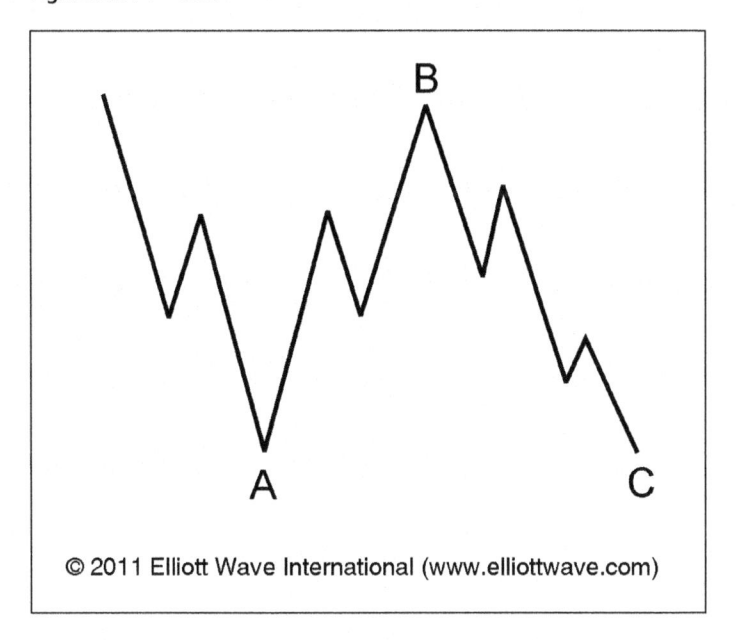

Figure A1.15 – Expanded flat

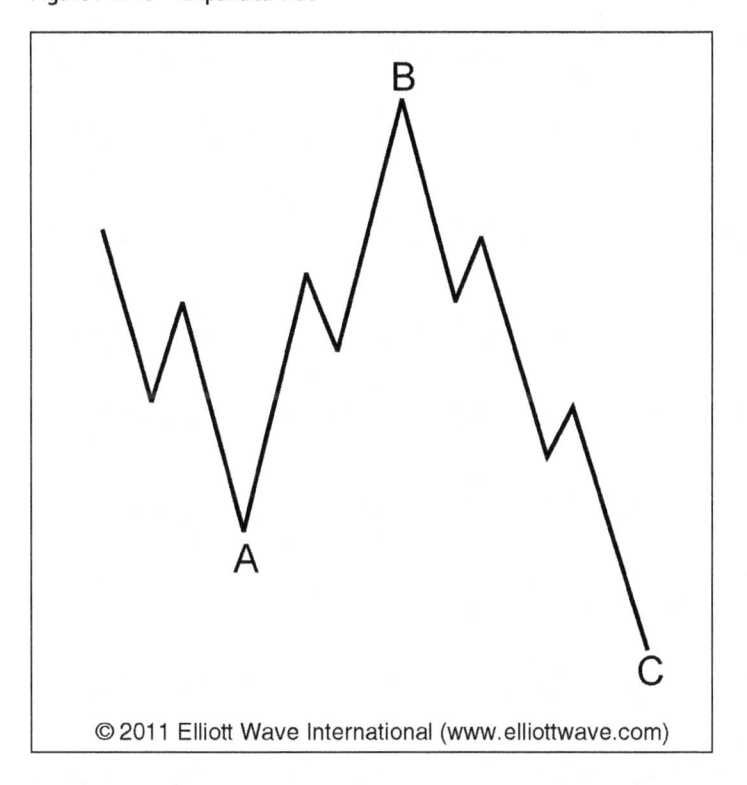

Appendix 2: FLD Code

The code for the FLD – as well as all of the code used in this book – is provided in Updata's proprietary language as well as TradeStation's Easy Language. For users of other trading platforms, you will either need to translate the code yourself or contact the development team at your vendor. However, if there is enough interest, I will commission a developer in Metastock, CQG or Ninja to convert all of the code shown in the Appendices. I will charge a small fee for this to cover costs. Please email me on **cgrafton@vectisma.com** if you are interested.

Updata

```
Programmer - Christopher Grafton
NAME FLD
PARAMETER #PERIOD=80
PARAMETER #SETBACK=20
PARAMETER #R=0
PARAMETER #G=0
PARAMETER #B=0

INDICATORTYPE TOOL
DISPLAYSTYLE  DASH
COLOUR RGB(#R,#G,#B)

@FLD=0

FOR #CURDATE=#PERIOD TO #LASTDATE+(#PERIOD/2)
@FLD=HIST((HIGH+LOW)/2,(#PERIOD/2)+1)

IF #CURDATE>#LASTDATE-#SETBACK

@PLOT=@FLD

ENDIF

NEXT
```

Notes
- You will need to run the code separately for each FLD you wish to display on the chart. The setback period as well as the actual cycle period and colour will need to be changed manually each time.

- #PERIOD refers to the nominal cycle period. Stick to the time units of the chart you are looking at. For example if you want to plot an 18 month FLD on a weekly chart, you need to express the FLD in weeks, thus #PERIOD=80. On the monthly chart it is just 18. If you want to plot the 80 week FLD on a daily chart, then you need to express weeks in trading days. To do this simply multiply by five (the number of trading days in a week): thus in this case 80W = 18M = 400 days.

- Remember: you need to use the average cycle periods actually derived from your phasing analysis or scans. If you just use the nominal periods (80W, 40W and so on), the FLDs will be out of kilter with the actual cycles on the chart. The Nominal Model in months, weeks and days for both calendar and trading time can be found in Chapter 1, Table 1.3.

- Also remember that FLDs on the daily chart always need to be expressed in trading days. If you express them in calendar days, the FLDs will be too long and will not do their job. The conversion again is: calendar to trading multiply by 0.7; trading to calendar divide by 0.7.

- #SETBACK refers to how much of the FLD in past time you wish to see. If you are plotting a historical FLD, then this value needs to be at least the same as the number of bars displayed on the chart. If you are doing current FLDs you may find you need to adjust between 0 and 20. It is a matter of personal preference. If the setback is too long, then the chart can look too busy. If the setback is too short, then it will convey too little information.

- #DISPLAYSTYLE THICK2 is the thickness of the FLD line. If this setting is too thick, then change it to #DISPLAYSTYLE LINE.

- #COLOUR: Updata uses the additive primary colour RGB system. You can choose whatever colours you like for FLDs, and the full table of colours can be found at http://www.tayloredmktg.com/rgb. Remember though that your colour code needs to be uniform across all of your analysis components: FLDs, VTLs and phasing diamonds. For example, a forty day (nominal) FLD – which is blue in the scheme used in this book – has to be the same colour as both the 40-day diamond and VTL. If you do not do this, you will get into a dreadful muddle. Finally, if you choose to use the colour scheme shown in this book (shown in Table A2.1) and prefer to display your charts with a black background, you will need to change the 80W to white RGB (255,255,255), otherwise it will not show up on your chart.

- The actual Updata file can be downloaded from:
  vectisma.com/resources/downloads/fldcode

Colour coding

Table A2.1: RGB colour codes for cycles in the Nominal Model

Nom.			Colour	RGB code	
18Y			Brown	139,69,19	
9Y			Turqoiuse	0,134,139	
54M	230W		Grey	105,105,105	
18M	80W		Black	0,0,0	
9M	40W		Purple	148,0,211	
	20W		Olive	107,142,35	
	10W	80D	Red	255,0,0	
		40D	Blue	0,0,255	
		20D	Green	0,100,0	
		10D	Orange	255,165,0	
		5D	Light Blue	0,191,255	

TradeStation

```
/// Program Name - FLD ///

/// Programmer - Mark Cotton ///

/// Website - www.7GTradingTools.com ///

/// Skype - markcottons.skype ///

/// Email - markcottons.email@gmail.com ///


inputs: int PERIOD( 80 ) ;
inputs: int SETBACK( 0 ) ;
inputs: int COLOR( RGB( 241, 31, 15 ) ) ;
inputs: int THICKNESS( 0 { 0 to 6 } ) ;


variables: bool vFIRSTBAR( true ) ;
variables: int vTEXTID( 0 ), double vPREVLASTBARDATE(
JuliantoDate( LastCalcJDate ) ) ;
variables: int vCOUNT( 0 ), int vb( 0 ) ;
if vFIRSTBAR = true then

  begin

    while vPREVLASTBARDATE = JuliantoDate(
LastCalcJDate )

      begin

        vCOUNT = vCOUNT + 1 ;

        vTEXTID = Text_New( JuliantoDate( LastCalcJDate
- vCOUNT ), time, high + ( high - low ), " " ) ;

        Text_SetStyle( vTEXTID, 1, 1 ) ;

        vPREVLASTBARDATE = Text_GetDate( vTEXTID ) ;

      end ;
```

```
            vFIRSTBAR = false ;

    end ;


if GetAppInfo( aiSpaceToRight ) >= ( ( PERIOD * 0.5 ) +
1 ) then

    begin

        if SETBACK > 0 then

            begin

                if LastBarOnChart = true then

                    begin

                        for vb = 0 to ( SETBACK + ( ( PERIOD * 0.5
) + 1 ) ) - 1

                            begin

                                plot1[( -( PERIOD * 0.5 ) + 1 ) +
vb]( ( high[vb] + low[vb] ) * 0.5, "FLD1", COLOR,
default, THICKNESS ) ;

                            end ;

                    end ;

            end

        else

            begin

                plot2[-( PERIOD * 0.5 ) + 1]( ( high + low ) *
0.5, "FLD2", COLOR, default, THICKNESS ) ;

                end ;

    end
```

```
else

  begin

    value1 = Text_SetString( vTEXTID, "Set Spaces to
the Right to " + numtostr( ( ( PERIOD * 0.5 ) + 1 ), 0
) + " in Format Window" ) ;

  end ;
```

Appendix 3: Inverse Moving Average Code

Updata

```
Programmer – Christopher Grafton
NAME INVERSE MOVING AVERAGE
PARAMETER @PERIOD=20

INDICATORTYPE CHART
DISPLAYSTYLE HISTOGRAM

@SMA=0
@CLOSE=0
@DETREND=0

FOR #CURDATE=@PERIOD TO #LASTDATE
@SMA=HIST(MAVE(@PERIOD),(-@PERIOD/2))
@CLOSE=CLOSE

@DETREND=@CLOSE-@SMA

IF @DETREND>0
  COLOUR RGB(0,0,255)
ENDIF

IF @DETREND<0
  COLOUR RGB(255,0,0)
ENDIF

@PLOT=@DETREND
NEXT

FOR #CURDATE=(#LASTDATE-@PERIOD/2)+1 TO #LASTDATE
@PLOT=-10000
NEXT
```

Notes

- This indicator, also called a Detrender is displayed as a histogram in the lower window of the chart. When the close is above the moving average, the histogram bars are coloured blue; and when the close is below the moving average, the bars are coloured red.

- The closing price has been used, although you could equally use any other price level: for example High or Low. In which case, simply change the line: @CLOSE=CLOSE to @CLOSE=HIGH or @CLOSE=LOW.

- Similarly, the moving average does not need to be a simple moving average. If you wish to use an exponential moving average for example simply replace MAVE with EAVE in the line @SMA=HIST(MAVE(@PERIOD),(-@PERIOD/2))

- The Parameter @PERIOD is a manual input and the choice of moving average period is yours.

- The Updata code can be downloaded from: vectisma.com/downloads/inversema

Appendix 4: Cycle Envelope Code

Updata

```
Programmer – Christopher Grafton
NAME CYCLE ENVELOPE
PARAMETER @PERIOD=20
PARAMETER @ADJUST=1.5
PARAMETER #R=0
PARAMETER #G=0
PARAMETER #B=0

INDICATORTYPE TOOL
DISPLAYSTYLE 3LINES
PLOTSTYLE LINE RGB(#R,#G,#B)
PLOTSTYLE2 LINE RGB(#R,#G,#B)
PLOTSTYLE3 DASH RGB(#R,#G,#B)

@SMA=0
@UPPER=0
@LOWER=0
@HIGH=0
@LOW=0
@MID=0
@MID1=0
@MID2=0
@RANGE=@PERIOD/2
@AVG=0
#SUM=0
#ADD=0
@BAND=0
@DEV=0
@DEN=0

FOR #CURDATE=@PERIOD TO (#LASTDATE-@PERIOD/2)
@DEV=MAX(@DEV,(HIGH(0)-LOW(0)))
@DEN=@DEN+1
NEXT
@BAND=@DEV/@ADJUST
FOR #CURDATE=@PERIOD TO (#LASTDATE-@PERIOD/2)
@SMA=HIST(MAVE(@PERIOD),(-@PERIOD/2))
@UPPER=@SMA+@BAND
@LOWER=@SMA-@BAND
@RANGE=(@PERIOD/2)
@PLOT=@UPPER
@PLOT2=@LOWER
@PLOT3=@SMA
```

```
NEXT

FOR #CURDATE=(#LASTDATE-@PERIOD/2)+1 TO (#LASTDATE-1)
@PLOT=-10000
@PLOT2=-10000
@PLOT3=-10000
NEXT

#CURDATE=#LASTDATE
@MID=MAVE(@RANGE)
@MID1=MAVE(@RANGE)+@BAND
@MID2=MAVE(@RANGE)-@BAND
DRAWLINESTYLE DASH
DRAWCOLOUR RGB(#R,#G,#B)
DRAWLINE  @RANGE,@UPPER,0,@MID1
DRAWLINE  @RANGE,@LOWER,0,@MID2
DRAWLINE  @RANGE,@SMA,0,@MID
```

Notes

This tool is simply centred moving average bands, but with straight lines drawn from the last plot of each line (centred MA, upper band and lower band) to the simple moving average value at the end of the data, thereby plotting in an approximation for the final lagging range.

- #PERIOD refers to the moving average period. This needs to be between one quarter and a half of the cycle around which you wish to draw the envelope. For example, a 40 day cycle will need an envelope period of between 10 and 20 days. Half is standard, but sometimes this may be too smooth. If the envelope period is the same length as the cycle, the envelope will not pick out the fluctuation of the cycle of interest.

- Any number of envelopes can be drawn and they can be differentiated by choosing different colours. Remember, you need to input the appropriate RGB number in each case, for example red would #R=255, #G=0, #B=0.

- #ADJUST: this automatically adjusts the width of the envelope to enclose most of the price action. The default setting is 1.5, however sometimes you will find that the bands are too narrow. In this case, decrease the number. If the bands are too wide, then increase the number. Often it is a case of experimenting to get the best fit.

- The Updata code can be downloaded from: vectisma.com/downloads/envelope

TradeStation

```
/// Program Name - Cycle Envelope ///
/// Programmer - Mark Cotton ///
/// Website - www.7GTradingTools.com ///
/// Skype - markcottons.skype ///
/// Email - markcottons.email@gmail.com ///


inputs: int PERIOD( 20 ) ;
inputs: int CHANNELWIDTH( 30 ) ;
inputs: int COLOR( RGB( 241, 31, 15 ) ) ;
inputs: int COLORPRO( RGB( 20, 241, 15 ) ) ;


variables: double vDEV( 0 ), int vb( 0 ) ;
variables: double vSMA( 0 ), double vUPPER( 0 ), double vLOWER( 0 ) ;
variables: double vCLOSETOT( 0 ), double vAVGPRO( 0 ), double vAVGPROPLOT( 0 ) ;
variables: double vINCREMENT( 0 ) ;


vSMA = Average( close, PERIOD ) ;
vUPPER = vSMA + ( CHANNELWIDTH * 0.5 ) ;
vLOWER = vSMA - ( CHANNELWIDTH * 0.5 ) ;


plot1[( Period * 0.5 )]( vSMA, "SMA", COLOR ) ;
plot2[( Period * 0.5 )]( vUPPER, "UPPER", COLOR ) ;
plot3[( Period * 0.5 )]( vLOWER, "LOWER", COLOR ) ;


vCLOSETOT = 0 ;

for vb = 0 to ( PERIOD * 0.5 ) - 1

  begin

    vCLOSETOT = vCLOSETOT + close ;

  end ;

vAVGPRO = vCLOSETOT / ( PERIOD * 0.5 ) ;
```

```
vINCREMENT = absvalue( vAVGPRO - vSMA ) / ( PERIOD *
0.5 ) ;


for vb = 0 to ( PERIOD * 0.5 ) - 1

  begin

    if vAVGPRO >= vSMA then vAVGPROPLOT = vAVGPRO - (
vb * vINCREMENT ) else vAVGPROPLOT = vAVGPRO + ( vb *
vINCREMENT ) ;

    plot1[vb]( vAVGPROPLOT, "SMA", COLORPRO ) ;

    plot2[vb]( vAVGPROPLOT + ( CHANNELWIDTH * 0.5 ),
"UPPER", COLORPRO ) ;

    plot3[vb]( vAVGPROPLOT - ( CHANNELWIDTH * 0.5 ),
"LOWER", COLORPRO ) ;

  end ;
```

Appendix 5: Diamonds Grid and Numbers

Updata

Diamonds Grid

```
Programmer — Christopher Grafton
NAME DIAMONDS GRID
PARAMETER "GAPSIZE" #GAPSIZE=10
PARAMETER "PROJECT" #PROJECT=50
PARAMETER "DAY" #D=8
PARAMETER "MONTH" #M=2
PARAMETER "YEAR" #Y=2010
PARAMETER "WHITE" #WHITE=1
PARAMETER "DAILY" #DAILY=1
PARAMETER "ADJUST" #GAP=20

INDICATORTYPE TOOL

#GAPHOR=10
#PERIOD0=#LASTDATE-DATE(#D,#M,#Y)

#CURDATE=#LASTDATE-1
@LOW=PLOW(LOW,#PERIOD0)
@HIGH=PHIGH(HIGH,#PERIOD0)
@LOWEST=PLOW(LOW,#PERIOD0+#GAPHOR)
@HIGHEST=PHIGH(HIGH,#PERIOD0+#GAPHOR)
@GAPHIGH=0.05 * (@HIGHEST-@LOWEST)
@GAPLOW=0.1 * (@HIGHEST-@LOWEST)
@GAPLEVEL=0.035 * (@HIGHEST-@LOWEST)
@LOWEST=@LOWEST - @GAPLOW
@HIGHEST=@LOWEST + @GAPHIGH
@LEVEL=@LOWEST-@GAPLEVEL*0.5
@LEVEL=@LOWEST-@GAPLEVEL*1.5
@LEVEL=@LOWEST-@GAPLEVEL*2.5
@LEVEL=@LOWEST-@GAPLEVEL*3.5
@LEVEL=@LOWEST-@GAPLEVEL*4.5
@LEVEL=@LOWEST-@GAPLEVEL*5.5
@LEVEL=@LOWEST-@GAPLEVEL*6.5

#I=0
@LEVEL=0.0
```

```
FOR #I=0 TO 7
@LEVEL=@LOWEST-#I*@GAPLEVEL
IF #WHITE=0
DRAWLEVEL DOT,@LEVEL,RGB(105,105,105)
ELSEIF #WHITE=1
DRAWLEVEL DOT,@LEVEL,RGB(0,0,0)
ENDIF
NEXT

IF #WHITE=0
COLOUR RGB(255,255,255)
ELSEIF #WHITE=1
COLOUR RGB(0,0,0)
ENDIF
#CURDATE=DATE(#D,#M,#Y)- #GAP
IF #DAILY=1
@LEVEL=@LOWEST-@GAPLEVEL*0.5
DRAWTEXT @LEVEL AT "80W (18M)"
ELSEIF #DAILY=0
@LEVEL=@LOWEST-@GAPLEVEL*0.5
DRAWTEXT @LEVEL AT "18Y"
ENDIF
IF #DAILY=1
@LEVEL=@LOWEST-@GAPLEVEL*1.5
DRAWTEXT @LEVEL AT "40W (200D)"
ELSEIF #DAILY=0
@LEVEL=@LOWEST-@GAPLEVEL*1.5
DRAWTEXT @LEVEL AT "9Y (460W)"
ENDIF
IF #DAILY=1
@LEVEL=@LOWEST-@GAPLEVEL*2.5
DRAWTEXT @LEVEL AT "20W (100D)"
ELSEIF #DAILY=0
@LEVEL=@LOWEST-@GAPLEVEL*2.5
DRAWTEXT @LEVEL AT "54M (230W)"
ENDIF
IF #DAILY=1
@LEVEL=@LOWEST-@GAPLEVEL*3.5
DRAWTEXT @LEVEL AT "80D (55D)"
ELSEIF #DAILY=0
@LEVEL=@LOWEST-@GAPLEVEL*3.5
DRAWTEXT @LEVEL AT "18M (80W)"
ENDIF
IF #DAILY=1
@LEVEL=@LOWEST-@GAPLEVEL*4.5
DRAWTEXT @LEVEL AT "40D (28D)"
```

```
ELSEIF #DAILY=0
@LEVEL=@LOWEST-@GAPLEVEL*4.5
DRAWTEXT @LEVEL AT "9M (40W)"
ENDIF
IF #DAILY=1
@LEVEL=@LOWEST-@GAPLEVEL*5.5
DRAWTEXT @LEVEL AT "20D (14D)"
ELSEIF #DAILY=0
@LEVEL=@LOWEST-@GAPLEVEL*5.5
DRAWTEXT @LEVEL AT "20W (100D)"
ENDIF
IF #DAILY=1
@LEVEL=@LOWEST-@GAPLEVEL*6.5
DRAWTEXT @LEVEL AT "10D (7D)"
ELSEIF #DAILY=0
@LEVEL=@LOWEST-@GAPLEVEL*6.5
DRAWTEXT @LEVEL AT "10W (55D)"
ENDIF

@LEVEL = @LOWEST + @GAPLEVEL
IF #WHITE=0
COLOUR RGB(255,255,255)
ELSEIF #WHITE=1
COLOUR RGB(0,0,0)
ENDIF

#COUNT=0
#COUNT1=0
FOR #CURDATE=(#LASTDATE-#PERIOD0) TO (#LASTDATE+#PROJECT)
  IF MOD(#COUNT,#GAPSIZE) != 0
    DRAWTEXT @LEVEL AT "."
  ELSEIF MOD(#COUNT,#GAPSIZE) = 0
    DRAWTEXT @LEVEL AT #COUNT
  ENDIF
    #COUNT=#COUNT+1
NEXT
```

Notes

The diamonds grid superimposes at the bottom of the price chart and does not create a new sub-window. You will need to manually adjust the chart to fit the screen once the grid has been placed.

- #GAPSIZE: this is the gap between the sequence of consecutive numbers running along the top of the grid and serving as a proxy for date. You can choose any number, but for most purposes 10 is sufficient. This will just count up in tens, leaving dots instead of numbers in-between. If you are looking at shorter periods, then you should choose a lower value, say 1 or 5. If you are looking at longer periods choose 20 or more.

- #PROJECT: this sets how far into the future the numbers keep counting. You should leave a space at the right side of your chart to allow the FLDs to project into and place future potential diamonds.

- #DAY, #MONTH, #YEAR: you need to choose the start date of the grid, inputting day, month and year. For the year, do not abbreviate, write 2009, 2010 etc.

- #WHITE: this sets the colour of the lines and the numbers in the grid. If you are using a white background chart, then you need to select #WHITE=1. If you are using a black background chart, select #WHITE=0.

- #DAILY: if you are conducting an analysis on a daily chart you need to select #DAILY=1. If you are conducting analysis on a weekly chart, select #DAILY=0.

- #ADJUST: this adjusts the position of the nominal periods on the far left of the grid either closer to the start (0) or further away, depending on the timeframe or the size of your chart. The default setting is 10, which means the values are written ten bars back from the zero. Five is closer, 20 is further away.

- The actual Updata file can be downloaded from: vectisma.com/downloads/diamondgrid

Numbers from fixed date

You may just want to have the sequence of consecutive numbers at the bottom of the chart, but not the grid, for example if you are scanning through charts to pick out likely candidates for further analysis. In this case you can run the following code. The parameters are the same, but there is no need to distinguish daily from weekly.

```
Programmer – Christopher Grafton
NAME NUMBERS
PARAMETER "GAPSIZE" #GAPSIZE=10
PARAMETER "PROJECT" #PROJECT=50
PARAMETER "DAY" #D=9
PARAMETER "MONTH" #M=3
PARAMETER "YEAR" #Y=2009
PARAMETER "WHITE" #WHITE=1

INDICATORTYPE TOOL
DISPLAYSTYLE 2LINES
PLOTSTYLE1 LINE RGB(0,0,0)
PLOTSTYLE2 LINE RGB(0,0,0)
#GAPHOR=10
#PERIOD0=#LASTDATE-DATE(#D,#M,#Y)

#CURDATE=#LASTDATE-1
@LOW=PLOW(LOW,#PERIOD0)
@HIGH=PHIGH(HIGH,#PERIOD0)
@LOWEST=PLOW(LOW,#PERIOD0+#GAPHOR)
@HIGHEST=PHIGH(HIGH,#PERIOD0+#GAPHOR)
@GAPHIGH=0.05 * (@HIGHEST-@LOWEST)
@GAPLOW=0.1 * (@HIGHEST-@LOWEST)
@GAPLEVEL=0.035 * (@HIGHEST-@LOWEST)
@LOWEST=@LOWEST - @GAPLOW
@HIGHEST=@LOWEST + @GAPHIGH
@LEVEL9Y=@LOWEST-@GAPLEVEL*0.5
@LEVEL54M=@LOWEST-@GAPLEVEL*1.5
@LEVEL18M=@LOWEST-@GAPLEVEL*2.5
@LEVEL9M=@LOWEST-@GAPLEVEL*3.5
@LEVEL20W=@LOWEST-@GAPLEVEL*4.5
@LEVEL10W=@LOWEST-@GAPLEVEL*5.5

#I=0
@LEVEL=0.0
FOR #I=0 TO 1
```

```
@LEVEL=@LOWEST-#I*@GAPLEVEL
NEXT

@LEVEL = @LOWEST - @GAPLEVEL*0.5

#COUNT=0
#COUNT1=0
FOR #CURDATE=(#LASTDATE-
#PERIOD0) TO (#LASTDATE+#PROJECT)
IF MOD(#COUNT,#GAPSIZE) != 0
DRAWTEXT @LEVEL AT "."
ELSEIF #WHITE=1
COLOUR RGB(0,0,0)
ENDIF
IF MOD(#COUNT,#GAPSIZE) = 0
DRAWTEXT @LEVEL AT #COUNT
ELSEIF #WHITE=0
COLOUR RGB(255,255,255)
ENDIF
#COUNT=#COUNT+1
NEXT
```

Numbers from period back

Instead of starting the numbers from a fixed date, you may wish to choose a period back, for example to start counting 125 bars back from the last date. The code for this is as follows:

```
NAME NUMBERS PERIOD
PARAMETER "GAPSIZE" #GAPSIZE=10
PARAMETER "PROJECT" #PROJECT=30
PARAMETER "PERIOD" #PERIOD1=125
PARAMETER "WHITE" #WHITE=1

INDICATORTYPE TOOL
DISPLAYSTYLE 2LINES
PLOTSTYLE1 LINE RGB(0,0,0)
PLOTSTYLE2 LINE RGB(0,0,0)
#GAPHOR=10
#PERIOD0=#PERIOD1

#CURDATE=#LASTDATE-1
@LOW=PLOW(LOW,#PERIOD0)
@HIGH=PHIGH(HIGH,#PERIOD0)
@LOWEST=PLOW(LOW,#PERIOD0+#GAPHOR)
```

```
@HIGHEST=PHIGH(HIGH,#PERIOD0+#GAPHOR)
@GAPHIGH=0.05 * (@HIGHEST-@LOWEST)
@GAPLOW=0.1 * (@HIGHEST-@LOWEST)
@GAPLEVEL=0.035 * (@HIGHEST-@LOWEST)
@LOWEST=@LOWEST - @GAPLOW
@HIGHEST=@LOWEST + @GAPHIGH
@LEVEL9Y=@LOWEST-@GAPLEVEL*0.5
@LEVEL54M=@LOWEST-@GAPLEVEL*1.5
@LEVEL18M=@LOWEST-@GAPLEVEL*2.5
@LEVEL9M=@LOWEST-@GAPLEVEL*3.5
@LEVEL20W=@LOWEST-@GAPLEVEL*4.5
@LEVEL10W=@LOWEST-@GAPLEVEL*5.5

#I=0
@LEVEL=0.0
FOR #I=0 TO 1
@LEVEL=@LOWEST-#I*@GAPLEVEL
NEXT

@LEVEL = @LOWEST - @GAPLEVEL*0.5

#COUNT=0
#COUNT1=0
FOR #CURDATE=(#LASTDATE-
#PERIOD1) TO (#LASTDATE+#PROJECT)
IF MOD(#COUNT,#GAPSIZE) != 0
DRAWTEXT @LEVEL AT "."
ELSEIF #WHITE=1
COLOUR RGB(0,0,0)
ENDIF
IF MOD(#COUNT,#GAPSIZE) = 0
DRAWTEXT @LEVEL AT #COUNT
ELSEIF #WHITE=0
COLOUR RGB(255,255,255)
ENDIF
#COUNT=#COUNT+1
NEXT
```

- Updata code can be downloaded from **vectisma.com/downloads/numbers**

TradeStation

```
/// Program Name - Diamonds Grid ///
/// Programmer - Mark Cotton ///
/// Website - www.7GTradingTools.com ///
/// Skype - markcottons.skype ///
/// Email - markcottons.email@gmail.com ///


inputs: int GAPSIZE( 10 ) ;
inputs: int STARTDAY( 6 ) ;
inputs: int STARTMONTH( 3 ) ;
inputs: int STARTYEAR( 2009 ) ;
inputs: int TEXTPOSITION( 25 { Bars back from start
date } ) ;
inputs: int TEXTCOLOR( White ) ;
inputs: int LINEGAPSIZE( 100 ) ;
inputs: int LINEPROJECT( 5 { Bars into future } { Set
Spaces to the Right to 50 in Format Window } ) ;
inputs: int LINECOLOR( DarkGray ) ;


variables: bool vFIRSTBAR( true ) ;
variables: int vTEXTID( 0 ), double vPREVLASTBARDATE(
JuliantoDate( LastCalcJDate ) ) ;
variables: bool vHILOCALC( False ), int vPERIOD(
TEXTPOSITION ) ;
variables: double vSTARTDATE( 0 ), double vSTARTTIME( 0
) ;
variables: double vLOWEST( 999999999 ), intrabarpersist
bool vFINISHED( False ) ;
variables: double vTICK( ( MinMove / PriceScale ) *
iff( Category = 12, 10, 1 ) ) ;
variables: int vPLOT( 0 ), int vCOUNT( 0 ), int vTEXT(
0 ), int va1( 0 ), int va2( 0 ) ;


arrays: string aTEXT[7]( "" ) ;
arrays: int aTEXTID[]( 0 ) ; Array_SetMaxIndex(
aTEXTID[], LINEPROJECT * 40 ) ;
arrays: double aTEXTDATEID[]( 0 ) ; Array_SetMaxIndex(
aTEXTDATEID[], LINEPROJECT + 1 ) ;
```

/// Retrieve Date previous to Last Chart Date ///

if vFIRSTBAR = true then

  begin

    while vPREVLASTBARDATE = JuliantoDate(LastCalcJDate)

      begin
        vCOUNT = vCOUNT + 1 ;
        vTEXTID = Text_New(JuliantoDate(LastCalcJDate - vCOUNT), time, high + (high - low), " ") ;
        Text_SetStyle(vTEXTID, 1, 1) ;
        vPREVLASTBARDATE = Text_GetDate(vTEXTID) ;
      end ;

    vFIRSTBAR = false ;

  end ;

if GetAppInfo(aiSpaceToRight) < LINEPROJECT then
  begin
    value1 = Text_SetString(vTEXTID, "Set Spaces to the Right to " + numtostr(LINEPROJECT, 0) + " in Format Window") ;
  end ;

/// Find grid start position / Calculate Lowest Low to plot grid below ///

if date >= ELDate(STARTMONTH, STARTDAY, STARTYEAR) and vHILOCALC = false and GetAppInfo(aiSpaceToRight) >= LINEPROJECT then

  begin
    if vPERIOD = TEXTPOSITION then
      begin
        vSTARTDATE = date[TEXTPOSITION] ;
        vSTARTTIME = time[TEXTPOSITION] ;
      end ;

```
    vPERIOD = vPERIOD + 1 ;


    if low < vLOWEST then vLOWEST = low ;

    if date = vPREVLASTBARDATE then vHILOCALC = true ;
  end ;


/// Draw Grid ///

if vHILOCALC = true and vHILOCALC[1] = false and
barstatus( 1 ) = 2 then

  begin

    /// Numeric Series ///

    vCOUNT = 0 ;

    for vPLOT = vPERIOD - ( TEXTPOSITION + 1 ) downto -
LINEPROJECT

      begin

        /// Dots History ///
        if mod( vCOUNT, GAPSIZE ) <> 0 and vPLOT >= 0
then
          begin

            value1 = Text_New( date[vPLOT],
time[vPLOT], vLOWEST - ( 1 * ( LINEGAPSIZE * vTICK ) ),
"." ) ;
            Text_SetColor( value1, TEXTCOLOR ) ;
            Text_SetStyle( value1, 2, 2 ) ;
          end ;


        /// Numbers History ///

        if mod( vCOUNT, GAPSIZE ) = 0 and vPLOT >= 0
then

          begin
```

```
            value1 = Text_New( date[vPLOT],
time[vPLOT], vLOWEST - ( 1 * ( LINEGAPSIZE * vTICK ) ),
numtostr( vCOUNT, 0 ) ) ;
            Text_SetColor( value1, TEXTCOLOR ) ;
            Text_SetStyle( value1, 2, 1 ) ;
          end ;


        /// Dots Future / Calculate Future Dates ///

        if vPLOT = -1 then

          begin
            va1 = 0 ; va2 = 0 ;
            while va2 < LINEPROJECT
              begin
                 va1 = va1 + 1 ;
                 aTEXTID[va1] = Text_New(
JuliantoDate( DateToJulian( Date ) + va1 ) , time,
vLOWEST - ( 1 * ( LINEGAPSIZE * vTICK ) ), "." ) ;

                 Text_SetColor( aTEXTID[va1],
TEXTCOLOR ) ;
                 Text_SetStyle( aTEXTID[va1], 2, 2 ) ;

                 if va1 = 1 or Text_GetDate(
aTEXTID[va1] ) <> Text_GetDate( aTEXTID[va1 - 1] ) then

                       begin
                           va2 = va2 + 1 ;
                           aTEXTDATEID[va2] =
aTEXTID[va1] ;


                       end ;


                 if va1 > 1 and Text_GetDate(
aTEXTID[va1] ) = Text_GetDate( aTEXTID[va1 - 1] ) then

                       begin
                           Text_SetString(
aTEXTID[va1], " " ) ;
                           Text_SetColor(
aTEXTID[va1], TEXTCOLOR ) ;
```

```
                              Text_SetStyle(
aTEXTID[val], 2, 2 ) ;
                    end ;

            end ;

         end ;


      /// Numbers Future ///

      if mod( vCOUNT, GAPSIZE ) = 0 and vPLOT < 0
then
         begin
            Text_SetString( aTEXTDATEID[ absvalue(
vPLOT ) ], numtostr( vCOUNT, 0 ) ) ;
            Text_SetColor( aTEXTDATEID[ absvalue( vPLOT
) ], TEXTCOLOR ) ;
            Text_SetStyle( aTEXTDATEID[ absvalue( vPLOT
) ], 2, 1 ) ;
         end ;

      vCOUNT = vCOUNT + 1 ;
   end ;


   /// Lines 1 to 7 ///

   for vPLOT = vPERIOD downto -LINEPROJECT

      begin
         plot1[vPLOT]( vLOWEST - ( 2 * ( LINEGAPSIZE *
vTICK ) ), "Line1", LINECOLOR ) ;
         plot2[vPLOT]( vLOWEST - ( 3 * ( LINEGAPSIZE *
vTICK ) ), "Line2", LINECOLOR ) ;
         plot3[vPLOT]( vLOWEST - ( 4 * ( LINEGAPSIZE *
vTICK ) ), "Line3", LINECOLOR ) ;
         plot4[vPLOT]( vLOWEST - ( 5 * ( LINEGAPSIZE *
vTICK ) ), "Line4", LINECOLOR ) ;
         plot5[vPLOT]( vLOWEST - ( 6 * ( LINEGAPSIZE *
vTICK ) ), "Line5", LINECOLOR ) ;
         plot6[vPLOT]( vLOWEST - ( 7 * ( LINEGAPSIZE *
vTICK ) ), "Line6", LINECOLOR ) ;
         plot7[vPLOT]( vLOWEST - ( 8 * ( LINEGAPSIZE *
```

```
          vTICK ) ), "Line7", LINECOLOR ) ;
            end ;



        /// Grid Text ///

        if bartype = 2 then

          begin
            aTEXT[1] = "20W (100D)" ;
            aTEXT[2] = "80D (55D)" ;
            aTEXT[3] = "40D (28D)" ;
            aTEXT[4] = "20D (14D)" ;
            aTEXT[5] = "10D (7D)" ;
            aTEXT[6] = "5D (3.5D)" ;
          end ;


        if bartype = 3 then

          begin
            aTEXT[1] = "54M (230W)" ;
            aTEXT[2] = "18M (80W)" ;
            aTEXT[3] = "9M (40W)" ;
            aTEXT[4] = "20W (100D)" ;
            aTEXT[5] = "10W (55D)" ;
            aTEXT[6] = "5W (28D)" ;
          end ;



        for vTEXT = 3 to 9

          begin
            value1 = Text_New( vSTARTDATE, vSTARTTIME,
vLOWEST - ( vTEXT * ( LINEGAPSIZE * vTICK ) ),
aTEXT[vTEXT - 2] ) ;
            Text_SetColor( value1, TEXTCOLOR ) ;
Text_SetStyle( value1, 0, 1 ) ;
          end ;

    end ;
```

Appendix 6: Diamond Placement Code

Updata

Diamond placement on monthly chart

Programmer – Christopher Grafton

```
NAME DIAMOND - MONTHLY
PARAMETER "PROJECT" #PROJECT=50
PARAMETER "STARTGAP" #STARTGAP=-10
PARAMETER "ENDGAP" #ENDGAP=20
INDICATORTYPE TOOL
DISPLAYSTYLE 3LINES
PLOTSTYLE LINE RGB(255,0,0)
PLOTSTYLE2 LINE RGB(255,255,255)
PLOTSTYLE3 LINE RGB(0,0,0)
```

'Copy the contents of the Code Variables column from the Phasing Model spreadsheet and paste this into the space between the two rows of hash marks below. Before you do this you will need to Save As the code here and name it for the security being analysed. You will also need to change the NAME in row 0 from DIAMOND MONTHLY to that of the security, for example in this case it would be $ UKX MONTHLY. The pasted contents will need to overwrite whatever is in the space already. Take cake not to overwrite anything below the second row of hash marks. Also, there is no need to copy the entire column from the spreadsheet, just the rows containing the code variables. For example copy A3:A43, not A:A.

'################################

```
#D=31
#M=3
#Y=1995
#18YAV=168.857142857143
#9YAV=84.4285714285714
#54MAV=42.2142857142857
#18MAV=14.0714285714286
#LASTGRID=199
```

```
#18YLAST=96
#9YLAST=168
#54MLAST=168
#18MLAST=197
#18Y1=96
#18Y2=-50
#9Y1=0
#9Y2=168
#9Y3=-50
#9Y4=-50
#9Y5=-50
#9Y6=96
#9Y7=-50
#54M1=43
#54M2=135
#54M3=-50
#54M4=-50
#54M5=-50
#54M6=-50
#54M7=-50
#54M8=0
#54M9=168
#54M10=-50
#54M11=-50
#54M12=-50
#54M13=96
#54M14=-50
#18M1=16
#18M2=31
#18M3=61
#18M4=78
#18M5=113
#18M6=122
#18M7=154
#18M8=144
#18M9=184
#18M10=197
#18M11=-50
#18M12=-50
#18M13=-50
#18M14=-50
#18M15=43
#18M16=135
#18M17=-50
#18M18=-50
```

```
#18M19=-50
#18M20=-50
#18M21=-50
#18M22=0
#18M23=168
#18M24=-50
#18M25=-50
#18M26=-50
#18M27=96
#18M28=-50


'################################

@REM=0
@NEWNUM=0
@REM1=0
@NEWNUM1=0
@REM2=0
@NEWNUM2=0
@REM3=0
@NEWNUM3=0
#GAP=10
#GAPSIZE=10
#GAPHOR=10
#PERIOD0=#LASTDATE-DATE(#D,#M,#Y)
@LEVEL1=0

#CURDATE=#LASTDATE-1
@LOW=PLOW(LOW,#PERIOD0)
@HIGH=PHIGH(HIGH,#PERIOD0)
@LOWEST=PLOW(LOW,#PERIOD0+#GAPHOR)
@HIGHEST=PHIGH(HIGH,#PERIOD0+#GAPHOR)
@GAPHIGH=0.05*(@HIGHEST-@LOWEST)
@GAPLOW=0.1*(@HIGHEST-@LOWEST)
@GAPLEVEL=0.035*(@HIGHEST-@LOWEST)
@LOWEST=@LOWEST-@GAPLOW
@HIGHEST=@LOWEST+@GAPHIGH
@LEVEL=@LOWEST-@GAPLEVEL*0.5
@LEVEL=@LOWEST-@GAPLEVEL*1.5
@LEVEL=@LOWEST-@GAPLEVEL*2.5
@LEVEL=@LOWEST-@GAPLEVEL*3.5
@LEVEL=@LOWEST-@GAPLEVEL*4.5
@LEVEL18Y=@LOWEST-@GAPLEVEL*0.5
@LEVEL9Y=@LOWEST-@GAPLEVEL*1.5
```

```
@LEVEL54M=@LOWEST-@GAPLEVEL*2.5
@LEVEL18M=@LOWEST-@GAPLEVEL*3.5

#I=0
@LEVEL=0.0
FOR #I=0 TO 5
@LEVEL=@LOWEST-#I*@GAPLEVEL
DRAWCOLOUR RGB(0,0,0)
DRAWLEVEL DOT,@LEVEL,RGB(0,134,139)
NEXT

@LEVEL=@LOWEST+@GAPLEVEL
COLOUR RGB(0,0,0)
#COUNT=0
#COUNT1=0
FOR #CURDATE=DATE(#D,#M,#Y) TO #LASTDATE+#PROJECT
   IF MOD(#COUNT,#GAPSIZE) != 0
      DRAWTEXT @LEVEL AT "."
   ELSEIF MOD(#COUNT,#GAPSIZE) = 0
      DRAWTEXT @LEVEL AT #COUNT
   ENDIF
   #COUNT=#COUNT+1
NEXT

COLOUR RGB(0,0,0)
#CURDATE=DATE(#D,#M,#Y)+#STARTGAP
@LEVEL1=@LOWEST+@GAPLEVEL*0.3
DRAWTEXT @LEVEL1 AT "Nom"
@LEVEL=@LOWEST-@GAPLEVEL*0.5
DRAWTEXT @LEVEL AT "18Y"
@LEVEL=@LOWEST-@GAPLEVEL*1.5
DRAWTEXT @LEVEL AT "9Y"
@LEVEL=@LOWEST-@GAPLEVEL*2.5
DRAWTEXT @LEVEL AT "54M"
@LEVEL=@LOWEST-@GAPLEVEL*3.5
DRAWTEXT @LEVEL AT "18M"

@REM=MOD((#18YAV/12)*10,INT((#18YAV/12)*10))
IF @REM>0.5
   @REM=1
ELSE
   @REM=0
ENDIF
@NEWNUM=(INT((#18YAV/12)*10)+@REM)/10
```

```
@REM1=MOD((#9YAV/12)*10,INT((#9YAV/12)*10))
IF @REM1>0.5
    @REM1=1
ELSE
    @REM1=0
ENDIF
@NEWNUM1=(INT((#9YAV/12)*10)+@REM1)/10

@REM2=MOD((#54MAV)*10,INT((#54MAV)*10))
IF @REM2>0.5
    @REM2=1
ELSE
    @REM2=0
ENDIF
@NEWNUM2=(INT((#54MAV)*10)+@REM2)/10

@REM3=MOD((#18MAV*4.333)*10,INT((#18MAV*4.333)*10))
IF @REM3>0.5
    @REM3=1
ELSE
    @REM3=0
ENDIF
@NEWNUM3=(INT((#18MAV*4.333)*10)+@REM3)/10

COLOUR RGB(0,0,0)
#CURDATE=#LASTDATE+#ENDGAP
@LEVEL1=@LOWEST+@GAPLEVEL*0.3
DRAWTEXT @LEVEL1 AT "Avg"
@LEVEL=@LOWEST-@GAPLEVEL*0.5
DRAWTEXT @LEVEL AT @NEWNUM "Y"
@LEVEL=@LOWEST-@GAPLEVEL*1.5
DRAWTEXT @LEVEL AT @NEWNUM1 "Y"
@LEVEL=@LOWEST-@GAPLEVEL*2.5
DRAWTEXT @LEVEL AT @NEWNUM2 "M"
@LEVEL=@LOWEST-@GAPLEVEL*3.5
DRAWTEXT @LEVEL AT @NEWNUM3 "W"

'18Y DIAMONDS
#CURDATE=DATE(#D,#M,#Y)+#18Y1
DRAWIMAGE AT,#CURDATE,@LEVEL18Y,Diamond 8,RGB(139,69,19)
DRAWIMAGE AT,#CURDATE,@LEVEL9Y,Diamond 8,RGB(0,134,139)

DRAWIMAGE AT,#CURDATE,@LEVEL54M,Diamond 8,RGB(105,105,105)
DRAWIMAGE AT,#CURDATE,@LEVEL18M,Diamond 8,RGB(0,0,0)
#CURDATE=DATE(#D,#M,#Y)+#18Y2
```

```
DRAWIMAGE AT,#CURDATE,@LEVEL18Y,Diamond 8,RGB(139,69,19)
DRAWIMAGE AT,#CURDATE,@LEVEL9Y,Diamond 8,RGB(0,134,139)

DRAWIMAGE AT,#CURDATE,@LEVEL54M,Diamond 8,RGB(105,105,105)
DRAWIMAGE AT,#CURDATE,@LEVEL18M,Diamond 8,RGB(0,0,0)

'9Y DIAMONDS
#CURDATE=DATE(#D,#M,#Y)+#9Y1
DRAWIMAGE AT,#CURDATE,@LEVEL9Y,Diamond 8,RGB(0,134,139)

DRAWIMAGE AT,#CURDATE,@LEVEL54M,Diamond 8,RGB(105,105,105)
DRAWIMAGE AT,#CURDATE,@LEVEL18M,Diamond 8,RGB(0,0,0)
#CURDATE=DATE(#D,#M,#Y)+#9Y2
DRAWIMAGE AT,#CURDATE,@LEVEL9Y,Diamond 8,RGB(0,134,139)

DRAWIMAGE AT,#CURDATE,@LEVEL54M,Diamond 8,RGB(105,105,105)
DRAWIMAGE AT,#CURDATE,@LEVEL18M,Diamond 8,RGB(0,0,0)
#CURDATE=DATE(#D,#M,#Y)+#9Y3
DRAWIMAGE AT,#CURDATE,@LEVEL9Y,Diamond 8,RGB(0,134,139)

DRAWIMAGE AT,#CURDATE,@LEVEL54M,Diamond 8,RGB(105,105,105)
DRAWIMAGE AT,#CURDATE,@LEVEL18M,Diamond 8,RGB(0,0,0)
#CURDATE=DATE(#D,#M,#Y)+#9Y4
DRAWIMAGE AT,#CURDATE,@LEVEL9Y,Diamond 8,RGB(0,134,139)

DRAWIMAGE AT,#CURDATE,@LEVEL54M,Diamond 8,RGB(105,105,105)
DRAWIMAGE AT,#CURDATE,@LEVEL18M,Diamond 8,RGB(0,0,0)
#CURDATE=DATE(#D,#M,#Y)+#9Y5
DRAWIMAGE AT,#CURDATE,@LEVEL9Y,Diamond 8,RGB(0,134,139)

DRAWIMAGE AT,#CURDATE,@LEVEL54M,Diamond 8,RGB(105,105,105)
DRAWIMAGE AT,#CURDATE,@LEVEL18M,Diamond 8,RGB(0,0,0)
#CURDATE=DATE(#D,#M,#Y)+#9Y6
DRAWIMAGE AT,#CURDATE,@LEVEL9Y,Diamond 8,RGB(0,134,139)

DRAWIMAGE AT,#CURDATE,@LEVEL54M,Diamond 8,RGB(105,105,105)
DRAWIMAGE AT,#CURDATE,@LEVEL18M,Diamond 8,RGB(0,0,0)
#CURDATE=DATE(#D,#M,#Y)+#9Y7
DRAWIMAGE AT,#CURDATE,@LEVEL9Y,Diamond 8,RGB(0,134,139)

DRAWIMAGE AT,#CURDATE,@LEVEL54M,Diamond 8,RGB(105,105,105)
DRAWIMAGE AT,#CURDATE,@LEVEL18M,Diamond 8,RGB(0,0,0)

'54M DIAMONDS
#CURDATE=DATE(#D,#M,#Y)+#54M1
```

Appendices | Appendix 6: Final Diamond Placement Code

```
DRAWIMAGE AT,#CURDATE,@LEVEL54M,Diamond 8,RGB(105,105,105)
DRAWIMAGE AT,#CURDATE,@LEVEL18M,Diamond 8,RGB(0,0,0)
#CURDATE=DATE(#D,#M,#Y)+#54M2
DRAWIMAGE AT,#CURDATE,@LEVEL54M,Diamond 8,RGB(105,105,105)
DRAWIMAGE AT,#CURDATE,@LEVEL18M,Diamond 8,RGB(0,0,0)
#CURDATE=DATE(#D,#M,#Y)+#54M3
DRAWIMAGE AT,#CURDATE,@LEVEL54M,Diamond 8,RGB(105,105,105)
DRAWIMAGE AT,#CURDATE,@LEVEL18M,Diamond 8,RGB(0,0,0)
#CURDATE=DATE(#D,#M,#Y)+#54M4
DRAWIMAGE AT,#CURDATE,@LEVEL54M,Diamond 8,RGB(105,105,105)
DRAWIMAGE AT,#CURDATE,@LEVEL18M,Diamond 8,RGB(0,0,0)
#CURDATE=DATE(#D,#M,#Y)+#54M5
DRAWIMAGE AT,#CURDATE,@LEVEL54M,Diamond 8,RGB(105,105,105)
DRAWIMAGE AT,#CURDATE,@LEVEL18M,Diamond 8,RGB(0,0,0)
#CURDATE=DATE(#D,#M,#Y)+#54M6
DRAWIMAGE AT,#CURDATE,@LEVEL54M,Diamond 8,RGB(105,105,105)
DRAWIMAGE AT,#CURDATE,@LEVEL18M,Diamond 8,RGB(0,0,0)
#CURDATE=DATE(#D,#M,#Y)+#54M7
DRAWIMAGE AT,#CURDATE,@LEVEL54M,Diamond 8,RGB(105,105,105)
DRAWIMAGE AT,#CURDATE,@LEVEL18M,Diamond 8,RGB(0,0,0)
#CURDATE=DATE(#D,#M,#Y)+#54M8
DRAWIMAGE AT,#CURDATE,@LEVEL54M,Diamond 8,RGB(105,105,105)
DRAWIMAGE AT,#CURDATE,@LEVEL18M,Diamond 8,RGB(0,0,0)
#CURDATE=DATE(#D,#M,#Y)+#54M9
DRAWIMAGE AT,#CURDATE,@LEVEL54M,Diamond 8,RGB(105,105,105)
DRAWIMAGE AT,#CURDATE,@LEVEL18M,Diamond 8,RGB(0,0,0)
#CURDATE=DATE(#D,#M,#Y)+#54M10
DRAWIMAGE AT,#CURDATE,@LEVEL54M,Diamond 8,RGB(105,105,105)
DRAWIMAGE AT,#CURDATE,@LEVEL18M,Diamond 8,RGB(0,0,0)
#CURDATE=DATE(#D,#M,#Y)+#54M11
DRAWIMAGE AT,#CURDATE,@LEVEL54M,Diamond 8,RGB(105,105,105)
DRAWIMAGE AT,#CURDATE,@LEVEL18M,Diamond 8,RGB(0,0,0)
#CURDATE=DATE(#D,#M,#Y)+#54M12
DRAWIMAGE AT,#CURDATE,@LEVEL54M,Diamond 8,RGB(105,105,105)
DRAWIMAGE AT,#CURDATE,@LEVEL18M,Diamond 8,RGB(0,0,0)
#CURDATE=DATE(#D,#M,#Y)+#54M13
DRAWIMAGE AT,#CURDATE,@LEVEL54M,Diamond 8,RGB(105,105,105)
DRAWIMAGE AT,#CURDATE,@LEVEL18M,Diamond 8,RGB(0,0,0)
#CURDATE=DATE(#D,#M,#Y)+#54M14
DRAWIMAGE AT,#CURDATE,@LEVEL54M,Diamond 8,RGB(105,105,105)
DRAWIMAGE AT,#CURDATE,@LEVEL18M,Diamond 8,RGB(0,0,0)

'18M DIAMONDS
#CURDATE=DATE(#D,#M,#Y)+#18M1
DRAWIMAGE AT,#CURDATE,@LEVEL18M,Diamond 8,RGB(0,0,0)
```

```
#CURDATE=DATE(#D,#M,#Y)+#18M2
DRAWIMAGE AT,#CURDATE,@LEVEL18M,Diamond 8,RGB(0,0,0)
#CURDATE=DATE(#D,#M,#Y)+#18M3
DRAWIMAGE AT,#CURDATE,@LEVEL18M,Diamond 8,RGB(0,0,0)
#CURDATE=DATE(#D,#M,#Y)+#18M4
DRAWIMAGE AT,#CURDATE,@LEVEL18M,Diamond 8,RGB(0,0,0)
#CURDATE=DATE(#D,#M,#Y)+#18M5
DRAWIMAGE AT,#CURDATE,@LEVEL18M,Diamond 8,RGB(0,0,0)
#CURDATE=DATE(#D,#M,#Y)+#18M6
DRAWIMAGE AT,#CURDATE,@LEVEL18M,Diamond 8,RGB(0,0,0)
#CURDATE=DATE(#D,#M,#Y)+#18M7
DRAWIMAGE AT,#CURDATE,@LEVEL18M,Diamond 8,RGB(0,0,0)
#CURDATE=DATE(#D,#M,#Y)+#18M8
DRAWIMAGE AT,#CURDATE,@LEVEL18M,Diamond 8,RGB(0,0,0)
#CURDATE=DATE(#D,#M,#Y)+#18M9
DRAWIMAGE AT,#CURDATE,@LEVEL18M,Diamond 8,RGB(0,0,0)
#CURDATE=DATE(#D,#M,#Y)+#18M10
DRAWIMAGE AT,#CURDATE,@LEVEL18M,Diamond 8,RGB(0,0,0)
#CURDATE=DATE(#D,#M,#Y)+#18M11
DRAWIMAGE AT,#CURDATE,@LEVEL18M,Diamond 8,RGB(0,0,0)
#CURDATE=DATE(#D,#M,#Y)+#18M12
DRAWIMAGE AT,#CURDATE,@LEVEL18M,Diamond 8,RGB(0,0,0)
#CURDATE=DATE(#D,#M,#Y)+#18M13
DRAWIMAGE AT,#CURDATE,@LEVEL18M,Diamond 8,RGB(0,0,0)
#CURDATE=DATE(#D,#M,#Y)+#18M14
DRAWIMAGE AT,#CURDATE,@LEVEL18M,Diamond 8,RGB(0,0,0)
#CURDATE=DATE(#D,#M,#Y)+#18M15
DRAWIMAGE AT,#CURDATE,@LEVEL18M,Diamond 8,RGB(0,0,0)
#CURDATE=DATE(#D,#M,#Y)+#18M16
DRAWIMAGE AT,#CURDATE,@LEVEL18M,Diamond 8,RGB(0,0,0)
#CURDATE=DATE(#D,#M,#Y)+#18M17
DRAWIMAGE AT,#CURDATE,@LEVEL18M,Diamond 8,RGB(0,0,0)
#CURDATE=DATE(#D,#M,#Y)+#18M18
DRAWIMAGE AT,#CURDATE,@LEVEL18M,Diamond 8,RGB(0,0,0)
#CURDATE=DATE(#D,#M,#Y)+#18M19
DRAWIMAGE AT,#CURDATE,@LEVEL18M,Diamond 8,RGB(0,0,0)
#CURDATE=DATE(#D,#M,#Y)+#18M20
DRAWIMAGE AT,#CURDATE,@LEVEL18M,Diamond 8,RGB(0,0,0)
#CURDATE=DATE(#D,#M,#Y)+#18M21
DRAWIMAGE AT,#CURDATE,@LEVEL18M,Diamond 8,RGB(0,0,0)
#CURDATE=DATE(#D,#M,#Y)+#18M22
DRAWIMAGE AT,#CURDATE,@LEVEL18M,Diamond 8,RGB(0,0,0)
#CURDATE=DATE(#D,#M,#Y)+#18M23
DRAWIMAGE AT,#CURDATE,@LEVEL18M,Diamond 8,RGB(0,0,0)
#CURDATE=DATE(#D,#M,#Y)+#18M24
```

```
DRAWIMAGE AT,#CURDATE,@LEVEL18M,Diamond 8,RGB(0,0,0)
#CURDATE=DATE(#D,#M,#Y)+#18M25
DRAWIMAGE AT,#CURDATE,@LEVEL18M,Diamond 8,RGB(0,0,0)
#CURDATE=DATE(#D,#M,#Y)+#18M26
DRAWIMAGE AT,#CURDATE,@LEVEL18M,Diamond 8,RGB(0,0,0)
#CURDATE=DATE(#D,#M,#Y)+#18M27
DRAWIMAGE AT,#CURDATE,@LEVEL18M,Diamond 8,RGB(0,0,0)
#CURDATE=DATE(#D,#M,#Y)+#18M28
DRAWIMAGE AT,#CURDATE,@LEVEL18M,Diamond 8,RGB(0,0,0)

'FUTURE DIAMONDS
#CURDATE=DATE(#D,#M,#Y)+#18YLAST+#18YAV
DRAWIMAGE AT,#CURDATE,@LEVEL18Y,DOT 8,RGB(255,0,0)
#CURDATE=DATE(#D,#M,#Y)+#9YLAST+#9YAV
DRAWIMAGE AT,#CURDATE,@LEVEL9Y,DOT 8,RGB(255,0,0)
#CURDATE=DATE(#D,#M,#Y)+#54MLAST+#54MAV
DRAWIMAGE AT,#CURDATE,@LEVEL54M,DOT 8,RGB(255,0,0)
#CURDATE=DATE(#D,#M,#Y)+#18MLAST+#18MAV
DRAWIMAGE AT,#CURDATE,@LEVEL18M,DOT 8,RGB(255,0,0)


FOR #CURDATE=#LASTDATE TO #LASTDATE+#PROJECT
   @PLOT=@HIGHEST
NEXT
FOR #CURDATE=0 TO #LASTDATE
   @PLOT2=@HIGHEST
NEXT
#CURDATE=#LASTDATE
DRAWLINESTYLE DOT
DRAWCOLOUR RGB(255,0,0)
DRAWLINE 0,LOW,0,@LOWEST
```

Notes

This is the code for semi-automatic diamond placement on a monthly chart – in this case FTSE100 (UKX) from March 1995 to October 2011. There are separate codes for the weekly and daily charts. The Code Variables are copied and pasted from a spreadsheet and of course vary from analysis to analysis.

The code has only been written for Updata. If you would like this programmed into TradeStation, Metastock, CQG or Ninja, please email me on cgrafton@vectisma.com. If there is sufficient interest, I will commission a developer. There will be small fee for this to cover costs.

It is not absolutely imperative to use the Diamond Placement Code, but it is a good idea. For my own work, I always use it. The advantages are that the finish is neat, polished and consistent. Furthermore, your analyses can be quickly updated as new data comes through and saved for future reference. In many ways it is easier to save the code for each security and just rerun it that it is to save charts.

The code and inputs for the diamond placement can be found on the Phasing Model spreadsheet which can be downloaded from **vectisma.com/downloads/phasingmodel**. Because considerable time and effort were spent programming this spreadsheet. I will be charging US $199 for the download. The model can be platform and country specific – i.e. to take national holidays into account for future projections. Included for free in this one off fee are three one hour plus long online videos showing a full Hurst cycle analysis on three different securities.

The Updata code for monthly, weekly and daily diamond placements can be found at the following locations, respectively:

- vectisma.com/downloads/diamondplacement_monthly;
- vectisma.com/downloads/diamondplacement_weekly; and
- vectisma.com/downloads/diamondplacement_daily

Appendix 7: Discrete Fourier Transform Code

Updata – Visual Basic DFT (VB.Net)

Discrete Fourier Transform

Developed by John F. Ehlers

Coded in VB.NET by Paolo Barletta PhD

Produces a spectrum measured by a Discrete Fourier Transform (DFT) but with a music-based transform applied to it.

The color in the heatmap indicates the cycle amplitude and the cycle period is the vertical scale, scaled from 8 to 50 bars.

The heatmap is in time synchronism with the barchart.

The additional transformation makes it easier to identify the variable dominant cycle.

Reference: *Stocks & Commodities* Magazine, January 2007.

```
Imports Microsoft.VisualBasic
Imports System.Windows.Forms
Imports System.Drawing
Imports Updata
Imports System.IO
Imports System.Text

Public Class Updata_TestIndicator
  Implements ICustomIndicator

  ' the init() function will be called once each time the indicator is created, before everything
  ' else is called
  Public Sub init() Implements ICustomIndicator.init
  End Sub

  ' the getLines() function returns the number of lines displayed, and also
  ' how to display them
' iLineStyles is an array of values from the linestyles list in the header, eg BAR, CANDLE
' iToolStyles is an array of values from the linestyles
```

```
list in the header, eg CHART, TOOL
' sNames is an array of names for each of the
individual lines
' iColours is the default up colour, and iColours2 the
default down colour for each bar
  Public Function getLines(ByVal iLineStyles() As
LineStyles, ByVal iChartStyles() As ChartStyles, ByVal
sNames() As String, ByVal iColours() As Integer, ByVal
iColours2() As Integer)  As Integer Implements
ICustomIndicator.getLines
iLineStyles(0) = LineStyles.Dot
    iChartStyles(0) = ChartStyles.Chart
    iColours(0) = Color.Red.ToArgb()
    iColours2(0) = Color.Red.ToArgb()
    sNames(0) = "Discrete Fourier Transform"
    getLines = 1
  End Function


' the queryForParameters function needs to fill up the
arrays that are passed in, and return the
  ' number of parameters that the indicator refers to.
  ' iRets - returns types of the variables required –
eg PRICEVARIABLE, INDICATORVARIABLE
  ' sNames - returns the short name for the parameter
  ' sDescrips – returns the long descriptive text for
the variable shown on the prompt dialog
  ' defaults – returns the default value (must be of
the correct type) for this parameter

  Public Function queryForParameters(ByVal iRets() As
Updata.VariableTypes, ByVal sNames() As String, ByVal
sDescrips() As String, ByVal defaults As Object()) As
Integer Implements ICustomIndicator.queryForParameters
    iRets(0) = VariableTypes.PriceVariable
    sNames(0) = "Period"
    sDescrips(0) = "Period"
    defaults(0) = CType(50, Integer)
    queryForParameters = 1
  End Function


  ' these global variables are maintained between the
last calculation, and the current paint
  ' all this information is required to plot the heatmap
    Private Colour1(50, 1) As Integer
```

```vb
    Private Colour2(50, 1) As Integer
    Private cycledata(50, 1) As Double

    ' recalculateAll does the full recalculation of your
indicator based on source data
    ' you need to fill up the dRet double array with
return values
    ' dSrc: the data of the main chart is drawn on, first
index=point, second=field OHLCV
    '        note that study lines may only return one
point per field
    ' oParams: returns the values of the parameters
specified in queryForParameters, correctly formatted
    '        note that lines and lists will be returned as
price arrays, again OHLCV or just c if a study
    ' dRet: The data to be returned, this has one
Double()() for each line returned.
    '        each Double()() is the same length as the
source data, and each index in
    '        the source data should match the same index
in the dest data
    ' iTradeTypes: return values from the tradetypes
above, or ignore if not a system above,
    ' dTradeOpenPrices: return price to open a new
position at
    ' dTradeClosePrices: return price to close a position
at
    ' iTradeAmount: return size of holding place, leave
blank to use defaults


Public Function recalculateAll(ByVal dSrc()() As Double
, ByVal oParams() As Object, ByVal dRet()()() As
Double, ByVal iTradeTyles()() As Integer, ByVal
dTradeOpenPrices()() As Double, ByVal
dTraderClosePrices()() As Double, ByVal
iTradeAmounr()() As Integer, ByVal dStopLevels()() As
Double) As Boolean Implemets ICustom
Indicator.recalculateAll
        If dSrc.Length = 0 Then
    recalculateAll = False
    End If
    Dim i As Integer
    Dim alpha1 As Double
    Dim HP(dRet(0).Length - 1) As Double
```

```
Dim CleanedData(dRet(0).Length - 1) As Double
Dim Period As Integer
Dim n As Integer
Dim MaxPwr As Double
Dim Num As Double
Dim Denom As Double
Dim price(dRet(0).Length - 1) As Double
Dim k As Integer
'meant to set size of display window
Dim Window As Integer = CType(oParams(0), Integer)
Dim CosinePart(50) As Double
Dim SinePart(50) As Double
Dim Pwr(50) As Double
Dim DB(50) As Double

ReDim cycledata(50, dRet(0).Length)
ReDim Colour1(50, dRet(0).Length)
ReDim Colour2(50, dRet(0).Length)

For i = 2000 To dRet(0).Length - 1

    price(i) = (dSrc(i)(1) + dSrc(i)(2)) / 2

    'Get a detrended version of the data by High Pass
Filtering with a 40 Period cutoff
If i <= 5 Then
        HP(i) = price(i)
        CleanedData(i) = price(i)
    End If

    If i > 5 Then

alpha1 = (1 - System.Math.Sin(360 / 40)) / system.math.
Cos(360 / 40)
        HP(i) = 0.5 * (1 + alpha1) * (price(i) -
price(i — 1)) + alpha1 * (HP(i — 1)
        CleanedData(i) = (HP(i) + 2 * HP(i - 1) + 3 *
HP(i - 2) + 3 * HP(i - 3) + 2 * HP(I — 4) + HP(I — 5))
/ 12
    End If

    If i > Window Then

        'This is the DFT
        For Period = 8 To 50
```

```
          CosinePart(Period) = 0
          SinePart(Period) = 0
          For n = 0 To Window - 1

             CosinePart(Period) = CosinePart(Period) +
CleanedData(i-n) * system.math.Cos(2*system.Math.Pi *
(i - n) / Period)
             SinePart(Period) = SinePart(Period) +
CleanedData(i-n) *
system.math.Sin(2*system.math.Sin(2*system.Math.Pi * (i
- n) / Period)
          Next n

Pwr(Period) = CosinePart(Period) * CosinePart(Period) +
SinePart(Period) * SinePart(Period)
        Next Period

        'Find Maximum Power Level for Normalization
        MaxPwr = Pwr(8)
        For Period = 8 To 50
          If Pwr(Period) > MaxPwr Then
            MaxPwr = Pwr(Period)
          End If
        Next Period

        'Normalize Power Levels and Convert to Decibels
        For Period = 8 To 50
          If MaxPwr > 0 And Pwr(Period) > 0 Then
            DB(Period) = - 10 * system.math.log10(0.01
/ (1 - 0.99 * Pwr(Period) / MaxPwr)) /
system.math.log10(10)
          End If
          If DB(Period) > 20 Then
            DB(Period) = 20
          End If
        Next Period

        'Find Dominant Cycle using CG algorithm
        Num = 0
        Denom = 0
        For Period = 8 To 50
          cycledata(period, i) = 0
          If DB(Period) < 3 Then
            Num = Num + Period * (3 - DB(Period))
            Denom = Denom + (3 - DB(Period))
```

```
            End If

cycledata(period, i) = DB(Period)    '!!!! is this what we're meant to plot?
            Next Period

            ' store the dominant cycle in period 7
            If Denom <> 0 Then
              cycledata(7, i) = Num / Denom
            End If


            'Plot the Spectrum as a Heatmap
            For Period = 8 To 50
              'Convert Decibels to RGB Color for Display
              If DB(Period) > 10 Then
                Colour1(Period, i) =255 * (2 - DB(Period) / 10)
                Colour2(Period, i) = 0
              End If
              If DB(Period) <= 10 Then
                Colour1(Period, i) = 255
                Colour2(Period, i) = 255 * (1 - DB(Period) / 10)
              End If


            Next Period


            ' force a 0 to 50 range
            For k = 0 To dRet(0)(i).Length - 1
              dRet(0)(i)(k) = 8
              If i Mod 2 = 0 Then
                dRet(0)(i)(k) = 50
              End If
            Next k


        End If

    Next i

    recalculateAll = True
```

End Function

  ' reserved for future support
  Public Function recalculateLast(ByVal dSrc()() As Double, ByVal oParams() As Object, ByVal dRet()()() As Double) As Boolean Implements ICustomIndicator.recalculateLast
      recalculateLast = False
  End Function

  ' override the default paint function with this code
  ' return false if you want Updata to paint the line as per normal
  ' inputs: g is the Graphics object to draw to
  '   oParams are the current values for the parameters of this indicator
  '   ds are the current price values for this indicator
  '   iFirstVisible is the first bar to be visible on the screen area
  '   iLastVisible is the last bar to be visible on the screen area
  '   iGraphFunctions is the object that holds info about the physical chart displayed
  '   iLineNumber is the number of the line being drawn iLineNumber is the number of the line being drawn

  Public Function paint(ByVal g As System.Drawing.Graphics, ByVal oParams() As Object, ByVal ds()()() As Double, ByVal iFirstVisible As Integer, ByVal iLastVisible As Integer, ByVal c As iGraphFunctions, ByVal iLineNum As Integer) As Boolean Implements ICustomIndicator.paint
      If iLineNum = 1 Then
        paint = False
      Else
        'Line Conditions
        Dim x, y, y2, i, Period As Integer
        Dim pLastPoint As Point
        If (iFirstVisible < iLastVisible − 10) Then ' checks to see it's not just refreshing the last point
            ' shade the background in black

Using b As SolidBrush = New SolidBrush(Color.fromArgb(0, 0, 0))

```
g.FillRectangle(b, c.getLocation().x, c.getLocation().y
, c.getSize().Width, c.getSize().Height)
        End Using
      End If

    ' now show the colour spectrum

Using brush As SolidBrush = New SolidBrush(Color.fromAr
gb(0, 0, 0))
        For period = 8 To 50
           y = c.DataToY(period)
           y2 = c.DataToY(period + 1)
           For i = iFirstVisible To iLastVisible

brush.Color = Color.fromArgb(Colour1(period, i), Colour
2(period, i), 0)
            x = c.DataToX(i)
            If i <> iFirstVisible Then
              If y - y2 > 1 Then
                g.FillRectangle(brush, x, y2, x -
pLastPoint.x + 1, y - y2 + 1)

 'g.FillRectangle(brush, x, y, x, pLastPoint.y)
              Else

g.FillRectangle(brush, x, y2, x - pLastPoint.x + 1, 1)
              End If
            End If
            pLastPoint = New Point(x, y)
          Next i
        Next period
      End Using


    Dim showdc As Boolean

showdc = not True '!!!! change this to not show the
dominant cycle

    If showdc Then   ' show dominant cycle

Using pUp As Pen = New pen(Color.fromArgb(255, 255, 255
))
        pUp.Width = 2
```

```vb
            period = 7
            y = c.DataToY(period)
            y2 = c.DataToY(period + 1)
            For i = iFirstVisible To iLastVisible
               If period <> 7 Then

pUp.Color = Color.fromArgb(Colour1(period, i), Colour2(period, i), 0)
               Else
                  pUp.Width = 4
               End If
               y = c.DataToY(cycledata(7, i))
               x = c.DataToX(i)
               If i <> iFirstVisible Then

g.DrawLine(pUp, x, y, pLastPoint.x, pLastPoint.y)
               End If
               pLastPoint = New Point(x, y)
            Next i
         End Using
      End If

      paint = True
    End If
  End Function

End Class
```

- The VB Code for Updata can be downloaded from: vectisma.com/downloads/dft

TradeStation – Easy Language

{Discrete Fourier Transform, Copyright (c) 2006 John F. Ehlers}

```
Inputs:
  Price((H+L)/2),
  Window(50),
  ShowDC(False);

Vars:
  alpha1(0),
  HP(0),
  CleanedData(0),
  Period(0),
  n(0),
  MaxPwr(0),
  Num(0),
  Denom(0),
  DominantCycle(0),
  Color1(0),
  Color2(0);

//Arrays are sized to have a maximum Period of 50 bars
Arrays:
  CosinePart[50](0),
  SinePart[50](0),
  Pwr[50](0),
  DB[50](0);

//Get a detrended version of the data by High Pass
Filtering with a 40 Period cutoff
If CurrentBar <= 5 Then Begin
  HP = Price;
  CleanedData = Price;
End;
If CurrentBar > 5 Then Begin
  alpha1 = (1 - Sine(360/40))/Cosine(360/40);
  HP = .5*(1 + alpha1)*(Price - Price[1]) +
alpha1*HP[1];
  CleanedData = (HP + 2*HP[1] + 3*HP[2] + 3*HP[3] +
2*HP[4] + HP[5])/12;
End;

//This is the DFT
```

```
For Period = 8 to 50 Begin
  CosinePart[Period] = 0;
  SinePart[Period] = 0;
  FOR n = 0 to Window - 1 Begin
    CosinePart[Period] = CosinePart[Period] +
CleanedData[n]*Cosine(360*n/Period);
    SinePart[Period] = SinePart[Period] +
CleanedData[n]*Sine(360*n/Period);
  End;
  Pwr[Period] = CosinePart[Period]*CosinePart[Period] +
SinePart[Period]*SinePart[Period];
End;

//Find Maximum Power Level for Normalization
MaxPwr = Pwr[8];
For Period = 8 to 50 Begin
  If Pwr[Period] > MaxPwr Then MaxPwr = Pwr[Period];
End;

//Normalize Power Levels and Convert to Decibels
For Period = 8 to 50 Begin
  IF MaxPwr > 0 and Pwr[Period] > 0 Then DB[Period] = -
10*LOG(.01 / (1 - .99*Pwr[Period] / MaxPwr))/Log(10);
  If DB[Period] > 20 then DB[Period] = 20;
End;

//Find Dominant Cycle using CG algorithm
Num = 0;
Denom = 0;
For Period = 8 to 50 Begin
  If DB[Period] < 3 Then Begin
    Num = Num + Period*(3 - DB[Period]);
    Denom = Denom + (3 - DB[Period]);
  End;
End;
If Denom <> 0 then DominantCycle = Num/Denom;
If ShowDC = True Then Plot1(DominantCycle, "S1", RGB(0,
0, 255),0,2);

//Plot the Spectrum as a Heatmap
For Period = 8 to 50 Begin
  //Convert Decibels to RGB Color for Display
  If DB[Period] > 10 Then Begin
    Color1 = 255*(2 - DB[Period]/10);
    Color2 = 0;
  End;
```

```
  If DB[Period] <= 10 Then Begin
    Color1 = 255;
    Color2 = 255*(1 - DB[Period]/10);
  End;
  If Period = 8 Then Plot8(8, "S8", RGB(Color1, Color2,
0),0,4);
  If Period = 9 Then Plot9(9, "S9", RGB(Color1, Color2,
0),0,4);
  If Period = 10 Then Plot10(10, "S10", RGB(Color1,
Color2, 0),0,4);
  If Period = 11 Then Plot11(11, "S11", RGB(Color1,
Color2, 0),0,4);
  If Period = 12 Then Plot12(12, "S12", RGB(Color1,
Color2, 0),0,4);
  If Period = 13 Then Plot13(13, "S13", RGB(Color1,
Color2, 0),0,4);
  If Period = 14 Then Plot14(14, "S14", RGB(Color1,
Color2, 0),0,4);
  If Period = 15 Then Plot15(15, "S15", RGB(Color1,
Color2, 0),0,4);
  If Period = 16 Then Plot16(16, "S16", RGB(Color1,
Color2, 0),0,4);
  If Period = 17 Then Plot17(17, "S17", RGB(Color1,
Color2, 0),0,4);
  If Period = 18 Then Plot18(18, "S18", RGB(Color1,
Color2, 0),0,4);
  If Period = 19 Then Plot19(19, "S19", RGB(Color1,
Color2, 0),0,4);
  If Period = 20 Then Plot20(20, "S20", RGB(Color1,
Color2, 0),0,4);
  If Period = 21 Then Plot21(21, "S21", RGB(Color1,
Color2, 0),0,4);
  If Period = 22 Then Plot22(22, "S22", RGB(Color1,
Color2, 0),0,4);
  If Period = 23 Then Plot23(23, "S23", RGB(Color1,
Color2, 0),0,4);
  If Period = 24 Then Plot24(24, "S24", RGB(Color1,
Color2, 0),0,4);
  If Period = 25 Then Plot25(25, "S25", RGB(Color1,
Color2, 0),0,4);
  If Period = 26 Then Plot26(26, "S26", RGB(Color1,
Color2, 0),0,4);
  If Period = 27 Then Plot27(27, "S27", RGB(Color1,
Color2, 0),0,4);
  If Period = 28 Then Plot28(28, "S28", RGB(Color1,
Color2, 0),0,4);
```

```
  If Period = 29 Then Plot29(29, "S29", RGB(Color1,
Color2, 0),0,4);
  If Period = 30 Then Plot30(30, "S30", RGB(Color1,
Color2, 0),0,4);
  If Period = 31 Then Plot31(31, "S31", RGB(Color1,
Color2, 0),0,4);
  If Period = 32 Then Plot32(32, "S32", RGB(Color1,
Color2, 0),0,4);
  If Period = 33 Then Plot33(33, "S33", RGB(Color1,
Color2, 0),0,4);
  If Period = 34 Then Plot34(34, "S34", RGB(Color1,
Color2, 0),0,4);
  If Period = 35 Then Plot35(35, "S35", RGB(Color1,
Color2, 0),0,4);
  If Period = 36 Then Plot36(36, "S36", RGB(Color1,
Color2, 0),0,4);
  If Period = 37 Then Plot37(37, "S37", RGB(Color1,
Color2, 0),0,4);
  If Period = 38 Then Plot38(38, "S38", RGB(Color1,
Color2, 0),0,4);
  If Period = 39 Then Plot39(39, "S39", RGB(Color1,
Color2, 0),0,4);
  If Period = 40 Then Plot40(40, "S40", RGB(Color1,
Color2, 0),0,4);
  If Period = 41 Then Plot41(41, "S41", RGB(Color1,
Color2, 0),0,4);
  If Period = 42 Then Plot42(42, "S42", RGB(Color1,
Color2, 0),0,4);
  If Period = 43 Then Plot43(43, "S43", RGB(Color1,
Color2, 0),0,4);
  If Period = 44 Then Plot44(44, "S44", RGB(Color1,
Color2, 0),0,4);
  If Period = 45 Then Plot45(45, "S45", RGB(Color1,
Color2, 0),0,4);
  If Period = 46 Then Plot46(46, "S46", RGB(Color1,
Color2, 0),0,4);
  If Period = 47 Then Plot47(47, "S47", RGB(Color1,
Color2, 0),0,4);
  If Period = 48 Then Plot48(48, "S48", RGB(Color1,
Color2, 0),0,4);
  If Period = 49 Then Plot49(49, "S49", RGB(Color1,
Color2, 0),0,4);
  If Period = 50 Then Plot50(50, "S50", RGB(Color1,
Color2, 0),0,4);
End;
```

Appendix 8: Volatility Index code

Updata

```
Programmer - Christopher Grafton
NAME VOLATILITY INDEX
PARAMETER "INDEX" ~INDEX="$UKX-FTSE"
PARAMETER "LEVEL" @LEVEL=0

INDICATORTYPE TOOL

#PERIOD1=14
@SUM=0
@ATRSEC=0
@ATRSECNORM=0
@ATRIND=0
@ATRINDNORM=0
@RV=0
@LOW=0
@HIGH=0
@SMASEC=0
@SMAIND=0
@LASTPRICE=0
@FIRSTPRICE=0
#TIMEFRAME=250
@LEVEL=0
FOR #CURDATE=#LASTDATE-#TIMEFRAME TO #LASTDATE

@LEVEL=PHIGH(HIGH,#TIMEFRAME)
    @ATRSEC=ATR(#PERIOD1)
    @SMASEC=MAVE(#PERIOD1)
    @ATRSECNORM=(@ATRSEC/@SMASEC)*100

    SOURCEDATA ~INDEX
    @ATRIND=ATR(#PERIOD1)
    @SMAIND=MAVE(#PERIOD1)
    @ATRINDNORM=(@ATRIND/@SMAIND)*100
    @RV=@ATRSECNORM/@ATRINDNORM

NEXT
#CURDATE=#LASTDATE
ENDIF
DRAWCOLOUR RGB(0,0,0)
DRAWFONT ARIAL 15
```

```
DRAWTEXT @LEVEL AT "RV" @RV
'DRAWTEXT @LEVEL ABOVE "SEC" @ATRSECNORM
'DRAWTEXT @LEVEL BELOW "INDEX" @ATRINDNORM

QUOTENOTE RV=@RV
```

Notes

The parameter "Index" is the index you wish to compare the security to. In this case it is the FTSE 100 as an ESignal ticker ($UKX-FTSE).

The Updata code can be downloaded from: vectisma.com/downloads/volatility

Recommended further reading

Constance Brown, *Technical Analysis for the Trading Professional* (McGraw Hill, 1999)

Thomas Bulkowski, *Encyclopaedia of Chart Patterns* (Wiley, 2005)

Cherubini et al, *Fourier Transforms in Finance* (Wiley, 2009)

Thomas DeMark & Jason Perl, *DeMark Indicators* (Bloomberg Press, 2008)

Edward Dewey & Edwin Dakin, *Cycles: The Science of Prediction* (Kessinger, 2010)

Edward Dewey & Og Mandino, *Cycles: the Mysterious Forces that Trigger Events* (Hawthorn, 1971)

Mark Douglas, *Trading in the Zone* (New York Institute of Finance, 2000)

Jeremy Du Plessis, *The Definitive Guide to Point and Figure* (Harriman House, 2005)

Edwards, Magee & Bassetti, *Technical Analysis of Stock Trends* (CRC Amacom, 2007)

Alexander Elder, *Come into My Trading Room* (Wiley, 2002)

R.N. Elliott, *Masterworks* (including *Nature's Law – The Secret of the Universe*) (New Classics Library, 2005)

A.J. Frost & Robert Prechter, *The Elliott Wave Principle* (New Classic Library, 2005)

J.M. Hurst, *The Profit Magic of Stock Transaction Timing* (Traders Press, 2000)

Kirkpatrick & Dahlquist, *Technical Analysis* (FT Press, 2007)

Brain Millard, *Channels and Cycles* (Traders Press, 1999)

Tony Plummer, *Forecasting Financial Markets* (Kogan Page, 2008)

Malcolm Pryor, *The Financial Spread Betting Handbook* (Harriman House, 2011)

J. Welles Wilder, *New Concepts in Technical Trading Systems* (Trend Research, 1978)

The Sentient Trader

The Sentient Trader – Hurst Trading System (**www.sentienttrader.com**) is the only software available today that is based on the advanced techniques described in *JM Hurst's Cycles Course* as well as *The Profit Magic of Stock Transaction Timing*.

David Hickson, creator of Sentient Trader, has developed a trading system that compresses hours and hours of Hurst's *ruler and pencil* analysis into just seconds of computer time. The software includes a Sentient Trading option, which refines Hurst's trading methodology with advanced pattern recognition techniques, leading to improved trading performance and profitability.

Sentient Trader is offered as both an EOD and Intraday trading system and is compatible with major market data feeds.

Index

Note:

Page numbers in *italic* refer to diagrams and tables.

A

acceleration, 6, 9, 237
action signal, 197, 202, 206, 216, 220, 226, 255, 277
actual current volatility. *see* volatility
actual low, 153, 227–228
amplitude, 3, 5–6
    attenuation, 110
    estimating, 181–182
    physical model, 8–9
    proportional to period, 8, 39, 43
    represented by price change, 6
    and volatility, 181
arithmetic scale, 117
astrology, 279
ATR. *See* average true range (ATR)
attenuation, amplitude, 110
average cycle periods, 69, *70*, 97, 148, 160, 189, 247, 296
average true range (ATR), 173, 174–175, 207

B

bandwidth, 112, 113–114
bearish divergence, 251, 254–255
behaviour, trader, 23–25
benchmarking, 176
Bernanke, Ben, 249
Beta, 176, 209
Boeing
    18-month cycle phasing analysis, *122*
    20-week cycle phasing analysis, 128–131, *154*
    40 and 80-week cycle envelopes, *115*
    40-week moving average bands, *113*
    54 month cycle phasing analysis, *121*
    80-week cycles with moving averages, *112*
    9-month cycle phasing analysis, *125*
    comparison of conventional and centred moving average, *108*
    cycle envelopes, *115*
    daily chart with Ehlers' DFT, *150*
    phasing analysis chart set up, *116*
    phasing analysis final version, *138*
    phasing analysis in daily chart, *149*
    phasing analysis weekly abstract, *153*
    phasing model abstract, *136*
    price data, *109*
    price data periodogram, *149*
breakouts, 171
British Airways

average cycle periods, 70
non valid trendlines, 73
valid downtrend lines, 71
valid uptrend lines, 67
bullish divergence, 251, 254–255
business cycle, 28

C

calendar time, 26–27
candlestick chart, 173–174, *174*
capital risk, 168, 192–193, 194, 196, 204, 208, 217, 221, 223, 225, 227, 228, 232, 243
Cardwell, Andrew, 242–243, 251, 270
cascades, 96–100, 101, 187, 216, 220, 230
Caterpillar (CAT), *174*
   daily chart final scan, *188*
   final scan weekly chart, *186*
   initial scan weekly chart, *179*, *184*
   set up and entry, 193–194
   trading the 20W cycle post, *195*
   weekly chart detail, *187*
centred moving average, 106, 108, 110, 112, 304
charts
   composite chart, 62–63, *63*
   phasing analysis, *116*
   point and figure technique, 47
   scanning, 178–185, 189–190
   trendlines, *45*, *46*
coding
   cycle envelopes, 303–304
   forward line of demarcation (FLD), 86, 295–296
   inverse moving average, 301–302
   phasing model, 137
   TradeStation, 314–319
   Volatility Index (VI), 357–358
coherence, 7

colour coding, 54, 75, 97, 99, 102, 111, 118, 160, 297
commonality, 17
complex composites, 13–15
   showing four component cycles, *13*
   showing individual components, *14*
complex forward line of demarcation, 85
composite cycles, 269
complex composites, 13–15
creation of, 12
data extract, *13*, *15*
and FLD, 96
periodogram, *147*
and price movement, 43
principle of summation, 11–15
showing 15% trend, *17*
showing 5% trend, *16*
swamped cycles, 16–17
trendlines, 59–60
and underlying trend distortion, 15–16
underlying trend in 156-day cycle, *59*
underlying trend in 78-day cycle, *60*
valid trendline (VTL), 66
confirmation, 126, 195, 198, 201, 202, 206, 216, 228, 251, 265, 267
consolidation pattern, 8
constructive interference, 7, 12
convergence, 30
corona chart, 151
corrective waves, 243, 245–247, 257–258, 264, *289*
credit easing, 249
cycle energy, 24–25
cycle envelopes, 105–106
   Boeing examples, *115*
   coding, 303–304
   dominancy envelope, 113

edge band, 196
multiple envelopes, 114–115
uses and limitations, 138
cycles
   causes of, 277–280
   composite cycles, 11–15
   fractal nature of, 43
   harmonic relationships between, 18–20, *19*
   identification of, 4
   interaction in the market, 3–4, 10
   and market energy, 24
   the Nominal Model, 25–26
   non-harmonic relationships, 19
   physical properties, 3, 5–10, 39, 273
   principle of cyclicity, 17
   swings, 25
   trading, 191–193
cyclic correlation, 7
cyclicity, principle of, 17–18, 170

D

daily phasing model, 160
damped oscillation, *10*
data filters, 109–111
data visualisation, 107
DeMark indicators, 47
destructive interference, 7, 12
detrending, 30, 31, 110–111
Dewey, Edward, 277–278
diamond placing code, 321–330
diamonds grid, 118–119, 307–310
directional movement index (DMI), 27
discrete Fourier transform (DTF), 144, 148, 163
   Boeing daily chart, *151*
   coding, 331–343
   estimating cycle periods, 180–181
   spectral analysis, 150–152
   uses and limitations, 152
displaced cycle, 7, 74, 80
   mechanics of, 80–83
   offset sine waves, 80
divergence, 30, 169, 242, 243, 251, 254, 266, 286
DMI. *see* directional movement index (DMI)
dominancy envelope, 113
double bottom, 11, *11*, 12, 124, 260, 263
double top, 203
Dow Jones Eurostoxx 50
   FLD falling cascade, *99*
   FLD rising cascade, 50, *97*
   rising cascade, *98*
   through falling cascade, *100*
Dow Jones Industrial Average Index, 28–37
   1900-1921, *29*
   1921-1942, *31*
   1942-1962, *32*
   1961-1982, *33*
   1982-2002, *34*
   periodicity, *36*
   relative and average true range values, *175*
drawdown, 191, 194, 198, 218, 233
DTF. *see* discrete Fourier transform (DTF)

E

edge band, 196
Elliot Wave theory, 12, 47, 237–238, 243–249
   and cycles, 247–249
   Euro/USD, case study analysis, 262–266
   Euro-USD weekly data, *263*
   gold case study analysis, 255–258, *256*

harmonicity, 247–248
impulse motive waves, 244–245, 256–257
motive and corrective waves, 243–247, 257–258
patterns, 285–290
emotionality, 23–25, 278, 279
empirical roots, cycle analysis, 274
entry conditions, 195–196
nest of lows, 195–196
price, 193, 202–203
trade risk, 195–196
valid trendline (VTL) breaks, 196
equidistant cycle finder, 117
Eurostoxx. *see* Dow Jones Eurostoxx 50
Euro/USD, case study, 260–268
cyclic status and VTLs, 261
daily chart post entry, *269*
Elliot Wave theory analysis, 262–266
FLDs and underlying trend, 262
relative strength index (RSI) analysis, 266–268, *267*
Excel, spreadsheet, 135–137
expanded flat, 245, *293*
extrapolating bands, 114, 198
extraterrestrial causes of cycles, 278

F

falling cascade, 100
Fibonacci ratio, 246, 258, 265
filters, analysis, 169–177
cyclicity, 170
volatility, 170–177
final scan (FS), 178
daily charts, 188–189
phasing analysis, 186
weekly charts, 185–187
five-wave decline, 12

flag, 33
flat, 53, 57, 95, 128, 245, 293
FLD. *see* forward line of demarcation (FLD)
fluctuation, variable, 5
forward line of demarcation (FLD)
18-day FLD, *84*
31-day FLD, *85*
70.5 day FLD, *87*
70.5 day FLD upward cross, *92*
70.5-day FLD downward cross, *90*
calculation of, 82–83
cascades, 96–100
coding, 86, 295–296
complex, 85
in composite cycles, 96
daily charts, 189
definition, 275
estimating underlying trend direction, 182–185
Final Scan (FS), 187
FLD falling cascade DJ Eurostoxx 50, *99*
FLD number, 83
FLD rising cascade DJ Eurostoxx 50, *97*
historical, 182–185
inactive projections, 182
open position management, 214
open projections, 182
patterns, 96–100
pause zones, 96–100
plotting examples, 83–85
price intersection, 88–89
projecting prices, 91–94
projections summary, *94*
proxy, 94
trend projections, 182–185
and underlying trend, 93–94, 262
Foundation for the Study of Cycles, 277, 279

frequency, cycle. *see* period
FTSE 100
    80-day cycle, *15*
    non-trading days, *27*
    sharp bottoms and rounded tops, *22*

G

gold case study, 249–259
    Elliot Wave theory analysis, 255–258, *256*
    post analysis, *259*
    relative strength index (RSI) analysis, 251–255
    weekly phasing analysis, *250*
    weekly RSI data, *252*
gravitational vector, 280
grids, *126*, *127*

H

harmonicity, 4, 17–21, 39
    analogy with music, 4, 20–21
    Elliot Wave theory, 247–248
    and market cycle periods, 20
    multiples of three, 20
    multiples of two, 20
head and shoulder top, *11*
heat map. *see* corona chart
height, cycle. *see* amplitude
herding instinct, 279
Hickson, David, 360
histograms, 111
horizontal tool line, 119–120

I

impulse motive waves, 244–245, 256–257, 264

Initial Cyclic Model, 148
initial scan (IS), 178
    Caterpillar (CAT) weekly chart, *179*
    readability, 179–180
interference, 7, 12
internal trendlines, 47
invalid trendlines, 72–73
inverse moving average, 110, *111*
    code, 301–302
investment strategy, 169–170
ionisation, 279–280
iShares Spain country ETF, 205

J

JPMorgan Chase, case study, 214–234
    20-week cycle set up, *224*
    phasing model, *226*
    second cycle low and recovery, *218*
    trade overview, *233*
    trading: final leg, *232*
    trading: first leg, *227*
    trading: second leg, *229*
    trading the recovery, daily chart, *220*
    weekly phasing analysis, *215*

K

Kennedy, Jeffrey, 249, 264
Kondratieff cycle, 20, 25
K-wave. *see* Kondratieff cycle

L

lag, time, 107–108
left translation, 162
    in the S&P 500, *162*
length, cycle. *see* period

liquidity, 167–168, 170, 207
long cycles, 28–37, 39
low pass filter, 109

M

MACD. *see* moving-average convergence-divergence (MACD)
magnetic field, 279–280
market bottom, 23
market mood, 23–25
Market Vectors Egypt country ETF, 207
mass spring oscillator, 9, 10
measurement, phasing analysis, 119–120
MESA, software, 152
mid-channel pause, 202, 205, 206
momentum, 237, 239–243, 275–276. *see also* velocity, cycle
motivation, 25
motive waves, 243–245
moving averages, 107–115, 275
    bands, 106, 112–114, 304
    Boeing showing three 80-week cycles with MAs, *112*
    centring, 107–108
    constructing bands, 112–114
    as data filters, 109–111
    detrending data, *111*
    highlighting cycles, 111–112
    inverse, 301–302
    period of centred MA, 114
    moving-average convergence-divergence (MACD), 27, 30, 242
MSCI Spain, case study, 204–207
multiple envelopes, 114–115
multiple time frames, 274

N

Nature's Law-The Secret of the Universe, 247
negative reversal, 266–268
nest of lows, 72, 130, 132, 133, 153, 154, 156, 158, 186, 189, 190, 194, 195–196, 217, 218, 219, 221, 223, 224, 226, 227, 228, 230, 231, 233, 251, 252, 253, 258–259, 262
    Telefonica case study, *197*, 198–199, 199
net trend direction, 53–54. *see also* trendlines
Nominal Model, 25–38. *see also* nominality
    alternative cycles, 28
    calendar time and trading days, 26
    comparing cycles in Periodogram, 148
    cycles, 25–26
nominality, 4, 17, 39. *see also* Nominal Model
    in the Dow Jones Industrial Average index, 28–37
    in the Topix (Japan) index, 37–38
non-trading days, 27
non-valid trendlines, 72–73

O

offset sine waves, 80
open positions, 213
    JPMorgan Chase, case study, 214–234
orthodox low, 227
oscillation, 8, 9

P

pause zones, 80, 95, 96–100, 101
    and falling cascade, 100

and rising cascade, 97–98
peak translation, 161–162
peaks and troughs, 66
    estimation using FLDs, 86
    identification of using VTLs, 65
    location, 82
    projection, 81–82
period
    calculating in phasing analysis, 133–134
    definition, 3, 6
    Dow Jones Industrial Average Index, *36*
    estimating, 179–181
    and harmonicity, 20
    moving averages, 114
    physical model, 8–9
    proportional to amplitude, 8, 39, 43
    quarter-cycle rule, 202
    and relative strength index (RSI), 242
periodicity
    BA data, *70*
    in the Dow Jones Industrial Average index, *36*
    in the Topix (Japan) index, *38*
periodogram, 137, 144, 145–150, 163
    Boeing price data, *150*
    comparing cycles in Nominal Model, 148
    estimating cycle periods, 180–181
    interpretation, 146–148
    key data, *147*
    showing composite cycles, *147*
phase
    definition, 3, 7
    in the market, 7
    in phase vs. out of phase, 108–109
    of a single cycle, 7
phasing analysis, 105, 121–137. *see also* phasing model

10-week cycles, 131–133, *132*
18 month cycles, 122–124
20-week cycles, 128–131, 153–155, *154*
40-day cycles, *157*, 157–159
54 month cycles, 121–122
80-day cycles, 155–157, *156*
9-month cycles, 124–128
analysis timeframe, 117
Boeing final version, *138*
Boeing weekly abstract, *153*
calculating period, 133–134
chart setup, *116*
cycle status, 134–135
daily charts, 144, 152–160
diamonds grid, 118–119
Euro-USD weekly data, 261
final scan (FS), 186
function of, 115, 139
gold case study, *250*
measuring cycle periods, 119–120
the periodogram, 145–150
software, 117
synchronicity, 123
phasing model, 7, 115, 133–138. *see also* phasing analysis
Boeing abstract, *136*
coding, 137
daily detail, *160*
data entry, 133–134
JPMorgan Chase, case study, *226*
preparation of, 135–137
use of, 160
point and figure charts, 47
portfolio selection, 169–170
positive reversal, 251, 252–253
Prechter, Robert, 243, 264
presidential cycle, 28
price
    first and second derivatives, *240*
    fluctuation around a mean, 5

interaction, 88
price action, 39
price movement, 43
    FLD forecasting, 80
price patterns, *11*
price projecting, 91–92
price shocks, 274
projection formula, 253
projection summary, *94*
projection targets, 93, 93
    Elliot Wave theory analysis, 263
proportionality, 8, 39
proxy, forward line of demarcation, 94

Q

quarter-cycle rule, 202

R

range rules, 251, 253–254
relative strength index (RSI), 27, 237, 254–255
    bull and bear ranges, 254–255
    Euro/USD, case study, 266–268, 267
    gold case study, 251–255
    gold data, 252
    positive reversal, 252–253
    range rules, 252–253
    rising wedge, 268
    Wilder formula, 241–243
relative volatility, 174–175
    limitations, 176–177
    weekly and daily, 175
resistance, 275–276
retracement, *248*
reversals, 89–91, 101
    vs. long-term investment, 170–171
    negative reversal, 266–268

reward-to-risk ratio, 93, 168, 193, 208
right translation, 161–162
    in the S&P 500, *161*
rising cascade, 97–98
rising wedge, 268
risk, 168, 169, 192–193, 208
    and entry conditions, 195–196, 203–204
    and volatility, 171
Rolls-Royce, *174*
rounded tops, 23
RSI. *see* relative strength index (RSI)

S

S&P 500
    daily bar chart December 2009 - October 2010, *49*
    daily bar chart February 2009 - October 2010, *51*
    daily bar chart February 2010 - October 2010, *50*
    daily bar chart January 2005 - October 2010, *52*
    left translation in, *162*
    monthly bar chart 1970 - October 2010, *53*
    right translation in, *161*
    trend mix Oct 2010, *54*
    trend strength March 2009 - October 2010, *55*
Sarubbi, Bill, 279
scanning, charts, 178–185
    final scan (FS), 185–190
    initial scan (IS), 178–185
    volatility, 189–190
screening software, 169–170
Sentient Trader, software, 27, 348
serotonin, 279–280
short cycles, 39
short selling, 168, 199

MSCI Spain, case study, 204–207
risk, 200, 203–204
Verizon Communications, case study, 199–207
shortlisting, stocks, 169–170
sine waves, *132*
   averaging out, 110
   components and phasing analysis, *146*
   downtrend channel, *58*
   horizontal trend channel, *58*
   with offset replica, *81*
   offset with no underlying trend, *94*
   offset with no underlying uptrend or downtrend, *95*
   showing double bottom and head and shoulders top, *11*
   showing harmonicity and synchronisation, *21*
   showing period, amplitude and phase, *5*
   showing trend, 57–58
   uptrend channel, *58*
smoothed data, 110
social mood, 25
sovereign debt crisis, 260
spectral analysis, 145–150
   market data, 148–150
   using discrete Fourier transform (DFT), 150–152
speed, cycle, 6
statistics, phasing analysis, 133–134
Stochastics, 27
stops loss, 192–193, 208
subprime mortgage crisis, 260
summation, 8, 10–11
superposition, 11
support, 275
swamped cycles, 16–17
synchronicity, 4, 17, 21–23, 39, 105
   peaks and troughs, 21–22
   phasing analysis, 123

T

technical analysis, 276
Telefonica, set up and entry case study, 197–199
time lag, 107
Topix index, 28, 37, 37–38
   period, *38*
TradeStation, 152, 298–300, 304–306
   coding, 314–319
   easy language, 352–355
trading, 190–192
   entering and exiting, 191–193
   the set-up, 190–191
trading cycle, 191–193
   selection of, 192
trading risk, 193, 203
   short selling, 200
trading time, 26–27
trend, 45. *see also* trendlines
   as cyclic action, 45
   direction, 48–50
   estimating underlying trend, 182
   and forward line demarcation projections, 93–94
   identification of, 48
   isolating net trend direction, 53–54
   maturity, 53
   nature of, 56–58, 74
   S&P 500 daily bar chart, *49*
   strength, *54*
   timeframes, 48
   underlying distortion, 15–16, 44
   underlying in 156-day cycle, *59*
   underlying in 78-day cycle, *60*
   underlying in 9-day cycle, *60*
   underlying in 18-day cycle, *60*
trend channels, 49–50, 58
   S&P 500 Daily bar chart, *50*
trendlines, 44, 275. *see also* trend; valid trendline (VTL)

breaks in, 55–56
connecting price levels, 46–47
internal trendlines, 47
interpretation of, 50–52
methodologies, 47
positioning of, 46
sine waves, 57–58
subjective nature of, 45, 56
trend channels, 49–50
uses and limitations, 56
using the close behind the spike, 47
trigger, 168, 190, 193, 219, 225
troughs, market
and phasing analysis, 115
and synchronicity, 23

U

unsynchronised tops, 203
USD case study. *see* Euro/USD, case study

V

valid downtrend line
BA data chart, 71
breaks in, 66
connecting price extremes, 46
constructing, 70–72, 74
in valid trendlines, 61, 63
valid trendline (VTL), 39, 44. *see also* trendlines
breaks in, 66, 196
composite cycles, 62–63, 63
construction rules, 61, 74
correct and incorrect, 64
daily charts, 189
differentiated from traditional trendlines, 61
downtrend and uptrend, 63

drawing uptrend lines, 66–70
Euro/USD, case study, 261
final scan (FS), 186
identifying peaks and troughs, 65
incorrect examples, 72–73
objective nature of, 74
open position management, 214
valid uptrend line
BA data chart, 67
breaks in, 66
connecting price extremes, 46
constructing, 66–70, 74
in valid trendlines, 61, 63
variation, principle of, 17, 39, 274
Vedanta Resources, 86–87, 89–91
velocity, cycle, 6, 237, 239–240. *see also* momentum
Verizon Communications, case study, 199, 199–207
20-week cycle, 201
visualising data, 107
volatility, 170, 171–177, 207. *see also* Volatility Index (VI)
and amplitude, 181
Average True Range (ATR) formula, 173
relative volatility, 174–176
and risk, 171
screening for, 171
Volatility Index (VI), 171–172, 207
code, 345-346
formula, 172
relative volatility, 174–175

W

Wall, P.Q., 278
wave energy, 24
Welles Wilder, J., 173, 238
RSI formula, 241–243

Y

yield, 177, 208

Z

zigzag waves, 47, 245–246, 246, 257, 258, 264

Lightning Source UK Ltd.
Milton Keynes UK
UKOW06f1119020317
295705UK00004B/15/P